Student Solutions Manual

BASIC BUSINESS STATISTICS:
Concepts and Applications

Student Solutions Manual

BASIC BUSINESS STATISTICS:
Concepts and Applications
Tenth Edition

Mark. L Berenson
David M. Levine
Timothy C. Krehbiel

Pin T. Ng
Northern Arizona University

PEARSON
Prentice
Hall

Upper Saddle River, New Jersey 07458

VP/Editorial Director: Jeff Shelstad
Executive Editor: Mark Pfaltzgraff
Supplement Coordinator: Kathryn Madara
Senior Editorial Assistant: Jane Avery
Manufacturing Manager: Vincent Scelta
Production Editor & Buyer: Carol O'Rourke
Printer/Binder: Bind-Rite Graphics

10 9 8 7 6 5 4 3 2 1
ISBN 0-13-185203-5

Table of Contents

Chapter 1	Introduction and Data Collection	1
Chapter 2	Presenting Data in Tables and Charts	6
Chapter 3	Numerical Descriptive Measures	59
Chapter 4	Basic Probability	83
Chapter 5	Some Important Discrete Probability Distributions	92
Chapter 6	The Normal Distribution and Other Continuous Distributions	109
Chapter 7	Sampling Distributions	124
Chapter 8	Confidence Interval Estimation	137
Chapter 9	Fundamentals of Hypothesis Testing: One-Sample Tests	152
Chapter 10	Two-Sample Tests	173
Chapter 11	Analysis of Variance	214
Chapter 12	Chi-Square Tests and Nonparametric Tests	243
Chapter 13	Simple Linear Regression	274
Chapter 14	Introduction to Multiple Regression Models	301
Chapter 15	Multiple Regression Model Building	324
Chapter 16	Time-Series Forecasting and Index Numbers	355
Chapter 17	Decision Making	392
Chapter 18	Statistical Applications in Quality and Production Management	411

Preface

The *Student's Solutions Manual* consists of three major sections. The *Objective* section summarizes what is expected of a student after reading a chapter. The *Overview and Key Concepts* section provides an overview of the major topics covered in a chapter and lists the important key concepts. The overview and listing of the key concepts are meant not to replace but to supplement the textbook and to reinforce understanding. The *Solutions to End of Section and Chapter Review Even Problems* section provides extra detail in the problem solutions.

CHAPTER 1

OBJECTIVES
- To understand how statistics can be used in business
- To be able to identify sources of data
- To learn the different types of data used in business

OVERVIEW AND KEY CONCEPTS
The Growth and Development of Modern Statistics

Needs of government to collect data on its citizens

⇩

The development of the mathematics of probability theory

⇩

The advent of the computer

Key Definitions
- **Population (universe):** The whole collection of things under consideration, e.g., all the students enrolled at a university.
- **Sample:** A portion of the population selected for analysis, e.g., all the freshmen at a university.
- **Parameter:** A summary measure computed to describe a characteristic of the population, e.g., the population average weight of all the students enrolled at a university.
- **Statistic:** A summary measure computed to describe a characteristic of the sample, e.g., the average weight of sample of freshmen at a university.

Relationship between Population and Sample

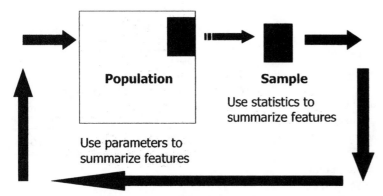

Inference on the population from the sample

The Difference between Descriptive Statistics and Inferential Statistics
- **Descriptive statistics:** Deal with collecting, presenting, summarizing, and analyzing data.
- **Inferential statistics:** Deal with drawing conclusions and/or making decisions concerning a population based only on sample data.

The Primary Goal of the Text
To understand how the methods of statistics can be used in decision-making process. This understanding includes the following objectives:
- To properly present and describe business data and information
- To draw conclusions about large populations based solely on information collected from samples
- To make reliable forecasts about business trends
- To improve business processes

The Different Types of Data Sources

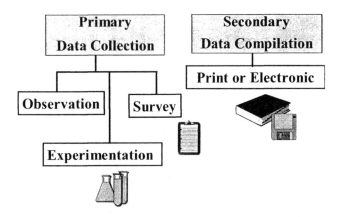

The Different Types of Data
- **Qualitative (categorical) variable**: A nonnumeric variable, e.g., male or female.
- **Quantitative (numerical) variable:** A numeric variable, e.g., weight, exam score.
- **Discrete variable:** A variable with only certain values, there are usually gaps between values, e.g., the number of cars a company owns.
- **Continuous variable:** A variable that can have any value within a specified range, e.g., atmospheric temperature.

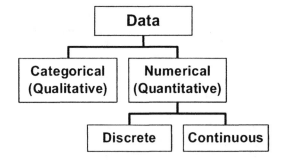

Levels of Measurement and Types of Measurement Scales

- **Nominal scale**: Categorical data that are classified into distinct categories in which no ranking is implied, e.g. male or female.
- **Ordinal scale:** Categorical data that are classified into distinct categories in which ranking is implied, e.g. a letter grade of A, B, C, D or F.
- **Interval scale:** Numerical data that are measured using an ordered scale in which the difference between measurements is meaningful but does not involve a true zero point, e.g. standardized exam score.
- **Ratio scale:** Numerical data that are measured using an ordered scale in which the difference between the measurements is meaningful and involves a true zero point, e.g. height, weight.

SOLUTIONS TO END OF SECTION
AND CHAPTER REVIEW EVEN PROBLEMS

1.2   Three sizes of soft drink are classified into distinct categories—small, medium, and large—in which order is implied.

1.4   (a)   numerical, discrete, ratio scale
        (b)   numerical, continuous, ratio scale
        (c)   categorical, nominal scale
        (d)   categorical, nominal scale

1.6   (a)   categorical, nominal scale
        (b)   numerical, continuous, ratio scale
        (c)   numerical, discrete, ratio scale
        (d)   numerical, discrete, ratio scale

1.8   (a)   numerical, continuous, ratio scale *
        (b)   numerical, discrete, ratio scale
        (c)   numerical, continuous, ratio scale *
        (d)   categorical, nominal
           *Some researchers consider money as a discrete numerical variable because it can be counted
            to the nearest penny.

1.10   While it is theoretically true that ties cannot occur with continuous data, the grossness of the
        measuring instruments used often leads to the reporting of ties in practical applications.
        Hence two students may both score 90 on an exam—not because they possess identical
        ability but rather because the grossness of the scoring method used failed to detect a
        difference between them.

1.12   A population contains all the items of interest whereas a sample contains only a portion of the
        items in the population.

1.14   Descriptive statistical methods deal with the collection, presentation, summarization, and
        analysis of data whereas inferential statistical methods deal with decisions arising from the
        projection of sample information to the characteristics of a population.

1.16   Discrete random variables produce numerical responses that arise from a counting process.
        Continuous random variables produce numerical responses that arise from a measuring
        process.

1.18   The four types of measurement scales are (i) nominal scale, (ii) ordinal scale, (iii) interval
        scale and (iv) ratio scale.

Answers for 1.20 through 1.24 provided below are just some of the many different possible answers.

1.20   Microsoft Excel could be used to perform various statistical computations that were possible
        only with a slide-rule or hand-held calculator in the old days.

1.22   SPSS could be used to obtain various summary statistics and to perform inferential statistical analysis.

1.24   (a)   The American Housing Survey (AHS) collects data on the Nation's housing, including apartments, single-family homes, mobile homes, vacant housing units, household characteristics, income, housing and neighborhood quality, housing costs, equipment and fuels, size of housing unit, and recent movers. National data are collected in odd numbered years, and data for each of 47 selected Metropolitan Areas are collected currently about every six years. The national sample covers an average 55,000 housing units. Each metropolitan area sample covers 4,100 or more housing units.
         (b)   Neighborhood quality is a categorical variable.
         (c)   Size of the housing unit is a numerical variable.
         (d)   Size of the housing unit is a continuous variable.

1.26   (a)   The data were distributed by the U.S. Transportation Department and were obtained from a survey.
         (b)   Categorical variables: quality of service; on-time performance.
         (c)   Numerical variables: % arriving on-time; number of complaints.

1.28   (a)   Population: U.S. cat owners
         (b)   (1)   categorical   (3) numerical, discrete
                (2)   categorical   (4) categorical

CHAPTER 2

OBJECTIVES

- To be able to develop tables and charts for numerical data
- To be able to develop tables and charts for categorical data
- To understand the principles of proper graphical presentation

OVERVIEW AND KEY CONCEPTS
Organizing Numerical Data

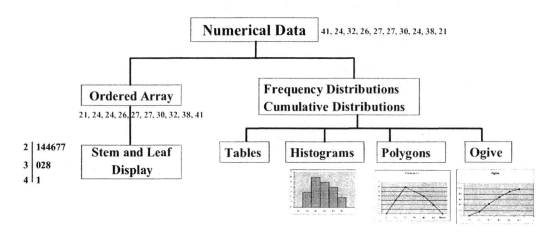

- **Ordered array:** Ordered sequence of raw data.
    - Ordered array makes it easier to pick out extremes, typical values, and concentrations of values.
- **Stem-and-leaf display:** Data are separated into leading digits (stems) and trailing digits (leaves).
    - Allows easy understanding of how the values distribute and cluster over the range of the observations in the data set.
- **Frequency distribution:** A summary table in which the data are arranged into numerically ordered class groupings or categories.
    - Makes the process of data analysis and interpretation much more manageable and meaningful
    - **Selecting the number of classes**: At least 5 but no more than 15 groupings
    - **Obtaining the class intervals:** $\text{width of interval} = \dfrac{\text{range}}{\text{number of desired class groupings}}$.
    - **Establishing the boundaries of the classes**: Non-overlapping classes must include the entire range of observations
    - **Class midpoint:** The point halfway between the boundaries of each class and is representative of the data within that class
- **Relative frequency distribution**: Formed by dividing the frequencies in each class of the frequency distribution by the total number of observations

- Essential whenever one set of data is being compared with other sets of data if the number of observations in each set differs
- **Percentage distribution:** Formed by multiplying the relative frequencies by 100%
- **Cumulative distribution:** Formed from the frequency distribution, relative frequency distribution or percentage distribution by accumulating the frequencies, relative frequencies or percentages
  - It shows the number of observations below given values (lower boundaries)
- **Histogram:** Vertical bar chart in which the rectangular bars are constructed at the boundaries of each class
- **Percentage polygon:** Formed by having the midpoint of each class represent the data in that class and then connecting the sequence of midpoints at their respective class percentages
  - Useful when comparing two or more sets of data
- **Cumulative polygon (Ogive):** Formed by plotting cumulative percentages against the lower boundaries of the classes and connecting the cumulative percentages
  - It is useful when comparing two or more sets of data

Graphing Bivariate Numerical Data

- **Scatter diagram (scatter plot):** Two-dimensional graph depicting how two numerical variables relate to each other
- **Time-series plot:** Two-dimensional graph that illustrates how a series of numerical data changes over time

Table and Charts for Categorical Data

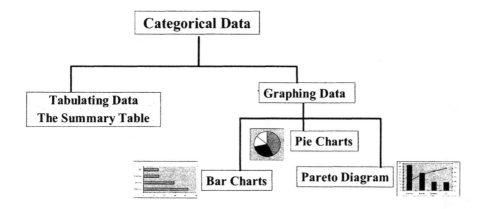

- **Summary table:** Similar to frequency distribution table for numerical data except there is no natural order of the classes
- **Bar chart:** Each category is depicted by a bar, the length of which represents the frequency or percentage of observations falling into a category
- **Pie chart:** The circle of 360^0 is divided into slices according to the percentage in each category
- **Pareto diagram:** A special type of vertical bar chart in which the categorized responses are plotted in the descending rank order of their frequencies and combined with a cumulative polygon on the same scale
  - Useful when the number of classification increases. Enables the separation of the "vital few" from the "trivial many"

Tabulating and Graphing Bivariate Categorical Data
- Contingency table (cross-classification table): Two-way table of cross-classification
- Side-by-side bar chart: Bar charts arranged side-by-side according to the different categories or the two categorical variables; useful when looking for patterns or relationship

Principles of Graphical Excellence
- Well-designed presentation of data that provides substance, statistics and design
- Communicates complex ideas with clarity, precision and efficiency
- Gives the viewer the largest number of ideas in the shortest time with the least ink
- Almost always involves several dimensions
- Requires telling the truth about the data

Common Errors in Presenting Data
- Using "chart junk"
- No relative basis in comparing data between groups
- Compressing the vertical axis
- No zero point on the vertical axis

SOLUTIONS TO END OF SECTION
AND CHAPTER REVIEW EVEN PROBLEMS

2.2   (a)

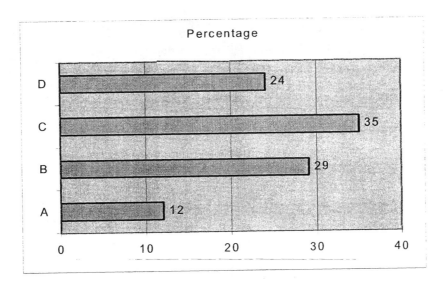

(b)

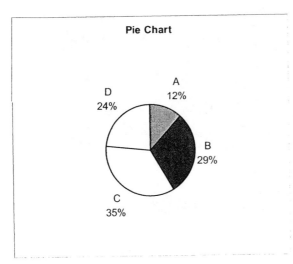

2.2   (c)
cont.

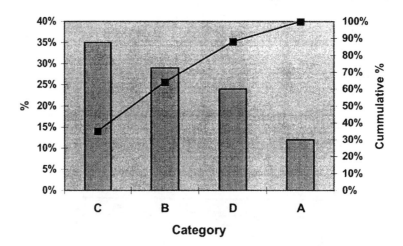

2.4   (a)

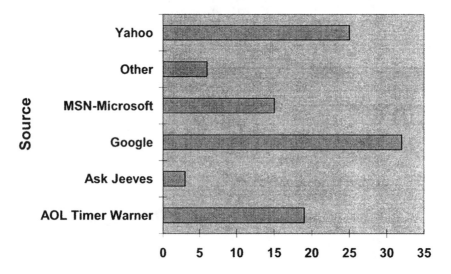

2.4   (a)
cont.

Pie Chart

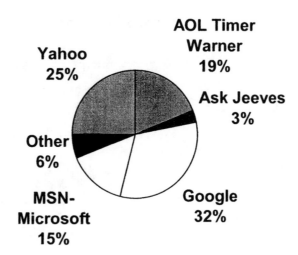

Pareto Diagram

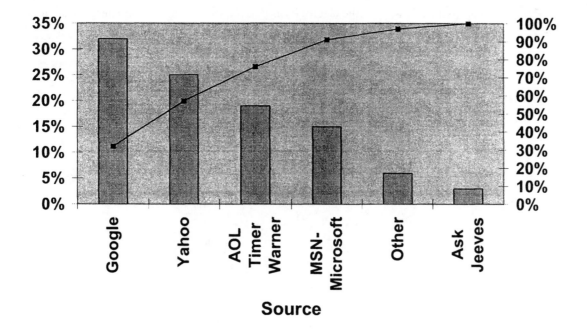

2.4   (b)   The Pareto diagram is better than the pie chart to portray these data because it not
cont.   only sorts the frequencies in descending order, it also provides the cumulative
                   polygon on the same scale. From the Pareto diagram, it is obvious that "Google" has
                   the largest market share at 32%.[*]
                   * Note: This is one of the many possible solutions for the question.

2.6   (a)

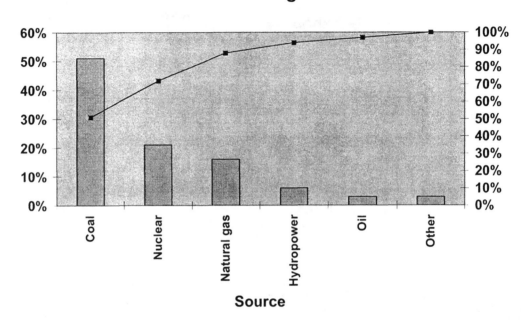

        (b)   Approximately 88% of the electricity is derived from coal, nuclear energy or natural
                 gas.

2.6   (c)
cont.

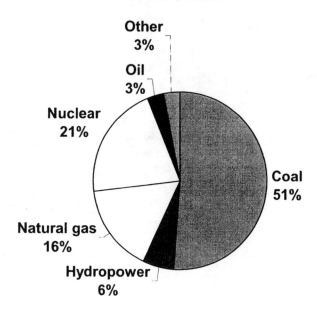

(d)   The Pareto diagram is better than the pie chart because it not only sorts the
frequencies in descending order, it also provides the cumulative polygon on the same
scale. From the Pareto diagram, it is obvious that almost 90% of the electricity is
derived from coal, nuclear energy or natural gas. [*]
* Note: This is one of the many possible solutions for the question.

2.8   (a)

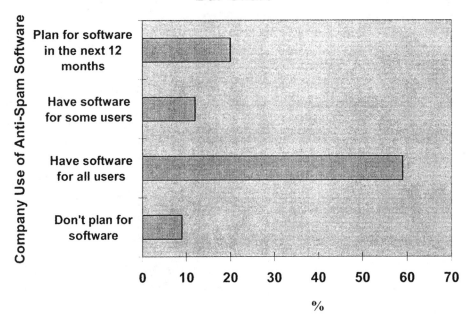

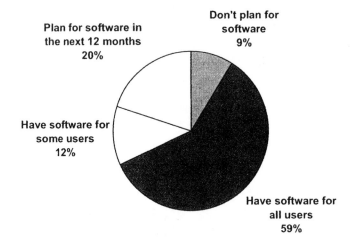

2.8   (b)   The bar chart is more suitable if the purpose is to compare the categories. The pie
cont.   chart is more suitable if the main objective is to investigate the portion of the
                whole that is in a particular category. *
                * Note: This is one of the many possible solutions for the question.

2.10   (a)

Pareto Diagram

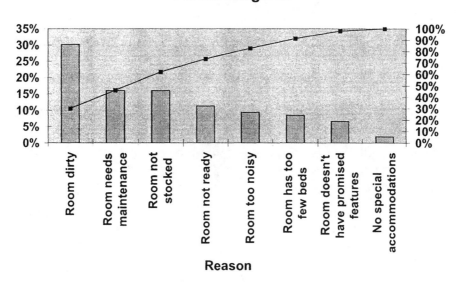

(b)   The most frequent complain is about "room being dirty" followed by "room needs
        maintenance" and "room not stocked". The remaining complaints are the "trivial
        many" reasons.

2.12   Stem-and-leaf of Finance Scores
                5   34
                6   9
                7   4
                8   0
                9   38
                        $n = 7$

2.14   Ordered array: 50 74 74 76 81 89 92

2.16   (a)   Ordered array: $15 $15 $18 $18 $20 $20 $20 $20 $20 $21 $22 $22 $25 $25 $25 $25 $25 $26 $28 $29 $30 $30 $30

        (b)   **PHStat output:**
Stem-and-Leaf Display
for Bounced-Check Fee
Stem unit: 10

```
1|5 5 8 8
2|0 0 0 0 0 1 2 2 5 5 5 5 5 6 8 9
3|0 0 0
```

        (c)   The stem-and-leaf display provides more information because it not only orders observations from the smallest to the largest into stems and leaves, it also conveys information on how the values distribute and cluster over the range of the observations in the data set.

        (d)   The bounced checked fees seem to be concentrated around $22 which is the center of the 20-row and also the median of the 23 observations.

2.18   (a)   Ordered array for chicken: 7, 9, 15, 16, 16, 18, 22, 25, 27, 33, 39
Ordered array for burger: 19, 31, 34, 35, 39, 39, 43

        (b)   **PHStat output:**

Stem-and-Leaf Display	**Stem-and-Leaf Display**
for Burger	**for Chicken**
Stem unit: 10	**Stem unit:** 10

```
1|9                      0|7 9
2|                       1|5 6 6 8
3|1 4 5 9 9              2|2 5 7
4|3                      3|3 9
```

        (c)   The stem-and-leaf display provides more information because it not only orders observations from the smallest to the largest into stems and leaves, it also conveys information on how the values distribute and cluster over the range of the observations in the data set.

        (d)   There seems to be higher fat content for burgers because 6 observations in the sample of 7 have fat content higher than 30 as compared to only 2 observations in the sample of 11 chicken items. Also, there is only 1 observation with a fat content lower than 20 for burgers as compared to 6 observations in the sample of 11 chicken items.

2.20   (a)   The class boundaries of the 9 classes can be "10 to less than 20", "20 to less than 30", "30 to less than 40", "40 to less than 50", "50 to less than 60", "60 to less than 70", "70 to less than 80", "80 to less than 90", and "90 to less than 100".

        (b)   The class-interval width is $= \dfrac{97.8 - 11.6}{9} = 9.58 \cong 10$.

        (c)   The nine class midpoints are: 15, 25, 35, 45, 55, 65, 75, 85, and 95.

2.22   (a)

Electricity Costs	Frequency	Percentage
$80 up to $99	4	8%
$100 up to $119	7	14
$120 up to $139	9	18
$140 up to $159	13	26
$160 up to $179	9	18
$180 up to $199	5	10
$200 up to $219	3	6

(b)

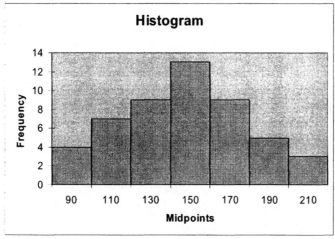

Monthly Electricity Costs

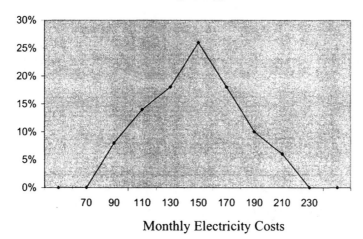

Monthly Electricity Costs

2.22   (c)
cont.

Electricity Costs	Frequency	Percentage	Cumulative %
$99	4	8%	8%
$119	7	14%	22%
$139	9	18%	40%
$159	13	26%	66%
$179	9	18%	84%
$199	5	10%	94%
$219	3	6%	100%

Cumulative Percentage Polygon

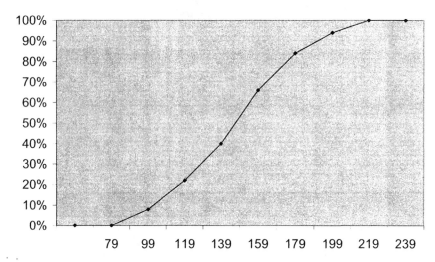

(d)   Monthly electricity costs are most concentrated between $140 and $160 a month, with better than one-fourth of the costs falling in that interval.

2.24   (a)

Width	Frequency	Percentage
8.310 -- 8.329	3	6.12%
8.330 -- 8.349	2	4.08%
8.350 -- 8.369	1	2.04%
8.370 -- 8.389	4	8.16%
8.390 -- 8.409	4	8.16%
8.410 -- 8.429	15	30.61%
8.430 -- 8.449	7	14.29%
8.450 -- 8.469	5	10.20%
8.470 -- 8.489	5	10.20%
8.490 -- 8.509	3	6.12%

2.24   (b)
cont.

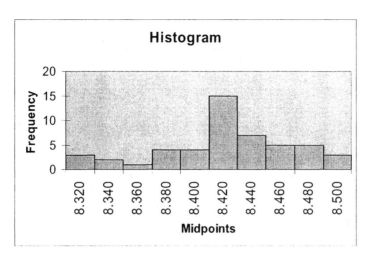

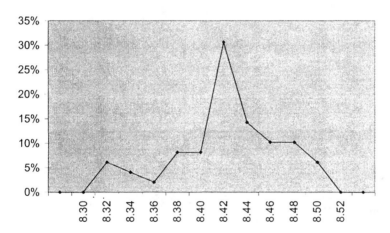

(c)

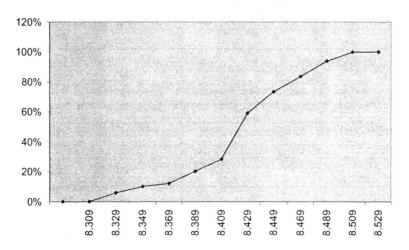

2.24   (d)   All the troughs will meet the company's requirements of between 8.31 and 8.61
cont.   inches wide.

2.26   (a)

Bulb Life (hrs)	Frequency Manufacturer A	Bulb Life (hrs)	Frequency Manufacturer B
650 -- 749	3	750 -- 849	2
750 -- 849	5	850 -- 949	8
850 -- 949	20	950 -- 1049	16
950 -- 1049	9	1050 -- 1149	9
1050 -- 1149	3	1150 -- 1249	5

Bulb Life (hrs)	Percentage, Mfgr A	Percentage, Mfgr B
650 – 749	7.5%	0.0%
750 – 849	12.5	5.0
850 – 949	50.0	20.0
950 – 1049	22.5	40.0
1050 – 1149	7.5	22.5
1150 – 1249	0.0	12.5

(b)

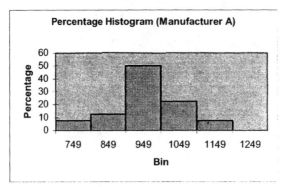

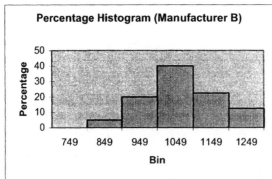

2.26   (b)
cont.

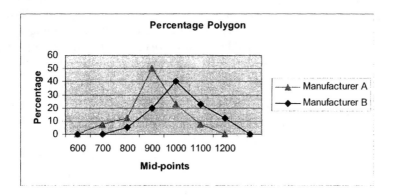

(c)

Bulb Life (hrs)	Frequency Less Than, Mfgr A	Frequency Less Than, Mfgr B
650 – 749	3	0
750 – 849	8	2
850 – 949	28	10
950 – 1049	37	26
1050 – 1149	40	35
1150 – 1249	40	40

(c)

Bulb Life (hrs)	Percentage Less Than, Mfgr A	Percentage Less Than, Mfgr B
650 – 749	7.5%	0.0%
750 – 849	20.0	5.0
850 – 949	70.0	25.0
950 – 1049	92.5	65.0
1050 – 1149	100.0	87.5
1150 – 1249	100.0	100.0

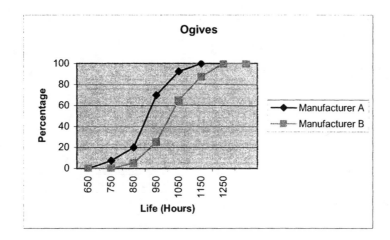

2.26   (d)   Manufacturer B produces bulbs with longer lives than Manufacturer A. The
cont.   cumulative percentage for Manufacturer B shows 65% of their bulbs lasted 1049
                 hours or less contrasted with 70% of Manufacturer A's bulbs which lasted 949 hours
                 or less. None of Manufacturer A's bulbs lasted more than 1149 hours, but 12.5% of
                 Manufacturer B's bulbs lasted between 1150 and 1249 hours. At the same time, 7.5%
                 of Manufacturer A's bulbs lasted less than 750 hours, while all of Manufacturer B's
                 bulbs lasted at least 750 hours.

2.28   (a)   Table frequencies for all student responses
                 Student Major Categories

Gender	A	C	M	Totals
Male	14	9	2	25
Female	6	6	3	15
Totals	20	15	5	40

(b)   Table percentages based on overall student responses
                 Student Major Categories

Gender	A	C	M	Totals
Male	35.0%	22.5%	5.0%	62.5%
Female	15.0%	15.0%	7.5%	37.5%
Totals	50.0%	37.5%	12.5%	100.0%

Table based on row percentages
                 Student Major Categories

Gender	A	C	M	Totals
Male	56.0%	36.0%	8.0%	100.0%
Female	40.0%	40.0%	20.0%	100.0%
Totals	50.0%	37.5%	12.5%	100.0%

Table based on column percentages
                 Student Major Categories

Gender	A	C	M	Totals
Male	70.0%	60.0%	40.0%	62.5%
Female	30.0%	40.0%	60.0%	37.5%
Totals	100.0%	100.0%	100.0%	100.0%

(c)

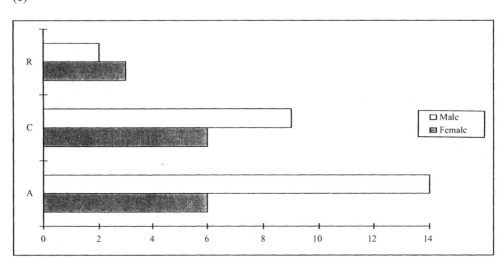

2.30   (a)   **Contingency Table**

Condition of Die

Quality	No Particles	Particles	Totals
Good	320	14	334
Bad	80	36	116
Totals	400	50	450

Table of Total Percentages

Condition of Die

Quality	No Particles	Particles	Totals
Good	71%	3%	74%
Bad	18%	8%	26%
Totals	89%	11%	100%

Table of Row Percentages

Condition of Die

Quality	No Particles	Particles	Totals
Good	96%	4%	100%
Bad	69%	31%	100%
Totals	89%	11%	100%

Table of Column Percentages

Condition of Die

Quality	No Particles	Particles	Totals
Good	80%	28%	74%
Bad	20%	72%	26%
Totals	100%	100%	100%

(b)

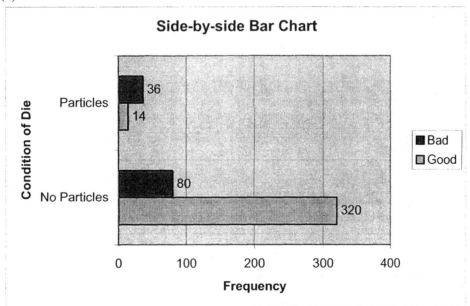

(c)   The data suggests that there is some association between condition of the die and the quality of wafer because more good wafers are produced when no particles are found in the die and more bad wafers are produced when there are particles found in the die.

2.32   (a)   Table of total percentages

	Gender		
Enjoy Shopping for Clothing	Male	Female	Total
Yes	27%	45%	72%
No	21%	7%	28%
Total	48%	52%	100%

Table of row percentages

	Gender		
Enjoy Shopping for Clothing	Male	Female	Total
Yes	38%	62%	100%
No	74%	26%	100%
Total	48%	52%	100%

Table of column percentages

	Gender		
Enjoy Shopping for Clothing	Male	Female	Total
Yes	57%	86%	72%
No	43%	14%	28%
Total	100%	100%	100%

(b)

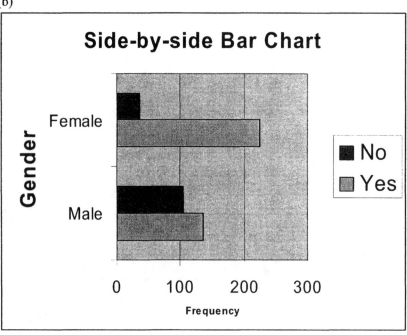

(c)   The percentage of shoppers who enjoy shopping for clothing is higher among females than males.

2.34   (a)

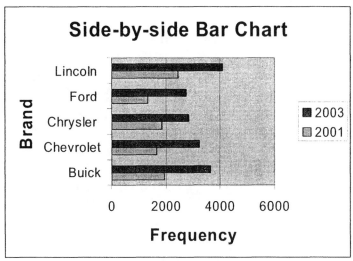

(b)   All five brands increased the amount of rebates from 2001 to 2003 with Ford more than doubling, Chevrolet and Buick almost doubling the amount of rebates.

2.36   (a)

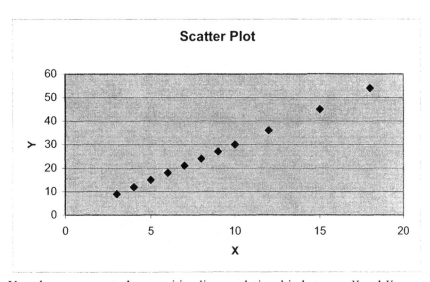

(b)   Yes, there appears to be a positive linear relationship between X and Y.

2.38   (a)

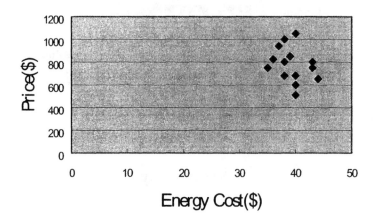

(b)   There does not appear to be any relationship between price and energy cost.

(c)   The data do not seem to indicate that higher-priced refrigerators have greater energy efficiency.

2.40   (a)

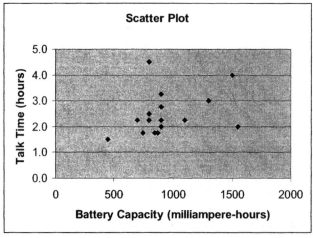

(b)   There does not appear to be any relationship between the battery capacity and the digital-mode talk time.

(c)   No, the data do not support the expectation that higher battery capacity is associated with higher talk time.

2.42 (a)

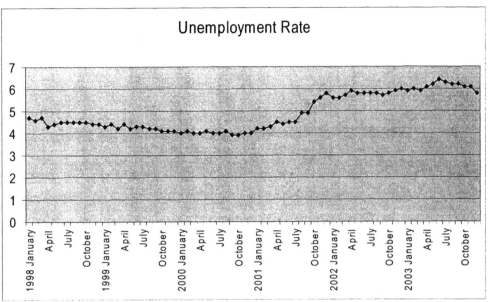

(b) The unemployment rate followed a downward trend from January of 1998 to September of 2000 and changed to an upward trend from there onwards.

2.44 (a)

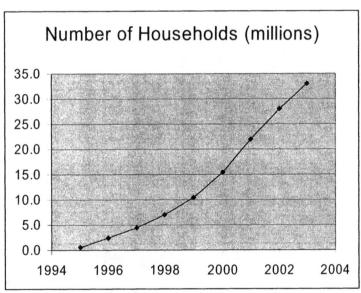

(b) There is an upward trend in the number of households using online banking and/or online bill payment.

(c) The number of U.S. households actively using online banking and/or online bill payment in 2004 will be around 36 millions.

2.50   (a)   The size of the policeman for Washington is not only taller but also bigger in overall size. This has a tendency to distort the actual difference in the size of the police forces. A simple bar chart would do a much better job.

2.54   (a)

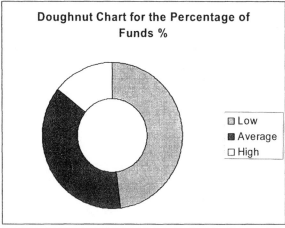

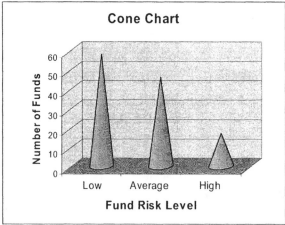

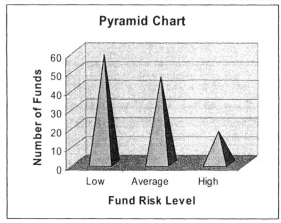

(b)   The bar chart, the pie chart and the Pareto diagram should be preferred over the doughnut chart, the cone chart and the pyramid chart since the former set is simpler and easier to interpret.

2.56   A summary table allows one to determine the frequency or percentage of occurrences in each category.

2.58   The bar chart for categorical data is plotted with the categories on the vertical axis and the frequencies or percentages on the horizontal axis. In addition, there is a separation between categories. The histogram is plotted with the class grouping on the horizontal axis and the frequencies or percentages on the vertical axis. This allows one to more easily determine the distribution of the data. In addition, there are no gaps between classes in the histogram.

2.60   Because the categories are arranged according to frequency or importance, it allows the user to focus attention on the categories that have the greatest frequency or importance.

2.62   (a)

Bar Chart

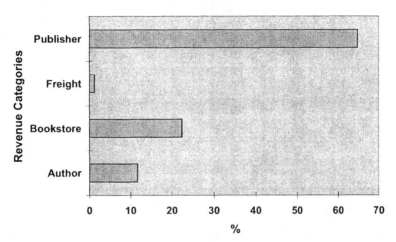

Pie Chart

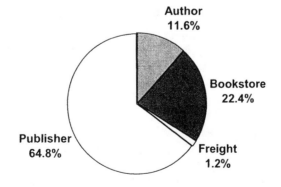

2.62   (a)
cont.

Pareto Diagram

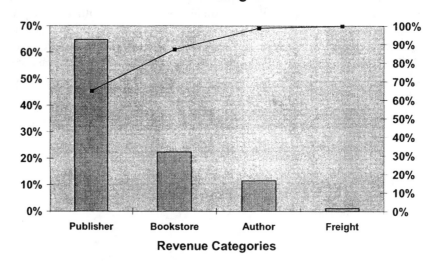

Bar Chart

(b)

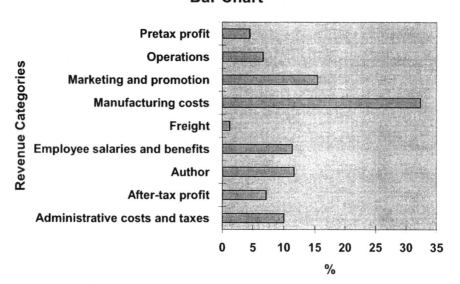

2.62   (b)
cont.

Pie Chart

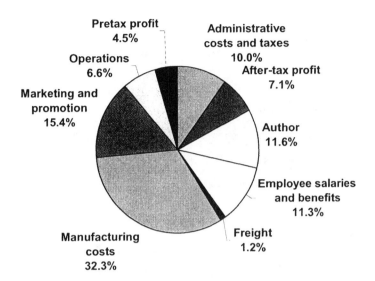

Pareto Diagram

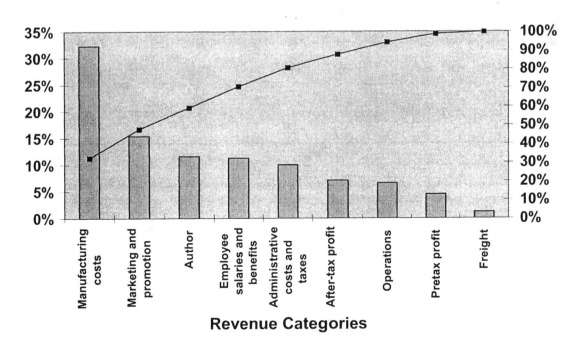

2.62   (c)   The publisher gets the largest portion (64.8%) of the revenue. About half (32.2%) of
cont.   the revenue received by the publisher is used for manufacturing costs. Bookstore
                marketing and promotion account for the next larger share of the revenue at 15.4%.
                Author, bookstore employee salaries and benefits, and publisher administrative costs
                and taxes each accounts for around 10% of the revenue while the publisher after-tax
                profit, bookstore operations, bookstore pretax profit and freight constitute the "trivial
                few" allocations of the revenue.

2.64   (a)

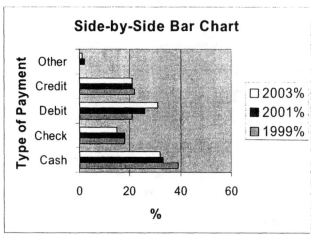

        (b)   From 1999 to 2003, payment by cash and check had declined while payment by debit
               and other type of payment had increased. The percentage of payment by credit had
               remained more or less constant.

2.66   (a)

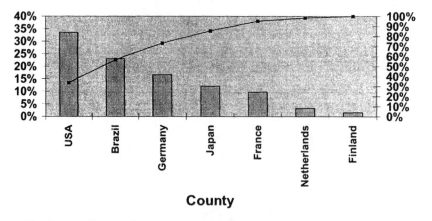

               The Pareto diagram is most appropriate because it not only sorts the frequencies in
               descending order, it also provides the cumulative polygon on the same scale. From
               the Pareto diagram, it is obvious that USA and Brazil make up more than half of the
               coffee consumption in major markets in 2000.

2.66   (b)
cont.

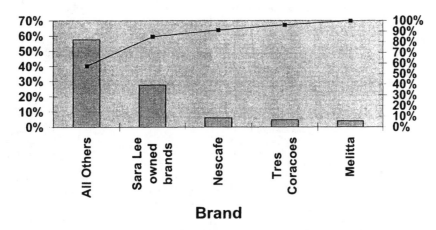

The Pareto diagram is most appropriate because it not only sorts the frequencies in descending order, it also provides the cumulative polygon on the same scale. From the Pareto diagram, it is obvious that no single major corporation dominates the coffee market in Brazil. The corporation that owns the largest share of the market, Sara Lee owned brands, captures only less than 30% of the market share.

2.68   (a)

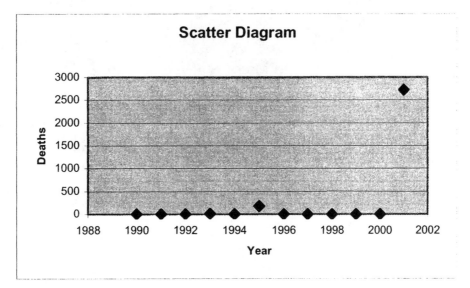

There is no particular pattern to the deaths due to terrorism on U.S. soil between 1990 and 2001. There are exceptionally high death counts in 1995 and 2001 due to the Okalahoma City and New York City bombings.

2.68   (b)
cont.

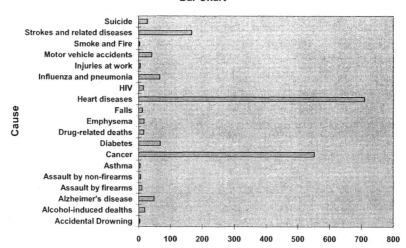

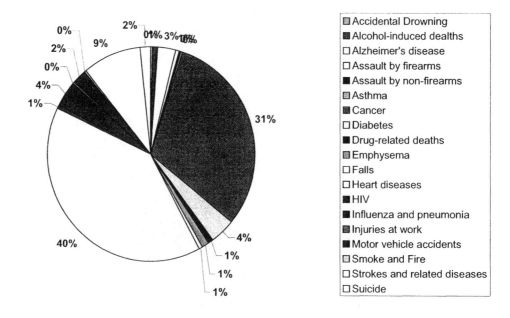

2.68 (b)
cont.

Pareto Diagram

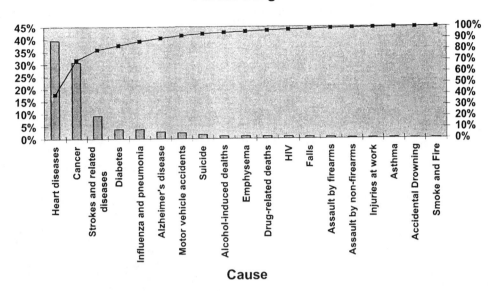

(c) The Pareto diagram is best to portray these data because it not only sorts the
frequencies in descending order, it also provides the cumulative polygon on the same
scale. The labels in the pie chart are unreadable because there are too many
categories in the causes of death.

(d) The major causes of death in the U.S. in 2000 are heart diseases followed by cancer.
These two accounted for more than 70% of the total deaths.

2.70 (a)

Dessert Ordered	Gender			Dessert Ordered	Beef Entrée		
	Male	Female	Total		Yes	No	Total
Yes	71%	29%	100%	Yes	52%	48%	100%
No	48%	52%	100%	No	25%	75%	100%
Total	53%	47%	100%	Total	31%	69%	100%

(g)

Dessert Ordered	Gender			Dessert Ordered	Beef Entrée		
	Male	Female	Total		Yes	No	Total
Yes	30%	14%	23%	Yes	38%	16%	23%
No	70%	86%	77%	No	62%	84%	77%
Total	100%	100%	100%	Total	100%	100%	100%

(h)

Dessert Ordered	Gender			Dessert Ordered	Beef Entrée		
	Male	Female	Total		Yes	No	Total
Yes	16%	7%	23%	Yes	12%	11%	23%
No	37%	40%	77%	No	19%	58%	77%
Total	53%	47%	100%	Total	31%	69%	100%

2.70   (b)   If the owner is interested in finding out the percentage of joint occurrence of gender
cont.   and ordering of dessert or the percentage of joint occurrence of ordering a beef entrée
               and a dessert among all patrons, the table of total percentages is most informative. If
               the owner is interested in the effect of gender on ordering of dessert or the effect of
               ordering a beef entrée on the ordering of dessert, the table of column percentages will
               be most informative. Since dessert will usually be ordered after the main entree and
               the owner has no direct control over the gender of patrons, the table of row
               percentages is not very useful here.

        (c)   30% of the men sampled ordered desserts compared to 14% of the women. Men are
               more than twice as likely to order desserts as women. Almost 38% of the patrons
               ordering a beef entree ordered dessert compared to less than 16% of patrons ordering
               all other entrees. Patrons ordering beef are better than 2.3 times as likely to order
               dessert as patrons ordering any other entree.

2.72   (a)

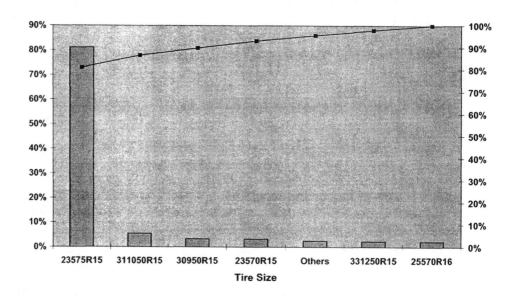

23575R15 accounts for over 80% of the warranty claims.

2.72   (b)
cont.

Pie Chart

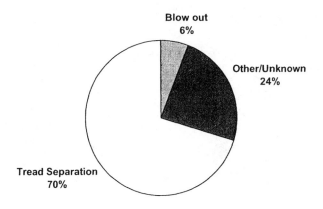

Tread separation accounts for the majority (70%) of the warranty claims.

(c)

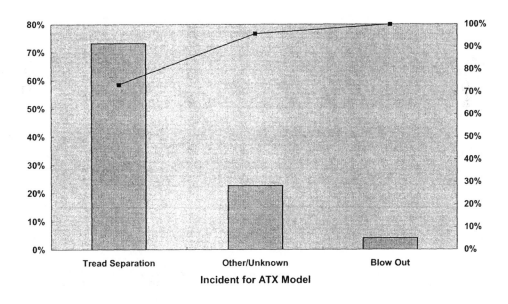

Tread separation accounts for more than 70% of the warranty claims among the ATX model.

2.72   (d)
cont.

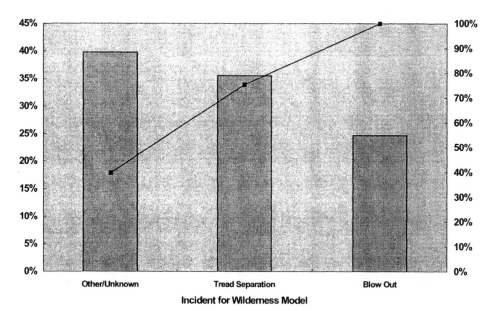

The number of claims is quite evenly distributed among the three incidents. The incident of "other/unknown" accounts for almost 40% of the claims, the incident of "tread separation" accounts for about 35% of the claims while the incident of "blow out" accounts for about 25% of the claims.

2.74   (a), (c)

Cost	Frequency	Percentage	Cumulative Percentage
Less than 0.75	4	11.11%	11.11%
0.75 but less than 1	16	44.44%	55.56%
1 but less than 1.25	3	8.33%	63.89%
1.25 but less than 1.5	8	22.22%	86.11%
1.5 but less than 1.75	4	11.11%	97.22%
1.75 but less than 2	1	2.78%	100.00%

Calories	Frequency	Percentage	Cumulative Percentage
280 but less than 310	5	13.89%	13.89%
310 but less than 340	9	25.00%	38.89%
340 but less than 370	10	27.78%	66.67%
370 but less than 400	8	22.22%	88.89%
400 but less than 430	4	11.11%	100.00%

Fat	Frequency	Percentage	Cumulative Percentage
Less than 5	1	2.78%	2.78%
5 but less than 10	4	11.11%	13.89%
10 but less than 15	13	36.11%	50.00%
15 but less than 20	9	25.00%	75.00%
20 but less than 25	7	19.44%	94.44%
25 but less than 30	2	5.56%	100.00%

2.74   (b)
cont.

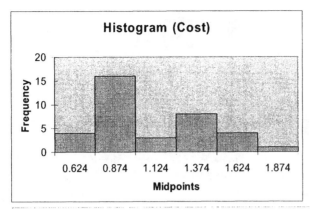

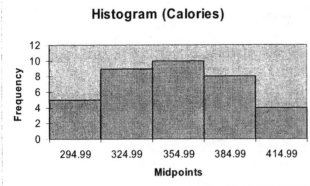

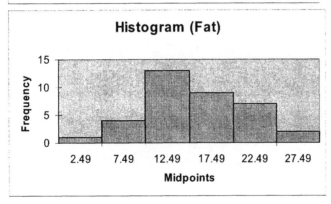

2.74   (b)
cont.

Percentage Polygon for Cost

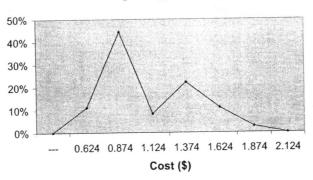

Percentage Polygon for Calories

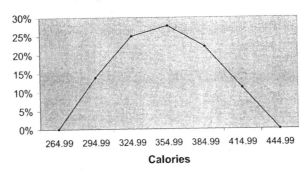

Percentage Polygon for Fat

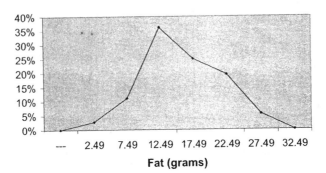

2.74   (c)
cont.

Cumulative Percentage Polygon for Cost

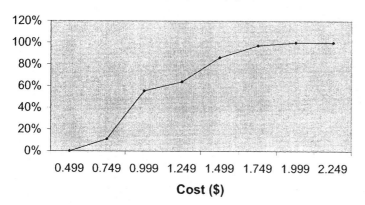

Cumulative Percentage Polygon for Calories

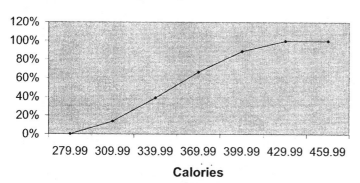

Cumulative Percentage Polygon for Fat

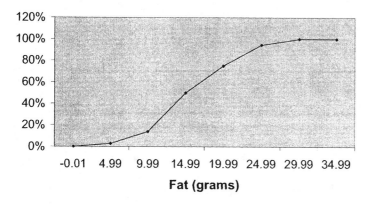

2.74   (d)
cont.

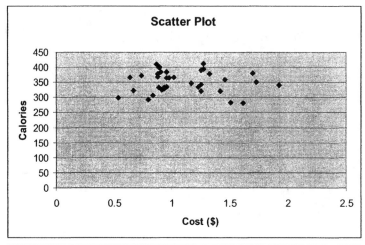

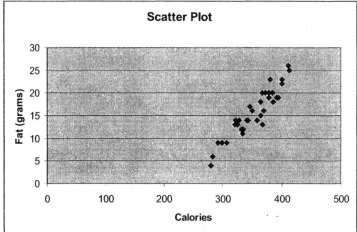

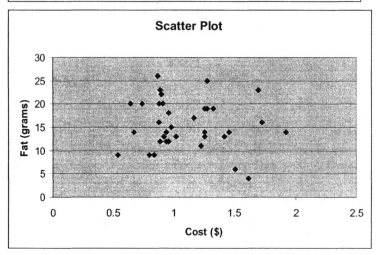

2.74 (e)   The typical cost for a slice of pizza is between $.75 and $1.00 since that is the most
cont.   frequently occurring interval and better than 50% of the sample is less than or equal to
            $1.00. The typical caloric content for a slice of pizza is between 310 and 400 calories
            since better than 80% of the sample falls in that range. More than 73% of the pizzas have
            between 10 to 20 grams of fat. Based on the results of the pair-wise scatter diagrams,
            calories and fat seem to be related. Other variables do not show any particular pattern in
            the scatter plot. But the graph of calories and fat has a positive slope because it rises
            from left to right, showing that as one variable increases, the other tends to also increase.
            The data points are tightly distributed within the cloud of points, indicating that the
            relationship between calories and fat content is strong.

2.76 (a)

Frequencies (Boston)

Weight (Boston)	Frequency	Percentage
3015 but less than 3050	2	0.54%
3050 but less than 3085	44	11.96%
3085 but less than 3120	122	33.15%
3120 but less than 3155	131	35.60%
3155 but less than 3190	58	15.76%
3190 but less than 3225	7	1.90%
3225 but less than 3260	3	0.82%
3260 but less than 3295	1	0.27%

(b)

Frequencies (Vermont)

Weight (Vermont)	Frequency	Percentage
3550 but less than 3600	4	1.21%
3600 but less than 3650	31	9.39%
3650 but less than 3700	115	34.85%
3700 but less than 3750	131	39.70%
3750 but less than 3800	36	10.91%
3800 but less than 3850	12	3.64%
3850 but less than 3900	1	0.30%

2.76   (c)
cont.

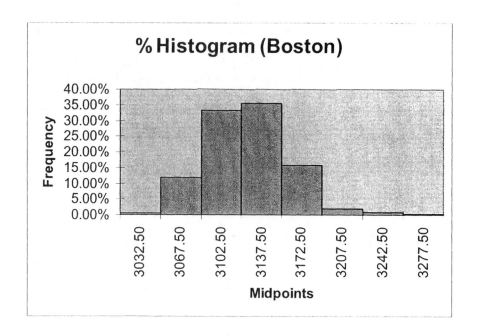

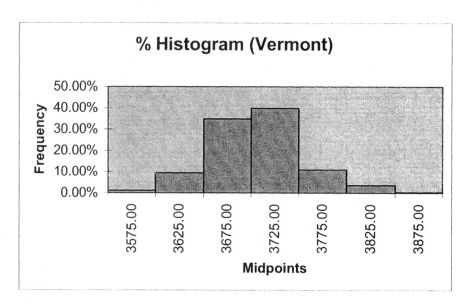

(d)   0.54% of the "Boston" shingles pallets are underweight while 0.27% are overweight. 1.21% of the "Vermont" shingles pallets are underweight while 3.94% are overweight.

2.78   (a), (c)

Calories	Frequency	Percentage	Percentage Less Than
50 up to 100	3	12%	12%
100 up to 150	3	12	24
150 up to 200	9	36	60
200 up to 250	6	24	84
250 up to 300	3	12	96
300 up to 350	0	0	96
350 up to 400	1	4	100
Protein	**Frequency**	**Percentage**	**Percentage Less Than**
16 up to 20	1	4	4
20 up to 24	5	20	24
24 up to 28	8	32	56
28 up to 32	9	36	92
32 up to 36	2	8	100
Calories from Fat	**Frequency**	**Percentage of Percentage**	**Percentage Less Than**
0% up to 10%	3	12	12
10% up to 20%	4	16	28
20% up to 30%	2	8	36
30% up to 40%	5	20	56
40% up to 50%	3	12	68
50% up to 60%	5	20	88
60% up to 70%	2	8	96
70% up to 80%	1	4	100
Calories from Saturated Fat	**Frequency**	**Percentage of Percentage**	**Percentage Less Than**
0% up to 5%	6	24	24
5% up to 10%	2	8	32
10% up to 15%	5	20	52
15% up to 20%	5	20	72
20% up to 25%	5	20	92
25% up to 30%	2	8	100
Cholesterol	**Frequency**	**Percentage**	**Percentage Less Than**
0 up to 50	2	8	8%
50 up to 100	17	68	76
100 up to 150	4	16	92
150 up to 200	1	4	96
200 up to 250	0	0	96
250 up to 300	0	0	96
300 up to 350	0	0	96
350 up to 400	0	0	96
400 up to 450	0	0	96
450 up to 500	1	4	100

2.78   (b)
cont.

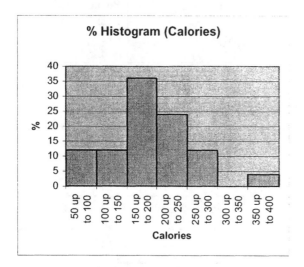

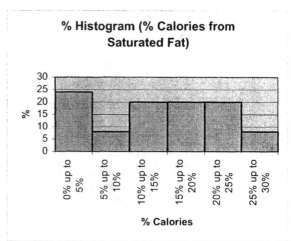

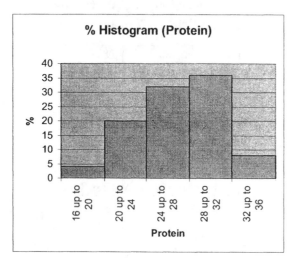

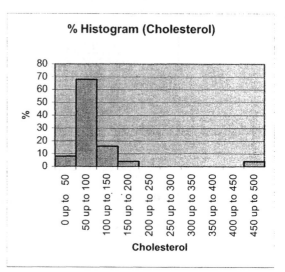

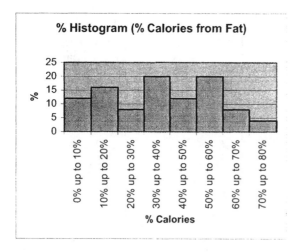

2.78 (b)
cont.

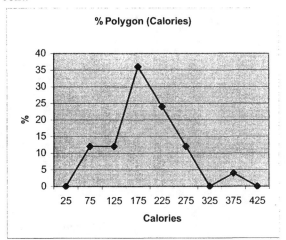

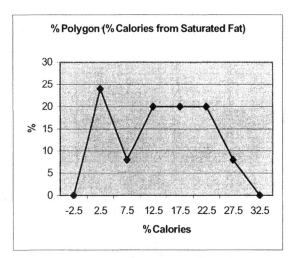

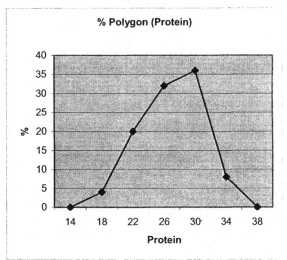

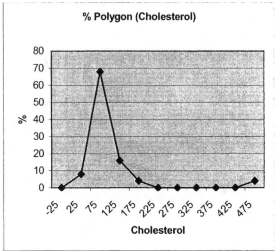

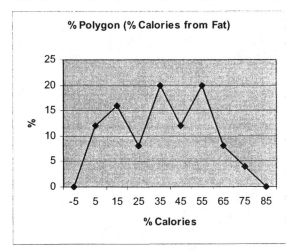

2.78   (c)
cont.

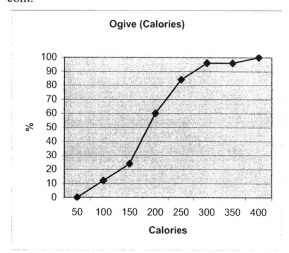

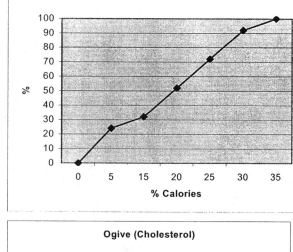

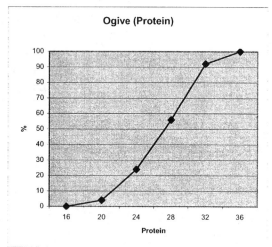

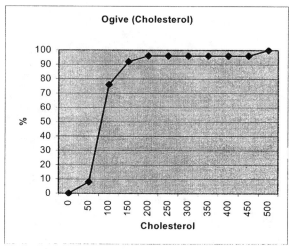

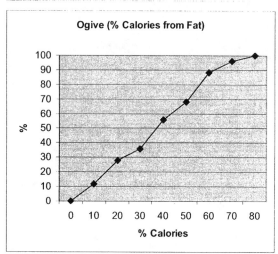

2.78   (d)   The sampled fresh red meats, poultry, and fish vary from 98 to 397 calories per
cont.   serving with the highest concentration between 150 to 200 calories. One protein
                 source, spareribs with 397 calories, was over 100 calories beyond the next highest
                 caloric food. The protein content of the sampled foods varies from 16 to 33 grams
                 with 68% of the data values falling between 24 and 32 grams. Spareribs and fried
                 liver are both very different from other foods sampled, the former on calories and the
                 latter on cholesterol content.

2.80   (a)

Count of Drive Type	Fuel Type			
Drive Type	Diesel	Premium	Regular	Grand Total
AWD	0	5	2	7
Front	1	18	63	82
Front, AWD	0	0	1	1
Permanent 4WD	0	3	0	3
Rear	0	11	17	28
Grand Total	1	37	83	121

(b)

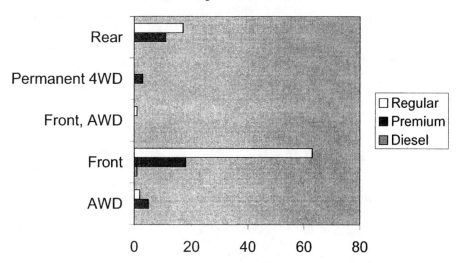

Side-By-Side Chart

(c)   Based on the results of (a) and (b), the percentage of front-wheels drive cars that use
       regular gasoline appears to be higher than that for rear-wheel drive cars.

2.82 (a), (c)

Average Ticket$	Frequency	Percentage	Cumulative %
More than 6 and up to 12	3	10.00%	10.00%
More than 12 and up to 18	12	40.00%	50.00%
More than 18 and up to 24	11	36.67%	86.67%
More than 24 and up to 30	3	10.00%	96.67%
More than 30 and up to 36	0	0.00%	96.67%
More than 36 and up to 42	1	3.33%	100.00%

Fan Cost Index	Frequency	Percentage	Cumulative %
More than 80 and up to 105	2	6.67%	6.67%
More than 105 and up to 130	7	23.33%	30.00%
More than 130 and up to 155	10	33.33%	63.33%
More than 155 and up to 180	9	30.00%	93.33%
More than 180 and up to 205	1	3.33%	96.67%
More than 205 and up to 230	1	3.33%	100.00%

Regular season game receipts ($millions)	Frequency	Percentage	Cumulative %
More than 5 and up to 20	5	16.67%	16.67%
More than 20 and up to 35	7	23.33%	40.00%
More than 35 and up to 50	5	16.67%	56.67%
More than 50 and up to 65	6	20.00%	76.67%
More than 65 and up to 80	5	16.67%	93.33%
More than 80 and up to 95	1	3.33%	96.67%
More than 95 and up to 110	1	3.33%	100.00%

Local TV, radio and cable ($millions)	Frequency	Percentage	Cumulative %
More than 0 and up to 10	7	23.33%	23.33%
More than 10 and up to 20	13	43.33%	66.67%
More than 20 and up to 30	5	16.67%	83.33%
More than 30 and up to 40	3	10.00%	93.33%
More than 40 and up to 50	1	3.33%	96.67%
More than 50 and up to 60	1	3.33%	100.00%

Other Local Operating Revenue	Frequency	Percentage	Cumulative %
More than 0 and up to 10	6	20.00%	20.00%
More than 10 and up to 20	3	10.00%	30.00%
More than 20 and up to 30	8	26.67%	56.67%
More than 30 and up to 40	8	26.67%	83.33%
More than 40 and up to 50	3	10.00%	93.33%
More than 50 and up to 60	1	3.33%	96.67%
More than 60 and up to 70	1	3.33%	100.00%

2.82
cont.

(a), (c)

Player compensation and benefits	Frequency	Percentage	Cumulative %
More than 30 and up to 45	5	16.67%	16.67%
More than 45 and up to 60	8	26.67%	43.33%
More than 60 and up to 75	4	13.33%	56.67%
More than 75 and up to 90	5	16.67%	73.33%
More than 90 and up to 105	5	16.67%	90.00%
More than 105 and up to 120	3	10.00%	100.00%

National and other local Expenses	Frequency	Percentage	Cumulative %
More than 30 and up to 40	4	13.33%	13.33%
More than 40 and up to 50	10	33.33%	46.67%
More than 50 and up to 60	9	30.00%	76.67%
More than 60 and up to 70	2	6.67%	83.33%
More than 70 and up to 80	3	10.00%	93.33%
More than 80 and up to 90	2	6.67%	100.00%

Income from Baseball Operations	Frequency	Percentage	Cumulative %
More than -60 and up to -45	2	6.67%	6.67%
More than -45 and up to -30	2	6.67%	13.33%
More than -45 and up to −15	8	26.67%	40.00%
More than -15 and up to 0	8	26.67%	66.67%
More than 0 and up to 15	7	23.33%	90.00%
More than 15 and up to 30	1	3.33%	93.33%
More than 30 and up to 45	2	6.67%	100.00%

(b), (c)

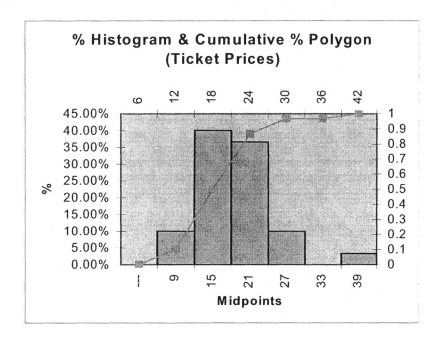

2.82   (b), (c)
cont.

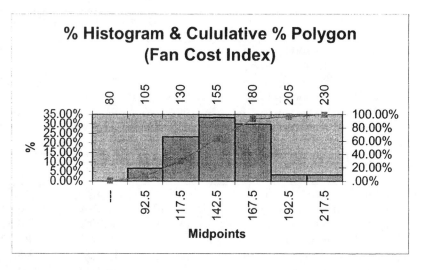

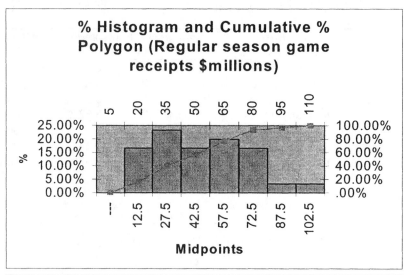

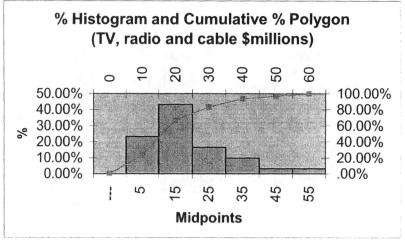

2.82 (b), (c)
cont.

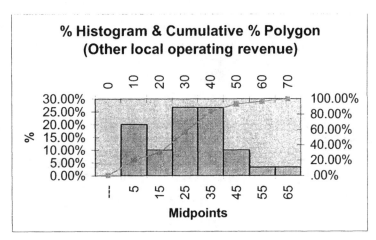

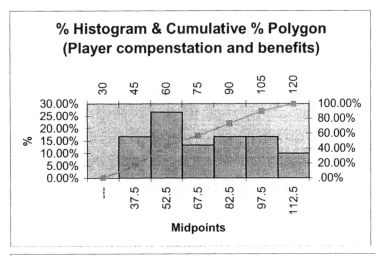

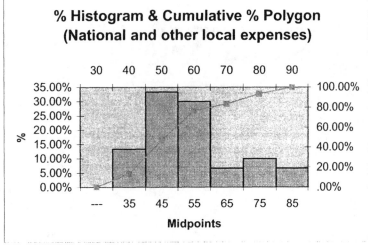

2.82   (b), (c)
cont.

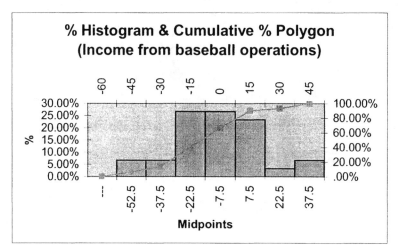

(b)

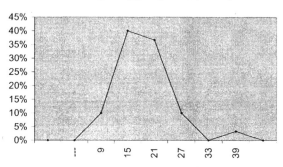

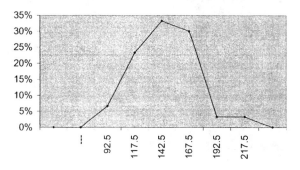

2.82   (b)
cont.

Percentage Polygon (Regular season game receipts)

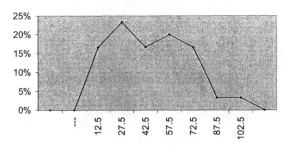

Percentage Polygon (Local TV, radio and cable ($millions))

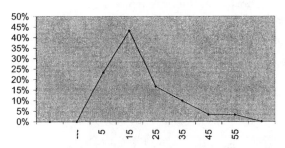

Percentage Polygon (Other Local Operating Revenue)

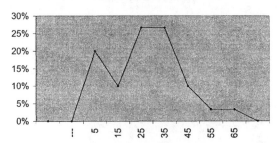

Percentage Polygon (Player compensation and benefits)

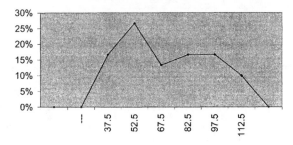

2.82   (b)
cont.

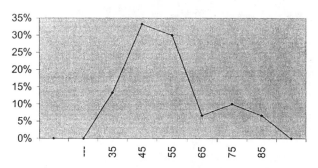

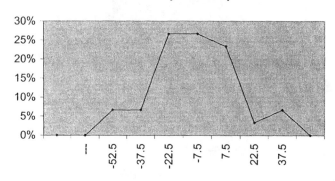

(d)

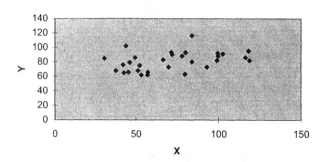

There appears to be a positive linear relationship between number of wins and player compensation and benefits.

2.84   (a)

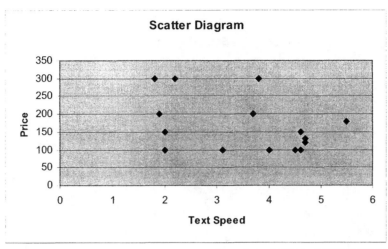

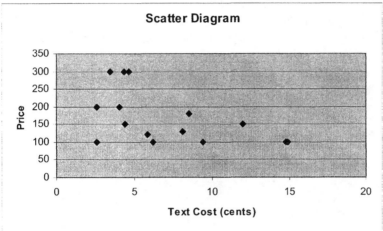

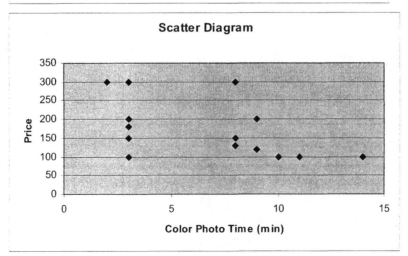

2.84   (a)
cont.

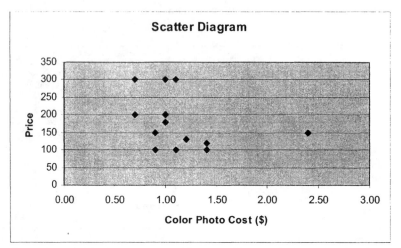

(b)   The only variable that appears to be useful in predicting printer price is text cost. There appears to be a negative relationship between price and text cost. The higher the text cost, the lower the printer cost.

CHAPTER 3

OBJECTIVES

- To be able to describe the properties of central tendency, variation, and shape in numerical data
- To be able to calculate descriptive summary measures from population
- To be able to develop and interpret a box-and-whisker plot
- To be able to calculate the coefficient of correlation

OVERVIEW AND KEY CONCEPTS

Measures of Central Tendency

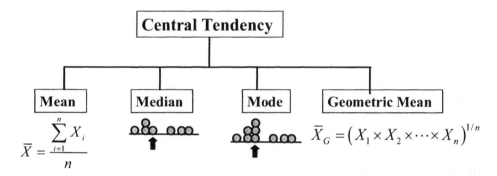

- **Arithmetic mean:** The sum of all the observations in a set of data divided by the total number of observations.

  - $$\overline{X} = \frac{\sum_{i=1}^{n} X_i}{n}$$

  - The arithmetic mean is the most common measure of central tendency.
  - It is very sensitive to extreme values, called outliers.
- **Median:** The value such that 50% of the observations are smaller and 50% of the observations are larger.

  - Median $= \dfrac{n+1}{2}$ ranked observation.

  - If n is odd, the median is the middle ranked observation.
  - If n is even, the median is the average of the two middle ranked observations.
  - The median is not affected by extreme values.

- **Mode:** The value that occurs most often in a set of data.
  - It is not affected by extreme values.
  - There may be several modes or there may be no mode in a set of data.
  - It can be used for either numerical or categorical data.
- **Geometric mean:** The nth root of the product of n values.
  - $$\bar{X}_G = \left(X_1 \times X_2 \times \cdots \times X_n \right)^{1/n}$$
  - It is useful in the measure of rate of change of a variable over time.
  - The geometric mean rate of return can be used to measure the status of an investment over time. $\bar{R}_G = \left[\left(1 + R_1 \right) \times \left(1 + R_2 \right) \times \cdots \times \left(1 + R_n \right) \right]^{1/n} - 1$
- **Quartiles:** The most widely used measures of noncentral location.
  - The ordered data is split into four equal portions.
  - The first quartile (Q_1) is the value for which 25% of the observations are smaller and 75% are larger.

    $Q_1 = \dfrac{n+1}{4}$ ordered observation.
  - The third quartile (Q_3) is the value for which 75% of the observations are smaller and 25% are larger.

    $Q_3 = \dfrac{3(n+1)}{4}$ ordered observation.
  - The median is the second quartile.

    $Q_2 = \dfrac{(n+1)}{2}$ ordered observation.

Measures of Variation

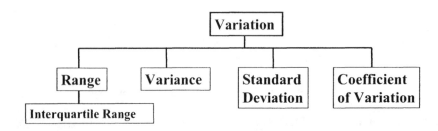

- **Range:** The largest value minus the smallest value.
  - The range ignores how the data are distributed.
  - It is very sensitive to extreme values.
- **Interquartile range (mid-spread):** The 3rd quartile minus the 1st quartile.
  - It is not affected by extreme values.
  - It measures the spread of the middle 50% of the observations.

- **Sample variance:** The sum of the squared differences around the arithmetic mean divided by the sample size minus 1.

  - $$S^2 = \frac{\sum_{i=1}^{n}(X_i - \bar{X})^2}{n-1}$$

    - Sample variance measures the average scatter around the mean.
- **Sample standard deviation:** The square root of the sample variance.

  - $$S = \sqrt{\frac{\sum_{i=1}^{n}(X_i - \bar{X})^2}{n-1}}$$

    - Sample standard deviation has the same units of measurement as the original data.
- **Coefficient of Variation:** The standard deviation divided by the arithmetic mean, multiplied by 100%.

  - $$CV = \left(\frac{S}{\bar{X}}\right)100\%$$

    - It is a relative measure of variation.
    - It is used in comparing two or more sets of data measured in different units.

Shape of a Distribution

- The shape describes how data is distributed.
- Measures of shapes can be symmetric or skewed.

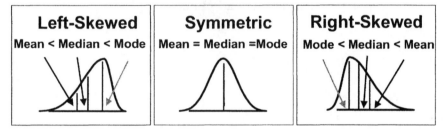

| **Left-Skewed** | **Symmetric** | **Right-Skewed** |
| Mean < Median < Mode | Mean = Median =Mode | Mode < Median < Mean |

Exploratory Data Analysis

- A five-number summary consists of X_{smallest}, Q_1, Median, Q_3, X_{largest}.
- **Box-and-whisker plot:** Provides a graphical representation of the data based on the five-number summary.

Distribution Shape and Box-and-Whisker Plot

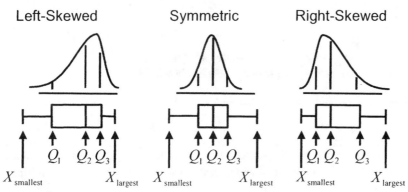

- In right-skewed distributions, the distance from the median to $X_{largest}$ is greater than the distance from $X_{smallest}$ to the median.
- In right-skewed distribution, the distance from Q_3 to $X_{largest}$ is greater than the distance from $X_{smallest}$ to Q_1.
- In left-skewed distributions, the distance from the median to $X_{largest}$ is smaller than the distance from $X_{smallest}$ to the median.
- In left-skewed distribution, the distance from Q_3 to $X_{largest}$ is smaller than the distance from $X_{smallest}$ to Q_1.

Obtaining Descriptive Summary Measures from a Population

- **Population mean:** $\mu = \dfrac{\sum\limits_{i=1}^{N} X_i}{N}$

- **Population variance:** $\sigma^2 = \dfrac{\sum\limits_{i=1}^{N}(X_i - \mu)^2}{N}$

- **Population standard deviation:** $\sigma = \sqrt{\dfrac{\sum\limits_{i=1}^{N}(X_i - \mu)^2}{N}}$

- **The empirical rule:** In bell-shaped distributions, roughly 68% of the observations are contained within a distance of ± 1 standard deviation around the mean, approximately 95% of the observations are contained within a distance of ± 2 standard deviation around the mean and approximately 99.7% are contained within a distance of ± 3 standard deviation around the mean.

- **The Bienaymé-Chebyshev rule:** Regardless of how skewed a set of data is distributed, the percentage of observations that are contained within distances of k standard deviations around the mean must be at least $\left(1 - \dfrac{1}{k^2}\right)100\%$

  - At least 75% of the observations must be contained within distances of ± 2 standard deviation around the mean.
  - At least 88.89% of the observations must be contained within distances of ± 3 standard deviation around the mean.
  - At least 93.75% of the observations must be contained within distances of ± 4 standard deviation around the mean.

Computing Numerical Descriptive Measures from a Frequency Distribution

- **Approximating the sample mean:** $\overline{X} = \dfrac{\displaystyle\sum_{j=1}^{c} m_j f_j}{n}$

  where c = number of classes
  m_j = midpoint of the jth class
  f_j = frequency of the jth class

- **Approximating the sample standard deviation:** $S = \sqrt{\dfrac{\displaystyle\sum_{j=1}^{c} \left(m_j - \overline{X}\right)^2 f_j}{n-1}}$

Correlation Coefficient as a Measure of Strength between Two Numerical Variables

- **The coefficient of correlation:** $r = \dfrac{\displaystyle\sum_{i=1}^{n}\left(X_i - \overline{X}\right)\left(Y_i - \overline{Y}\right)}{\sqrt{\displaystyle\sum_{i=1}^{n}\left(X_i - \overline{X}\right)^2 \sum_{i=1}^{n}\left(Y_i - \overline{Y}\right)^2}}$

  - Measures the strength of a linear relationship between 2 numerical variables X and Y.
  - Is unit free.
  - The values are between -1 and 1.
  - The closer r is to -1, the stronger the negative linear relationship.
  - The closer r is to $+1$, the stronger the positive linear relationship.
  - If r is close to 0, little or no linear relationship exists.

SOLUTIONS TO END OF SECTION
AND CHAPTER REVIEW EVEN PROBLEMS

3.2   (a)   Mean = 7   Median = 7   Mode = 7
       (b)   Range = 9   Variance = 10.8   Interquartile range = 5
              Standard deviation = 3.286   Coefficient of variation = (3.286/7)•100% = 46.94%
       (c)   Z scores: 0, -0.913, 0.609, 0, -1.217, 1.522
              None of the Z scores is larger than 3.0 or smaller than -3.0. There is no outlier.
       (d)   Since the mean equals the median, the distribution is symmetrical.

3.4   (a)   Mean = 2   Median = 7   Mode = 7
       (b)   Range = 17   Variance = 62   Interquartile range = 14.5
              Standard deviation = 7.874   Coefficient of variation = (7.874/2)•100% = 393.7%
       (c)   Since the mean is less than the median, the distribution is left-skewed.

3.6   (a)
	Grade X	Grade Y
Mean	575	575.4
Median	575	575
Standard deviation	6.4	2.1

       (b)   If quality is measured by the average inner diameter, Grade X tires provide slightly better
              quality because X's mean and median are both equal to the expected value, 575 mm. If,
              however, quality is measured by consistency, Grade Y provides better quality because,
              even though Y's mean is only slightly larger than the mean for Grade X, Y's standard
              deviation is much smaller. The range in values for Grade Y is 5 mm compared to the
              range in values for Grade X which is 16 mm.
       (c)
	Grade X	Grade Y, Altered
Mean	575	577.4
Median	575	575
Standard deviation	6.4	6.1

              In the event the fifth Y tire measures 588 mm rather than 578 mm, Y's average inner
              diameter becomes 577.4 mm, which is larger than X's average inner diameter, and Y's
              standard deviation swells from 2.07 mm to 6.11 mm. In this case, X's tires are providing
              better quality in terms of the average inner diameter with only slightly more variation
              among the tires than Y's.

3.8   (a)   The distribution of family incomes will most likely be skewed to the right due to the
              presence of a few millionaires and billionaires. As a result, the median income is a better
              measure of central tendency than the mean income.
       (b)   The article reports the median home price and not the mean home price because it is a
              better measure of central tendency in the presence of some extremely expensive homes
              that will drive the mean home price upward.

3.10 Excel output:

Product	Calories	Fat	Calories Z Score	Fat Z Score
Dunkin' Donuts Iced Mocha Swirl latte (whole milk)	240	8	-1.24	-1.07
Starbucks Coffee Frappuccino blended coffee	260	3.5	-1.06	-1.69
Dunkin' Donuts Coffee Coolatta (cream)	350	22	-0.27	0.86
Starbucks Iced Coffee Mocha Expresso (whole milk and whipped cream)	350	20	-0.27	0.58
Starbucks Mocha Frappuccino blended coffee (whipped cream)	420	16	0.35	0.03
Starbucks Chocolate Brownie Frappuccino blended coffee (whipped cream)	510	22	1.15	0.86
Starbucks Chocolate Frappuccino Blended Crème (whipped cream)	530	19	1.33	0.44

(a)   Calories: mean = 380   median = 350 1st quartile = 260 3rd quartile = 510
     Fat: mean = 15.8   median = 19 1st quartile = 8 3rd quartile = 22

(b)   Calories: variance = 12800   standard deviation = 113.1   range = 290
     interquartile range = 250   CV = 29.77%
     None of the Z scores are less than -3 or greater than 3. There is no outlier in calories.
     Fat: variance = 52.82   standard deviation = 7.3   range = 18.5
     Interquartile range = 14   CV = 46.04%
     None of the Z scores are less than -3 or greater than 3. There is no outlier in fat.

(c)   Calories are slightly right-skewed while fat is slightly left-skewed.

(d)   The mean calories is 380 while the middle ranked calorie is 350. The average scatter of calories around the mean is 113.14. 50% of the calories are scattered over 250 while the difference between the highest and the lowest calories is 290.
     The mean fat is 15.79 grams while the middle ranked fat is 19 grams. The average scatter of fat around the mean is 7.27 grams. 50% of the fat is scattered over 14 grams while the difference between the highest and the lowest fat is 18.5 grams.

3.12 Excel output:

Price($)	Price Z Score
340	-0.1121
450	1.4576
450	1.4576
280	-0.9684
220	-1.8246
340	-0.1121
290	-0.8257
370	0.3160
400	0.7441
310	-0.5402
340	-0.1121
430	1.1722
270	-1.1111
380	0.4587

3.12 (a) mean = \$348   median = \$340   1st quartile = \$290   3rd quartile = \$400
cont. (b) variance = 4910   standard deviation = \$70   range = \$230
           interquartile range = \$110   CV = 20.14%
           None of the Z scores are less than -3 or greater than 3. There is no outlier in the price.
      (c) The price of 3-megapixel cameras is rather symmetrical.
      (d) The mean price is \$348 while the middle ranked price is \$340. The average scatter of
           price around the mean is \$70. 50% of the price is scattered over \$110 while the
           difference between the highest and the lowest price is \$230.

3.14 (a) Mean = 473.5   Median = 451   There is no mode.
           The median seems to be a better descriptive measure of the data, since it is closer to the
           observed values than is the mean. Also the outlier of 1049 affects the mean.
      (b) Range = 785   Variance = 44,422.44   Standard deviation = 210.77
      (c) From the manufacturer's viewpoint, the worst measure would be to compute the
           percentage of batteries that last over 400 hours (8/13 = .61). The median (451) and the
           mean (473.5) are both over 400, and would be better measures for the manufacturer to
           use in advertisements.
      (d) (a), (b)

	Original Data	Altered Data
Mean	473.5	550.4
Median	451	492
Mode	none	none
Range	785	1,078
Variance	44,422.44	99,435.26
Standard deviation	210.77	315.33

           (c) From the manufacturer's viewpoint, the worst measure remains the percentage of
           batteries that last over 400 hours (9/13 = .69). The median (492) and the mean
           (550.38) are both well over 400, and would be better measures for the manufacturer
           to use in advertisements.
           The shape of the distribution of the original data is right-skewed, since the mean is
           larger than the median.
           The shape of the distribution of the altered data set is right-skewed as well, since its
           mean is also larger than its median.

3.16 (a) Mean = 7.114   Median = 6.68 Q_1 = 5.64 Q_3 = 8.73
      (b) Variance = 4.336   Standard deviation = 2.082   Range = 6.67
           Interquartile range = 3.09   Coefficient of variation = 29.27%
      (c) Since the mean is greater than the median, the distribution is right-skewed.
      (d) The mean and median are both well over 5 minutes and the distribution is right-skewed,
           meaning that there are more unusually high observations than low. Further, 13 of the 15
           bank customers sampled (or 86.7%) had wait times in excess of 5 minutes. So, the
           customer is more likely to experience a wait time in excess of 5 minutes. The manager
           overstated the bank's service record in responding that the customer would "almost
           certainly" not wait longer than 5 minutes for service.

3.18 (a)

Year	DJIA	SP500	Russell2000	Wilshire5000
2003	25.30	26.40	45.40	29.40
2002	-15.01	-22.10	-21.58	-20.90
2001	-5.44	-11.90	-1.03	-10.97
2000	-6.20	-9.10	-3.02	-10.89
Geometric mean	-1.42%	-5.77%	2.28%	-5.07%

(b) The rate of return of SP500 is the worst at -5.77% followed by Wilshire 5000 at -5.07% and DJIA -1.42%. Russell 2000 is the only stock among the four that has a positive rate of return at 2.28% over the four-year period.

(c) In general, investments in the metal market achieved a higher rate of return than investments in the certificate of deposit market from 2000 to 2003. Investments in the stock market had the worse rate of return.

3.20 (a)

Year	Platinum	Gold	Silver
2003	34.2	19.5	24.0
2002	24.5	24.5	5.5
2001	-21.3	1.2	-3.0
2000	-23.3	1.8	-5.9
Geometric Mean	0.21%	11.27%	4.53%

(b) All three metals achieved positive rate of returns over the four-year period with gold yielding the highest rate of return at 11.27%, followed by silver at 4.53% and platinum at 0.21%.

(c) In general, investments in the metal market achieved a higher rate of return than investments in the certificate of deposit market from 2000 to 2003. Investments in the stock market had the worse rate of return.

3.22 (a) Population Mean = 6

(b) $\sigma = 1.67$ $\sigma^2 = 2.8$

3.24 (a) 68% (b) 95% (c) not calculable 75% 88.89%

(d) $\mu - 4\sigma$ to $\mu + 4\sigma$ or -2.8 to 19.2

3.26 (a) mean = 12999.2158, variance = 14959700.52, std. dev. = 3867.7772

(b) 64.71%, 98.04% and 100% of these states have average per capita energy consumption within 1, 2 and 3 standard deviation of the mean, respectively.

(c) This is consistent with the 68%, 95% and 99.7% according to the empirical rule.

(d) (a) mean = 12857.7402, variance = 14238110.67, std. dev. = 3773.3421

(b) 66%, 98% and 100% of these states have average per capita energy consumption within 1, 2 and 3 standard deviation of the mean, respectively.

(c) This is consistent with the 68%, 95% and 99.7% according to the empirical rule.

3.28

m_j	f_j	$m_j f_j$	$(m_j - \overline{X})^2 f_j$
5	10	50	4000
15	20	300	2000
25	40	1000	0
35	20	700	2000
45	10	450	4000
	$n = 100$	$\Sigma(m_j f_j) = 2500$	$\Sigma(m_j - \overline{X})^2 f_j = 12000$

(a) $\overline{X} = \dfrac{\sum\limits_{j=1}^{c} m_j f_j}{n} = \dfrac{2500}{100} = 25$

(b) $S = \sqrt{\dfrac{\sum\limits_{j=1}^{c}(m_j - \overline{X})^2 f_j}{n-1}} = 11.01$

3.30   Excel output for March:

m_j	f_j	$m_j f_j$	$(m_j - \overline{X})^2 f_j$
1000	6	6000	83030400
3000	13	39000	38459200
5000	17	85000	1332800
7000	10	70000	51984000
9000	4	36000	73273600
11000	0	0	0
	$n = 50$	$\Sigma(m_j f_j) = 236000$	$\Sigma(m_j - \overline{X})^2 f_j = 2.48\text{E}+08$

Excel output for April:

m_j	f_j	$m_j f_j$	$(m_j - \overline{X})^2 f_j$
1000	10	10000	1.16E+08
3000	14	42000	27440000
5000	13	65000	4680000
7000	10	70000	67600000
9000	0	0	0
11000	3	33000	1.31E+08
	$n = 50$	$\Sigma(m_j f_j) = 220000$	$\Sigma(m_j - \overline{X})^2 f_j = 3.46\text{E}+08$

(a)   March: $\overline{X} = \dfrac{\sum\limits_{j=1}^{c} m_j f_j}{n} = \dfrac{236000}{50} = 4720$ April: $\overline{X} = \dfrac{\sum\limits_{j=1}^{c} m_j f_j}{n} = \dfrac{220000}{50} = 4400$

3.30 (b)
cont.

$$\text{March: } S = \sqrt{\dfrac{\sum_{j=1}^{c}\left(m_j - \bar{X}\right)^2 f_j}{n-1}} = 2250.08$$

$$\text{April: } S = \sqrt{\dfrac{\sum_{j=1}^{c}\left(m_j - \bar{X}\right)^2 f_j}{n-1}} = 2657.30$$

(c)   The arithmetic mean has declined by \$320 while the standard deviation has increased by \$407.22.

3.32 Excel output:

Division A				Division B			
m_j	f_j	$m_j f_j$	$\left(m_j - \bar{X}\right)^2 f_j$	m_j	f_j	$m_j f_j$	$\left(m_j - \bar{X}\right)^2 f_j$
25	8	200	1905.86	25	15	375	2099.583
35	17	595	502.1267	35	32	1120	107.2803
45	11	495	229.2533	45	20	900	1334.656
55	8	440	1697.164	55	4	220	1320.452
65	2	130	1206.9	65	0	0	0
	$n = 46$	$\Sigma\left(m_j f_j\right) =$ 1860	$\Sigma\left(m_j - \bar{X}\right)^2 f_j =$ 5541.304		$n = 71$	$\Sigma\left(m_j f_j\right) =$ 2615	$\Sigma\left(m_j - \bar{X}\right)^2 f_j =$ 4861.972

(a)   Division A: $\bar{X} = 40.4348$ Division B: $\bar{X} = 36.8310$
(b)   Division A: $S = 11.0969$ Division B: $S = 8.3341$
(c)   Division A has a higher mean and standard deviation in age than division B.

3.34 (a)   Five-number summary: 3 4 7 9 12
(b)

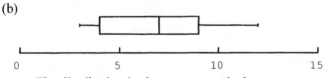

The distribution is almost symmetrical.
(c)   The data set is almost symmetrical since the median line almost divides the box in half but the whiskers show right skewness.

3.36 (a)   Five-number summary: −8 −6.5 7 8 9
(b)

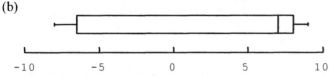

The distribution is left-skewed.
(c)   The box-and-whisker plot shows a longer left box from Q_1 to Q_2 than from Q_2 to Q_3, visually confirming our conclusion that the data are left-skewed.

3.38 (a)   Five-number summary: 309   593   895.5   1425   1720

(b)   PHStat output:

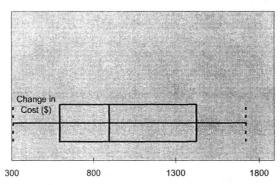

The distribution is skewed slightly to the right.

3.40 (a)   **Bounced check fee:** Five-number summary: 15 20 22 26 30
Monthly service fee: Five-number summary: 0 5 7 10 12

(b)

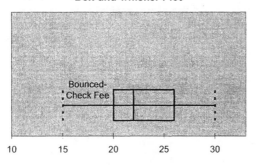

The distribution of bounced-check fee is skewed slightly to the right

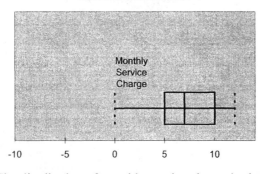

The distribution of monthly service charge is skewed to the left.

(c)   The central tendency of the bounced-check fee is substantially higher than that of monthly service fee. While the distribution of the bounced-check fee is quite symmetrical, the distribution of monthly service fee is skewed more to the left with a few banks charging very low or no monthly service fee.

3.42 (a)   **Commercial district**: Five-number summary: 0.38 3.2 4.5 5.55 6.46
            Residential area: Five-number summary: 3.82 5.64 6.68 8.73 10.49

   (b)   **Commercial district:**

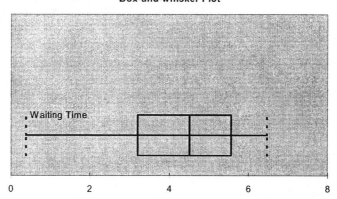

The distribution is skewed to the left.
Residential area:

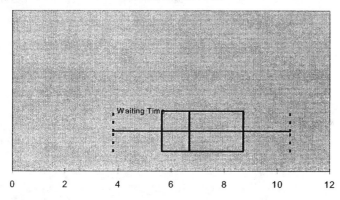

The distribution is skewed slightly to the right.

   (c)   The central tendency of the waiting times for the bank branch located in the commercial
          district of a city is lower than that of the branch located in the residential area. There are
          a few longer than normal waiting times for the branch located in the residential area
          whereas there are a few exceptionally short waiting times for the branch located in the
          commercial area.

3.44 (a)

Pair of Investments	Relationship
U.S. stocks and the International Large Cap stocks	strong positive linear relationship
U.S. stocks and Emerging market stocks	strong positive linear relationship
U.S. stocks and International Small Cap stocks	moderate positive linear relationship
U.S. stocks and Emerging market debt stocks	moderate positive linear relationship
U.S. stocks and International Bonds	very weak positive linear

(b)   In general, there is a positive linear relationship between the return on investment of U.S. stocks and international stocks, U.S. bonds and international bonds, U.S. stocks and Emerging market debt, and a very weak negative linear relationship, if any, between the return on investment of U.S. bonds and international stocks.

3.46 (a) $$\text{cov}(X,Y) = \frac{\sum_{i=1}^{n}(X_i - \bar{X})(Y_i - \bar{Y})}{n-1} = \frac{3550}{6} = 591.6667$$

(b) $$r = \frac{\text{cov}(X,Y)}{S_X S_Y} = \frac{591.6667}{(113.1371)(7.2678)} = 0.7196$$

(c)   The correlation coefficient is more valuable for expressing the relationship between calories and fat because it does not depend on the units used to measure calories and fat.

(d)   There is a rather strong positive linear relationship between calories and fat.

3.48 (a) $$\text{cov}(X,Y) = \frac{\sum_{i=1}^{n}(X_i - \bar{X})(Y_i - \bar{Y})}{n-1} = \frac{-6065.2421}{18} = -336.9579$$

(b) $$r = \frac{\text{cov}(X,Y)}{S_X S_Y} = \frac{-336.9579}{(105.3617)(7.9670)} = -0.4014$$

(c)   The coefficient of correlation between turnover rate and security violations indicates that there is a moderate negative linear relationship between the two.

3.50   We should look for ways to describe the typical value, the variation, and the distribution of the data within a range.

3.52   The arithmetic mean is a simple average of all the values, but is subject to the effect of extreme values. The median is the middle ranked value, but varies more from sample to sample than the arithmetic mean, although it is less susceptible to extreme values. The mode is the most common value, but is extremely variable from sample to sample.

3.54   Variation is the amount of dispersion, or "spread," in the data.

3.56   The range is a simple measure, but only measures the difference between the extremes. The interquartile range measures the range of the center fifty percent of the data. The standard deviation measures variation around the mean while the variance measures the squared variation around the mean, and these are the only measures that take into account each observation. The coefficient of variation measures the variation around the mean relative to the mean.

3.58   The Chebyshev rule applies to any type of distribution while the empirical rule applies only to data sets that are approximately bell-shaped. The empirical rule is more accurate than Chebyshev rule in approximating the concentration of data around the mean.

3.60   The covariance measures the strength of the linear relationship between two numerical variables while the coefficient of correlation measures the relative strength of the linear relationship. The value of the covariance depends very much on the units used to measure the two numerical variables while the value of the coefficient of correlation is totally free from the units used.

3.62   (a)   mean = 43.89   median = 45 1st quartile = 18 3rd quartile = 63
       (b)   range = 76   interquartile range = 45   variance = 639.2564
             standard deviation = 25.28   coefficient of variation = 57.61%
       (c)

Box-and-whisker Plot

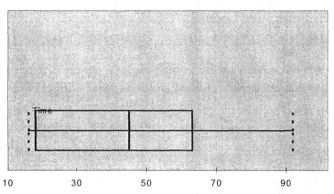

10	30	50	70	90

The distribution is skewed to the right because there are a few policies that require an exceptionally long period to be approved. However, if one compares the mean with the median, one can conclude that the distribution is skewed to the left because the mean is smaller than the median.

       (d)   The mean approval process takes 43.89 days with 50% of the policies being approved in less than 45 days. 50% of the applications are approved between 18 and 63 days. About 67% of the applications are approved between 18.6 to 69.2 days.

3.64 (a)   mean = 8.421, median = 8.42, range = 0.186 and standard deviation = 0.0461. On average, the width is 8.421 inches. The width of the middle ranked observation is 8.42. The difference between the largest and smallest width is 0.186 and majority of the widths fall between 0.0461 inches around the mean of 8.421 inches.

(b)   Minimum = 8.312, 1st quartile = 8.404, median = 8.42, 3rd quartile = 8.459 and maximum = 8.498

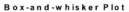

Box-and-whisker Plot

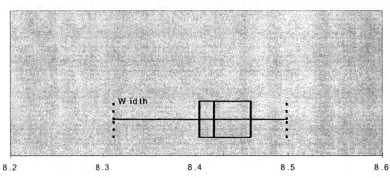

(c)

Even though the median is equal to the mean, the distribution is not symmetrical but skewed to the left.

(d)   All the troughs fall within the limit of 8.31 and 8.61 inches.

3.66 (a), (b)

	Time	
	Office I	Office II
Mean	2.214	2.012
Median	1.54	1.505
Standard Deviation	1.7180	1.8917
Sample Variance	2.9517	3.5786
Range	5.8	7.47
First Quartile	0.93	0.6
Third Quartile	3.93	3.75
Interquartile Range	3	3.15
Coefficient of Variation	77.60%	94.04%

3.66 (c)
cont.

Box-and-whisker Plot

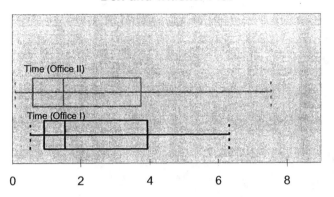

Times to clear problems at both central offices are right-skewed.

(d)   Times to clear problems for Office I are less dispersed about the mean than times to clear
        problems for Office II, even though the mean for Office I times is higher (2.214) than that
        for Office II (2.012).

3.68 (a), (b)

	Cost (per ounce)	Calories	Fiber (grams)	Sugar (grams)
Minimum	0.100000	50.000000	5.000000	0.000000
First Quartile	0.130000	135.000000	5.000000	6.000000
Median	0.170000	190.000000	6.000000	11.000000
Third Quartile	0.200000	200.000000	8.000000	17.500000
Maximum	0.270000	210.000000	13.000000	23.000000
Mean	0.170606	165.757576	6.909091	11.393939
Standard Deviation	0.046900	51.782617	2.402650	6.651783
Sample Variance	0.002200	2681.439394	5.772727	44.246212
Range	0.170000	160.000000	8.000000	23.000000
Interquartile range	0.070000	65.000000	3.000000	11.500000
Coefficient of Variations	27.4903%	31.2400%	34.7752%	58.3800%

3.68   (c)
cont.

Box-and-whisker Plot (Cost per ounce)

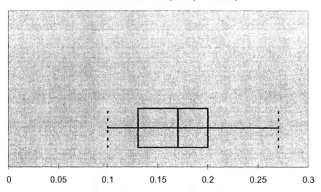

Box-and-whisker Plot (Calories)

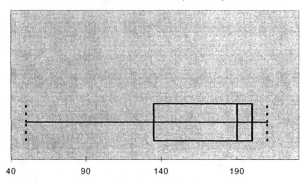

Box-and-whisker Plot (Fiber)

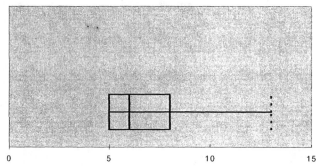

Box-and-whisker Plot (Sugar)

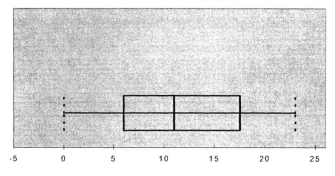

3.68   (c)   The distribution for fiber content is skewed to the right while the distribution for calories
cont.   is skewed to the left. The distributions for cost per ounce and sugar content are quite
              symmetrical.

    (d)   Cost: The mean cost is about 17 cents per ounce; most cereals cluster around this cost
              with a few high priced cereals. The average scatter around the mean is about 5 cents per
              ounce.
              Calories: The mean calories is about 166 and a middle value of 190, with an average
              scatter around the mean of about 52. Since the data are left skewed most of the calories
              are clustered at the high end with a few lower calorie cereals.

3.70   (a)   With promotion: mean = 20748.93, standard deviation = 8109.50
              Without promotion: mean = 13935.70, standard deviation = 4437.92

    (b)   With promotion: minimum = 10470, 1st quartile = 14905, median = 19775,
              3rd quartile = 24456, maximum = 40605
              Without promotion: minimum = 9555, 1st quartile = 11779, median = 12952,
              3rd quartile = 14367, maximum = 28834

    (c)

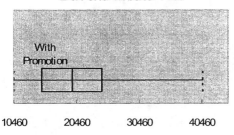

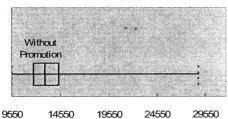

    (d)   The mean attendance is 6813 more when there is a promotion than when there is not, and
              the variation in attendance when there is a promotion is larger than when there is no
              promotion. There are many factors that can cause variation in the paid attendance. Some
              of them are weather condition, time and day of the game, home or visiting team, etc.

3.72 (a)   Excel output:
                   Five-number Summary

	Boston	Vermont
Minimum	0.04	0.02
First Quartile	0.17	0.13
Median	0.23	0.2
Third Quartile	0.32	0.28
Maximum	0.98	0.83

(b)

Box-and-whisker Plot

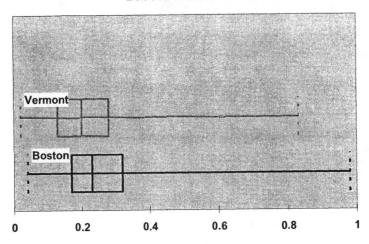

Both distributions are right skewed.

(c)   Majority (75%) of the Boston and Vermont shingles are able to achieve a granule
          loss of 0.8 grams or less. However, the highest amount of granule loss of the Boston
          and Vermont shingles are 0.98 grams and 0.83 grams, respectively, which are above
          the 0.8 grams threshold.

3.74 (a), (b) Excel output:

	Average Ticket$	Fan Cost Index	Regular season gate receipts ($millions)	Local TV, radio and cable ($millions)	Other Local Operating Revenue	Player compensation and benefits	National and other local Expenses	Income from Baseball Operations
Minimum	6.61	84.89	6.4	0.5	2.8	30.5	35	-52.9
First Quartile	15.2	124.25	30.2	10.9	13.9	49.4	46.9	-18.5
Median	17.83	143.475	47.55	16.35	29.05	70.8	50.5	-8.35
Third Quartile	20.84	160.76	62.1	23.6	37	92.8	58.5	1.9
Maximum	39.68	228.73	98	56.8	61.5	118.5	84.2	40.9
Mean	18.1333	144.5737	46.1367	19.0467	27.5933	71.3567	54.6467	-8.3733
Variance	35.9797	843.4552	512.5445	151.0184	234.6186	663.8405	176.4081	428.1531
Standard Dev	5.9983	29.0423	22.6394	12.2890	15.3173	25.7651	13.2819	20.6919
Range	33.07	143.84	91.60	56.30	58.70	88.00	49.20	93.80
Interquartile Range	5.64	36.51	31.90	12.70	23.10	43.40	11.60	20.40
Coefficient of Variation	33.08%	20.09%	49.07%	64.52%	55.51%	36.11%	24.30%	-247.12%

(c)

Box-and-whisker Plot

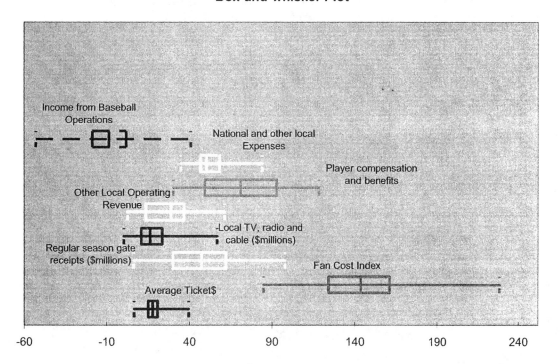

Average ticket prices, local TV, radio and cable receipts, national and other local expenses are skewed to the right; fan cost index is slightly skewed to the right; all other variables are pretty symmetrical.

3.74   (d) $r = 0.3985$. There is a moderate positive linear relationship between the number of wins
cont.   and player compensation and benefits.

3.76   (a)   Price and text speed: $r = -0.3842$
             Price and text cost: $r = -0.5123$
             Price and color photo time: $r = -0.5443$
             Price and color photo cost: $r = -0.2614$
       (b)   Color photo time has the strongest relationship with price of the four variables, although
             it is still only a moderate relationship, so it would be the most helpful in predicting price.
             As the price increases the color photo time tends to decrease. All four variables have a
             negative (inverse) relationship with price.

3.78   **For not SUV:**
       (a), (b)

	MPG	Length	Width	Cargo Volume	Turning Circle	Weight
Minimum	17	155	65	5	33	2150
First Quartile	19	178	68	13	38	3095
Median	21	189	71	15	40	3427.5
Third Quartile	23	198	73	19	41	3750
Maximum	41	215	79	75.5	45	4315
Mean	22.1556	187.9778	71.0000	22.3944	39.7000	3391.7222
Variance	18.7396	161.4377	9.8652	323.7837	6.3247	232210.7647
Std. Dev	4.3289	12.7058	3.1409	17.9940	2.5149	481.8825
Range	24	60	14	70.5	12	2165
Interquartile Range	4	20	5	6	3	655
Coefficient Variation	19.54%	6.76%	4.42%	80.35%	6.33%	14.21%

       (c)

Not SUV Box-and-whisker Plot

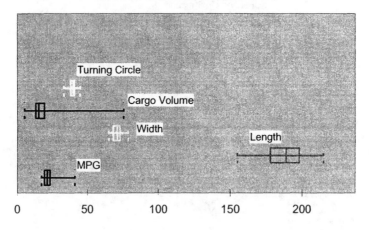

3.78 (c)
cont.

Not SUV Box-and-whisker Plot

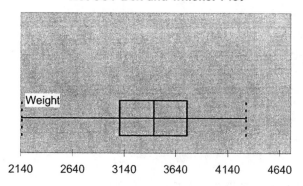

Miles per gallon and luggage capacity (cargo volume) are skewed to the right; length
and weight are skewed to the left; width is slightly skewed to the right and turning
circle requirement is quite symmetrical.

For SUV
(a), (b)

	MPG	Length	Width	Cargo Volume	Turning Circle	Weight
Minimum	10	163	67	28	37	3055
First Quartile	15	175	70	34.5	39	3590
Median	16	183	72	37.5	40	4135
Third Quartile	18	190	74	45.5	41	4715
Maximum	22	227	80	84	52	7270
Mean	16.4839	184.9032	72.3226	42.3548	40.5806	4267.4194
Variance	7.2581	209.5570	11.0925	183.7532	11.3183	783086.4516
Std. Dev	2.6941	14.4761	3.3305	13.5556	3.3643	884.9217
Range	12	64	13	56	15	4215
Interquartile Range	3	15	4	11	2	1125
Coefficient Variation	16.34%	7.83%	4.61%	32.00%	8.29%	20.74%

3.78   (c)
cont.

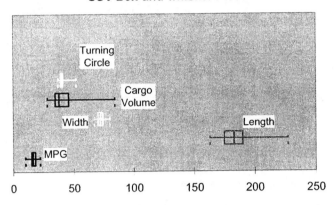

SUV Box-and-whisker Plot

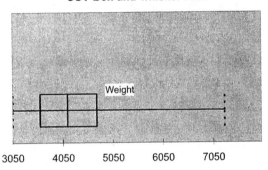

SUV Box-and-whisker Plot

All variables are skewed to the right except miles per gallon is only slightly skewed to the right.

CHAPTER 4

OBJECTIVES
- To understand the basic probability concepts
- To understand conditional probability
- To use Bayes theorem to revise probability in the light of new information
- To use rules for counting the number of possible events

OVERVIEW AND KEY CONCEPTS
Some Basic Probability Concepts
- **A priori probability:** The probability is based on prior knowledge of the process involved.
- **Empirical probability:** The probability is based on observed data.
- **Subjective probability:** Chance of occurrence assigned to an event by particular individual.
- **Sample space:** Collection of all possible outcomes, e.g., the set of all six faces of a die.
- **Simple event:** Outcome from a sample space with one characteristic, e.g., a red card from a deck of cards.
- **Joint event:** Involves two or more characteristics simultaneously, e.g., an Ace that is also a Red Card from a deck of cards.
- **Impossible event:** Event that will never happen, e.g., a club and diamond on a single card.
- **Complement event:** The complement of event A, denoted as A', includes all events that are not part of event A, e.g., If event A is the queen of diamonds, then the complement of event A is all the cards in a deck that are not the queen of diamonds.
- **Mutually exclusive events:** Two events are mutually exclusive if they cannot occur together. E.g., If event A is the queen of diamonds and event B is the queen of clubs, then both event A and event B cannot occur together on one card. An event and its complement are always mutually exclusive.
- **Collectively exhaustive events:** A set of events is collectively exhaustive if one of the events must occur. The set of collectively exhaustive events covers the whole sample space. E.g., Event A: all the aces, event B: all the black cards, event C: all the diamonds, event D: all the hearts. Then events A, B, C, and D are collectively exhaustive and so are events B, C, and D. An event and its complement are always collectively exhaustive.
- **Rules of probability:** (1) Its value is between 0 and 1; (2) the sum of probabilities of all collectively exhaustive and mutually exclusive events is 1.
- **The addition rule:** $P(A \text{ or } B) = P(A) + P(B) - P(A \text{ and } B)$
  - For two mutually exclusive events: $P(A \text{ and } B) = 0$
- **The multiplication rule:** $P(A \text{ and } B) = P(A \mid B)P(B) = P(B \mid A)P(A)$
- **Conditional probability:** $P(A \mid B) = \dfrac{P(A \text{ and } B)}{P(B)}$; $P(B \mid A) = \dfrac{P(A \text{ and } B)}{P(A)}$
- **Statistically independent events:** Two events are statistically independent if $P(A \mid B) = P(A)$, $P(B \mid A) = P(B)$ or $P(A \text{ and } B) = P(A)P(B)$. That is, any information about a given event does not affect the probability of the other event.

- **Bayes theorem:** $P\left(B_i \mid A\right) = \dfrac{P\left(A \mid B_i\right)P\left(B_i\right)}{P\left(A \mid B_1\right)P\left(B_1\right) + \cdots + P\left(A \mid B_k\right)P\left(B_k\right)} = \dfrac{P\left(B_i \text{ and } A\right)}{P\left(A\right)}$

  - **E.g.** We know that 50% of borrowers repaid their loans. Out of those who repaid, 40% had a college degree. Ten percent of those who defaulted had a college degree. What is the probability that a randomly selected borrower who has a college degree will repay the loan?
    Solution: Let R represent those who repaid and C represent those who have a college degree. $P\left(R\right) = 0.50$, $P\left(C \mid R\right) = 0.4$, $P\left(C \mid R'\right) = 0.10$.

$$P\left(R \mid C\right) = \frac{P\left(C \mid R\right)P\left(R\right)}{P\left(C \mid R\right)P\left(R\right) + P\left(C \mid R'\right)P\left(R'\right)} = \frac{(.4)(.5)}{(.4)(.5) + (.1)(.5)} = \frac{.2}{.25} = .8$$

  - Bayes theorem is used if $P\left(A \mid B\right)$ is needed when $P\left(B \mid A\right)$ is given or vice-versa.

Viewing and Computing Marginal (Simple) Probability and Joint Probability Using a

Event	Event B$_1$	B$_2$	Total
A$_1$	P(A$_1$ and B$_1$)	P(A$_1$ and B$_2$)	P(A$_1$)
A$_2$	P(A$_2$ and B$_1$)	P(A$_2$ and B$_2$)	P(A$_2$)
Total	P(B$_1$)	P(B$_2$)	1

Joint Probability   Marginal (Simple) Probability   Contingency Table

Viewing and Computing Compound Probability Using a Contingency Table

P(A$_1$ or B$_1$) = P(A$_1$) + P(B$_1$) - P(A$_1$ and B$_1$)

Event	Event B$_1$	B$_2$	Total
A$_1$	P(A$_1$ and B$_1$)	P(A$_1$ and B$_2$)	P(A$_1$)
A$_2$	P(A$_2$ and B$_1$)	P(A$_2$ and B$_2$)	P(A$_2$)
Total	P(B$_1$)	P(B$_2$)	1

For Mutually Exclusive Events: P(A or B) = P(A) + P(B)

Viewing and Computing Conditional Probability Using a Contingency Table

First setup the contingency table.

Type	Color Red	Black	Total
Ace	2	2	4
Non-Ace	24	24	48
Total	26	26	52

Revised Sample Space

To find $P(\text{Ace}|\text{Red})$, we only need to focus on the revised sample space of $P(\text{Red}) = 26/52$.
Out of this, 2/52 belongs to Ace and Red.
Hence, $P(\text{Ace}|\text{Red})$ is the ratio of 2/52 to 26/52 or 2/26.

Likewise, $P(\text{Red}|\text{Ace}) = \dfrac{P(\text{Ace and Red})}{P(\text{Ace})} = \dfrac{2/52}{4/52} = \dfrac{2}{4}$

Applying Bayes theorem Using a Contingency Table

- **E.g.** We know that 50% of borrowers repaid their loans. Out of those who repaid, 40% had a college degree. Ten percent of those who defaulted had a college degree. What is the probability that a randomly selected borrower who has a college degree will repay the loan?
  Solution: Let R represents those who repaid and C represents those who have a college degree. We know that $P(R) = 0.50$, $P(C|R) = 0.4$, $P(C|R') = 0.10$.

	Repay	$\overline{\text{Repay}}$	Total
College	.2	.05	.25
College	.3	.45	.75
Total	.5	.5	1.0

First we fill in the marginal probabilities of $P(R) = 0.5$ and $P(R') = 0.5$ in the contingency table. Then we make use of the conditional probability $P(C|R) = 0.4$. It says that if R has already occurred, the probability of C is 0.4. Since R has already occurred, we are restricted to the revised sample space of $P(R) = 0.5$. Forty percent or 0.4 of this $P(R) = 0.5$ belongs to $P(C \text{ and } R)$. Hence, the $0.4(0.5) = 0.2$ for $P(C \text{ and } R)$ in the contingency table. Likewise, given that R' has already occurred, the probability of C is 0.10. Hence, $P(C \text{ and } R')$ is 10% of $P(R') = 0.5$, which is 0.05. Utilizing the fact that the joint probabilities add up vertically and horizontally to their respective marginal probabilities, the contingency table is completed.
We want the probability of R given C. Now we are restricted to the revised sample space of $P(C) = 0.25$ since we know that C has already occurred. Out of this 0.25, 0.2 belongs to $P(C \text{ and } R)$. Hence, $P(R|C) = \dfrac{0.2}{0.25} = 0.8$

Counting Rules

- If any one of the k different mutually exclusive and collectively exhaustive events can occur on each of the n trials, the number of possible outcomes is equal to k^n
- If there are k_1 events on the first trial, k_2 events on the second trials, ..., and k_n events on the nth trial, then the number of possible outcomes is $(k_1)(k_2)\cdots(k_n)$
- The number of ways that all n objects can be arranged in order is $n! = n(n-1)\cdots(1)$
  - $n!$ is called n *factorial*
  - $0! = 1$
- **Permutation**: The number of ways of arranging X objects selected from n objects in order is
$$\frac{n!}{(n-X)!}$$
- **Combination**: The number of ways of selecting X objects out of n objects, irrespective or order, is $\begin{pmatrix} n \\ X \end{pmatrix} = \frac{n!}{X!(n-X)!}$

SOLUTIONS TO END OF SECTION
AND CHAPTER REVIEW EVEN PROBLEMS

4.2   (a)   Simple events include selecting a red ball.   (b)   Selecting a white ball

4.4   (a) $60/100 = 3/5 = 0.6$ (b) $10/100 = 1/10 = 0.1$

    (c) $35/100 = 7/20 = 0.35$ (d) $\dfrac{60}{100} + \dfrac{65}{100} - \dfrac{35}{100} = \dfrac{90}{100} = \dfrac{9}{10} = 0.9$

4.6   (a)   Mutually exclusive, not collectively exhaustive. "Registered voters in the United States were asked whether they registered as Republicans, Democrats, or none of the above." will be mutually exclusive and collectively exhaustive.

    (b)   Mutually exclusive, not collectively exhaustive. "Respondents were classified by country of manufacture of car owned into the categories American, European, Japanese, or none of the above." will be mutually exclusive and collectively exhaustive.

    (c)   Mutually exclusive, not collectively exhaustive. "People were asked, "Do you currently live in (i) an apartment, (ii) a house or (iii) none of the above?" will be mutually exclusive and collectively exhaustive.

    (d)   Mutually exclusive, collectively exhaustive

4.8   (a)   "Is a homeowner."
    (b)   "A homeowner who drives to work."
    (c)   "Does not drive to work."
    (d)   A person can drive to work and is also a homeowner.

4.10   (a)   "A wafer is good."
    (b)   "A wafer is good and no particle was found on the die."
    (c)   "bad wafer."
    (d)   A wafer can be a "good wafer" and was produced by a die "with particles".

4.12

		Company Size		
		Large	Small-to-midsized	
Stock	Yes	40	43	83
Options	No	149	137	286
		189	180	369

    (a) P(offered stock options) $= 83/369 = 0.2249$
    (b) P(small-to-midsized and did not offer stock options) $= 137/369 = 0.3713$
    (c) P(small-to-midsized or offered stock options) $= (180 + 83 - 43)/369 = 0.5962$
    (d)   The probability of "small-to-midsized or offered stock options" includes the probability of "small-to-midsized and offered stock options", the probability of "small-to-midsized but did not offer stock options" and the probability of "large and offered stock options".

4.14   Enjoy Clothes

Shopping	Male	Female	Total
Yes	136	224	360
No	104	36	140
Total	240	260	500

(a) P(enjoys clothes shopping) = 360/500 = 18/25 = 0.72
(b) P(female *and* enjoys clothes shopping) = 224/500 = 56/125 = 0.448
(c) P(female *or* enjoys clothes shopping) = 396/500 = 99/125 = 0.792
(d) P(male *or* female) = 500/500 = 1.00

4.16   (a) $P(A \mid B)$ = 10/30 = 1/3 = 0.33
         (b) $P(A \mid B')$ = 20/60 = 1/3 = 0.33
         (c) $P(A' \mid B')$ = 40/60 = 2/3 = 0.67
         (d)   Since $P(A \mid B) = P(A) = 1/3$, events A and B are statistically independent.

4.18 $P(A \mid B) = \dfrac{P(A \text{ and } B)}{P(B)} = \dfrac{0.4}{0.8} = \dfrac{1}{2} = 0.5$

4.20   Since $P(A \text{ and } B) = .20$ and $P(A)\,P(B) = 0.12$, events A and B are not statistically independent.

4.22   (a) P(had particles | bad) = 36/116 = 0.3103
         (b) P(had particles | good) = 14/334 = 0.0419
         (c) P(no particles | good) = 320/334 = 0.9581
               P(no particles) = 400/450 = 0.8889
               Since P(no particles | good) $\neq P$(no particles), "a good wafer" and "a die with no particle" are not statistically independent.

4.24   (a) P(claimed bias | white) = 29/56 = 0.5179
         (b) P(while | claim bias) = 29/155 = 0.1871
         (c)   The conditional events are reversed.
         (d)   Since P(white | claim bias) = 0.1871 is not equal to P(white) = 0.1210, being white and claiming bias are not statistically independent.

4.26   (a) P(needs warranty repair | manufacturer based in U.S.) = 0.025/0.6 = 0.0417
         (b) P(needs warranty repair | manufacturer not based in U.S.) = 0.015/0.4
               = 0.0375
         (c)   Since P(needs warranty repair | manufacturer based in U.S.) = 0.0417 and P(needs warranty repair) = 0.04, the two events are not statistically independent.

4.28   (a) P(both queens) = $\dfrac{4}{52} \cdot \dfrac{3}{51} = \dfrac{12}{2,652} = \dfrac{1}{221} = 0.0045$

         (b) P(10 followed by 5 or 6) = $\dfrac{4}{52} \cdot \dfrac{8}{51} = \dfrac{32}{2,652} = \dfrac{8}{663} = 0.012$

         (c) P(both queens) = $\dfrac{4}{52} \cdot \dfrac{4}{52} = \dfrac{16}{2,704} = \dfrac{1}{169} = 0.0059$

         (d) P(blackjack) = $\dfrac{16}{52} \cdot \dfrac{4}{51} + \dfrac{4}{52} \cdot \dfrac{16}{51} = \dfrac{128}{2,652} = \dfrac{32}{663} = 0.0483$

4.30

$$P(B \mid A) = \frac{P(A \mid B) \cdot P(B)}{P(A \mid B) \cdot P(B) + P(A \mid B') \cdot P(B')}$$

$$= \frac{0.8 \cdot 0.05}{0.8 \cdot 0.05 + 0.4 \cdot 0.95} = \frac{0.04}{0.42} = 0.095$$

4.32   (a) D = has disease T = tests positive

$$P(D \mid T) = \frac{P(T \mid D) \cdot P(D)}{P(T \mid D) \cdot P(D) + P(T \mid D') \cdot P(D')}$$

$$= \frac{0.9 \cdot 0.03}{0.9 \cdot 0.03 + 0.01 \cdot 0.97} = \frac{0.027}{0.0367} = 0.736$$

(b)

$$P(D' \mid T') = \frac{P(T' \mid D') \cdot P(D')}{P(T' \mid D') \cdot P(D') + P(T' \mid D) \cdot P(D)}$$

$$= \frac{0.99 \cdot 0.97}{0.99 \cdot 0.97 + 0.10 \cdot 0.03} = \frac{0.9603}{0.9633} = 0.997$$

4.34   (a) B = Base Construction Co. enters a bid
O = Olive Construction Co. wins the contract

$$P(B' \mid O) = \frac{P(O \mid B') \cdot P(B')}{P(O \mid B') \cdot P(B') + P(O \mid B) \cdot P(B)}$$

$$= \frac{0.5 \cdot 0.3}{0.5 \cdot 0.3 + 0.25 \cdot 0.7} = \frac{0.15}{0.325} = 0.4615$$

(b) $P(O) = 0.175 + 0.15 = 0.325$

4.36   (a) P(huge success | favorable review) = 0.099/0.459 = 0.2157
P(moderate success | favorable review) = 0.14/0.459 = 0.3050
P(break even | favorable review) = 0.16/0.459 = 0.3486
P(loser | favorable review) = 0.06/0.459 = 0.1307
(b) P(favorable review) = 0.99(0.1) + 0.7(0.2) + 0.4(0.4) + 0.2(0.3) = 0.459

4.38 $3^{10} = 59049$

4.40   (a) $2^7 = 128$ (b) $6^7 = 279936$
(c) There are two mutually exclusive and collectively exhaustive outcomes in (a) and six in (b).

4.42 $(8)(4)(3)(3) = 288$

4.44 $5! = (5)(4)(3)(2)(1) = 120$. Not all these orders are equally likely because the players are different in each team.

4.46 $n! = 6! = 720$

4.48 $\dfrac{n!}{X!(n-X)!} = \dfrac{8!}{2!(6!)} = \dfrac{(8)(7)}{2} = 28$

4.50 $\dfrac{n!}{X!(n-X)!} = \dfrac{100!}{2!(98!)} = \dfrac{(100)(99)}{2} = 4950$

4.54   With a priori probability, the probability of success is based on prior knowledge of the process involved. With empirical probability, outcomes are based on observed data. Subjective probability refers to the chance of occurrence assigned to an event by a particular individual.

4.56   The addition rule is used by adding the probability of A and the probability of B and then subtracting the joint probability of A and B.

4.58   If events A and B are statistically independent, the conditional probability of event A given B is equal to the probability of A.

4.60   Bayes theorem uses conditional probabilities to revise the probability of an event in the light of new information.

4.62   (a) P(nonconforming bottle) = 0.01 + 0.025 = 0.035
       (b) P(machine I *and* conforming bottle) = 0.49
       (c) P(machine I *or* conforming bottle) = 0.5 + 0.965 – 0.49 = 0.5 + 0.475 = 0.975
       (d) P(nonconforming | machine I) = 0.02
       (e) P(machine I | nonconforming) = 0.01/0.035 = 0.2857
       (f)   The conditions are switched. Part (d) answers $P(A|B)$ and part (e) answers $P(B|A)$.

4.64   (a)   A simple event can be "a firm that has a transactional public web site" and a joint event can be "a firm that has a transactional public web site and has sales greater than $10 billion".
       (b) P(transactional public web site) = 170/490 = 0.3469
       (c) P(transactional public web site and sales in excess of $10 billion) = 71/490 = 0.1449
       (d)   Since P(transactional public web site) $\times P$(sales in excess of $10 billion) $\neq$ P(transactional public web site and sales in excess of $10 billion), the two events, "sales in excess of ten billion dollars" and "has a transactional publicWeb site" are not independent.

4.66   R = read the advertisement,   O = place an order
       $P(R) = 0.15$ $P(O \mid R) = 0.15$
       (a) P(R and O) = $P(O \mid R) P(R) = 0.0225$
       (b)   (175000)(0.0225) = 3937.5 $\cong$ 3938 can be expected to read the advertisement and place an order.
       (c) $P(R) = 0.20.$ P(R and O) = $P(O \mid R) P(R) = (0.15)(0.20) = 0.03$
       (d)   (175000)(0.03) = 5250 can be expected to read the advertisement and place an order.

4.68   (a) $P(B \mid A) = (0.158)(0.24)/((0.158)(0.24)+(0.056)(0.76)) = 0.4712$

(b)   Since the probability that a fatality involved a rollover given that the fatality involved an SUV, van or pickup is 0.4712, which is almost twice the probability that a fatality involved a rollover with any vehicle type at 0.24, SUV's, vans or pickups are generally more prone to rollover accidents.

CHAPTER 5

OBJECTIVES

- To understand the properties of a probability distribution
- To be able to compute the expected value and variance of a probability distribution
- To be able to calculate the covariance and understand its use in finance
- To understand how to compute probabilities from binomial, hypergeometric, and Poisson distributions
- To know when and how to use the binomial, hypergeometric, and Poisson distributions to solve business problems

OVERVIEW AND KEY CONCEPTS

Some Basic Concepts of Discrete Probability Distribution

- **Random variable:** Outcomes of an experiment expressed numerically, e.g., Toss a die twice and count the number of times the number four appears (0, 1 or 2 times).
- **Discrete random variable:** A random variable that can have only certain distinct values. It is usually obtained by counting. E.g., Toss a coin five times and count the number of tails (0, 1, 2, 3, 4 or 5 tails).
- **Discrete probability distribution:** A mutually exclusive listing of all possible numerical outcomes for a discrete random variable such that a particular probability of occurrence is associated with each outcome.

Concepts of Expectation for a Discrete Random Variable

- **Expected value of a discrete random variable:** A weighted average over all possible outcomes.
  - The weights being the probabilities associated with each of the outcomes.
  - $$\mu = E(X) = \sum_{i=1}^{N} X_i P(X_i)$$

- **Variance of a discrete random variable:** The weighted average of the squared differences between each possible outcome and its mean
  - The weights being the probabilities of each of the respective outcomes.
  - $$\sigma^2 = \sum_{i=1}^{N} \left[X_i - E(X) \right]^2 P(X_i)$$

- **Standard deviation of a discrete random variable:** The square root of the variance.
  - $$\sigma = \sqrt{\sum_{i=1}^{N} \left[X_i - E(X) \right]^2 P(X_i)}$$

Covariance and Its Applications

- **Covariance:** $\sigma_{XY} = \sum_{i=1}^{N} \left[X_i - E(X) \right] \left[Y_i - E(Y) \right] P(X_i Y_i)$

  - A positive covariance indicates a positive relationship between the two discrete random variables.
  - A negative covariance indicates a negative relationship between the two discrete random variables.
  - The unit of the covariance depends on the units of the two discrete random variables, hence, its magnitude cannot be used to measure the strength of the relationship but only the direction of the relationship.

- **The expected value of the sum of two discrete random variables:** The expected value of the sum equals to the sum of the expected values.

  - $E(X + Y) = \mu_{X+Y} = E(X) + E(Y) = \mu_X + \mu_Y$

- **The variance of the sum of two discrete random variables:** The variance of the sum equals the sum of the variances plus twice the covariance.

  - $Var(X + Y) = \sigma_{X+Y}^2 = \sigma_X^2 + \sigma_Y^2 + 2\sigma_{XY}$

- **The standard deviation of the sum of two discrete random variables:**

  $\sigma_{X+Y} = \sqrt{\sigma_{X+Y}^2}$

- **Portfolio expected return:** The portfolio expected returns for a two-asset investment is equal to the weight (w) assigned to asset X multiplied by the expected return of asset X plus the weight ($1-w$) assigned to asset Y multiplied by the expected return of asset Y.

  - $E(P) = \mu_P = wE(X) + (1-w)E(Y)$

- **Portfolio risk:** The standard deviation of the portfolio.

  - $\sigma_P = \sqrt{w^2 \sigma_X^2 + (1-w)^2 \sigma_Y^2 + 2w(1-w)\sigma_{XY}}$

  - The smaller the value of σ_P, the less risky is an investment portfolio.

The Binomial Distribution

- **Properties of the binomial distribution:**
  - The sample has n observations.
  - Each observation is classified into one of the two mutually exclusive and collectively exhaustive categories, usually called *success* and *failure*.
  - The probability of getting a *success* is p while the probability of a *failure* is $(1-p)$.
  - The outcome (i.e., *success* or *failure*) of any observation is independent of the outcome of any other observation. This can be achieved by selecting each observation randomly either from an *infinite population without replacement* or from a *finite population with replacement*.

- **The binomial probability distribution function:**

  - $$P(X) = \frac{n!}{X!(n-X)!} p^X (1-p)^{n-X}$$

    where

    $P(X)$: probability of X successes given n and p

    X: number of "successes" in the sample $(X = 0, 1, \cdots, n)$

    p: the probability of "success"

    $(1-p)$: the probability of "failure"

    n: sample size

- **The mean and variance of a binomial distribution:**

  - $\mu = E(X) = np$

  - $\sigma^2 = np(1-p)$

  - $\sigma = \sqrt{np(1-p)}$

- **Applications:** Useful in evaluating the probability of X successes in a sample of size n drawn with replacement from a finite population or without replacement from an infinite population.

The Poisson Distribution

- **Properties of the Poisson distribution:**
    1. The area of opportunity, in which the number of times a particular event occurs is of interest, is defined by time, length, surface area, etc.
    2. The probability that an event occurs in a given area of opportunity is the same for all of the areas of opportunity.
    3. The number of events that occur in one area of opportunity is independent of the number of events that occur in other areas of opportunity.
    4. The probability that two or more events will occur in an area of opportunity approaches zero as the area of opportunity becomes smaller.

- **The Poisson probability distribution function:**

  - $$P(X) = \frac{e^{-\lambda} \lambda^X}{X!}$$

    where

    $P(X)$: probability of X "successes" given λ

    X: number of "successes" per unit

    λ: expected (average) number of "successes"

    e: 2.71828 (base of natural logs)

- **The mean and variance of a Poisson Distribution**

  - $\mu = E(X) = \lambda$

  - $\sigma^2 = \lambda$

  - $\sigma = \sqrt{\lambda}$

- **Applications:** Useful in modeling the number of successes in a given continuous interval of time, length, surface area, etc.

The Hypergeometric Distribution

- **Properties of the hypergeometric distribution:**
  - There are "n" trials in a sample taken randomly from a finite population of size N.
  - The sample is drawn without replacement.
  - The "n" trials are dependent.
- **The hypergeometric probability distribution function:**

  - $$P(X) = \frac{\binom{A}{X}\binom{N-A}{n-X}}{\binom{N}{n}}$$

  where

  $P(X)$: probability that X successes given $n, N,$ and A

  n: sample size

  N: population size

  A: number of "successes" in population

  X: number of "successes" in sample $(X = 0, 1, 2, \cdots, n)$

- **The mean and variance of a hypergeometric distribution:**

  - $$\mu = E(X) = \frac{nA}{N}$$

  - $$\sigma = \sqrt{\frac{nA(N-A)}{N^2}}\sqrt{\frac{N-n}{N-1}}$$

- **Applications:** Useful in evaluating the probability of A successes in a sample containing n observations drawn without replacement from a finite population of N observations.

SOLUTIONS TO END OF SECTION
AND CHAPTER REVIEW EVEN PROBLEMS

5.2   (a)   Distribution C   Distribution D

X	P(X)	X*P(X)		X	P(X)	X*P(X)
0	0.20	0.00		0	0.10	0.00
1	0.20	0.20		1	0.20	0.20
2	0.20	0.40		2	0.40	0.80
3	0.20	0.60		3	0.20	0.60
4	0.20	0.80		4	0.10	0.40
	1.00	2.00 $\mu = 2.00$			1.00	2.00 $\mu = 2.00$

(b)   Distribution C

X	$(X-\mu)^2$	P(X)	$(X-\mu)^2*P(X)$
0	$(-2)^2$	0.20	0.80
1	$(-1)^2$	0.20	0.20
2	$(0)^2$	0.20	0.00
3	$(1)^2$	0.20	0.20
4	$(2)^2$	0.20	0.80
		$\sigma^2=$	2.00

$$\sigma = \sqrt{\sum (X-\mu)^2 \cdot P(X)} = \sqrt{2.00} = 1.414$$

Distribution D

X	$(X-\mu)^2$	P(X)	$(X-\mu)^2*P(X)$
0	$(-2)^2$	0.10	0.40
1	$(-1)^2$	0.20	0.20
2	$(0)^2$	0.40	0.00
3	$(1)^2$	0.20	0.20
4	$(2)^2$	0.10	0.40
		$\sigma^2=$	1.20

$$\sigma = \sqrt{\sum (X-\mu)^2 \cdot P(X)} = \sqrt{1.20} = 1.095$$

(c)   Distribution C is uniform and symmetric; D is unimodal and symmetric. Means are the same but variances are different.

5.4   (a)-(b)

X	P(x)	X*P(X)	$(X-\mu_X)^2$	$(X-\mu_X)^2*P(X)$
0	0.10	0.00	4	0.40
1	0.20	0.20	1	0.20
2	0.45	0.90	0	0.00
3	0.15	0.45	1	0.15
4	0.05	0.20	4	0.20
5	0.05	0.25	9	0.45
	(a) Mean =	2.00	Variance =	1.40
			(b) Stdev =	1.18321596

5.6   (a)

X	P(X)
$-1	21/36
$+1	15/36

(b)

X	P(X)
$-1	21/36
$+1	15/36

(c)

X	P(X)
$-1	30/36
$+4	6/36

    (d) -0.167 for each method of play

5.8   (a) $E(X) = (0.2)(\$ -100) + (0.4)(\$50) + (0.3)(\$ 200) + (0.1)(\$300) = \$90$
            $E(Y) = (0.2)(\$50) + (0.4)(\$30) + (0.3)(\$ 20) + (0.1)(\$20) = \$30$

     (b)

$$\sigma_X = \sqrt{(0.2)(-100-90)^2 + (0.4)(50-90)^2 + (0.3)(200-90)^2 + (0.1)(300-90)^2}$$
$$= \sqrt{15900} = 126.10$$

$$\sigma_Y = \sqrt{(0.2)(50-30)^2 + (0.4)(30-30)^2 + (0.3)(20-30)^2 + (0.1)(20-30)^2}$$
$$= \sqrt{120} = 10.95$$

     (c) $\sigma_{XY} = (0.2)(-100-90)(50-30) + (0.4)(50-90)(30-30)$
               $+ (0.3)(200-90)(20-30) + (0.1)(300-90)(20-30) = -1300$

     (d) $E(X + Y) = E(X) + E(Y) = \$90 + \$30 = \$120$

5.10   (a) $E(\text{total time}) = E(\text{time waiting}) + E(\text{time served}) = 4 + 5.5 = 9.5$ minutes

      (b) $\sigma(\text{total time}) = \sqrt{1.2^2 + 1.5^2} = 1.9209$ minutes

5.12   PHStat output for (a)-(c):

Covariance Analysis			
Probabilities & Outcomes:	**P**	**X**	**Y**
	0.1	-100	50
	0.3	0	150
	0.3	80	-20
	0.3	150	-100
Weight Assigned to X	0.5		
Statistics			
E(X)	59		
E(Y)	14		
Variance(X)	6189		
Standard Deviation(X)	78.6702		
Variance(Y)	9924		
Standard Deviation(Y)	99.61928		
Covariance(XY)	-6306		
Variance(X+Y)	3501		
Standard Deviation(X+Y)	59.16925		
Portfolio Management			
Weight Assigned to X	0.5		
Weight Assigned to Y	0.5		
Portfolio Expected Return	36.5		
Portfolio Risk	29.58462		

5.12   (a) $E(X) = \sum_{i=1}^{N} X_i P(X_i) = 59$

cont. $E(Y) = \sum_{i=1}^{N} Y_i P(Y_i) = 14$

     (b) $\sigma_X = \sqrt{\sum_{i=1}^{N} \left[X_i - E(X)\right]^2 P(X_i)} = 78.6702$

             $\sigma_Y = \sqrt{\sum_{i=1}^{N} \left[Y_i - E(Y)\right]^2 P(Y_i)} = 99.62$

     (c) $\sigma_{XY} = \sum_{i=1}^{N} \left[X_i - E(X)\right]\left[Y_i - E(Y)\right] P(X_i Y_i) = -6306$

     (d)   Stock X gives the investor a lower standard deviation while yielding a higher expected return so the investor should select stock X.

5.14   (a) $E(X) = \$71$ $E(Y) = \$97$
      (b) $\sigma_X = 61.88$ $\sigma_Y = 84.27$
      (c) $\sigma_{XY} = 5113$
      (d)   Stock Y gives the investor a higher expected return than stock X, but also has a higher standard deviation. A risk-averse investor should invest in stock X, but an investor willing to sustain a higher risk can expect a higher return from stock Y.

5.16   Let X = corporate bond fund Y = common stock fund
      (a) $E(X) = \$77$ $E(Y) = \$97$
      (b) $\sigma_X = 39.76$ $\sigma_Y = 108.95$
      (c) $\sigma_{XY} = 4161$
      (d)   Common stock fund gives the investor a higher expected return than corporate bond fund, but also has a standard deviation better than 2.5 times higher than that for corporate bond fund. An investor should carefully weigh the increased risk.

5.18   (a)   0.5997   (c)   0.0439
      (b)   0.0016   (d)   0.4018

5.20   Mean   Standard Deviation
      (a)   0.40   0.60
      (b)   1.60   0.980
      (c)   4.00   0.894
      (d)   1.50   0.866

5.22   Given $p = .6$ and $n = 5$,
      (a) $P(X = 5) = 0.0778$
      (b) $P(X \geq 3) = 0.6826$
      (c) $P(X < 2) = 0.0870$
      (d)   (a) $P(X = 5) = 0.3277$
             (b) $P(X \geq 3) = 0.9421$
             (c) $P(X < 2) = 0.0067$

5.24   Given $p = 0.90$ and $n = 3$,

(a) $P(X = 3) = \dfrac{n!}{X!(n-X)!} p^X (1-p)^{n-X} = \dfrac{3!}{3!0!}(.9)^3(.1)^0 = 0.729$

(b) $P(X = 0) = \dfrac{n!}{X!(n-X)!} p^X (1-p)^{n-X} = \dfrac{3!}{0!3!}(.9)^0(.1)^3 = 0.001$

(c) $P(X \geq 2) = P(X = 2) + P(X = 3) = \dfrac{3!}{2!1!}(.9)^2(.1)^1 + \dfrac{3!}{3!0!}(.9)^3(.1)^0 = 0.972$

(d) $E(X) = np = 3(.9) = 2.7$

$\sigma_X = \sqrt{np(1-p)} = \sqrt{3(.9)(.1)} = 0.5196$

5.26   (a) $P(X = 0) = 1.0 \times 10^{-10}$ (b) $P(X = 1) = 9.0 \times 10^{-9}$

(c) $P(X \leq 2) = 3.74 \times 10^{-7}$ (d) $P(X \geq 3) = 1.0$

5.28   (a)   Since the 68% and 24% figures are obtained from the survey results conducted by the networks, they are best classified as empirical classical probability.

(b) $P(X < 5) = 1.4 \times 10^{-5} = 0.000014$ (c) $P(X \geq 10) = 0.9721$

(d) $P(X = 20) = 0.000447$

5.30   (a)   Using the equation, if $\lambda = 2.5$, $P(X = 2) = \dfrac{e^{-2.5} \cdot (2.5)^2}{2!} = 0.2565$

(b)   If $\lambda = 8.0$, $P(X = 8) = 0.1396$

(c)   If $\lambda = 0.5$, $P(X = 1) = 0.3033$

(d)   If $\lambda = 3.7$, $P(X = 0) = 0.0247$

5.32   PHStat output for (a) – (d)

Poisson Probabilities Table						
	X	P(X)	P(<=X)	P(<X)	P(>X)	P(>=X)
	0	0.006738	0.006738	0.000000	0.993262	1.000000
	1	0.033690	0.040428	0.006738	0.959572	0.993262
	2	0.084224	0.124652	0.040428	0.875348	0.959572
	3	0.140374	0.265026	0.124652	0.734974	0.875348
	4	0.175467	0.440493	0.265026	0.559507	0.734974
	5	0.175467	0.615961	0.440493	0.384039	0.559507
	6	0.146223	0.762183	0.615961	0.237817	0.384039
	7	0.104445	0.866628	0.762183	0.133372	0.237817
	8	0.065278	0.931906	0.866628	0.068094	0.133372
	9	0.036266	0.968172	0.931906	0.031828	0.068094
	10	0.018133	0.986305	0.968172	0.013695	0.031828
	11	0.008242	0.994547	0.986305	0.005453	0.013695
	12	0.003434	0.997981	0.994547	0.002019	0.005453
	13	0.001321	0.999302	0.997981	0.000698	0.002019
	14	0.000472	0.999774	0.999302	0.000226	0.000698
	15	0.000157	0.999931	0.999774	0.000069	0.000226
	16	0.000049	0.999980	0.999931	0.000020	0.000069
	17	0.000014	0.999995	0.999980	0.000005	0.000020
	18	0.000004	0.999999	0.999995	0.000001	0.000005
	19	0.000001	1.000000	0.999999	0.000000	0.000001
	20	0.000000	1.000000	1.000000	0.000000	0.000000

Given $\lambda = 5.0$,

(a) $P(X = 1) = 0.0337$
(b) $P(X < 1) = 0.0067$
(c) $P(X > 1) = 0.9596$
(d) $P(X \leq 1) = 0.0404$

5.34   (a) – (c) Portion of PHStat output

Data					
Average/Expected number of successes:			6		
Poisson Probabilities Table					
X	P(X)	P(<=X)	P(<X)	P(>X)	P(>=X)
0	0.002479	0.002479	0.000000	0.997521	1.000000
1	0.014873	0.017351	0.002479	0.982649	0.997521
2	0.044618	0.061969	0.017351	0.938031	0.982649
3	0.089235	0.151204	0.061969	0.848796	0.938031
4	0.133853	0.285057	0.151204	0.714943	0.848796
5	(b) 0.160623	0.445680	(a) 0.285057	0.554320	(c) 0.714943
6	0.160623	0.606303	0.445680	0.393697	0.554320
7	0.137677	0.743980	0.606303	0.256020	0.393697
8	0.103258	0.847237	0.743980	0.152763	0.256020
9	0.068838	0.916076	0.847237	0.083924	0.152763
10	0.041303	0.957379	0.916076	0.042621	0.083924
11	0.022529	0.979908	0.957379	0.020092	0.042621
12	0.011264	0.991173	0.979908	0.008827	0.020092
13	0.005199	0.996372	0.991173	0.003628	0.008827
14	0.002228	0.998600	0.996372	0.001400	0.003628
15	0.000891	0.999491	0.998600	0.000509	0.001400
16	0.000334	0.999825	0.999491	0.000175	0.000509
17	0.000118	0.999943	0.999825	0.000057	0.000175

(a) $P(X < 5) = P(X = 0) + P(X = 1) + P(X = 2) + P(X = 3) + P(X = 4)$

$$= \frac{e^{-6}(6)^0}{0!} + \frac{e^{-6}(6)^1}{1!} + \frac{e^{-6}(6)^2}{2!} + \frac{e^{-6}(6)^3}{3!} + \frac{e^{-6}(6)^4}{4!}$$
$$= 0.002479 + 0.014873 + 0.044618 + 0.089235 + 0.133853 = 0.2851$$

(b) $P(X = 5) = \dfrac{e^{-6}(6)^5}{5!} = 0.1606$

(c) $P(X \geq 5) = 1 - P(X < 5) = 1 - 0.2851 = 0.7149$

(d) $P(X = 4 \text{ or } X = 5) = P(X = 4) + P(X = 5) = \dfrac{e^{-6}(6)^4}{4!} + \dfrac{e^{-6}(6)^5}{5!} = 0.2945$

5.36   Given $\lambda = 3.21$,
(a) $P(X = 0) = 0.0404$ (b) $P(X \geq 1) = 0.9596$
(c) $P(X \geq 2) = 0.8301$
(d)   Because Delta has a higher mean rate of mishandled bags per 1000 passengers than Jet Blue, its probability of mishandling at least a certain number of bags is higher than that of Jet Blue.

5.38   (a)   If $\lambda = 0.2$, $P(X \geq 2) = 1 - [P(X = 0) + P(X = 1)] = 1 - [0.8187 + 0.1637]$
$$= 0.0176$$

(b)   If there are 0.2 flaws per foot on the average, then there are 0.2•(12) or 2.4 flaws on the average in a 12-foot roll.
If $\lambda = 2.4$, then $P(X \geq 1) = 1 - P(X = 0) = 1 - 0.0907 = 0.9093$

(c)   If there are 0.2 flaws per foot on the average, then there are 0.2•(50) or 10 flaws on the average in a 50-foot roll.
If $\lambda = 10$, then $P(5 \leq X \leq 15) = 0.9220$

5.40   (a) $\lambda = 5.09$, $P(X = 0) = 0.0062$ (b) $\lambda = 5.09$, $P(X \leq 2) = 0.1173$

(c)   Because Kia had a higher mean rate of problems per car, the probability of a randomly selected Kia having no more than 2 problems is lower than that of a randomly chosen Lexus. Likewise, the probability of a randomly selected Kia having zero problems is lower than that of a randomly chosen Lexus

5.42   (a) $\lambda = 1.53$, $P(X = 0) = 0.2165$ (b) $\lambda = 1.53$, $P(X \leq 2) = 0.8013$

(c)   Because Kia had a lower mean rate of problems per car in 2004 compared to 2003, the probability of a randomly selected Kia having zero problems and the probability of no more than 2 problems are both higher than their values in 2003.

5.44   (a) $P(X = 3) = \dfrac{\dbinom{5}{3}\dbinom{10-5}{4-3}}{\dbinom{10}{4}} = \dfrac{\frac{5 \cdot 4 \cdot 3!}{3! \cdot 2 \cdot 1} \cdot \frac{5 \cdot 4!}{4! \cdot 1!}}{\frac{10 \cdot 9 \cdot 8 \cdot 7 \cdot 6!}{6! \cdot 4 \cdot 3 \cdot 2 \cdot 1}} = \dfrac{5}{3 \cdot 7} = 0.2381$

(b) $P(X = 1) = \dfrac{\dbinom{3}{1} \cdot \dbinom{6-3}{4-1}}{\dbinom{6}{4}} = \dfrac{\frac{3 \cdot 2!}{2! \cdot 1} \cdot \frac{3!}{3! \cdot 0!}}{\frac{6 \cdot 5 \cdot 4!}{4! \cdot 2 \cdot 1}} = \dfrac{1}{5} = 0.2$

(c) $P(X = 0) = \dfrac{\dbinom{3}{0} \cdot \dbinom{12-3}{5-0}}{\dbinom{12}{5}} = \dfrac{\frac{3!}{3! \cdot 0!} \cdot \frac{9 \cdot 8 \cdot 7 \cdot 6 \cdot 5!}{5! \cdot 4 \cdot 3 \cdot 2 \cdot 1}}{\frac{12 \cdot 11 \cdot 10 \cdot 9 \cdot 8 \cdot 7!}{7! \cdot 5 \cdot 4 \cdot 3 \cdot 2 \cdot 1}} = \dfrac{7}{44} = 0.1591$

(d) $P(X = 3) = \dfrac{\dbinom{3}{3} \cdot \dbinom{7-0}{3-3}}{\dbinom{10}{3}} = \dfrac{\frac{3!}{3! \cdot 0!} \cdot \frac{7!}{7! \cdot 0!}}{\frac{10 \cdot 9 \cdot 8 \cdot 7!}{7! \cdot 3 \cdot 2 \cdot 1}} = \dfrac{1}{120} = 0.0083$

5.46 (a) If $n = 6$, $A = 25$, and $N = 100$,

$$P(X \geq 2) = 1 - [P(X = 0) + P(X = 1)] = 1 - [\frac{\binom{25}{0}\binom{100-25}{6-0}}{\binom{100}{6}} + \frac{\binom{25}{1}\binom{100-25}{6-1}}{\binom{100}{6}}]$$

$$= 1 - [0.1689 + 0.3620] = 0.4691$$

(b) If $n = 6$, $A = 30$, and $N = 100$,

$$P(X \geq 2) = 1 - [P(X = 0) + P(X = 1)] = 1 - [\frac{\binom{30}{0}\binom{100-30}{6-0}}{\binom{100}{6}} + \frac{\binom{30}{1}\binom{100-30}{6-1}}{\binom{100}{6}}]$$

$$= 1 - [0.1100 + 0.3046] = 0.5854$$

(c) If $n = 6$, $A = 5$, and $N = 100$,

$$P(X \geq 2) = 1 - [P(X = 0) + P(X = 1)] = 1 - [\frac{\binom{5}{0}\binom{100-5}{6-0}}{\binom{100}{6}} + \frac{\binom{5}{1}\binom{100-5}{6-1}}{\binom{100}{6}}]$$

$$= 1 - [0.7291 + 0.2430] = 0.0279$$

(d) If $n = 6$, $A = 10$, and $N = 100$,

$$P(X \geq 2) = 1 - [P(X = 0) + P(X = 1)] = 1 - [\frac{\binom{10}{0}\binom{100-10}{6-0}}{\binom{100}{6}} + \frac{\binom{10}{1}\binom{100-10}{6-1}}{\binom{100}{6}}]$$

$$= 1 - [0.5223 + 0.3687] = 0.1090$$

(e) The probability that the entire group will be audited is very sensitive to the true number of improper returns in the population. If the true number is very low ($A = 5$), the probability is very low (0.0279). When the true number is increased by a factor of six ($A = 30$), the probability the group will be audited increases by a factor of almost 21 (0.5854).

5.48   (a)--(c) PHStat output:

Data		
Sample size	8	
No. of successes in population	12	
Population size	48	
Hypergeometric Probabilities Table		
	X	P(X)
	0	(b) 0.080192
	1	0.265463
	2	0.340677
	3	0.219792
	4	0.077271
	5	0.014986
	6	0.001543
	7	7.56E-05
	8	(a) 1.31E-06

$P(X = 8) = 1.31178 \times 10^{-6}$
$P(X = 0) = 0.0802$
$P(X \geq 1) = 0.9198$

(d) PHStat output:

Data		
Sample size	8	
No. of successes in population	6	
Population size	48	
Hypergeometric Probabilities Table		
	X	P(X)
	0	0.312788
	1	0.428966
	2	0.208525
	3	0.045087
	4	0.004449
	5	0.000183
	6	2.28E-06

$P(X = 6) = 2.28 \times 10^{-6}$
$P(X = 0) = 0.3128$
$P(X \geq 1) = 0.6872$

5.50 (a)--(c)

	A	B	C
1	Defective Disks		
2			
3	Sample size	4	
4	No. of successes in population	5	
5	Population size	15	
6			
7	Hypergeometric Probabilities Table		
8		X	P(x)
9		0	0.153846
10		1	0.43956
11		2	0.32967
12		3	0.07326
13		4	0.003663

(a)   0.43956   (b) 0.84615   (c) 0.92308

(d) $\mu = n \cdot A/N = 4 \cdot (5)/15 = 1.33$

5.52   The four properties of a situation that must be present in order to use the binomial distribution are (i) the sample consists of a fixed number of observations, n, (ii) each observation can be classified into one of two mutually exclusive and collectively exhaustive categories, usually called success and failure, (iii) the probability of an observation being classified as success, p, is constant from observation to observation and (iv) the outcome (i.e., success or failure) of any observation is independent of the outcome of any other observation.

5.54   The hypergeometric distribution should be used when the probability of success of a sample containing n observations is not constant from trial to trial due to sampling without replacement from a finite population.

5.56   (a)   0.74
       (b)   0.74
       $p = 0.74$, $n = 5$
       (c) $P(X = 4) = 0.3898$ (d) $P(X = 0) = 0.0012$
       (e)   Stock prices tend to rise in the years when the economy is expanding and fall in the years of recession or contraction. Hence, the probability that the price will rise in one year is not independent from year to year.

5.58   (a)   If $p = 0.50$ and $n = 10$, $P(X \geq 8) = 0.0547$
       (b)   If $p = 0.70$ and $n = 10$, $P(X \geq 8) = 0.3829$
       (c)   If $p = 0.90$ and $n = 10$, $P(X \geq 8) = 0.9298$
       (d)   If the indicator is a random event, the probability that it will make a correct prediction in 8 or more times out of 10 is 5.47%. If one is willing to accept the argument that the amount of campaign expenditures spent during an election year exerts some multiplying impact on the stock market, the probability that the Dow Jones Industrial Average will increase in a U.S. Presidential election year is likely to be near 0.90 based on the result of (a)-(c).

5.60   (a)-(d)   Portion of the PHStat output:

Binomial Probabilities					
Data					
Sample size	10				
Probability of success	0.33				
Statistics					
Mean	(d) 3.3				
Variance	2.211				
Standard deviation	(d) 1.486943				
Binomial Probabilities Table					
	X	P(X)	P(<=X)	P(>=X)	
	0	(a) 0.018228	0.018228	1	
	1	(b) 0.089782	0.10801	0.981772	
	2	0.198993	0.307003	(c) 0.89199	
	10	1.53E-05	1	1.53E-05	

5.62   (a)-(d)   Portion of the PHStat output:

Binomial Probabilities					
Data					
Sample size	10				
Probability of success	0.74				
Statistics					
Mean	7.4				
Variance	1.924				
Standard deviation	1.387083				
Binomial Probabilities Table					
	X	P(X)	P(<X)	P(>X)	P(>=X)
	0	(a) 1.41E-06	0	0.999999	1
	5	0.066439	0.023915	(c) 0.909646	0.976085
	8	0.273535	0.50422	0.222245	(d) 0.49578
	10	(b) 0.04924	0.95076	0	0.04924

5.64   (a) – (e) Portion of the PHStat output: $p = 1628/3700 = 0.44$

Binomial Probabilities						
Data						
Sample size	10					
Probability of success	0.44					
Statistics						
Mean	(f) 4.4					
Variance	2.464					
Standard deviation	1.569713					
Binomial Probabilities Table						
	X	P(X)	P(<=X)	P(<X)	P(>X)	P(>=X)
	0	0.003033	0.003033	0	0.996967	1
	5	(b) 0.228878	0.759297	(d) 0.530419	0.240703	(c),(e) 0.469581
	6	0.149861	0.909157	0.759297	0.090843	0.240703
	7	0.067284	0.976442	0.909157	0.023558	0.090843
	8	0.019825	0.996267	0.976442	0.003733	0.023558
	9	0.003461	0.999728	0.996267	0.000272	0.003733
	10	(a) 0.000272	1	0.999728	0	0.000272

(f)   On average 4.4 people will refuse to participate out of every 10 people. You would have to survey about 227 ($\approx 100 / 0.44$) people to get 100 responses

5.66   If $p = 0.88$ and $n = 20$,
   (a) $\mu = 17.6$ (b) $\sigma = 1.453$
   (c) $P(X = 20) = 0.0776$ (d) $P(X \geq 18) = 0.5631$
   (e) $P(X \geq 15) = 0.9740$

5.68   (a)   If $p = 0.50$ and $n = 34$, $P(X \geq 29) = 1.92791E\text{-}05$
   (b)   If $p = 0.70$ and $n = 34$, $P(X \geq 29) = 0.0334$
   (c)   If $p = 0.90$ and $n = 34$, $P(X \geq 29) = 0.8815$
   (d)   Based on the results in (a)-(c), the probability that the Standard & Poor's 500 index will increase if there is an early gain in the first five trading days of the year is very likely to be close to 0.90 because that yields a probability of 88.15% that at least 29 of the 34 years the Standard & Poor's 500 index will increase the entire year.

5.70   (a)   The assumptions needed are (i) the probability that a golfer loses a golf ball in a given interval in a game is constant, (ii) the probability that a golfer loses more than one golf ball in this interval is 0, (iii) the probability that a golfer loses a golf ball is independent from interval to interval.
   $\lambda = 4.5$
   (b) $P(X = 0) = 0.0111$
   (c) $P(X \leq 5) = 0.70293$
   (d) $P(X \geq 6) = 0.29707$

5.72 (a) $P(\text{jackpot}) = \dfrac{\dbinom{5}{5}\dbinom{47}{0}}{\dbinom{52}{5}} \dfrac{\dbinom{1}{1}}{\dbinom{52}{1}} = 7.39941 \cdot 10^{-9}$

(b) $P(\$175,000) = \dfrac{\dbinom{5}{5}}{\dbinom{52}{5}} \dfrac{\dbinom{1}{0}\dbinom{51}{1}}{\dbinom{52}{1}} = 3.77370 \cdot 10^{-7}$

(c) $P(\$5,000) = \dfrac{\dbinom{5}{4}\dbinom{47}{1}}{\dbinom{52}{5}} \dfrac{\dbinom{1}{1}}{\dbinom{52}{1}} = 1.73886 \cdot 10^{-6}$

(d) $P(\$150) = \dfrac{\dbinom{5}{4}\dbinom{47}{1}}{\dbinom{52}{5}} \dfrac{\dbinom{1}{0}\dbinom{51}{1}}{\dbinom{52}{1}} + \dfrac{\dbinom{5}{3}\dbinom{47}{2}}{\dbinom{52}{5}} \dfrac{\dbinom{1}{1}}{\dbinom{52}{1}}$

$= 8.86819 \cdot 10^{-5} + 7.99876 \cdot 10^{-5} = 1.68669 \cdot 10^{-4}$

(e) $P(\$10) = \dfrac{\dbinom{5}{2}\dbinom{47}{3}}{\dbinom{52}{5}} \dfrac{\dbinom{1}{1}}{\dbinom{52}{1}} = 0.00119981$

(f) $P(\$7) = \dfrac{\dbinom{5}{3}\dbinom{47}{2}}{\dbinom{52}{5}} \dfrac{\dbinom{1}{0}\dbinom{51}{1}}{\dbinom{52}{1}} = 0.00407937$

(g) $P(\$3) = \dfrac{\dbinom{5}{1}\dbinom{47}{4}}{\dbinom{52}{5}} \dfrac{\dbinom{1}{1}}{\dbinom{52}{1}} = 0.00659898$

(h) $P(\$2) = \dfrac{\dbinom{5}{0}\dbinom{47}{5}}{\dbinom{52}{5}} \dfrac{\dbinom{1}{1}}{\dbinom{52}{1}} = 0.0113502$

(i) $P(\$0) = 1 - P(\$2) - P(\$3) - P(\$7) - P(\$10) - P(\$150) - P(\$5,000) - P(\$175,000)$
$- P(\text{jackpot}) = 0.976601$

CHAPTER 6

OBJECTIVES

- To know how to compute probabilities from the normal distribution
- To be able to use the normal probability plot to determine whether a set of data is approximately normally distributed
- To know how to compute probabilities from the uniform distribution
- To know how to compute probabilities from the exponential distribution
- To be able to compute probabilities from the normal distribution to approximate probabilities from the binomial distribution

OVERVIEW AND KEY CONCEPTS

Some Basic Concepts of Continuous Probability Density Function

- **Continuous random variable:** A variable that can take an infinite number of values within a specific range, e.g. Weight, height, daily changes in closing prices of stocks, and time between arrivals of planes landing on a runway.
- **Continuous probability density function:** A mathematical expression that represents the continuous phenomenon of a continuous random variable, and can be used to calculate the probability that the random variable occurs within certain ranges or intervals.
- The probability that a continuous random variable is equal to a *particular value* is 0. This distinguishes continuous phenomena, which are measured, from discrete phenomena, which are counted. For example, the probability that a task can be completed in between 20 and 30 seconds can be measured. With a more precise measuring instrument, we can compute the probability that the task can be completed between a very small interval such as 19.99 to 20.01. However, the probability that the task can be completed in *exactly* 21 seconds is 0.
- Obtaining probabilities or computing expected values and standard deviations for continuous random variables involves mathematical expressions that require knowledge of integral calculus. In this book, these are achieved via special probability tables or computer statistical software like Minitab or PHStat.

The Normal Distribution

- **Properties of the normal distribution:**
    - Bell-shaped (and thus symmetrical) in its appearance.
    - Its measures of central tendency (mean, median, and mode) are all identical.
    - Its "middle spread" (interquartile range) is equal to 1.33 standard deviations.
    - Its associated random variable has an infinite range $(-\infty < X < +\infty)$.

- **The normal probability density function:**
  - $f(X) = \dfrac{1}{\sqrt{2\pi\sigma^2}} e^{-\frac{1}{2\sigma^2}(X-\mu)^2}$ where

    $f(X)$: density of random variable X

    $\pi = 3.14159;\quad e = 2.71828$

    μ: population mean

    σ: population standard deviation

    X: value of random variable $(-\infty < X < \infty)$
  - A particular combination of μ and σ will yield a particular normal probability distribution.
- **Standardization or normalization of a normal continuous random variable:** By standardizing (normalizing) a normal random variable, we need only one table to tabulate the probabilities of the whole family of normal distributions.
- **The transformation (standardization) formula:** $Z = \dfrac{X - \mu}{\sigma}$
  - The standardized normal distribution is one whose random variable Z always has a mean 0 and a standard deviation 1.
- **Finding range probability of a normal random variable:**
  1. Standardize the value of X into Z.
  2. Lookup the cumulative probabilities from the cumulative standardized normal distribution table.

     E.g., For $\mu = 5$ and $\sigma = 10$, $P(2.9 < X < 7.1) = ?$

$$Z = \frac{X - \mu}{\sigma} = \frac{2.9 - 5}{10} = -.21 \qquad Z = \frac{X - \mu}{\sigma} = \frac{7.1 - 5}{10} = .21$$

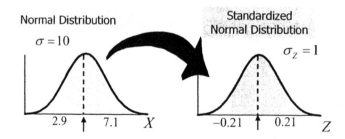

Cumulative Standardized Normal Distribution Table (Portion) $\mu_z = 0 \quad \sigma_z = 1$

Z	.00	.01	.02
0.0	.5000	.5040	.5080
0.1	.5398	.5438	.5478
0.2	.5793	.5832	.5871
0.3	.6179	.6217	.6255

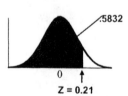

Cumulative Standardized Normal Distribution Table (Portion) $\mu_z = 0 \quad \sigma_z = 1$

Z	.00	.01	.02
-03	.3821	.3783	.3745
-02	.4207	.4168	.4129
-0.1	.4602	.4562	.4522
0.0	.5000	.4960	.4920

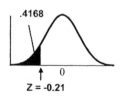

$$P(2.9 < X < 7.1) = P(-0.21 < Z < 0.21) = 0.5832 - 0.4168 = 0.1664$$

E.g., For $\mu = 5$ and $\sigma = 10$, $P(X \geq 8) = ?$

$$Z = \frac{X - \mu}{\sigma} = \frac{8 - 5}{10} = .30$$

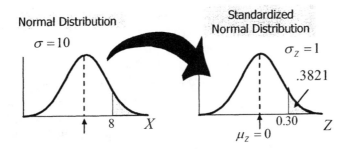

Cumulative Standardized Normal Distribution Table (Portion)

$\mu_z = 0$ $\sigma_z = 1$

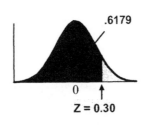

Z	.00	.01	.02
0.0	.5000	.5040	.5080
0.1	.5398	.5438	.5478
0.2	.5793	.5832	.5871
0.3	.6179	.6217	.6255

$$P(X \geq 8) = P(Z \geq 0.30) = 1 - 0.6179 = 0.3821$$

- **Recovering X values for known probabilities:**
    1. Lookup the Z value from the cumulative standardized normal distribution table.
    2. Recover the value of X using the formula $X = \mu + Z\sigma$

    E.g., For $\mu = 5$ and $\sigma = 10$, $P(X \leq A) = 0.6179$, what is the value of A?

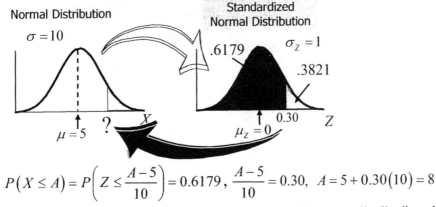

$$P(X \leq A) = P\left(Z \leq \frac{A-5}{10}\right) = 0.6179, \quad \frac{A-5}{10} = 0.30, \quad A = 5 + 0.30(10) = 8$$

- **Applications:** Many continuous random phenomena are either normally distributed or can be approximated by a normal distribution. Hence, it is important to know how to assess whether a distribution is normally distributed.

Evaluating the Normality Assumption

- For small and moderate-sized data sets, construct a stem-and-leaf display and box-and-whisker plot. For large data sets, construct the frequency distribution and plot the histogram or polygon.
- Obtain the mean, median, and mode, and note the similarities or differences among these measures of central tendency.
- Obtain the interquartile range and standard deviation. Note how well the interquartile range can be approximated by 1.33 times the standard deviation.
- Obtain the range and note how well it can be approximated by 6 times the standard deviation.
- Determine whether approximately 2/3 of the observations lie between the mean ± 1 standard deviation. Determine whether approximately 4/5 of the observations lie between the mean ± 1.28 standard deviations. Determine whether approximately 19/20 of the observations lie between the mean ± 2 standard deviations.
- Construct a normal probability plot and evaluate the likelihood that the variable of interest is at least approximately normally distributed by inspecting the plot for evidence of linearity (i.e., a straight line).

The Normal Probability Plot

- **The normal probability plot:** A two-dimensional plot of the observed data values on the vertical axis with their corresponding quantile values from a standardized normal distribution on the horizontal axis.

Left-Skewed

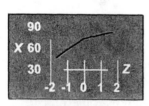

Right-Skewed

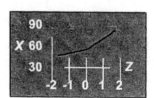

Rectangular

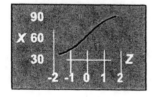

U-Shaped

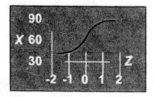

The Uniform Distribution

- **Properties of the uniform distribution:**
    - The probability of occurrence of a value is equally likely to occur anywhere in the range between the smallest value a and the largest value b.
    - Also called the **rectangular distribution.**
    - $\mu = \dfrac{a+b}{2}$
    - $\sigma^2 = \dfrac{(b-a)^2}{12}$
    - $\sigma = \sqrt{\dfrac{(b-a)^2}{12}}$
- **The uniform probability density function:**
    - $f(X) = \dfrac{1}{b-a}$ if $a \le X \le b$ and 0 elsewhere, where
    a is the minimum value of X and b is the maximum value of X
- **Applications:** Selection of random numbers.

The Exponential Distribution

- **The exponential distribution:**

    $P(\text{arrival time} < X) = 1 - e^{-\lambda X}$

    where

    X : any value of continuous random variable

    λ : the population average number of arrivals per unit of time

    $1/\lambda$: average time between arrivals

    $e = 2.71828$

- **Applications:** The exponential distribution is useful in waiting line (or queuing) theory to model the length of time between arrivals in processes such as customers at fast-food restaurants, and patients entering a hospital emergency room.

The Normal Approximation to the Binomial Distribution

- Whenever $np > 5$ and $np(1-p) > 5$, the normal distribution can be used to approximate the binomial distribution.
- For the discrete random variable X that has a binomial distribution, let A and B be integers. The various scenarios of computing the binomial probability using a normal approximation with a correction for continuity adjustment are presented below:
    - $P(A \le X) = P\left((A-0.5) \le X\right) = P\left(\dfrac{(A-0.5)-np}{\sqrt{np(1-p)}} \le Z\right)$

- $P(A < X) = P((A+1) \leq X) = P((A+0.5) \leq X) = P\left(\dfrac{(A+0.5)-np}{\sqrt{np(1-p)}} \leq Z\right)$

- $P(X \leq B) = P(X \leq (B+0.5)) = P\left(Z \leq \dfrac{(B+0.5)-np}{\sqrt{np(1-p)}}\right)$

- $P(X < B) = P(X \leq (B-1)) = P(X \leq (B-0.5)) = P\left(Z \leq \dfrac{(B-0.5)-np}{\sqrt{np(1-p)}}\right)$

- $P(A \leq X \leq B) = P((A-0.5) \leq X \leq (B+0.5)) = P\left(\dfrac{(A-0.5)-np}{\sqrt{np(1-p)}} \leq Z \leq \dfrac{(B+0.5)-np}{\sqrt{np(1-p)}}\right)$

- $P(A < X < B) = P((A+1) \leq X \leq (B-1)) = P((A+0.5) \leq X \leq (B-0.5))$

  $= P\left(\dfrac{(A+0.5)-np}{\sqrt{np(1-p)}} \leq Z \leq \dfrac{(B-0.5)-np}{\sqrt{np(1-p)}}\right)$

- $P(A < X \leq B) = P((A+1) \leq X \leq B) = P((A+0.5) \leq X \leq (B+0.5))$

  $= P\left(\dfrac{(A+0.5)-np}{\sqrt{np(1-p)}} \leq Z \leq \dfrac{(B+0.5)-np}{\sqrt{np(1-p)}}\right)$

- $P(A \leq X < B) = P(A \leq X \leq (B-1)) = P((A-0.5) \leq X \leq (B-0.5))$

  $= P\left(\dfrac{(A-0.5)-np}{\sqrt{np(1-p)}} \leq Z \leq \dfrac{(B-0.5)-np}{\sqrt{np(1-p)}}\right)$

- $P(X = A) = P((A-0.5) \leq X \leq (A+0.5)) = P\left(\dfrac{(A-0.5)-np}{\sqrt{np(1-p)}} \leq Z \leq \dfrac{(A+0.5)-np}{\sqrt{np(1-p)}}\right)$

SOLUTIONS TO END OF SECTION
AND CHAPTER REVIEW EVEN PROBLEMS

6.2   (a) $P(-1.57 < Z < 1.84) = 0.9671 - 0.0582 = 0.9089$
       (b) $P(Z < -1.57) + P(Z > 1.84) = 0.0582 + 0.0329 = 0.0911$
       (c)   If $P(Z > A) = 0.025$, $P(Z < A) = 0.975$. $A = +1.96$.
       (d)   If $P(-A < Z < A) = 0.6826$, $P(Z < A) = 0.8413$. So 68.26% of the area is captured between $-A = -1.00$ and $A = +1.00$.

6.4   (a) $P(Z > 1.08) = 1 - 0.8599 = 0.1401$
       (b) $P(Z < -0.21) = 0.4168$
       (c) $P(-1.96 < Z < -0.21) = 0.4168 - 0.0250 = 0.3918$
       (d) $P(Z > A) = 0.1587$, $P(Z < A) = 0.8413$. $A = +1.00$.

6.6   (a) $P(X > 43) = P(Z > -1.75) = 1 - 0.0401 = 0.9599$
       (b) $P(X < 42) = P(Z < -2.00) = 0.0228$
       (c) $P(X < A) = 0.05$,

$$Z = -1.645 = \frac{A - 50}{4} \qquad A = 50 - 1.645(4) = 43.42$$

       (d) $P(X_{lower} < X < X_{upper}) = 0.60$
             $P(Z < -0.84) = 0.20$ and $P(Z < 0.84) = 0.80$

$$Z = -0.84 = \frac{X_{lower} - 50}{4} \qquad Z = +0.84 = \frac{X_{upper} - 50}{4}$$

             $X_{lower} = 50 - 0.84(4) = 46.64$ and $X_{upper} = 50 + 0.84(4) = 53.36$

6.8   (a) $P(34 < X < 50) = P(-1.33 < Z < 0) = 0.4082$
       (b) $P(X < 30) + P(X > 60) = P(Z < -1.67) + P(Z > 0.83)$
             $= 0.0475 + (1.0 - 0.7967) = 0.2508$

       (c) $P(X > A) = 0.80 \qquad P(Z < -0.84) \cong 0.20 \qquad Z = -0.84 = \dfrac{A - 50}{12}$

             $A = 50 - 0.84(12) = 39.92$ thousand miles or 39,920 miles
       (d)   The smaller standard deviation makes the Z-values larger.
             (a) $P(34 < X < 50) = P(-1.60 < Z < 0) = 0.4452$
             (b) $P(X < 30) + P(X > 60) = P(Z < -2.00) + P(Z > 1.00)$
                  $= 0.0228 + (1.0 - 0.8413) = 0.1815$
             (c) $A = 50 - 0.84(10) = 41.6$ thousand miles or 41,600 miles

6.10   (a) $P(X < 91) = P(Z < 2.25) = 0.9878$
    (b) $P(65 < X < 89) = P(-1.00 < Z < 2.00) = 0.9772 - 0.1587 = 0.8185$
    (c) $P(X > A) = 0.05$ $P(Z < 1.645) = 0.9500$

$$Z = 1.645 = \frac{A - 73}{8} \quad A = 73 + 1.645(8) = 86.16\%$$

    (d)   Option 1: $P(X > A) = 0.10$ $P(Z < 1.28) \cong 0.9000$

$$Z = \frac{81 - 73}{8} = 1.00$$

Since your score of 81% on this exam represents a Z-score of 1.00, which is below the minimum Z-score of 1.28, you will not earn an "A" grade on the exam under this grading option.

Option 2: $Z = \dfrac{68 - 62}{3} = 2.00$

Since your score of 68% on this exam represents a Z-score of 2.00, which is well above the minimum Z-score of 1.28, you will earn an "A" grade on the exam under this grading option. You should prefer Option 2.

6.12   (a) $P(X < 1.7) = P(Z < 2.0) = 0.9772$
    (b) $P(X < 1.25) = P(Z < -1.0) = 0.1587$
    (c) $P(X < 1.0) = P(Z < -2.6667) = 0.0038$
    (d) $P(X > 1.0) = P(Z > -2.6667) = 0.9962$

6.14   With 39 observations, the smallest of the standard normal quantile values covers an area under the normal curve of 0.025. The corresponding Z-value is -1.96. The largest of the standard normal quantile values covers an area under the normal curve of 0.975 and its corresponding Z-value is $+1.96$.

6.16 $\text{mean} = \dfrac{\sum\limits_{i=1}^{n} X_i}{n} = \dfrac{2491.55}{25} = 99.662,$ $\text{median} = 95.78,$

range = max $-$ min $= 167.43 - 62.88 = 104.55,$

$$S_X = \sqrt{\frac{\sum\limits_{i=1}^{n}(X - \bar{X})^2}{n-1}} = \sqrt{\frac{14861.7724}{24}} = 24.8845,$$

$6 \cdot S_X = 6 \cdot 24.8845 = 149.3072,$

interquartile range $= Q_3 - Q_1 = 120.675 - 77.57 = 43.105,$

$1.33 \cdot S_X = 1.33 \cdot 24.8845 = 33.0964$

The mean is greater than the median; the range is smaller than 6 times the standard deviation and the interquartile range is larger than 1.33 times the standard deviation. The data do not appear to follow a normal distribution.

6.16   (b)
cont.

Normal Probability Plot

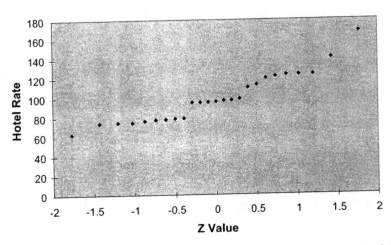

The normal probability plot suggests that the data are skewed to the right.

6.18   (a)   Plant A: $\bar{X} = 9.382$ $S = 3.998$
Five-number summary   4.42 7.29 8.515 11.42 21.62
Interquartile range = 4.13 $1.33\ S = 5.317$
Range = 17.2 $6\ S = 23.986$
Between $\bar{X} \pm 1S_X = 80\%$

Between $\bar{X} \pm 1.28S_X = 90\%$

Between $\bar{X} \pm 2S_X = 95\%$

The median is smaller than the mean. The interquartile range is smaller than 1.33 times the standard deviation and the range is much smaller than 6 times the standard deviation.
The distribution is right-skewed since the mean is greater than the median.

Note: The quartiles are obtained using PHStat without any interpolation.

Plant B: $\bar{X} = 11.354$ $S = 5.126$
Five-number summary   2.33 6.25 11.96 14.25 25.75
Interquartile range = 8 $1.33\ S = 6.818$
Range = 23.42 $6\ S = 30.757$
Between $\bar{X} \pm 1S_X = 75\%$

Between $\bar{X} \pm 1.28S_X = 95\%$

Between $\bar{X} \pm 2S_X = 95\%$

The median is slightly larger than the mean. The interquartile range is larger than 1.33 times the standard deviation and the range is smaller than 6 times the standard deviation.
Although the results are inconsistent due to an extreme value in the sample, since the mean is less than the median, we can say that the data for Plant B is left-skewed.

6.18   (a)   Note: The quartiles are obtained using PHStat without any interpolation
cont.

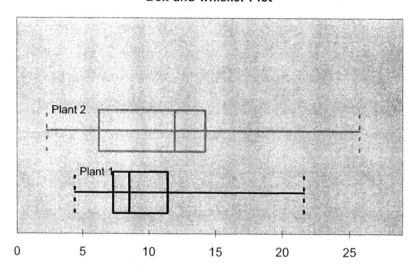

(b)

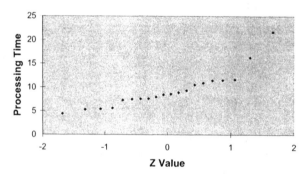

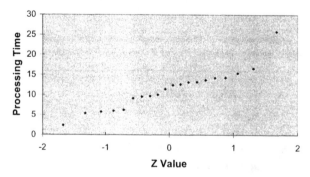

6.20   (a) $\bar{X} = -0.00023$ median = 0

Interquartile range = 0.0025 $S_X = 0.0017$ Range = 0.008

$1.33\ (S_X) = 0.0023$ $6\ (S_X) = 0.0102$

Between $\bar{X} \pm 1S_X = 61\%$ Between $\bar{X} \pm 1.28S_X = 72\%$

Between $\bar{X} \pm 2S_X = 98\%$

Since the interquartile range is quite close to $1.33\ (S_X)$ and the range is also quite close to $6\ (S_X)$, the data appear to be approximately normally distributed.

(b)

Normal Probability Plot

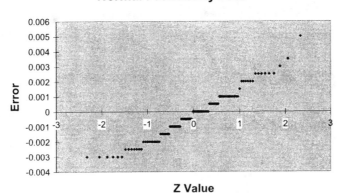

The normal probability plot suggests that the data appear to be approximately normally distributed.

6.22   (a)   Five-number summary: 82   127   148.5   168   213   mean = 147.06

range = 131   interquartile range = 41   standard deviation = 31.69

The mean is very close to the median. The five-number summary suggests that the distribution is quite symmetrical around the median. The interquartile range is very close to 1.33 times the standard deviation. The range is about $50 below 6 times the standard deviation. In general, the distribution of the data appears to closely resemble a normal distribution.

Note: The quartiles are obtained using PHStat without any interpolation.

6.22   (b)
cont.

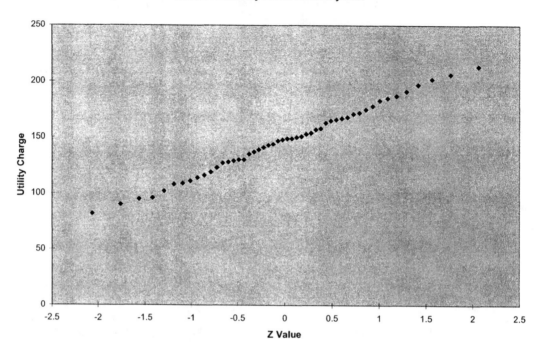

The normal probability plot confirms that the data appear to be approximately normally distributed.

6.24   (a) $P(0 < X < 20) = (20 - 0) /120 = 0.1667$
      (b) $P(10 < X < 30) = (30 - 10)/120 = 0.1667$
      (c) $P(35 < X < 120) = (120 - 35)/120 = 0.7083$

      (d) $\mu = \dfrac{0 + 120}{2} = 60$ $\sigma = \sqrt{\dfrac{(120-0)^2}{12}} = 34.6410$

6.26   (a) $P(5{:}55 \text{ a.m.} < X < 7{:}38 \text{ p.m.}) = P(355 < X < 1178) = (1178 - 355)/(1440) = 0.5715$
      (b) $P(10 \text{ p.m.} < X < 5 \text{ a.m.}) = P(1320 < X < 1440) + P(0 < X < 300)$
              $= (1440 - 1320)/1440 + (300)/1440 = 0.2917$
      (c)   Let X be duration between the occurrence of a failure and its detection.
           $a = 0, b = 60$
           $P(0 < X < 10) = P(0 < X < 10) = 10/60 = 0.1667$
      (d) $P(40 < X < 60) = (60 - 40)/60 = 0.3333$

6.28   (a) $P(\text{arrival time} < 0.1) = 1 - e^{-\lambda x} = 1 - e^{-(10)(0.1)} = 0.6321$
      (b) $P(\text{arrival time} > 0.1) = 1 - P(\text{arrival time} \le 0.1) = 1 - 0.6321 = 0.3679$
      (c) $P(0.1 < \text{arrival time} < 0.2) = P(\text{arrival time} < 0.2) - P(\text{arrival time} < 0.1)$
              $= 0.8647 - 0.6321 = 0.2326$
      (d) $P(\text{arrival time} < 0.1) + P(\text{arrival time} > 0.2) = 0.6321 + 0.1353 = 0.7674$

6.30   (a) $P(\text{arrival time} < 4) = 1 - e^{-(20)(4)} \cong 1$

(b) $P(\text{arrival time} > 0.4) = 1 - P(\text{arrival time} \leq 0.4) = 1 - 0.9997 = 0.0003$

     (c) $P(0.4 < \text{arrival time} < 0.5) = P(\text{arrival time} < 0.5) - P(\text{arrival time} < 0.4)$

          $= 0.99996 - 0.99967 = 0.00029$

     (d) $P(\text{arrival time} < 0.4) + P(\text{arrival time} > 0.5) = 0.999665 + 0.000045 = 0.99971$

6.32   (a)

	A	B
1	Fast Food Arrivals	
2		
3	Mean	2
4	X Value	1
5	P(<=X)	0.864665

(b) $P(\text{arrival time} \leq 5) = 0.99996$

     (c)   If $\lambda = 1$, $P(\text{arrival time} \leq 1) = 0.6321$,

                    $P(\text{arrival time} \leq 5) = 0.9933$

6.34   (a) $P(\text{time till next injury} \leq 10) = 1 - e^{-(0.1)(10)} = 0.6321$

(b) $P(\text{time till next injury} \leq 5) = 0.3935$

     (c) $P(\text{time till next injury} \leq 1) = 0.0952$

6.36   (a) $P(\text{arrival time} \leq 0.25) = 0.8647$

(b) $P(\text{arrival time} \leq 0.05) = 0.3297$

     (c)   If $\lambda = 15$, $P(\text{arrival time} \leq 0.25) = 0.9765$,

                  $P(\text{arrival time} \leq 0.05) = 0.5276$

6.38 $n = 100, p = 0.20.$ $np = 20 \geq 5$ and $n(1 - p) = 80 \geq 5$

     $\mu = np = 20$ $\sigma = \sqrt{np(1 - p)} = 4$

     (a) $P(X = 25) \cong P(24.5 \leq X \leq 25.5) = P(1.125 \leq Z \leq 1.375) = 0.0457$

     (b) $P(X > 25) = P(X \geq 26) \cong P(X \geq 25.5) = P(Z \geq 1.375) = 0.0846$

     (c) $P(X \leq 25) \cong P(X \leq 25.5) = P(Z \leq 1.375) = 0.9154$

     (d) $P(X < 25) = P(X \leq 24) \cong P(X \leq 24.5) = P(Z \leq 1.125) = 0.8697$

6.40 $n = 10, p = 0.50.$ $np = 5 \geq 5$ and $n(1-p) = 5 \geq 5$

   $\mu = np = 5$ $\sigma = \sqrt{np(1-p)} = 1.5811$

PHStat output:

X	P(X)	P(<=X)	P(<X)	P(>X)	P(>=X)
0	0.000977	0.000977	0	0.999023	1
1	0.009766	0.010742	0.000977	0.989258	0.999023
2	0.043945	0.054688	0.010742	0.945313	0.989258
3	0.117188	0.171875	0.054688	0.828125	0.945313
4	0.205078	0.376953	0.171875	0.623047	0.828125
5	0.246094	0.623047	0.376953	0.376953	0.623047
6	0.205078	0.828125	0.623047	0.171875	0.376953
7	0.117188	0.945313	0.828125	0.054687	0.171875
8	0.043945	0.989258	0.945313	0.010742	0.054687
9	0.009766	0.999023	0.989258	0.000977	0.010742
10	0.000977	1	0.999023	0	0.000977

(a) $P(X = 4) = 0.2051$
(b) $P(X \geq 4) = 0.8281$
(c) $P(4 \leq X \leq 7) = 0.9453 - 0.1719 = 0.7734$
(d)   (a) $P(X = 4) \cong P(3.5 \leq X \leq 4.5) = P(-0.9487 \leq Z \leq -0.3162) = 0.2045$
       (b) $P(X \geq 4) \cong P(X \geq 3.5) = P(Z \geq -0.9487) = 0.8286$
       (c) $P(4 \leq X \leq 7) \cong P(3.5 \leq X \leq 7.5) = P(-0.9487 \leq Z \leq 1.5812) = 0.7717$

6.42 $n = 200, p = 0.4.$ $np = 80 \geq 5$ and $n(1-p) = 120 \geq 5$

   $\mu = np = 80$ $\sigma = \sqrt{np(1-p)} = 6.9282$

(a) $P(X \geq 75) \cong P(X \geq 74.5) = P(Z \geq -0.7939) = 0.7864$
(b) $P(X \leq 70) \cong P(X \leq 70.5) = P(Z \leq -1.3712) = 0.0852$
(c) $P(70 \leq X \leq 75) \cong (69.5 \leq X \leq 75.5) = P(-1.5155 \leq Z \leq -0.6495) = 0.1932$

6.44   Using Table E.2, first find the cumulative area up to the largest value, and then subtract the cumulative area up to the smallest value.

6.46   The normal distribution is bell-shaped; its measures of central tendency are all equal; its middle 50% is within 1.33 standard deviations of its mean; and 99.7% of its values are contained within three standard deviations of its mean.

6.48   The exponential distribution is used to determine the probability that the next arrival will occur within a given length of time.

6.50   You can use the normal distribution to approximate the binomial distribution when both np and $n(1-p)$ are at least 5.

6.52   (a) $P(1.90 < X < 2.00) = P(-2.00 < Z < 0) = 0.4772$
       (b) $P(1.90 < X < 2.10) = P(-2.00 < Z < 2.00) = 0.9772 - 0.0228 = 0.9544$
       (c) $P(X < 1.90) + P(X > 2.10) = 1 - P(1.90 < X < 2.10) = 0.0456$
       (d) $P(X > A) = P(Z > -2.33) = 0.99$ $A = 2.00 - 2.33(0.05) = 1.8835$
       (e) $P(A < X < B) = P(-2.58 < Z < 2.58) = 0.99$
             $A = 2.00 - 2.58(0.05) = 1.8710$ $B = 2.00 + 2.58(0.05) = 2.1290$

6.54   (a) $P(4.70 < X < 5.00) = P(0 < Z < 0.75) = 0.2734$
     (b) $P(5.00 < X < 5.50) = P(0.75 < Z < 2.00) = 0.9772 - 0.7734 = 0.2038$
     (c) $P(X > A) = P(Z > -0.74) = 0.77$ $A = 4.70 - 0.74(0.40) = 4.404$ ounces
     (d) $P(A < X < B) = P(-1.28 < Z < 1.28) = 0.80$
           $A = 4.70 - 1.28(0.40) = 4.188$ ounces
           $B = 4.70 + 1.28(0.40) = 5.212$ ounces

6.56   (a) $P(X > 0) = P(Z > -0.6047) = 0.7273$
     (b) $P(X > 10) = P(Z > 0.5581) = 0.2884$
     (c) $P(X > 20) = P(Z > 1.7209) = 0.0426$
     (d) $P(X < -10) = P(Z < -1.7674) = 0.0386$
     (e)   The common stocks have higher mean annual returns than the long-term government bonds. But they also have higher volatility as reflected by their larger standard deviation. This is the usual trade-off between high return and high volatility in an investment instrument.
    Note: The above answers are obtained using PHStat. They may be slightly different when Table E.2 is used.

6.58   (a) $P(X < 1) = P(Z < 1) = 0.8413$
     (b) $P(0.5 < X < 1.5) = P(-1.5 < Z < 3.5) = 0.9330$
     (c) $P(0.5 < X) = P(-1.5 < Z) = 0.9332$
     (d) $P(A < X) = 0.99$ $\dfrac{A - 0.8}{0.2} = -2.3263$ $A = 0.3347$
     (e) $P(A < X < B) = 0.95$ $\dfrac{A - 0.8}{0.2} = -1.960$ $A = 0.4080$
           $\dfrac{B - 0.8}{0.2} = 1.96$ $B = 1.1920$

CHAPTER 7

OBJECTIVES

- To understand the concept of the sampling distribution
- To be able to compute probabilities related to the sample mean and sample proportion
- To understand and be able to apply the central limit theorem
- To be able to distinguish between different survey sampling methods

OVERVIEW AND KEY CONCEPTS

Some Basic Concepts on Sampling Distribution

- **Why do we study sampling distribution?**
    - Sample statistics are used to estimate population parameters, but different samples yield different estimates. The solution is to develop a theoretical basis based on sampling distribution.
- **What is a sampling distribution?**
    - A sampling distribution is a theoretical probability distribution of a sample statistic. A sample statistic (e.g., sample mean, sample proportion) is a random variable because a different sample will yield a different value for the statistic, and, hence, a different estimate for the parameter of interest. The sampling distribution is the probability distribution of the sample statistic as a result of taking all possible samples of the same size from the population.

Sampling Distribution of the Sample Mean

- **Population mean of the sample mean**
    - $\mu_{\bar{x}} = \mu$
    - This is the unbiased property of the sample mean.
- **Standard error (population standard deviation) of the sample mean**
    - $\sigma_{\bar{x}} = \dfrac{\sigma}{\sqrt{n}}$
    - Standard error of the sample mean is smaller than the standard deviation of the population.
    - The larger the sample size, the smaller the standard error.
- **The central limit theorem:** As the sample size (i.e., the number of the observations in a sample) gets *large enough*, the sampling distribution of the mean can be approximated by the normal distribution regardless of the distribution of the individual values in the population.
- **The distribution of the sample mean**
    - If the population is normally distributed, the sampling distribution of the mean is normally distributed regardless of the sample size.
    - If the population distribution is fairly symmetrical, the sampling distribution of the mean is approximately normal if sample size is at least 15.
    - For most population distributions, regardless of the shape, the sampling distribution of the mean is approximately normally distributed if the sample size is at least 30.

- **Finite population correction (Note: the finite population correction factor is covered in section 7.6 on the CD-ROM)**
    - Use the finite population correction factor to modify the standard error if sample size n is large relative to the population size N, i.e. $n/N > 0.05$.

    - Standard error with finite population correction factor: $\sigma_{\bar{X}} = \dfrac{\sigma}{\sqrt{n}} \sqrt{\dfrac{N-n}{N-1}}$

Finding Range Probability of the Sample Mean

1. Standardize the value of the sample mean using $Z = \dfrac{\bar{X} - \mu_{\bar{X}}}{\sigma_{\bar{X}}} = \dfrac{\bar{X} - \mu}{\dfrac{\sigma}{\sqrt{n}}}$.

2. Look up the cumulative probabilities from the cumulative standardized normal distribution table.

E.g., for $\mu = 8$, $\sigma = 2$, $n = 25$ and X normally distributed. $P\left(7.8 < \bar{X} < 8.2\right) = ?$

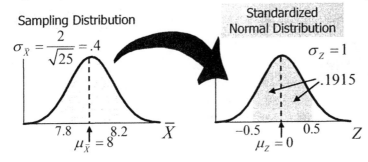

$$P\left(7.8 < \bar{X} < 8.2\right) = P\left(\frac{7.8 - 8}{2/\sqrt{25}} < \frac{\bar{X} - \mu_{\bar{X}}}{\sigma_{\bar{X}}} < \frac{8.2 - 8}{2/\sqrt{25}}\right) = P\left(-.5 < Z < .5\right) = .3830$$

Sampling Distribution of the Sample Proportion

- **Sample proportion:** $p = \dfrac{X}{n} = \dfrac{\text{number of items having the characteristic of interest}}{\text{sample size}}$

- **Population mean of the sample proportion**
    - $\mu_p = \pi$ where π is the population proportion.

- **Standard error of the sample proportion**
    - $\sigma_p = \sqrt{\dfrac{\pi\left(1 - \pi\right)}{n}}$

- **The distribution of the sample proportion**
    - When $n\pi$ and $n(1-\pi)$ are each at least 5, the sampling distribution of the sample proportion can be approximated by the normal distribution with mean μ_p and standard deviation σ_p.

- **Finite population correction (Note: the finite population correction factor is covered in section 7.6 on the CD-ROM)**
  - Use the finite population correction factor to modify the standard error if sample size n is large relative to the population size N, i.e. $n/N > 0.05$.

  - Standard error with finite population correction factor: $\sigma_p = \sqrt{\dfrac{\pi(1-\pi)}{n}}\sqrt{\dfrac{N-n}{N-1}}$

Finding Range Probability of the Sample Proportion

1. Standardize the value of the sample proportion using $Z = \dfrac{p - \mu_p}{\sigma_p} = \dfrac{p - \pi}{\sqrt{\dfrac{\pi(1-\pi)}{n}}}$.

2. Lookup the cumulative probabilities from the cumulative standardized normal distribution table.

E.g., for $n = 200$, $\pi = 0.4$. $P(p < 0.43) = ?$

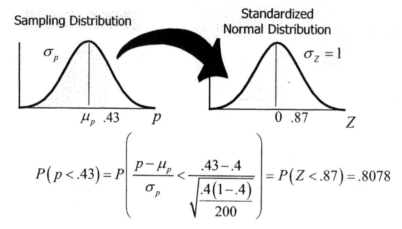

$$P(p<.43) = P\left(\frac{p - \mu_p}{\sigma_p} < \frac{.43 - .4}{\sqrt{\dfrac{.4(1-.4)}{200}}}\right) = P(Z < .87) = .8078$$

Reasons for Drawing Sample

- Less time consuming than a census
- Less costly to administer than a census
- Less cumbersome and more practical to administer than a census of the targeted population

The Different Methods of Sample Selection

- **A nonprobability sample:** Items or individuals are chosen without regard to their probability of occurrence.
- **A probability sample:** The subjects of the sample are chosen on the basis of known probability.
- **A simple random sample:** Every individual or item from the frame has an equal chance of being selected. Selection may be with replacement or without replacement.
- **A systematic sample:** Decide on a sample size, n; divide frame of N individuals into groups of k individuals, k = N/n; randomly select one individual from the first group; select every k[th] individual thereafter.

- **A stratified sample:** The population is divided into two or more groups according to some common characteristic, e.g., whether an employee is full-time or part-time; simple random sample is selected from each group; the two or more samples are combined into one.
- **A cluster sample:** The population is divided into several "clusters", e.g., counties or election districts, in which each is representative of the population; a simple random sample is selected from each cluster; the samples are combined into one.

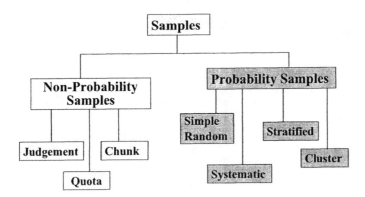

Evaluating Survey Worthiness

- What is the purpose of the survey?
- Is the survey based on a probability sample?
- **Coverage error:** Certain groups of subjects are excluded from the frame and have no chance of being selected in the sample.
- **Nonresponse error:** Failure to collect data on all subjects in the sample.
- **Measurement error:** Inaccuracies in the recorded responses that occur because of a weakness in question wording, an interviewer's effect on the respondent, or the effort made by the respondent.
- **Sampling error:** The chance differences from sample to sample based on the probability of particular individuals or items being selected in the particular samples. Sampling error always exists in a survey.

SOLUTIONS TO END OF SECTION
AND CHAPTER REVIEW EVEN PROBLEMS

7.2   (a) $P(\overline{X} < 47) = P(Z < -6.00) =$ virtually zero
       (b) $P(47 < \overline{X} < 49.5) = P(-6.00 < Z < -1.00) = 0.1587 - 0.00 = 0.1587$
       (c) $P(\overline{X} > 51.1) = P(Z > 2.20) = 1.0 - 0.9861 = 0.0139$
       (d) $P(\overline{X} > A) = P(Z > 0.39) = 0.35$ $\overline{X} = 50 + 0.39(0.5) = 50.195$

7.4   (a)   Sampling Distribution of the Mean for $n = 2$ (without replacement)

Sample Number	Outcomes	Sample Means $\overline{X}_i$
1	1, 3	$\overline{X}_1 = 2$
2	1, 6	$\overline{X}_2 = 3.5$
3	1, 7	$\overline{X}_3 = 4$
4	1, 9	$\overline{X}_4 = 5$
5	1, 10	$\overline{X}_5 = 5.5$
6	3, 6	$\overline{X}_6 = 4.5$
7	3, 7	$\overline{X}_7 = 5$
8	3, 9	$\overline{X}_8 = 6$
9	3, 10	$\overline{X}_9 = 6.5$
10	6, 7	$\overline{X}_{10} = 6.5$
11	6, 9	$\overline{X}_{11} = 7.5$
12	6, 10	$\overline{X}_{12} = 8$
13	7, 9	$\overline{X}_{13} = 8$
14	7, 10	$\overline{X}_{14} = 8.5$
15	9, 10	$\overline{X}_{15} = 9.5$

Mean of All Possible Sample Means: Mean of All Population Elements:

$$\mu_{\overline{X}} = \frac{90}{15} = 6 \qquad\qquad \mu = \frac{1+3+6+7+9+10}{6} = 6$$

Both means are equal to 6. This property is called unbiasedness.

7.4   (b)   Sampling Distribution of the Mean for $n = 3$ (without replacement)
cont.

Sample Number	Outcomes	Sample Means $\bar{X}_i$
1	1, 3, 6	$\bar{X}_1 = 3\ 1/3$
2	1, 3, 7	$\bar{X}_2 = 3\ 2/3$
3	1, 3, 9	$\bar{X}_3 = 4\ 1/3$
4	1, 3, 10	$\bar{X}_4 = 4\ 2/3$
5	1, 6, 7	$\bar{X}_5 = 4\ 2/3$
6	1, 6, 9	$\bar{X}_6 = 5\ 1/3$
7	1, 6, 10	$\bar{X}_7 = 5\ 2/3$
8	3, 6, 7	$\bar{X}_8 = 5\ 1/3$
9	3, 6, 9	$\bar{X}_9 = 6$
10	3, 6, 10	$\bar{X}_{10} = 6\ 1/3$
11	6, 7, 9	$\bar{X}_{11} = 7\ 1/3$
12	6, 7, 10	$\bar{X}_{12} = 7\ 2/3$
13	6, 9, 10	$\bar{X}_{13} = 8\ 1/3$
14	7, 9, 10	$\bar{X}_{14} = 8\ 2/3$
15	1, 7, 9	$\bar{X}_{15} = 5\ 2/3$
16	1, 7, 10	$\bar{X}_{16} = 6$
17	1, 9, 10	$\bar{X}_{17} = 6\ 2/3$
18	3, 7, 9	$\bar{X}_{18} = 6\ 1/3$
19	3, 7, 10	$\bar{X}_{19} = 6\ 2/3$
20	3, 9, 10	$\bar{X}_{20} = 7\ 1/3$

$$\mu_{\bar{X}} = \frac{120}{20} = 6 \qquad \text{This is equal to } \mu, \text{ the population mean.}$$

(c)   The distribution for $n = 3$ has less variability. The larger sample size has resulted in sample means being closer to μ.

7.4   (d)   (a)   Sampling Distribution of the Mean for $n = 2$ (with replacement)
cont.

Sample Number	Outcomes	Sample Means $\bar{X}_i$
1	1, 1	$\bar{X}_1 = 1$
2	1, 3	$\bar{X}_2 = 2$
3	1, 6	$\bar{X}_3 = 3.5$
4	1, 7	$\bar{X}_4 = 4$
5	1, 9	$\bar{X}_5 = 5$
6	1, 10	$\bar{X}_6 = 5.5$
7	3, 1	$\bar{X}_7 = 2$
8	3, 3	$\bar{X}_8 = 3$
9	3, 6	$\bar{X}_9 = 4.5$
10	3, 7	$\bar{X}_{10} = 5$
11	3, 9	$\bar{X}_{11} = 6$
12	3, 10	$\bar{X}_{12} = 6.5$
13	6, 1	$\bar{X}_{13} = 3.5$
14	6, 3	$\bar{X}_{14} = 4.5$
15	6, 6	$\bar{X}_{15} = 6$
16	6, 7	$\bar{X}_{16} = 6.5$
17	6, 9	$\bar{X}_{17} = 7.5$
18	6, 10	$\bar{X}_{18} = 8$
19	7, 1	$\bar{X}_{19} = 4$
20	7, 3	$\bar{X}_{20} = 5$
21	7, 6	$\bar{X}_{21} = 6.5$
22	7, 7	$\bar{X}_{22} = 7$
23	7, 9	$\bar{X}_{23} = 8$
24	7, 10	$\bar{X}_{24} = 8.5$
25	9, 1	$\bar{X}_{25} = 5$
26	9, 3	$\bar{X}_{26} = 6$
27	9, 6	$\bar{X}_{27} = 7.5$
28	9, 7	$\bar{X}_{28} = 8$
29	9, 9	$\bar{X}_{29} = 9$
30	9, 10	$\bar{X}_{30} = 9.5$
31	10, 1	$\bar{X}_{31} = 5.5$
32	10, 3	$\bar{X}_{32} = 6.5$

33	10, 6	$\overline{X}_{33} = 8$
34	10, 7	$\overline{X}_{34} = 8.5$
35	10, 9	$\overline{X}_{35} = 9.5$
36	10, 10	$\overline{X}_{36} = 10$

7.4
cont.   (d)   (a)

<table>
<tr><td>Mean of All Possible
Sample Means:</td><td>Mean of All
Population Elements:</td></tr>
<tr><td>$\mu_{\overline{X}} = \dfrac{216}{36} = 6$</td><td>$\mu = \dfrac{1+3+6+7+7+12}{6} = 6$</td></tr>
</table>

Both means are equal to 6. This property is called unbiasedness.

(b)   Repeat the same process for the sampling distribution of the mean for $n = 3$ (with replacement). There will be $6^3 = 216$ different samples.

$\mu_{\overline{X}} = 6$ This is equal to μ, the population mean.

(c)   The distribution for $n = 3$ has less variability. The larger sample size has resulted in more sample means being close to μ.

7.6   (a)   For samples of size 2, the sampling distribution of $\overline{X}$ will resemble the right-skewed population distribution.

(b)   When the sample size is 100, the sampling distribution of $\overline{X}$ will be very close to a normal distribution as a result of the central limit theorem.

(c) $P(\overline{X} < 250,000) = P(Z < -1.1111) = 0.1333$

7.8   (a) $P(\overline{X} > 3) = P(Z > -1.00) = 1 - 0.1587 = 0.8413$

(b) $P(\overline{X} < A) = P(Z < 1.04) = 0.85$ $\overline{X} = 3.10 + 1.04(0.1) = 3.204$

(c)   To be able to use the standard normal distribution as an approximation for the area under the curve, we must assume that the population is symmetrically distributed such that the central limit theorem will likely hold for samples of $n = 16$.

(d) $P(\overline{X} < A) = P(Z < 1.04) = 0.85$ $\overline{X} = 3.10 + 1.04(0.05) = 3.152$

7.10   (a) $P(\overline{X} < 2.75) = P(Z < 2.7386) = 0.9969$

(b) $P(2.7 < \overline{X} < 2.9) = P(2.1909 < Z < 4.3818) = 0.0142$

(c) $P(A < \overline{X} < B) = P(-1.2816 < Z < 1.2816) = 0.80$
       $A = 2.5 - 1.2816\,(0.0913) = 2.3830$ $B = 2.5 + 1.2816\,(0.0913) = 2.6170$

(d) $P(\overline{X} < A) = P(Z < 1.2816) = 0.90$ $A = 2.5 + 1.2816\,(0.0913) = 2.6170$

Note: The above answers are obtained using PHStat. They may be slightly different when Table E.2 is used.

7.12   (a) $p = 15/50 = 0.30$ (b) $\sigma_p = \sqrt{\dfrac{0.40(0.60)}{50}} = 0.0693$

7.14   (a) $\mu_p = \pi = 0.501$, $\sigma_p = \sqrt{\dfrac{\pi(1-\pi)}{n}} = \sqrt{\dfrac{0.501(1-0.501)}{100}} = 0.05$

$P(p > 0.55) = P(Z > 0.98) = 1 - 0.8365 = 0.1635$

(b) $\mu_p = \pi = 0.60$, $\sigma_p = \sqrt{\dfrac{\pi(1-\pi)}{n}} = \sqrt{\dfrac{0.6(1-0.6)}{100}} = 0.04899$

$P(p > 0.55) = P(Z > -1.021) = 1 - 0.1539 = 0.8461$

(c) $\mu_p = \pi = 0.49$, $\sigma_p = \sqrt{\dfrac{\pi(1-\pi)}{n}} = \sqrt{\dfrac{0.49(1-0.49)}{100}} = 0.05$

$P(p > 0.55) = P(Z > 1.20) = 1 - 0.8849 = 0.1151$

(d)   Increasing the sample size by a factor of 4 decreases the standard error by a factor of 2.

(a) $P(p > 0.55) = P(Z > 1.96) = 1 - 0.9750 = 0.0250$

(b) $P(p > 0.55) = P(Z > -2.04) = 1 - 0.0207 = 0.9793$

(c) $P(p > 0.55) = P(Z > 2.40) = 1 - 0.9918 = 0.0082$

7.16   (a) $P(p < 0.15) = P(Z < 0) = 0.50$

(b) $P(0.13 < p < 0.17) = P(-0.7921 < Z < 0.7921) = 0.5717$

(c) $P(0.10 < p < 0.20) = P(-1.9803 < Z < 1.9803) = 0.9523$

(d)   (a) $P(p < 0.15) = P(Z < 0) = 0.50$

(b) $P(0.13 < p < 0.17) = P(-0.5601 < Z < 0.5601) = 0.4246$

(c) $P(0.10 < p < 0.20) = P(-1.4003 < Z < 1.4003) = 0.8386$

7.18   (a) $P(0.75 < p < 0.80) = P(-0.6721 < Z < 1.0082) = 0.5926$

(b) $P(A < p < B) = P(-1.6449 < Z < 1.6449) = 0.90$

$A = 0.77 - 1.6449(0.0298) = 0.7211$

$B = 0.77 + 1.6449(0.0298) = 0.8189$

(c) $P(A < p < B) = P(-1.960 < Z < 1.960) = 0.95$

$A = 0.77 - 1.960(0.0298) = 0.7117$

$B = 0.77 + 1.96(0.0298) = 0.8283$

7.20   (a) $P(0.25 < p < 0.30) = P(-1.7630 < Z < 0.4408) = 0.6314$

(b) $P(p > .35) = P(Z > 2.6446) = 0.0041$

If the true population proportion is indeed 29%, the proportion of the samples with 35% or more who do not intend to work for pay at all is 0.41%, a very unlikely occurrence. Hence, the population estimate of 29% is very likely to be unrealistic and an under estimation.

(c) $P(p > .35) = P(Z > 1.3223) = 0.0930$

If the true population proportion is indeed 29%, the proportion of the samples with 35% or more who do not intend to work for pay at all is 9.3%, still a very unlikely occurrence. Hence, the population estimate of 29% is very likely to be unrealistic and an under estimation.

(d)   When the sample size is smaller in (c) compared to (b), the standard error of the sampling distribution of sample proportion is larger and, hence, a higher portion of the samples will have 35% or more who do not intend to work for pay at all.

7.22   (a) $P(0.89 < p < 0.91) = P(-0.4714 < Z < 0.4714) = 0.3626$
        (b) $P(0.85 < p < 0.95) = P(-2.3570 < Z < 2.3570) = 0.9816$
        (c) $P(p > 0.95) = P(Z > 2.3570) = 0.0092$
        Note: The above answers are obtained using PHStat. They may be slightly different when
                Table E.2 is used.

7.24   Sample without replacement: Read from left to right in 3-digit sequences and continue
                unfinished sequences from end of row to beginning of next row.
        Row 05: 338 505 855 551 438 855 077 186 579 488 767 833 170
        Rows 05-06: 897
        Row 06: 340 033 648 847 204 334 639 193 639 411 095 924
        Rows 06-07: 707
        Row 07: 054 329 776 100 871 007 255 980 646 886 823 920 461
        Row 08: 893 829 380 900 796 959 453 410 181 277 660 908 887
        Rows 08-09: 237
        Row 09: 818 721 426 714 050 785 223 801 670 353 362 449
        Rows 09-10: 406
        Note: All sequences above 902 are discarded.

7.26   A simple random sample would be less practical for personal interviews because of travel
        costs (unless interviewees are paid to attend a central interviewing location).

7.28   Here all members of the population are equally likely to be selected and the sample selection
        mechanism is based on chance. But not every sample of size 2 has the same chance of being
        selected. For example the sample "B and C" is impossible.

7.30   (a)   Row 16: 2323 6737 5131 8888 1718 0654 6832 4647 6510 4877
                Row 17: 4579 4269 2615 1308 2455 7830 5550 5852 5514 7182
                Row 18: 0989 3205 0514 2256 8514 4642 7567 8896 2977 8822
                Row 19: 5438 2745 9891 4991 4523 6847 9276 8646 1628 3554
                Row 20: 9475 0899 2337 0892 0048 8033 6945 9826 9403 6858
                Row 21: 7029 7341 3553 1403 3340 4205 0823 4144 1048 2949
                Row 22: 8515 7479 5432 9792 6575 5760 0408 8112 2507 3742
                Row 23: 1110 0023 4012 8607 4697 9664 4894 3928 7072 5815
                Row 24: 3687 1507 7530 5925 7143 1738 1688 5625 8533 5041
                Row 25: 2391 3483 5763 3081 6090 5169 0546
                Note: All sequences above 5000 are discarded. There were no repeating sequences.

        (b)   089   189   289   389   489   589   689   789   889   989
                1089 1189 1289 1389 1489 1589 1689 1789 1889 1989
                2089 2189 2289 2389 2489 2589 2689 2789 2889 2989
                3089 3189 3289 3389 3489 3589 3689 3789 3889 3989
                4089 4189 4289 4389 4489 4589 4689 4789 4889 4989
        (c)   With the single exception of invoice #0989, the invoices selected in the simple
                random sample are not the same as those selected in the systematic sample. It would
                be highly unlikely that a random process would select the same units as a systematic
                process.

7.32   Before accepting the results of a survey of college students, you might want to know, for
example:
> Who funded the survey? Why was it conducted?
> What was the population from which the sample was selected?
> What sampling design was used?
> What mode of response was used: a personal interview, a telephone interview, or a mail
> survey? Were interviewers trained? Were survey questions field-tested?
> What questions were asked? Were they clear, accurate, unbiased, valid?
> What operational definition of "vast majority" was used?
> What was the response rate?
> What was the sample size?

7.34   Before accepting the results of the survey on AOL subscribers, you might want to know, for
example:
> Who funded the study? Why was it conducted?
> What was the population from which the sample was selected?
> What sampling design was used?
> What mode of response was used: a personal interview, a telephone interview, or a mail
> survey? Were interviewers trained? Were survey questions field-tested?
> What other questions were asked? Were they clear, accurate, unbiased, and valid?
> What was the response rate?

7.36   Before accepting the results of the Maritz poll, you might want to know, for example:
> Who funded the study? Why was it conducted?
> What was the population from which the sample was selected?
> What sampling design was used?
> What mode of response was used: a personal interview, a telephone interview, or a mail
> survey? Were interviewers trained? Were survey questions field-tested?
> What operational definitions of "often or sometimes eating or drinking while driving"
> and "talking on cellphone" were used?
> What other questions were asked? Were they clear, accurate, unbiased, and valid?
> What was the response rate?

7.38   Before accepting the results of the survey conducted by Caravan, you might want to know, for
example:
> Who funded the study? Why was it conducted?
> What was the population from which the sample was selected?
> What was the sample size?
> What sampling design was used?
> What mode of response was used: a personal interview, a telephone interview, or a mail
> survey? Were interviewers trained? Were survey questions field-tested?
> What operational definitions of "great food", "reasonable prices", "atmosphere", "quick
> service" and "don't know" were used?
> What other questions were asked? Were they clear, accurate, unbiased, and valid?
> What was the response rate?

7.40 The variation of the sample means becomes smaller as larger sample sizes are taken. This is due to the fact that an extreme observation will have a smaller effect on the mean in a larger sample than in a small sample. Thus, the sample means will tend to be closer to the population mean as the sample size increases.

7.42 The probability distribution is the distribution of a particular variable of interest, while the sampling distribution represents the distribution of a statistic.

7.44 A probability sample is one in which the individuals or items are selected based on known probabilities. A nonprobability sample is one in which the individuals or items are selected without regard to their probability of occurrence.

7.46 Sampling with replacement means that once a person or item is selected, it is returned to the frame where it has the same probability of being selected again. Sampling without replacement means that a person or item once selected is not returned to the frame and therefore cannot be selected again.

7.48 In a stratified sample, the N individuals or items in the population are first subdivided into separate subpopulations, or strata, according to some common characteristic. In a simple random sample, each individual item is selected randomly.

7.50 $\mu_{\bar{X}} = 0.753$ $\sigma_{\bar{X}} = \dfrac{\sigma_X}{\sqrt{n}} = \dfrac{0.004}{5} = 0.0008$

(a) $P(0.75 < \bar{X} < 0.753) = P(-3.75 < Z < 0) = 0.5 - 0.00009 = 0.4999$
(b) $P(0.74 < \bar{X} < 0.75) = P(-16.25 < Z < -3.75) = 0.00009$
(c) $P(\bar{X} > 0.76) = P(Z > 8.75) =$ virtually zero
(d) $P(\bar{X} < 0.74) = P(Z < -16.25) =$ virtually zero
(e) $P(\bar{X} < A) = P(Z < -1.48) = 0.07$ $X = 0.753 - 1.48(0.0008) = 0.7518$

7.52 $\mu_{\bar{X}} = 4.7$ $\sigma_{\bar{X}} = \dfrac{\sigma_X}{\sqrt{n}} = \dfrac{0.40}{5} = 0.08$

(a) $P(4.60 < \bar{X}\ ) = P(-1.25 < Z) = 1 - 0.1056 = 0.8944$
(b) $P(A < \bar{X} < B) = P(-1.04 < Z < 1.04) = 0.70$
   $A = 4.70 - 1.04(0.08) = 4.6168$ ounces
   $X = 4.70 + 1.04(0.08) = 4.7832$ ounces
(c) $P(\bar{X} > A) = P(Z > -0.74) = 0.77$ $A = 4.70 - 0.74(0.08) = 4.6408$

7.54 (a) $P(\bar{X} < 0) = P(Z < -2.3559) = 0.0092$
(b) $P(0 < \bar{X} < 6) = P(-2.3559 < Z < 2.3875) = 0.9823$
(c) $P(\bar{X} > 10) = P(Z > 5.5498) =$ virtually zero

7.56 Even though Internet polling is less expensive, faster and offers higher response rates than telephone surveys, it is a self-selection response method. Because respondents who choose to participate in the survey may not represent the view of the public, the data collected may not be appropriate for making inference about the general population.

7.58   (a)   Given the low response rate (15.5%), the researchers should be especially concerned with nonresponse bias. The low response rate will also increase the sampling error.

   (b)   Researchers can follow up on the nonresponses by mail or telephone to encourage or remind those who have not returned the survey to complete it.

   (c)   The researchers can enlist the Chief of Police and the President of the Fraternal Order of Police to mobilize the supervisors of various units to convey to their subordinates the importance of completing the survey. Reminder memos can also be sent from the supervisors. Verbal reminders from the supervisors during weekly meetings will also serve the same purpose.

7.60   (a)   Before accepting the results of this survey, you would like to know (i) what is the purpose of the survey, (ii) what sampling method is being used, (iii) what is the response rate, (iv) what is the frame used in the survey, and (v) how are the questions being phrased.

   (b)   The population will be all the working women which includes both those who do and do not take advantage of family-friendly schedules in the geographic region. The frame can be compiled from the list of the women who file income tax returns in the region. Since there are two natural strata in the population, those who take advantage of family-friendly schedules and those who do not, a stratified sampling method should be used to better represent the population.

7.68 $\sqrt{\dfrac{N-n}{N-1}} = \sqrt{\dfrac{400-100}{400-1}} = 0.8671$ $\sqrt{\dfrac{N-n}{N-1}} = \sqrt{\dfrac{900-200}{900-1}} = 0.8824$

   A sample of size 100 selected without replacement from a population a population of size 400 has a greater effect in reducing the standard error.

7.70 $\mu = 1.30$, $\sigma = 0.04$

   Since $n/N = 16/500 > 0.05$ and the sample is selected without replacement, we need to perform the finite population correction.

   $\mu_{\bar{X}} = \mu = 1.3$ $\sigma_{\bar{X}} = \dfrac{\sigma}{\sqrt{n}}\sqrt{\dfrac{N-n}{N-1}} = 0.0096$

   $P(1.31 < \bar{X} < 1.33) = P(1.0417 < Z < 3.125) = 0.1479$

7.72 $\pi = .10$

   Since $n/N = 400/5000 > 0.05$ and the sample is selected without replacement, we need to perform the finite population correction.

   $\mu_p = .1$ $\sigma_p = \sqrt{\dfrac{\pi(1-\pi)}{n}}\sqrt{\dfrac{N-n}{N-1}} = 0.0144$

   (a) $P(0.09 < p < 0.10) = P(-0.6944 < Z < 0) = 0.2563$

   (b) $P(p < .08) = P(Z < -1.3889) = 0.0824$

CHAPTER 8

OBJECTIVES

- To be able to construct and interpret confidence interval estimates for the mean and the proportion
- To know how to determine the sample size necessary to develop a confidence interval for the mean and proportion
- To be able to apply confidence interval estimates in auditing

OVERVIEW AND KEY CONCEPTS

Why We Need Confidence Interval Estimates in Addition to Point Estimates

- Confidence interval estimates take into consideration variation in sample statistics from sample to sample.
- They provide information about closeness to unknown population parameters.
- The interval estimates are always stated in level of confidence, which is lower than 100%.

Confidence Interval Estimate for the Mean when the Population Variance is Known

- **Assumptions:**
    - Population variance σ^2 is known.
    - Population is normally distributed or the sample size is large.
- **Point estimate for the population mean, μ : $\overline{X}$**
- **Confidence interval estimate:**
    - $\overline{X} \pm Z_{\alpha/2} \dfrac{\sigma}{\sqrt{n}}$ where $Z_{\alpha/2}$ is the value corresponding to a cumulative area of

        $\left(1 - \dfrac{\alpha}{2}\right)$ from a standardized normal distribution, i.e., the right-tail probability of $\alpha/2$.
- **Elements of confidence interval estimate**
    - **Level of confidence:** Measures the level of confidence in which the interval will contain the unknown population parameter.
    - **Precision (range):** Represents the closeness to the unknown parameter.
    - **Cost:** The cost required to obtain a sample of size n.
- **Factors affecting interval width (precision)**
    - **Data variation measured by σ^2 :** The larger is the σ^2, the wider is the interval estimate.
    - **Sample size n:** The larger is the sample size, the narrower is the interval estimate.
    - **The level of confidence $100(1-\alpha)\%$:** The higher is the level of confidence, the wider is the interval estimate.

- **Interpretation of a** $100(1-\alpha)\%$ **confidence interval estimate:** If all possible samples of size n are taken and their sample means are computed, $100(1-\alpha)\%$ of the intervals contain the true population mean somewhere within the interval around their sample means and only $100(\alpha)\%$ of them do not.

Confidence Interval Estimate for the Mean when the Population Variance is Unknown

- **Assumptions:**
  - Population variance σ^2 is unknown.
  - Population is normally distributed or the sample size is large.
- **Confidence interval estimate:**
  - $\bar{X} \pm t_{\alpha/2,n-1} \dfrac{S}{\sqrt{n}}$ where $t_{\alpha/2,n-1}$ is the value corresponding to a cumulative area of

    $\left(1-\dfrac{\alpha}{2}\right)$ from a Student's distribution with n-1 degrees of freedom, i.e., the right-tail probability of $\alpha/2$.

Confidence Interval Estimate for the Proportion

- **Assumptions:**
  - Two categorical outcomes
  - Population follows Binomial distribution
  - Normal approximation can be used if $np \geq 5$ and $n(1-p) \geq 5$.
- **Point estimate for the population proportion of success,** π: $p = \dfrac{X}{n}$
- **Confidence interval estimate:**
  - $p \pm Z_{\alpha/2} \sqrt{\dfrac{p(1-p)}{n}}$

Confidence Interval Estimate for the Total Amount (Application of Confidence Interval Estimate in Auditing)

- **Point estimate for population total:** $N\bar{X}$
- **Confidence interval estimate:**
  - $N\bar{X} \pm N\left(t_{\alpha/2,n-1}\right) \dfrac{S}{\sqrt{n}} \sqrt{\dfrac{(N-n)}{(N-1)}}$

Confidence Interval Estimate for the Total Difference (Application of Confidence Interval Estimate in Auditing)

- **Point estimate for total difference:** $N\bar{D}$ where $\bar{D} = \dfrac{\sum\limits_{i=1}^{n} D_i}{n}$ is the sample average difference.
- **Confidence interval estimate:**

  - $N\bar{D} \pm N\left(t_{\alpha/2, n-1}\right)\dfrac{S_D}{\sqrt{n}}\sqrt{\dfrac{(N-n)}{(N-1)}}$ where $S_D = \sqrt{\dfrac{\sum\limits_{i=1}^{n}\left(D_i - \bar{D}\right)^2}{n-1}}$.

One-sided Confidence Interval Estimate for the Proportion (Application of Confidence Interval Estimate in Auditing)

- **Confidence interval estimate:**

  - $Upper\ Bound = p + Z_\alpha \sqrt{\dfrac{p(1-p)}{n}}\sqrt{\dfrac{N-n}{N-1}}$ where Z_α is the value corresponding to a cumulative area of $(1-\alpha)$ from a standardized normal distribution, i.e., the right-tail probability of α.

Determining Sample Size

- **The sample size needed when estimating the population mean:**

  - $n = \dfrac{Z^2\sigma^2}{e^2}$ where e is the acceptable sampling error and σ^2 is estimated from past data, by an educated guess or by the data obtained from a pilot study.
- **The sample size needed when estimating the population proportion:**

  - $n = \dfrac{Z^2\pi(1-\pi)}{e^2}$ where e is the acceptable sampling error and π is estimated from past information, by an educated guess or use 0.5.

SOLUTIONS TO END OF SECTION
AND CHAPTER REVIEW EVEN PROBLEMS

8.2 $\bar{X} \pm Z \cdot \dfrac{\sigma}{\sqrt{n}} = 125 \pm 2.58 \cdot \dfrac{24}{\sqrt{36}}$ $114.68 \le \mu \le 135.32$

8.4   Since the results of only one sample are used to indicate whether something has gone wrong in the production process, the manufacturer can never know with 100% certainty that the specific interval obtained from the sample includes the true population mean. In order to have 100% confidence, the entire population (sample size N) would have to be selected.

8.6   Approximately 5% of the intervals will not include the true population. Since the true population mean is not known, we do not know for certain whether it is contained in the interval (between 10.99408 and 11.00192 inches) that we have developed.

8.8   (a)

	A	B
1	Light Bulbs	
2		
3	Population Standard Deviation	100
4	Sample Mean	350
5	Sample Size	64
6	Confidence Level	95%
7	Standard Error of the Mean	12.5
8	Z Value	-1.95996108
9	Interval Half Width	24.49951353
10	Interval Lower Limit	325.5004865
11	Interval Upper Limit	374.4995135

$$\bar{X} \pm Z \cdot \frac{\sigma}{\sqrt{n}} = 350 \pm 1.96 \cdot \frac{100}{\sqrt{64}} \qquad\qquad 325.5 \le \mu \le 374.50$$

(b)   No. The manufacturer cannot support a claim that the bulbs last an average 400 hours. Based on the data from the sample, a mean of 400 hours would represent a distance of 4 standard deviations above the sample mean of 350 hours.

(c)   No. Since σ is known and $n = 64$, from the Central Limit Theorem, we may assume that the sampling distribution of $\bar{X}$ is approximately normal.

(d)   The confidence interval is narrower based on a process standard deviation of 80 hours rather than the original assumption of 100 hours.

       (a) $\bar{X} \pm Z \cdot \dfrac{\sigma}{\sqrt{n}} = 350 \pm 1.96 \cdot \dfrac{80}{\sqrt{64}}$ $330.4 \le \mu \le 369.6$

       (b)   Based on the smaller standard deviation, a mean of 400 hours would represent a distance of 5 standard deviations above the sample mean of 350 hours. No, the manufacturer cannot support a claim that the bulbs have a mean life of 400 hours.

8.10 (a) $t_9 = 2.2622$
      (b) $t_9 = 3.2498$
      (c) $t_{31} = 2.0395$
      (d) $t_{64} = 1.9977$
      (e) $t_{15} = 1.7531$

8.12 $\bar{X} \pm t \cdot \dfrac{S}{\sqrt{n}} = 50 \pm 2.9467 \cdot \dfrac{15}{\sqrt{16}}$ $38.9499 \le \mu \le 61.0501$

8.14 Original data: $5.8571 \pm 2.4469 \cdot \dfrac{6.4660}{\sqrt{7}}$ $-0.1229 \le \mu \le 11.8371$

      Altered data: $4.00 \pm 2.4469 \cdot \dfrac{2.1602}{\sqrt{7}}$ $2.0022 \le \mu \le 5.9978$

      The presence of an outlier in the original data increases the value of the sample mean and greatly inflates the sample standard deviation.

8.16 (a) $\bar{X} \pm t \cdot \dfrac{S}{\sqrt{n}} = 32 \pm 2.0096 \cdot \dfrac{9}{\sqrt{50}}$ $29.44 \le \mu \le 34.56$

      (b) The quality improvement team can be 95% confident that the population mean turnaround time is somewhere in between 29.44 hours and 34.56 hours.

      (c) The project was a success because the initial turnaround time of 68 hours does not fall inside the 95% confidence interval.

8.18 (a) $\bar{X} \pm t \cdot \dfrac{S}{\sqrt{n}} = 23 \pm 2.0739 \cdot \dfrac{4.6024}{\sqrt{23}}$ $\$21.01 \le \mu \le \$24.99$

      (b) You can be 95% confident that the mean bounced check fee for the population is somewhere between \$21.01 and \$24.99.

8.20 (a) $\bar{X} \pm t \cdot \dfrac{S}{\sqrt{n}} = 43.04 \pm 2.0096 \cdot \dfrac{41.9261}{\sqrt{50}}$ $31.12 \le \mu \le 54.96$

      (b) The population distribution needs to be normally distribution.

8.20   (c)
cont.

Normal Probability Plot

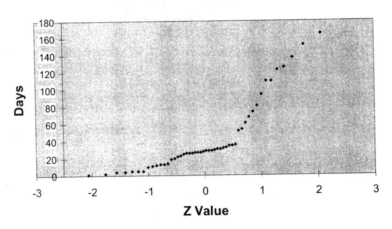

Both the normal probability plot and the box-and-whisker plot suggest that the
distribution is skewed to the right.

(d)   Even though the population distribution is not normally distributed, with a sample of
50, the t distribution can still be used due to the Central Limit Theorem.

8.22   (a) $\bar{X} \pm t \cdot \dfrac{S}{\sqrt{n}} = 182.4 \pm 2.0930 \cdot \dfrac{44.2700}{\sqrt{20}}$ $\$161.68 \le \mu \le \$203.12$

(b) $\bar{X} \pm t \cdot \dfrac{S}{\sqrt{n}} = 45 \pm 2.0930 \cdot \dfrac{10.0263}{\sqrt{20}}$ $\$40.31 \le \mu \le \$49.69$

(c)   The population distribution needs to be normally distributed.

Box-and-whisker Plot

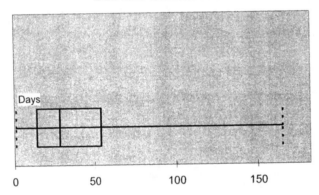

8.22   (d)
cont.

Normal Probability Plot

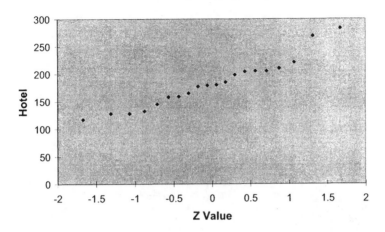

Box-and-whisker Plot

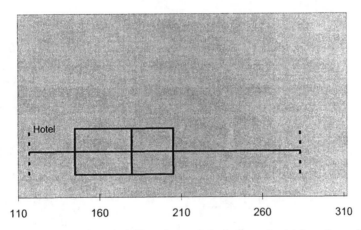

Both the normal probability plot and the box-and-whisker show that the population distribution for hotel cost is not normally distributed and is skewed to the right.

8.22   (d)
cont.

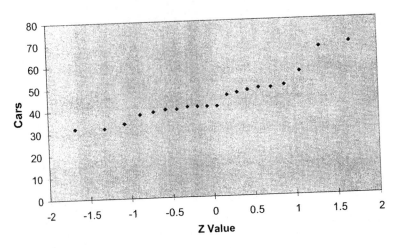

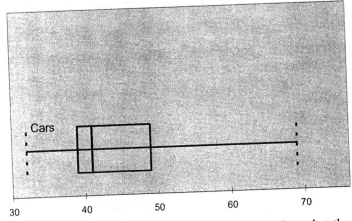

Both the normal probability plot and the box-and-whisker show that the population distribution for rental car cost is not normally distributed and is skewed to the right.

8.24 $p = \dfrac{X}{n} = \dfrac{50}{200} = 0.25$ $p \pm Z \cdot \sqrt{\dfrac{p(1-p)}{n}} = 0.25 \pm 1.96 \sqrt{\dfrac{0.25(0.75)}{200}}$

$0.19 \le \pi \le 0.31$

8.26   (a)

	A	B
1	Purchase Additional Telephone Line	
2		
3	Sample Size	500
4	Number of Successes	135
5	Confidence Level	99%
6	Sample Proportion	0.27
7	Z Value	-2.57583451
8	Standard Error of the Proportion	0.019854471
9	Interval Half Width	0.05114183
10	Interval Lower Limit	0.21885817
11	Interval Upper Limit	0.32114183

$$p = \frac{X}{n} = \frac{135}{500} = 0.27 \qquad p \pm Z \cdot \sqrt{\frac{p(1-p)}{n}} = 0.27 \pm 2.5758\sqrt{\frac{0.27(1-0.27)}{500}}$$

$$0.22 \leq \pi \leq 0.32$$

(b)   The manager in charge of promotional programs concerning residential customers can infer that the proportion of households that would purchase an additional telephone line if it were made available at a substantially reduced installation cost is between 0.22 and 0.32 with a 99% level of confidence.

8.28   (a) $p = 0.77 \qquad p \pm Z \cdot \sqrt{\frac{p(1-p)}{n}} = 0.77 \pm 1.96\sqrt{\frac{0.77(0.23)}{1000}}$

$$0.74 \leq \pi \leq 0.80$$

(b) $p = 0.77 \qquad p \pm Z \cdot \sqrt{\frac{p(1-p)}{n}} = 0.77 \pm 1.645\sqrt{\frac{0.77(0.23)}{1000}}$

$$0.75 \leq \pi \leq 0.79$$

(c)   The 95% confidence interval is wider. The loss in precision reflected as a wider confidence interval is the price you have to pay to achieve a higher level of confidence.

8.30   (a) $p = \frac{X}{n} = 0.46 \qquad p \pm Z \cdot \sqrt{\frac{p(1-p)}{n}} = 0.46 \pm 1.96\sqrt{\frac{0.46(1-0.46)}{500}}$

$$0.4163 < \pi < 0.5037$$

(b) $p = \frac{X}{n} = 0.10 \qquad p \pm Z \cdot \sqrt{\frac{p(1-p)}{n}} = 0.10 \pm 1.96\sqrt{\frac{0.10(1-0.10)}{500}}$

$$0.0737 < \pi < 0.1263$$

8.32   (a) $p = \dfrac{X}{n} = \dfrac{450}{1000} = 0.45$

$p \pm Z \cdot \sqrt{\dfrac{p(1-p)}{n}} = 0.45 \pm 1.96 \sqrt{\dfrac{0.45(1-0.45)}{1000}}$

$0.4192 < \pi < 0.4808$

(b)   You are 95% confidence that the proportion of all working women in North America who believe that companies should hold positions for those on maternity leave for more than six months is between 0.4192 and 0.4808.

8.34 $n = \dfrac{Z^2 \sigma^2}{e^2} = \dfrac{1.96^2 \cdot 15^2}{5^2} = 34.57$ Use $n = 35$

8.36 $n = \dfrac{Z^2 \pi(1-\pi)}{e^2} = \dfrac{2.58^2(0.5)(0.5)}{(0.04)^2} = 1{,}040.06$ Use $n = 1{,}041$

8.38   (a) $n = \dfrac{Z^2 \sigma^2}{e^2} = \dfrac{1.96^2 \cdot 400^2}{50^2} = 245.86$ Use $n = 246$

(b) $n = \dfrac{Z^2 \sigma^2}{e^2} = \dfrac{1.96^2 \cdot 400^2}{25^2} = 983.41$ Use $n = 984$

8.40 $n = \dfrac{Z^2 \sigma^2}{e^2} = \dfrac{1.96^2 \cdot (100)^2}{(20)^2} = 96.04$ Use $n = 97$

8.42   (a) $n = \dfrac{Z^2 \sigma^2}{e^2} = \dfrac{2.58^2 \cdot 25^2}{5^2} = 166.41$ Use $n = 167$

(b) $n = \dfrac{Z^2 \sigma^2}{e^2} = \dfrac{1.96^2 \cdot 25^2}{5^2} = 96.04$ Use $n = 97$

8.44 $n = \dfrac{Z^2 \sigma^2}{e^2} = \dfrac{1.96^2 \cdot 20^2}{5^2} = 61.47$ Use $n = 62$

8.46   (a) $n = \dfrac{Z^2 \pi(1-\pi)}{e^2} = \dfrac{1.96^2(0.45)(0.55)}{(0.02)^2} = 2376.8956$ Use $n = 2377$

(b) $n = \dfrac{Z^2 \pi(1-\pi)}{e^2} = \dfrac{1.96^2(0.29)(0.71)}{(0.02)^2} = 1977.3851$ Use $n = 1978$

(c)   The sample sizes differ because the estimated population proportions are different.
(d)   Since purchasing groceries at wholesale clubs and purchasing groceries at convenience stores are not necessary mutually exclusive events, it is appropriate to use one sample and ask the respondents both questions. However, drawing two separate samples is also appropriate for the setup.

8.48   (a) $p = \dfrac{X}{n} = \dfrac{303}{326} = 0.9294$

$p \pm Z \cdot \sqrt{\dfrac{p(1-p)}{n}} = 0.9294 \pm 1.96 \cdot \sqrt{\dfrac{0.9294(1-0.9294)}{326}}$

$0.9017 \le \pi \le 0.9572$

(b)   You are 95% confident that the population proportion of business men and women who have their presentations disturbed by cell phones is between 0.9017 and 0.9572.

(c) $n = \dfrac{Z^2 \pi(1-\pi)}{e^2} = \dfrac{1.96^2 (0.9294)(1-0.9294)}{(0.04)^2} = 157.5372$ Use $n = 158$

(d) $n = \dfrac{Z^2 \pi(1-\pi)}{e^2} = \dfrac{2.5758^2 (0.9294)(1-0.9294)}{(0.04)^2} = 272.0960$ Use $n = 273$

8.50 $N \cdot \bar{X} \pm N \cdot t \cdot \dfrac{S}{\sqrt{n}} \sqrt{\dfrac{N-n}{N-1}} = 500 \cdot 25.7 \pm 500 \cdot 2.7969 \cdot \dfrac{7.8}{\sqrt{25}} \cdot \sqrt{\dfrac{500-25}{500-1}}$

$\$10{,}721.53 \le \text{Population Total} \le \$14{,}978.47$

8.52   (a) $p + Z \cdot \sqrt{\dfrac{p(1-p)}{n}} = 0.04 + 1.2816 \cdot \sqrt{\dfrac{0.04(1-0.04)}{300}}$ $\pi < 0.0545$

(b) $p + Z \cdot \sqrt{\dfrac{p(1-p)}{n}} = 0.04 + 1.645 \cdot \sqrt{\dfrac{0.04(1-0.04)}{300}}$ $\pi < 0.0586$

(c) $p + Z \cdot \sqrt{\dfrac{p(1-p)}{n}} = 0.04 + 2.3263 \cdot \sqrt{\dfrac{0.04(1-0.04)}{300}}$ $\pi < 0.0663$

8.54 $N \cdot \bar{X} \pm N \cdot t \cdot \dfrac{S}{\sqrt{n}} \sqrt{\dfrac{N-n}{N-1}} = 3000 \cdot \$261.40 \pm 3000 \cdot 1.8331 \cdot \dfrac{\$138.8046}{\sqrt{10}} \cdot \sqrt{\dfrac{3000-10}{3000-1}}$

$\$543{,}176.96 \le \text{Population Total} \le \$1{,}025{,}223.04$

8.56 $N \cdot \bar{D} \pm N \cdot t \cdot \dfrac{S_D}{\sqrt{n}} \sqrt{\dfrac{N-n}{N-1}} = 4000 \cdot \$7.45907 \pm 4000 \cdot 2.6092 \cdot \dfrac{\$29.5523}{\sqrt{150}} \cdot \sqrt{\dfrac{4000-150}{4000-1}}$

$\$5{,}125.99 \le \text{Total Difference in the Population} \le \$54{,}546.57$

Note: The *t*-value of 2.6092 for 95% confidence and d.f. = 149 was derived on Excel.

8.58   (a) $p + Z \cdot \sqrt{\dfrac{p(1-p)}{n}} \sqrt{\dfrac{N-n}{N-1}} = 0.0367 + 1.645 \cdot \sqrt{\dfrac{0.0367(1-0.0367)}{300}} \sqrt{\dfrac{10000-300}{10000-1}}$

$\pi < 0.0542$

(b)   Since the upper bound is higher than the tolerable exception rate of 0.04, the auditor should request a larger sample.

8.60   The only way to have 100% confidence is to obtain the parameter of interest, rather than a sample statistic. From another perspective, the range of the normal and t distribution is infinite, so a Z or t value that contains 100% of the area cannot be obtained.

8.62   If the confidence level is increased, a greater area under the normal or t distribution needs to be included. This leads to an increased value of Z or t, and thus a wider interval.

8.64   In some applications such as auditing, interest is primarily on the total amount of a variable rather than the mean amount.

8.66   (a)   The population from which this sample was drawn was the collection of all the people who visited the magazine's web site.

(b)   The sample is not a random sample from this population. The sample consisted of only those who visited the magazine's web site and chose to fill out the survey.

(c)   This is not a statistically valid study. There was selection bias since only those who visited the magazine's web site and chose to answer the survey were represented. There was possibly nonresponse bias as well. Visitors to the web site who chose to fill out the survey might not answer all questions and there was no way for the magazine to get back to them to follow-up on the nonresponses if this was an anonymous survey.

(d)   To avoid the above potential pitfalls, the magazine could have drawn a random sample from the list of all subscribers to the magazine and offer them the option of filling out the survey over the Internet or on the survey form that is mailed to the subscribers. The magazine should also keep track of the subscribers who are invited to fill out the survey and follow up on the nonresponses after a specified period of time with mail or telephone to encourage them to participate in the survey.

The sample size needed is $n = \dfrac{Z^2 \cdot \pi \cdot (1-\pi)}{e^2} = \dfrac{1.96^2 \cdot (0.6195) \cdot (1-0.6195)}{(0.02)^2} = 2264$

8.68   (a) $p \pm Z \cdot \sqrt{\dfrac{p(1-p)}{n}} = 0.58 \pm 1.96 \cdot \sqrt{\dfrac{0.58(1-0.58)}{200}}$ $0.5116 < \pi < 0.6484$

(b) $p \pm Z \cdot \sqrt{\dfrac{p(1-p)}{n}} = 0.50 \pm 1.96 \cdot \sqrt{\dfrac{0.50(1-0.50)}{200}}$ $0.4307 < \pi < 0.5693$

(c) $p \pm Z \cdot \sqrt{\dfrac{p(1-p)}{n}} = 0.22 \pm 1.96 \cdot \sqrt{\dfrac{0.22(1-0.22)}{200}}$ $0.1626 < \pi < 0.2774$

(d) $p \pm Z \cdot \sqrt{\dfrac{p(1-p)}{n}} = 0.19 \pm 1.96 \cdot \sqrt{\dfrac{0.19(1-0.19)}{200}}$ $0.1356 < \pi < 0.2444$

(e) $n = \dfrac{Z^2 \cdot \pi \cdot (1-\pi)}{e^2} = \dfrac{1.96^2 \cdot (0.5) \cdot (0.5)}{(0.02)^2} = 2400.9 \cong 2401$

8.70 (a) $\bar{X} \pm t \cdot \dfrac{S}{\sqrt{n}} = 15.3 \pm 2.0227 \cdot \dfrac{3.8}{\sqrt{40}}$ $14.085 \le \mu \le 16.515$

(b) $p \pm Z \cdot \sqrt{\dfrac{p(1-p)}{n}} = 0.675 \pm 1.96 \cdot \sqrt{\dfrac{0.675(0.325)}{40}}$ $0.530 \le \pi \le 0.820$

(c) $n = \dfrac{Z^2 \cdot \sigma^2}{e^2} = \dfrac{1.96^2 \cdot 5^2}{2^2} = 24.01$ Use $n = 25$

(d) $n = \dfrac{Z^2 \cdot \pi \cdot (1-\pi)}{e^2} = \dfrac{1.96^2 \cdot (0.5) \cdot (0.5)}{(0.035)^2} = 784$ Use $n = 784$

(e)   If a single sample were to be selected for both purposes, the larger of the two sample sizes ($n = 784$) should be used.

8.72 (a) $\bar{X} \pm t \cdot \dfrac{S}{\sqrt{n}} = 9.7 \pm 2.0639 \cdot \dfrac{4}{\sqrt{25}}$ $8.049 \le \mu \le 11.351$

(b) $p \pm Z \cdot \sqrt{\dfrac{p(1-p)}{n}} = 0.48 \pm 1.96 \cdot \sqrt{\dfrac{0.48(0.52)}{25}}$ $0.284 \le \pi \le 0.676$

(c) $n = \dfrac{Z^2 \cdot \sigma^2}{e^2} = \dfrac{1.96^2 \cdot 4.5^2}{1.5^2} = 34.57$ Use $n = 35$

(d) $n = \dfrac{Z^2 \cdot \pi \cdot (1-\pi)}{e^2} = \dfrac{1.645^2 \cdot (0.5) \cdot (0.5)}{(0.075)^2} = 120.268$ Use $n = 121$

(e)   If a single sample were to be selected for both purposes, the larger of the two sample sizes ($n = 121$) should be used.

8.74 (a) $\bar{X} \pm t \cdot \dfrac{S}{\sqrt{n}} = \$28.52 \pm 1.9949 \cdot \dfrac{\$11.39}{\sqrt{70}}$ $\$25.80 \le \mu \le \$31.24$

(b) $p \pm Z \cdot \sqrt{\dfrac{p(1-p)}{n}} = 0.40 \pm 1.645 \cdot \sqrt{\dfrac{0.40(0.60)}{70}}$ $0.3037 \le \pi \le 0.4963$

(c) $n = \dfrac{Z^2 \cdot \sigma^2}{e^2} = \dfrac{1.96^2 \cdot 10^2}{2^2} = 96.04$ Use $n = 97$

(d) $n = \dfrac{Z^2 \cdot \pi \cdot (1-\pi)}{e^2} = \dfrac{1.645^2 \cdot (0.5) \cdot (0.5)}{(0.04)^2} = 422.82$ Use $n = 423$

(e)   If a single sample were to be selected for both purposes, the larger of the two sample sizes ($n = 423$) should be used.

8.76 (a) $\bar{X} \pm t \cdot \dfrac{S}{\sqrt{n}} = \$38.54 \pm 2.0010 \cdot \dfrac{\$7.26}{\sqrt{60}}$ $\$36.66 \le \mu \le \$40.42$

(b) $p \pm Z \cdot \sqrt{\dfrac{p(1-p)}{n}} = 0.30 \pm 1.645 \cdot \sqrt{\dfrac{0.30(0.70)}{60}}$ $0.2027 \le \pi \le 0.3973$

(c) $n = \dfrac{Z^2 \cdot \sigma^2}{e^2} = \dfrac{1.96^2 \cdot 8^2}{1.5^2} = 109.27$ Use $n = 110$

8.76   (d) $n = \dfrac{Z^2 \cdot \pi \cdot (1 - \pi)}{e^2} = \dfrac{1.645^2 \cdot (0.5) \cdot (0.5)}{(0.04)^2} = 422.82$ Use $n = 423$

cont.   (e)   If a single sample were to be selected for both purposes, the larger of the two sample sizes ($n = 423$) should be used.

8.78   (a) $p = \dfrac{7}{50} = 0.14$

$p + Z \cdot \sqrt{\dfrac{p(1-p)}{n}} \cdot \sqrt{\dfrac{N-n}{N-1}} = 0.14 + 1.2816 \cdot \sqrt{\dfrac{0.14(0.86)}{50}} \cdot \sqrt{\dfrac{1000-50}{1000-1}}$

$\pi \le 0.2013$

(b)   Since the upper bound is higher than the tolerable exception rate of 0.15, the auditor should request a larger sample.

8.80   (a) $n = \dfrac{Z^2 \cdot \sigma^2}{e^2} = \dfrac{2.58^2 \cdot 200^2}{100^2} = 26.5396$ Use $n = 27$

(b) $N \cdot \bar{X} \pm N \cdot t \cdot \dfrac{S}{\sqrt{n}} \cdot \sqrt{\dfrac{N-n}{N-1}} = 258 \cdot \$1654.27 \pm 258 \cdot 2.77872 \cdot \dfrac{\$184.62}{\sqrt{27}} \cdot \sqrt{\dfrac{258-27}{258-1}}$

$\$402{,}652.53 \le \text{Population Total} \le \$450{,}950.79$

8.82   (a) $\bar{X} \pm t \cdot \dfrac{S}{\sqrt{n}} = 8.4209 \pm 2.0106 \cdot \dfrac{0.0461}{\sqrt{49}}$ $8.41 \le \mu \le 8.43$

(b)   With 95% confidence, the population mean width of troughs is somewhere between 8.41 and 8.43 inches. Hence, the company's requirement of troughs being between 8.31 and 8.61 is being met with a 95% level of confidence.

8.84   (a) $\bar{X} \pm t \cdot \dfrac{S}{\sqrt{n}} = 0.2641 \pm 1.9741 \cdot \dfrac{0.1424}{\sqrt{170}}$ $0.2425 \le \mu \le 0.2856$

(b) $\bar{X} \pm t \cdot \dfrac{S}{\sqrt{n}} = 0.218 \pm 1.9772 \cdot \dfrac{0.1227}{\sqrt{140}}$ $0.1975 \le \mu \le 0.2385$

8.84 (c)
cont.

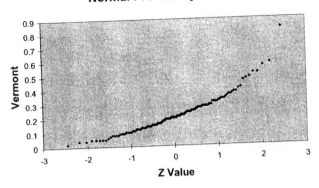

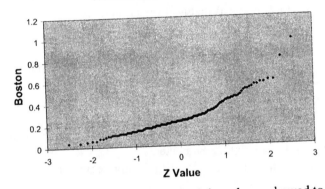

The amount of granule loss for both brands are skewed to the right.

(d) Since the two confidence intervals do not overlap, we can conclude that the mean granule loss of Boston shingles is higher than that of Vermont Shingles.

CHAPTER 9

OBJECTIVES
- To understand the basic hypothesis testing procedure
- To be able to use hypothesis testing to test a mean, proportion, or variance
- To be aware of the assumptions of each hypothesis testing procedure, how to evaluate the assumptions, and what will be the consequences if the assumptions are seriously violated
- To understand how to avoid the pitfalls involved in hypothesis testing
- To be familiar with the ethical issues involved in hypothesis testing

OVERVIEW AND KEY CONCEPTS
Some Basic Concepts in Hypothesis Testing
- **Null hypothesis** (H_0): The hypothesis that is always tested.
  - The null hypothesis always refers to a specified value of the population parameter, not a sample statistic.
  - The statement of the null hypothesis always contains an equal sign regarding the specified value of the population parameter.
- **Alternative hypothesis:** The opposite of the null hypothesis and represents the conclusion supported if the null hypothesis is rejected.
  - The statement of the alternative hypothesis never contains an equal sign regarding the specified value of the population parameter.
- **Critical value:** A value or values that separate the rejection region or regions from the remaining values.
- **Type I error:** A Type I error occurs if the null hypothesis is rejected when in fact it is true and should not be rejected.
- **Type II error:** A Type II error occurs if the null hypothesis is not rejected when in fact it is false and should be rejected.
- **Level of significance** (α): The probability of committing a Type I error.
- **The β risk (the consumer's risk level):** The probability of committing a Type II error.
- **Factors that affect the β risk:** Holding everything else constant,
  - β increases when the difference between the hypothesized parameter and its true value decreases.
  - β increases when α decreases.
  - β increases when σ increases.
  - β increases when the sample size n decreases.
- **The confidence coefficient** $(1-\alpha)$: The probability that the null hypothesis is not rejected when in fact it is true and should not be rejected.
- **The confidence level:** $100(1-\alpha)\%$
- **The power of a test** $(1-\beta)$: The probability of rejecting the null hypothesis when in fact it is false and should be rejected.

- **Risk in decision making:** There is a delicate balance between the probability of committing a Type I error and the probability of a Type II error.

H_0: Innocent

E.g. Jury Trial				Hypothesis Test		
	The Truth				The Truth	
Verdict	Innocent	Guilty	Decision	H_0 True	H_0 False
Innocent	Correct	Error	Do Not Reject H_0	$1 - \alpha$	Type II Error (β)
Guilty	Error	Correct	Reject H_0	Type I Error (α)	Power $(1 - \beta)$

- Reducing the probability of Type I error will inevitably increase the probability of committing a Type II error holding everything else constant.
- One should choose a smaller Type I error when the cost of rejecting the maintained hypothesis is high.
- One should choose a larger Type I error when there is an interest in changing the status quo.
- **p-value (the observed level of significance):** The probability of obtaining a test statistic equal to or more extreme than the result obtained from the sample data, given the null hypothesis is true.
  - It is also the smallest level of significance at which the null hypothesis can be rejected.
  - Roughly speaking, it measures the amount of evidence against the null hypothesis. The smaller the p-value, the stronger is the evidence against the null hypothesis.
  - The statistical decision rule is to reject the null hypothesis if the p-value is less than the level of significance (α), and do not reject otherwise.

The Six-Step Method in the Traditional Critical Value Approach to Hypothesis Testing

1. State the null hypothesis, H_0 and the alternative hypothesis, H_1.
2. Choose the level of significance, α and the sample size, n. The level of significance is specified according to the relative importance of the risks of committing Type I and Type II errors in the problem.
3. Determine the appropriate test statistic and sampling distribution.
4. Determine the critical values that divide the rejection and nonrejection regions.
5. Collect the data and compute the value of the test statistic.
6. Make the statistical decision and state the managerial conclusion. Compare the computed test statistic to the critical values. Reject H_0 when the computed test statistic falls in a rejection region; do not reject H_0 otherwise. The managerial conclusion is written in the context of the real-world problem.

The Five-Step Method in the p Value Approach to Hypothesis Testing

1. State the null hypothesis, H_0 and the alternative hypothesis, H_1.
2. Choose the level of significance, α and the sample size, n. The level of significance is specified according to the relative importance of the risks of committing Type I and Type II errors in the problem.
3. Determine the appropriate test statistic and sampling distribution.
4. Collect the data, compute the value of the test statistic and obtain the p-value based on the computed test statistic.
5. Make the statistical decision and state the managerial conclusion. If the p-value is greater than or equal to α, you do not reject the null hypothesis H_0. If the p-value is less than α, you reject the null hypothesis. Remember the mantra, if the p-value is low, the H_0 must go. The managerial conclusion is written in the context of the real-world problem.

Z Test for the Population Mean (μ) when σ is Known

*   **Assumptions:**
    *   Population is normally distributed or large sample size.
    * σ is known.
*   **Test statistic:**
    * $$Z = \frac{\overline{X} - \mu_{\overline{X}}}{\sigma_{\overline{X}}} = \frac{\overline{X} - \mu}{\sigma / \sqrt{n}}$$
    *   The alternative hypothesis can be one-tail with a right-tail rejection region, one-tail with a left-tail rejection region or two-tail with both right-tail and left-tail rejection regions.

t Test for the Population Mean (μ) when σ Is Unknown

*   **Assumptions:**
    *   Population is normally distributed or large sample size.
    * σ is unknown.
*   **Test statistic:**
    * $t = \dfrac{\overline{X} - \mu}{S / \sqrt{n}}$ with $(n-1)$ degrees of freedom.
    *   The alternative hypothesis can be one-tail with a right-tail rejection region, one-tail with a left-tail rejection region or two-tail with both right-tail and left-tail rejection regions.

Z Test for the Population Proportion (π)

*   **Assumptions:**
    *   Population involves 2 categorical values.
    *   Both np and $n(1-p)$ are at least 5.
*   **Test statistic:**
    * $$Z = \frac{p - \mu_p}{\sigma_p} = \frac{p - \pi}{\sqrt{\dfrac{\pi(1-\pi)}{n}}}$$

- The alternative hypothesis can be one-tail with a right-tail rejection region, one-tail with a left-tail rejection region or two-tail with both right-tail and left-tail rejection regions.

Potential Hypothesis-Testing Pitfalls

- To avoid potential hypothesis-testing pitfalls, you should:
    1. Consult with a person with substantial statistical training early in the process.
    2. Build in adequate controls from the beginning to avoid biases.
    3. Plan ahead by asking the following questions:
        i. What is the goal of the survey, study, or experiment? How can you translate into a null hypothesis and an alternative hypothesis?
        ii. Is the hypothesis test a two-tail test or one-tail test?
        iii. Can you select a random sample from the underlying population of interest?
        iv. What kinds of measurements will you collect from the sample? Are the sampled outcomes numerical or categorical?
        v. At what significance level, or risk of committing a Type I error, should you conduct the hypothesis test?
        vi. Is the intended sample size large enough to achieve the desired power of the test for the level of significance chosen?
        vii. What statistical test procedure should you use and why?
        viii. What conclusions and interpretations can you make from the results of the hypothesis test?

Ethical Issues

- Ethical considerations arise when the hypothesis-testing process is manipulated.
    - **Data collection method should be randomized:** The data must be the outcome of a random sample from a population or from an experiment in which a randomization process was used. .Potential respondents should not be permitted to self-select for a study nor should they be purposely selected.
    - **Informed Consent from Human Respondents Being "Treated":** Any individual who is to be subjected to some "treatment" in an experiment should be made aware of the research endeavor and any potential behavioral or physical side effects. The subject should also provide informed consent with respect to participation.
    - **Type of Test—Two-Tail or One-Tail:** If prior information is available that leads you to test the null hypothesis against a specifically directed alternative, then a one-tail test is more powerful than a two-tail test. On the other hand, if you are interested only in differences from the null hypothesis, not in the direction of the difference, the two-tail test is the appropriate procedure to use.
    - **Choice of Level of Significance:** The level of significance should be selected before data collection occurs. It is also good practice to always report the *p*-value, not just the conclusions of the hypothesis test.
    - **Data Snooping:** It is unethical to perform a hypothesis test on a set of data, look at the results, and then decide on the level of significance or decide between a one-tail or two-tail test.
    - **Cleansing and Discarding of Data:** If a measurement is incomplete or grossly in error because of some equipment problem or unusual behavioral occurrence unrelated to the study, you can discard the value. In a well-designed experiment or study, you should decide, in advance, on all rules regarding the possible discarding of data.
    - **Reporting of Findings:** In conducting research, you should document both good and bad results. It is inappropriate to report the results of hypothesis tests that show

statistical significance but not those for which there is insufficient evidence in the findings.

- **Statistical Significance versus Practical Significance:** You need to make the distinction between the existence of a statistically significant result and its practical significance in the context within a field of application. Sometimes, due to a very large sample size, you will get a result that is statistically significant, but has little practical significance.

SOLUTIONS TO END OF SECTION
AND CHAPTER REVIEW EVEN PROBLEMS

9.2 H_1 is used to denote the alternative hypothesis.

9.4 β is used to denote the risk or the chance of committing a Type II error.

9.6 α is the probability of making a Type I error – that is, the probability of incorrectly rejecting the null hypothesis when in reality the null hypothesis is true and should not be rejected.

9.8   The power of a test is the complement, which is $(1 - \beta)$, of the probability β of making a Type II error.

9.10   It is possible to not reject a false null hypothesis because the mean of a single sample can fall in the non-rejection region even though the hypothesized population mean is false.

9.12   Other things being equal, the closer the *hypothesized* mean is to the *actual* mean, the larger the risk of committing a Type II error will be.

9.14   Under the French judicial system, unlike ours in the United States, the null hypothesis assumes the defendant is guilty, the alternative hypothesis assumes the defendant is innocent. A Type I error would be not convicting a guilty person and a Type II error would be convicting an innocent person.

9.16 H_0: $\mu = 20$ minutes. 20 minutes is adequate travel time between classes.
        H_1: $\mu \neq 20$ minutes. 20 minutes is not adequate travel time between classes.

9.18 H_0: $\mu = 1.00$. The mean amount of paint per can is one gallon.
        H_1: $\mu \neq 1.00$. The mean amount of paint per can differs from one gallon.

9.20   Decision rule: Reject H_0 if $Z < -1.96$ or $Z > +1.96$.
        Decision: Since $Z_{calc} = +2.21$ is greater than $Z_{crit} = +1.96$, reject H_0.

9.22   Decision rule: Reject H_0 if $Z < -2.58$ or $Z > +2.58$.

9.24 p-value $= 2(1 - .9772) = 0.0456$

9.26 p-value $= 0.1676$

9.28 (a) H_0: $\mu = 70$ pounds. The cloth has a mean breaking strength of 70 pounds.
H_1: $\mu \neq 70$ pounds. The cloth has a mean breaking strength that differs from 70 pounds.
Decision rule: Reject H_0 if $Z < -1.96$ or $Z > +1.96$.
Test statistic: $Z = \dfrac{\overline{X} - \mu}{\sigma/\sqrt{n}} = \dfrac{69.1 - 70}{3.5/\sqrt{49}} = -1.80$

Decision: Since $Z_{calc} = -1.80$ is between the critical bounds of ± 1.96, do not reject H_0. There is not enough evidence to conclude that the cloth has a mean breaking strength that differs from 70 pounds.

(b) p-value $= 2(0.0359) = 0.0718$
Interpretation: The probability of getting a sample of 49 pieces that yield a mean strength that is farther away from the hypothesized population mean than this sample is 0.0718 or 7.18%.

(c)   Decision rule: Reject H_0 if $Z < -1.96$ or $Z > +1.96$.
Test statistic: $Z = \dfrac{\overline{X} - \mu}{\sigma/\sqrt{n}} = \dfrac{69.1 - 70}{1.75/\sqrt{49}} = -3.60$

Decision: Since $Z_{calc} = -3.60$ is less than the lower critical bound of -1.96, reject H_0. There is enough evidence to conclude that the cloth has a mean breaking strength that differs from 70 pounds.

(d)   Decision rule: Reject H_0 if $Z < -1.96$ or $Z > +1.96$.
Test statistic: $Z = \dfrac{\overline{X} - \mu}{\sigma/\sqrt{n}} = \dfrac{69 - 70}{3.5/\sqrt{49}} = -2.00$

Decision: Since $Z_{calc} = -2.00$ is less than the lower critical bound of -1.96, reject H_0. There is enough evidence to conclude that the cloth has a mean breaking strength that differs from 70 pounds.

9.30 (a) H_0: $\mu = 375$ hours. The mean life of the manufacturer's light bulbs is equal to 375 hours.
H_1: $\mu \neq 375$ hours. The mean life of the manufacturer's light bulbs differs from 375 hours.
Decision rule: Reject H_0 if $Z < -1.96$ or $Z > +1.96$.
Test statistic: $Z = \dfrac{\overline{X} - \mu}{\sigma/\sqrt{n}} = \dfrac{350 - 375}{100/\sqrt{64}} = -2.00$

Decision: Since $Z_{calc} = -2.00$ is below the critical bound of -1.96, reject H_0. There is enough evidence to conclude that the mean life of the manufacturer's light bulbs differs from 375 hours.

(b) p-value $= 2(0.0228) = 0.0456$.
Interpretation: The probability of getting a sample of 64 light bulbs that will yield a mean life that is farther away from the hypothesized population mean than this sample is 0.0456.

(c) $\overline{X} \pm Z \cdot \dfrac{\sigma}{\sqrt{n}} = 350 \pm 1.96 \cdot \dfrac{100}{\sqrt{64}}$ $325.50 \leq \mu \leq 374.50$

(d)   The results are the same. The confidence interval formed does not include the hypothesized value of 375 hours.

9.32

	A	B
1	Salad Dressings	
2		
3	Null Hypothesis $\mu=$	8
4	Level of Significance	0.05
5	Population Standard Deviation	0.15
6	Sample Size	50
7	Sample Mean	7.983
8	Standard Error of the Mean	0.021213203
9	Z Test Statistic	-0.80138769
10		
11	Two-Tailed Test	
12	Lower Critical Value	-1.95996108
13	Upper Critical Value	1.959961082
14	*p*-Value	0.422907113
15	Do not reject the null hypothesis	

(a) $H_0 : \mu = 8 \qquad H_1 : \mu \neq 8$

Decision rule: Reject H_0 if $Z < -1.96$ or $Z > 1.96$

Test statistic: $Z = \dfrac{7.983 - 8}{.15 / \sqrt{50}} = -0.8$

Decision: Do not reject H_0. There is insufficient evidence to conclude that the amount of salad dressing placed in 8 oz bottle is significantly different from 8 oz.

(b)   *p*-value = 0.4229. The probability of observing a Z test statistic more extreme than -0.8 is 0.4229 if the population mean is indeed 8 oz.

(c)   Decision rule: Reject H_0 if $Z < -1.96$ or $Z > +1.96$.

Test statistic: $Z = \dfrac{\overline{X} - \mu}{\sigma / \sqrt{n}} = \dfrac{7.983 - 8}{0.05 / \sqrt{50}} = -2.40$

Decision: Since $Z_{calc} = -2.40$ is less than the lower critical bound of -1.96, reject H_0. There is enough evidence to conclude that the machine is filling bottles improperly.

(d)   Decision rule: Reject H_0 if $Z < -1.96$ or $Z > +1.96$.

Test statistic: $Z = \dfrac{\overline{X} - \mu}{\sigma / \sqrt{n}} = \dfrac{7.952 - 8}{0.15 / \sqrt{50}} = -2.26$

Decision: Since $Z_{calc} = -2.26$ is less than the lower critical bound of -1.96, reject H_0. There is enough evidence to conclude that the machine is filling bottles improperly.

9.34 $Z = 2.33$

9.36 $Z = -2.33$

9.38   *p*-value $= 1 - 0.9772 = 0.0228$

9.40   *p*-value $= 0.0838$

9.42   *p*-value $= P(Z < 1.38) = 0.9162$

9.44 H_0: $\mu \geq 2.8$ feet.

The mean length of steel bars produced is at least 2.8 feet and the production equipment does not need immediate adjustment.

H_1: $\mu < 2.8$ feet.

The mean length of steel bars produced is less than 2.8 feet and the production equipment does need immediate adjustment.

(a)   Decision rule: If $Z < -1.645$, reject H_0.

Test statistic: $Z = \dfrac{\bar{X} - \mu}{\sigma / \sqrt{n}} = \dfrac{2.73 - 2.8}{0.2 / \sqrt{25}} = -1.75$

Decision: Since $Z_{calc} = -1.75$ is less than $Z_{crit} = -1.645$, reject H_0. There is enough evidence to conclude the production equipment needs adjustment.

(b)   Decision rule: If p-value < 0.05, reject H_0.

Test statistic: $Z = \dfrac{\bar{X} - \mu}{\sigma / \sqrt{n}} = \dfrac{2.73 - 2.8}{0.2 / \sqrt{25}} = -1.75$

p-value $= 0.0401$

Decision: Since p value $= 0.0401$ is less than $\alpha = 0.05$, reject H_0. There is enough evidence to conclude the production equipment needs adjustment.

(c)   The probability of obtaining a sample whose mean is 2.73 feet or less when the null hypothesis is true is 0.0401.

(d)   The conclusions are the same.

9.46   (a) H_0: $\mu \leq 5$

The mean number of trips that children take to the store is no more than 5.

H_1: $\mu > 5$

The mean number of trips that children take to the store is more than 5.

(b)   A Type I error occurs when you conclude the mean number of trips that children take to the store is more than 5 when in fact the mean number is not more than five.

A Type II error occurs when you conclude the mean number of trips that children take to the store is not more than 5 when in fact the mean number is more than five.

(c)   Decision rule: If $Z > 2.3263$ or when the p-value < 0.01, reject H_0.

Test statistic: $Z = \dfrac{\bar{X} - \mu}{\sigma / \sqrt{n}} = \dfrac{5.47 - 5}{1.6 / \sqrt{100}} = 2.9375$

p-value $= 0.0017$

Decision: Since $Z_{calc} = 2.9375$ is greater than $Z_{crit} = 2.3263$ or the p-value of 0.0017 is less than 0.01, reject H_0. There is enough evidence to conclude the population mean number of trips to the store is greater than 5 per week.

(d)   When the null hypothesis is true, the probability of obtaining a sample whose mean is 5.47 trips or more is 0.0017.

9.48 $t = \dfrac{\bar{X} - \mu}{S / \sqrt{n}} = \dfrac{56 - 50}{12 / \sqrt{16}} = 2.00$

9.50   (a) For a two-tailed test with a 0.05 level of confidence, $t_{crit} = \pm 2.1315$.

(b) For an upper-tailed test with a 0.05 level of confidence, $t_{crit} = +1.7531$.

9.52   No, you should not use the t test to test the null hypothesis that $\mu = 60$ on a population that is
left-skewed because the sample size ($n = 16$) is less than 30. The t test assumes that, if the
underlying population is not normally distributed, the sample size is sufficiently large to
enable the test statistic t to be influenced by the Central Limit Theorem. If sample sizes are
small ($n < 30$), the t test should not be used because the sampling distribution does not meet
the requirements of the Central Limit Theorem.

9.54   (a) H_0: $\mu \leq \$300$. The mean cost of textbooks per semester at a large university is no more
than \$300.
H_1: $\mu > \$300$. The mean cost of textbooks per semester at a large university is more
than \$300.
Decision rule: $d.f. = 99$. If $t > 1.2902$, reject H_0.

Test statistic: $t = \dfrac{\bar{X} - \mu}{S/\sqrt{n}} = \dfrac{\$315.40 - \$300.00}{\$43.20/\sqrt{100}} = 3.5648$

Decision: Since $t_{calc} = 3.5648$ is above the critical bound of $t = 1.2902$, reject H_0.
There is enough evidence to conclude that the mean cost of textbooks per semester at
a large university is more than \$300.

(b) H_0: $\mu \leq \$300$. The mean cost of textbooks per semester at a large university is no
more than \$300.
H_1: $\mu > \$300$. The mean cost of textbooks per semester at a large university is more
than \$300.
Decision rule: $d.f. = 99$. If $t > 1.6604$, reject H_0.

Test statistic: $t = \dfrac{\bar{X} - \mu}{S/\sqrt{n}} = \dfrac{\$315.40 - \$300.00}{\$75.00/\sqrt{100}} = 2.0533$

Decision: Since $t_{calc} = 2.0533$ is above the critical bound of $t = 1.6604$, reject H_0.
There is enough evidence to conclude that the mean cost of textbooks per semester at
a large university is more than \$300.

(c) H_0: $\mu \leq \$300$. The mean cost of textbooks per semester at a large university is no more
than \$300.
H_1: $\mu > \$300$. The mean cost of textbooks per semester at a large university is more
than \$300.
Decision rule: $d.f. = 99$. If $t > 1.2902$, reject H_0.

Test statistic: $t = \dfrac{\bar{X} - \mu}{S/\sqrt{n}} = \dfrac{\$305.11 - \$300.00}{\$43.20/\sqrt{100}} = 1.1829$

Decision: Since $t_{calc} = 1.1829$ is below the critical bound of $t = 1.2902$, do not reject
H_0. There is not enough evidence to conclude that the mean cost of textbooks per
semester at a large university is more than \$300.

9.56 H_0: $\mu \geq 3.7$ The mean waiting time is no less than 3.7 minutes.

H_1: $\mu < 3.7$ The mean waiting time is less than 3.7 minutes.

Decision rule: $d.f. = 63$. If $t < -1.6694$ or p-value < 0.05, reject H_0.

Test statistic: $t = \dfrac{\overline{X} - \mu}{S/\sqrt{n}} = \dfrac{3.57 - 3.7}{0.8/\sqrt{64}} = -1.3$

p-value $= 0.0992$

Decision: Since $t_{calc} = -1.3$ is $> t_{crit} = -1.6694$ and the p-value of 0.0992 is larger than 0.05, do not reject H_0. There is not enough evidence to conclude that the mean waiting time is less than 3.7 minutes.

9.58   (a) $H_0 : \mu \leq 400$ The mean life of the batteries is not more than 400 hours.

$H_1 : \mu > 400$ The mean life of the batteries is more than 400 hours.

Decision rule: Reject H_0 if $t > 1.7823$

Test statistic: $t = \dfrac{\overline{X} - \mu}{s/\sqrt{n}} = \dfrac{473.46 - 400}{210.77/\sqrt{13}} = 1.2567$

Decision: Since $t < 1.7823$, do not reject H_0. There is not enough evidence to conclude that the mean life of the batteries is more than 400 hours.

(b) p-value $= 0.1164$. If the population mean life is indeed no more than 400 hours, the probability of obtaining a sample of 13 batteries that result in a sample mean of 473.46 or more is 11.64%.

(c)   Allowing for only 5% probability of making a Type I error, the manufacturer should not say in advertisements that these batteries should last more than 400 hours. They can make the claim that these batteries should last more than 400 hours only if they are willing to raise the level of significance to more than 0.1164.

(d)   (a) $H_0 : \mu \leq 400$ The mean life of the batteries is not more than 400 hours.

$H_1 : \mu > 400$ The mean life of the batteries is more than 400 hours.

Decision rule: Reject H_0 if $t > 1.7823$

Test statistic: $t = \dfrac{\overline{X} - \mu}{s/\sqrt{n}} = \dfrac{550.38 - 400}{315.33/\sqrt{13}} = 1.7195$

Decision: Since $t < 1.7823$, do not reject H_0. There is not enough evidence to conclude that the mean life of the batteries is more than 400 hours.

(b) p-value $= 0.0556$. If the population mean life is indeed no more than 400 hours, the probability of obtaining a sample of 13 batteries that result in a sample mean of 550.38 or more is 5.56%.

(c)   Allowing for only 5% probability of making a Type I error, the manufacturer should not say in advertisements that these batteries should last more than 400 hours. They can make the claim that these batteries should last more than 400 hours only if they are willing to raise the level of significance to more than 0.0556.

The extremely larger value of 1342 raises the sample mean and sample standard deviation and, hence, results in a higher measured t statistic of 1.7195. This is, however, still not enough to offset the lower hours in the remaining sample to the degree that the null hypothesis can be rejected.

9.60   (a) $H_0 : \mu = 2$ $H_1 : \mu \neq 2$ $d.f. = 49$

Decision rule: Reject H_0 if $|t| > 2.0096$

Test statistic: $t = \dfrac{\overline{X} - \mu}{S / \sqrt{n}} = \dfrac{2.0007 - 2}{0.0446 / \sqrt{50}} = 0.1143$

Decision: Since $|t| < 2.0096$, do not reject H_0. There is not enough evidence to conclude that the mean amount of soft drink filled is different from 2.0 liters.

(b) p-value $= 0.9095$. If the population mean amount of soft drink filled is indeed 2.0 liters, the probability of observing a sample of 50 soft drinks that will result in a sample mean amount of fill more different from 2.0 liters is 0.9095.

(c)

Normal Probability Plot

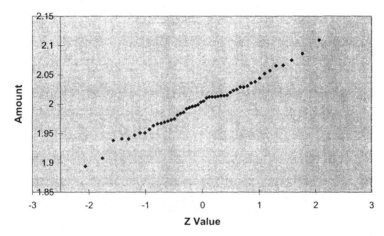

The normal probability plot suggests that the data are rather normally distributed. Hence, the results in (a) are valid in terms of the normality assumption.

(d)

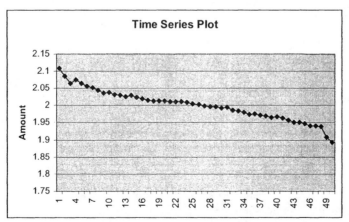

The time series plot of the data reveals that there is a downward trend in the amount of soft drink filled. This violates the assumption that data are drawn independently from a normal population distribution because the amount of fill in consecutive bottles appears to be closely related. As a result, the t test in (a) becomes invalid.

9.62   (a) $H_0 : \mu = 15.5$ $H_1 : \mu \neq 15.5$

Decision rule: Reject H_0 if $|t| > 2.6178$ $d.f. = 119$

Test statistic: $t = \dfrac{\bar{X} - \mu}{S/\sqrt{n}} = \dfrac{14.9775 - 15.5}{1.007/\sqrt{120}} = -5.684$

Decision: Since $|t| > 2.6178$, reject H_0. There is enough evidence to conclude that the mean viscosity has changed from 15.5.

(b)   The population distribution needs to be normal.

(c)

Normal Probability Plot

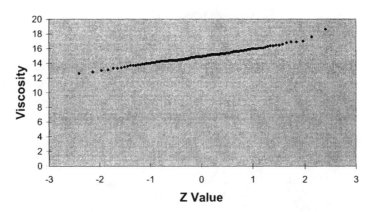

The normal probability plot indicates that the distribution is slightly skewed to the right. Even though the population distribution is probably not normally distributed, the result obtained in (a) should still be valid due to the Central Limit Theorem as a result of the relatively large sample size of 120.

9.64   (a) $H_0 : \mu = 5.5$ $H_1 : \mu \neq 5.5$

Decision rule: Reject H_0 if $|t| > 2.680$ $d.f. = 49$

Test statistic: $t = \dfrac{\bar{X} - \mu}{S/\sqrt{n}} = \dfrac{5.5014 - 5.5}{0.1058/\sqrt{50}} = 0.0935$

Decision: Since $|t| < 2.680$, do not reject H_0. There is not enough evidence to conclude that the mean amount of tea per bag is different than 5.5 grams.

(b) $\bar{X} \pm t \cdot \dfrac{S}{\sqrt{n}} = 5.5014 \pm 2.6800 \cdot \dfrac{0.1058}{\sqrt{50}}$ $5.46 < \mu < 5.54$

With 99% confidence, you can conclude that the population mean amount of tea per bag is somewhere between 5.46 and 5.54 grams.

(c)   The conclusions are the same.

9.66 $p = \dfrac{X}{n} = \dfrac{88}{400} = 0.22$

9.68 H_0: $\pi = 0.20$
H_1: $\pi \neq 0.20$
Decision rule: If $Z < -1.96$ or $Z > 1.96$, reject H_0.

Test statistic: $Z = \dfrac{p - \pi}{\sqrt{\dfrac{\pi(1-\pi)}{n}}} = \dfrac{0.22 - 0.20}{\sqrt{\dfrac{0.20(0.80)}{400}}} = 1.00$

Decision: Since $Z_{calc} = 1.00$ is between the critical bounds of $Z = \pm 1.96$, do not reject H_0.

9.70 H_0: $\pi \leq 0.43$ H_1: $\pi > 0.43$
Decision rule: If $Z > 1.645$ or p-value < 0.05, reject H_0.

Test statistic: $Z = \dfrac{p - \pi}{\sqrt{\dfrac{\pi(1-\pi)}{n}}} = \dfrac{0.5 - 0.43}{\sqrt{\dfrac{0.43(1-0.43)}{362}}} = 2.6902$

p-value $= 0.0036$
Decision: Since $Z_{calc} = 2.6902$ is above the critical bound of $Z = 1.645$ and the p-value of 0.0036 is less than 0.05, reject H_0. There is enough evidence to show that the proportion of employers that planned to hire new employees in 2004 is larger than the 2003 proportion of 0.43.

9.72   (a) H_0: $\pi = 0.50$
H_1: $\pi \neq 0.50$
Decision rule: If $Z < -1.96$ or $Z > 1.96$, reject H_0.

Test statistic: $Z = \dfrac{p - \pi}{\sqrt{\dfrac{\pi(1-\pi)}{n}}} = \dfrac{0.5097 - 0.50}{\sqrt{\dfrac{0.50(0.50)}{1083}}} = 0.6381$

Decision: Since $Z_{calc} = 0.6381$ is greater than the lower critical bound of $Z = -1.96$ and less than the upper critical bounds of $Z = 1.96$, do not reject H_0. You conclude that there is not enough evidence to show that the percentage of people who trust energy-efficiency ratings differs from 50%.

(b) H_0: $\pi = 0.50$
H_1: $\pi \neq 0.50$
Decision rule: If p-value < 0.05, reject H_0.

Test statistic: $Z = \dfrac{p - \pi}{\sqrt{\dfrac{\pi(1-\pi)}{n}}} = \dfrac{0.5097 - 0.50}{\sqrt{\dfrac{0.50(0.50)}{1083}}} = 0.6381$

p-value $= 0.5234$
Decision: Since the p-value of 0.5234 is greater than the 0.05 level of significance, do not reject H_0. You conclude that there is not enough evidence to show that the percentage of people who trust energy-efficiency ratings differs from 50%.
If the null hypothesis is true, the probability of obtaining a sample proportion further away from the hypothesized value of 0.50 is 0.5234.

9.74   (a) $p = 0.7112$

(b) $H_0: \pi \leq 0.50$

$H_1: \pi > 0.50$

Decision rule: If $Z > 1.6449$, reject H_0.

Test statistic: $Z = \dfrac{p_s - p}{\sqrt{\dfrac{p(1-p)}{n}}} = \dfrac{0.7112 - 0.50}{\sqrt{\dfrac{0.50(0.50)}{187}}} = 5.7771$

Decision: Since $Z_{calc} = 5.7771 > 1.6449$, reject H_0. There is enough evidence to conclude that more than half of all successful women executives have children.

(c) $H_0: \pi \leq 0.6667$

$H_1: \pi > 0.6667$

Decision rule: If $Z > 1.6449$, reject H_0.

Test statistic: $Z = \dfrac{p_s - p}{\sqrt{\dfrac{p(1-p)}{n}}} = \dfrac{0.7112 - 0.6667}{\sqrt{\dfrac{0.6667(0.3333)}{187}}} = 1.2927$

Decision: Since $Z_{calc} = 1.2927 < 1.6449$, do not reject H_0. There is not enough evidence to conclude that more than two-thirds of all successful women executives have children.

(d)   The random sample assumption is not likely to be valid because the criteria used in defining "successful women executives" is very likely to be quite different than those used in defining the "most powerful women in business" who attended the summit.

9.76 $H_0: \mu \geq 7, H_1: \mu < 7$, $\alpha = 0.01$, $n = 16$, $\sigma = 0.2$

Lower critical value: $Z_L = -2.3263$, $\bar{X}_L = \mu + Z_L\left(\dfrac{\sigma}{\sqrt{n}}\right) = 7 - 2.3263\left(\dfrac{.2}{\sqrt{16}}\right) = 6.8837$

(a) $Z = \dfrac{\bar{X}_L - \mu_1}{\dfrac{\sigma}{\sqrt{n}}} = \dfrac{6.8837 - 6.9}{\dfrac{.2}{\sqrt{16}}} = -0.3263$

power $= 1 - \beta = P\left(\bar{X} < \bar{X}_L\right) = P\left(Z < -0.3263\right) = 0.3721$

$\beta = 1 - 0.3721 = 0.6279$

(b) $Z = \dfrac{\bar{X}_L - \mu_1}{\dfrac{\sigma}{\sqrt{n}}} = \dfrac{6.8837 - 6.8}{\dfrac{.2}{\sqrt{16}}} = 1.6737$

power $= 1 - \beta = P\left(\bar{X} < \bar{X}_L\right) = P\left(Z < 1.6737\right) = 0.9529$

$\beta = 1 - 0.9529 = 0.0471$

(c)   Holding everything else constant, the greater the distance between the true mean and the hypothesized mean, the higher the power of the test will be and the lower the probability of committing a Type II error will be. Holding everything else constant, the smaller the level of significance, the lower the power of the test will be and the higher the probability of committing a Type II error will be.

9.78 $H_0 : \mu \geq 25,000, H_1 : \mu < 25,000$, $\alpha = 0.05$, $n = 100$, $\sigma = 3500$

Lower critical value: $Z_L = -1.6449$,

$$\overline{X}_L = \mu + Z_L \left(\frac{\sigma}{\sqrt{n}} \right) = 25,000 - 1.6449 \left(\frac{3,500}{\sqrt{100}} \right) = 24,424.3013$$

(a) $Z = \dfrac{\overline{X}_L - \mu_1}{\dfrac{\sigma}{\sqrt{n}}} = \dfrac{24,424.3012 - 24,000}{\dfrac{3500}{\sqrt{100}}} = 1.2123$

power = $1 - \beta = P(\overline{X} < \overline{X}_L) = P(Z < 1.2123) = 0.8873$

$\beta = 1 - 0.8873 = 0.1127$

(b) $Z = \dfrac{\overline{X}_L - \mu_1}{\dfrac{\sigma}{\sqrt{n}}} = \dfrac{24,424.3012 - 24,900}{\dfrac{3,500}{\sqrt{100}}} = -1.3591$

power = $1 - \beta = P(\overline{X} < \overline{X}_L) = P(Z < -1.3591) = 0.0871$

$\beta = 1 - 0.0871 = 0.9129$

9.80 $H_0 : \mu \geq 25,000$, $H_1 : \mu < 25,000$, $\alpha = 0.05$, $n = 25$, $\sigma = 3500$

Lower critical value: $Z_L = -1.6449$,

$$\overline{X}_L = \mu + Z_L \left(\frac{\sigma}{\sqrt{n}} \right) = 25,000 - 1.6449 \left(\frac{3,500}{\sqrt{25}} \right) = 23,848.6026$$

(a) $Z = \dfrac{\overline{X}_L - \mu_1}{\dfrac{\sigma}{\sqrt{n}}} = \dfrac{23,848.6026 - 24,000}{\dfrac{3,500}{\sqrt{25}}} = -0.2163$

power = $1 - \beta = P(\overline{X} < \overline{X}_L) = P(Z < -0.2163) = 0.4144$

$\beta = 1 - 0.4144 = 0.5856$

(b) $Z = \dfrac{\overline{X}_L - \mu_1}{\dfrac{\sigma}{\sqrt{n}}} = \dfrac{23,848.6026 - 24,900}{\dfrac{3,500}{\sqrt{25}}} = -1.5020$

power = $1 - \beta = P(\overline{X} < \overline{X}_L) = P(Z < -1.5020) = 0.0665$

$\beta = 1 - 0.0665 = 0.9335$

(c)   Holding everything else constant, the larger the sample size, the higher the power of the test will be and the lower the probability of committing a Type II error will be.

9.82   The null hypothesis represents the status quo or the hypothesis that is to be disproved. The null hypothesis includes an equal sign in its definition of a parameter of interest. The alternative hypothesis is the opposite of the null hypothesis and usually represents taking an action. The alternative hypothesis includes either a less than sign, a not equal to sign, or a greater than sign in its definition of a parameter of interest.

9.84   The power of a test is the probability that the null hypothesis will be rejected when the null hypothesis is false.

9.86   The *p*-value is the probability of obtaining a test statistic equal to or more extreme than the result obtained from the sample data, given that the null hypothesis is true.

9.88   The following steps would be used in all hypothesis tests: State the null hypothesis H_0. State the alternative hypothesis H_1. Choose the level of significance α. Choose the sample size *n*. Determine the appropriate statistical technique and corresponding test statistic to use. Set up the critical values that divide the rejection and nonrejection regions. Collect the data and compute the sample value of the appropriate test statistic. Determine whether the test statistic has fallen into the rejection or the nonrejection region. The computed value of the test statistic is compared with the critical values for the appropriate sampling distribution to determine whether it falls into the rejection or nonrejection region. Make the statistical decision. If the test statistic falls into the nonrejection region, the null hypothesis H_0 cannot be rejected. If the test statistic falls into the rejection region, the null hypothesis is rejected. Express the statistical decision in terms of a particular situation.

9.90   Among the questions to be raised are: What is the goal of the experiment or research? Can it be translated into a null and alternative hypothesis? Is the hypothesis test going to be two-tailed or one-tailed? Can a random sample be drawn from the underlying population of interest? What kinds of measurements will be obtained from the sample? Are the sampled outcomes of the random variable going to be numerical or categorical? At what significance level, or risk of committing a Type I error, should the hypothesis test be conducted? Is the intended sample size large enough to achieve the desired power of the test for the level of significance chosen? What statistical test procedure is to be used on the sampled data and why? What kind of conclusions and interpretations can be drawn from the results of the hypothesis test?

9.92   (a)   La Quinta Motor Inns commits a Type I error when it purchases a site that is not profitable.

   (b)   Type II error occurs when La Quinta Motor Inns fails to purchase a profitable site. The cost to the Inns when a Type II error is committed is the loss on the amount of profit the site could have generated had the Inns decided to purchase the site.

   (c)   The executives at La Quinta Motor Inns are trying to avoid a Type I error by adopting a very stringent decision criterion. Only sites that are classified as capable of generating high profit will be purchased.

   (d)   If the executives adopt a less stringent rejection criterion by buying sites that the computer model predicts will produce moderate or large profit, the probability of committing a Type I error will increase. On the other hand, the less stringent rejection criterion will lower the probability of committing a Type II error since now more potentially profitable sites will be purchased.

9.94 (a) H_0: $\mu = 10.0$ gallons. The mean gasoline purchase is equal to 10 gallons.
H_1: $\mu \neq 10.0$ gallons. The mean gasoline purchase differs from 10 gallons.
Decision rule: $d.f. = 59$. If $t < -2.0010$ or $t > 2.0010$, reject H_0.
Test statistic: $t = \dfrac{\overline{X} - \mu}{S/\sqrt{n}} = \dfrac{11.3 - 10.0}{3.1/\sqrt{60}} = 3.2483$

Decision: Since $t_{calc} = 3.2483$ is greater than the upper critical value of $t = 2.0010$, reject H_0. There is enough evidence to conclude that the mean gasoline purchase differs from 10 gallons.

(b) p-value $= 0.0019$.
Note: The-p value was found using Excel.

(c) H_0: $\pi \geq 0.20$. At least 20% of the motorists purchase super unleaded gasoline.
H_1: $\pi < 0.20$. Less than 20% of the motorists purchase super unleaded gasoline.
Decision rule: If $Z < -1.645$, reject H_0.
Test statistic: $Z = \dfrac{p - \pi}{\sqrt{\dfrac{\pi(1-\pi)}{n}}} = \dfrac{0.1833 - 0.20}{\sqrt{\dfrac{0.20(0.80)}{60}}} = -0.32$

Decision: Since $Z_{calc} = -0.32$ is greater than the critical bound of $Z = -1.645$, do not reject H_0. There is not sufficient evidence to conclude that less than 20% of the motorists purchase super unleaded gasoline.

(d) H_0: $\mu = 10.0$ gallons. The mean gasoline purchase is equal to 10 gallons.
H_1: $\mu \neq 10.0$ gallons. The mean gasoline purchase differs from 10 gallons.
Decision rule: $d.f. = 59$. If $t < -2.0010$ or $t > 2.0010$, reject H_0.
Test statistic: $t = \dfrac{\overline{X} - \mu}{S/\sqrt{n}} = \dfrac{10.3 - 10.0}{3.1/\sqrt{60}} = 0.7496$

Decision: Since the test statistic of $t_{calc} = 0.7496$ is between the critical bounds of $t = \pm 2.0010$, do not reject H_0. There is not enough evidence to conclude that the mean gasoline purchase differs from 10 gallons.

(e) H_0: $\pi \geq 0.20$. At least 20% of the motorists purchase super unleaded gasoline.
H_1: $\pi < 0.20$. Less than 20% of the motorists purchase super unleaded gasoline.
Decision rule: If $Z < -1.645$, reject H_0.
Test statistic: $Z = \dfrac{p - \pi}{\sqrt{\dfrac{\pi(1-\pi)}{n}}} = \dfrac{0.1167 - 0.20}{\sqrt{\dfrac{0.20(0.80)}{60}}} = -1.61$

Decision: Since $Z_{calc} = -1.61$ is greater than the critical bound of $Z = -1.645$, do not reject H_0. There is not sufficient evidence to conclude that less than 20% of the motorists purchase super unleaded gasoline.

9.96   (a) H_0: $\mu \geq 5$ minutes. The mean waiting time at a bank branch in a commercial district of the city is at least 5 minutes during the 12:00 p.m. to 1 p.m. peak lunch period.
H_1: $\mu < 5$ minutes. The mean waiting time at a bank branch in a commercial district of the city is less than 5 minutes during the 12:00 p.m. to 1 p.m. peak lunch period.
Decision rule: $d.f. = 14$. If $t < -1.7613$, reject H_0.

Test statistic: $t = \dfrac{\overline{X} - \mu}{S/\sqrt{n}} = \dfrac{4.28\overline{66} - 5.0}{1.637985/\sqrt{15}} = -1.6867$

Decision: Since $t_{calc} = -1.6867$ is greater than the critical bound of $t = -1.7613$, do not reject H_0. There is not enough evidence to conclude that the mean waiting time at a bank branch in a commercial district of the city is less than 5 minutes during the 12:00 p.m. to 1 p.m. peak lunch period.

(b)   To perform the t-test on the population mean, you must assume that the observed sequence in which the data were collected is random and that the data are approximately normally distributed.

(c)   Normal probability plot:

Normal Probability Plot

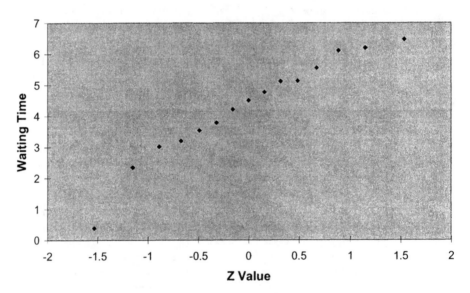

With the exception of one extreme point, the data are approximately normally distributed.

(d)   Based on the results of (a), the manager does not have enough evidence to make that statement.

9.98   (a) $H_0 : \mu \geq 0.35$ $H_1 : \mu < 0.35$

Decision rule: Reject H_0 if $t < -1.690$ $d.f. = 35$

Test statistic: $t = \dfrac{\overline{X} - \mu}{S / \sqrt{n}} = \dfrac{0.3167 - 0.35}{0.1357 / \sqrt{36}} = -1.4735$

Decision: Since $t > -1.690$, do not reject H_0. There is not enough evidence to conclude that the mean moisture content is less than 0.35 pounds per 100 square feet.

(b) p-value = 0.0748. If the population mean moisture content is in fact no less than 0.35 pounds per 100 square feet, the probability of observing a sample of 36 shingles that will result in a sample mean moisture content of 0.3167 pounds per 100 square feet or less is 7.48%.

(c) $H_0 : \mu \geq 0.35$ $H_1 : \mu < 0.35$

Decision rule: Reject H_0 if $t < -1.6973$ $d.f. = 30$

Test statistic: $t = \dfrac{\overline{X} - \mu}{S / \sqrt{n}} = \dfrac{0.2735 - 0.35}{0.1373 / \sqrt{31}} = -3.1003$

Decision: Since $t < -1.6973$, reject H_0. There is enough evidence to conclude that the mean moisture content is less than 0.35 pounds per 100 square feet.

(d) p-value = 0.0021. If the population mean moisture content is in fact no less than 0.35 pounds per 100 square feet, the probability of observing a sample of 31 shingles that will result in a sample mean moisture content of 0.2735 pounds per 100 square feet or less is 0.21%.

(e)   In order for the t test to be valid, the data are assumed to be independently drawn from a population that is normally distributed. Since the sample sizes are 36 and 31, respectively, which are considered quite large, the t distribution will provide a good approximation to the sampling distribution of the mean as long as the population distribution is not very skewed.

(f)

Box-and-whisker Plot (Boston)

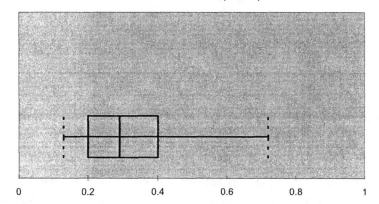

9.98   (f)
cont.

Box-and-whisker Plot (Vermont)

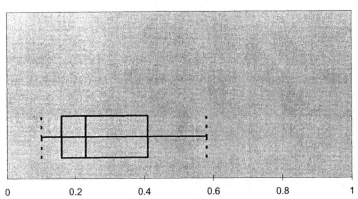

Both box-and-whisker plots suggest that the data are skewed slightly to the right, more so for the Boston shingles. To be more conservative, larger sample sizes should be used in both samples.

9.100   (a) $H_0 : \mu = 0.5$ $H_1 : \mu \neq 0.5$

Decision rule: Reject H_0 if $|t| > 1.9741$ $d.f. = 169$

Test statistic: $t = \dfrac{\overline{X} - \mu}{S / \sqrt{n}} = \dfrac{0.2641 - 0.5}{0.1424 / \sqrt{170}} = -21.6059$

Decision: Since $t < -1.9741$, reject H_0. There is enough evidence to conclude that the mean granule loss is different from 0.5 grams.

(b) p-value is virtually zero. If the population mean granule loss is in fact 0.5 grams, the probability of observing a sample of 170 shingles that will yield a test statistic more extreme than -21.6059 is virtually zero.

(c) $H_0 : \mu = 0.5$ $H_1 : \mu \neq 0.5$

Decision rule: Reject H_0 if $|t| > 1.977$ $d.f. = 139$

Test statistic: $t = \dfrac{\overline{X} - \mu}{S / \sqrt{n}} = \dfrac{0.218 - 0.5}{0.1227 / \sqrt{140}} = -27.1940$

Decision: Since $t < -1.977$, reject H_0. There is enough evidence to conclude that the mean granule loss is different from 0.5 grams.

(d) p-value is virtually zero. The probability of observing a sample of 140 shingles that will yield a test statistic more extreme than -27.1940 is virtually zero if the population mean granule loss is in fact 0.5 grams.

(e)   In order for the t test to be valid, the data are assumed to be independently drawn from a population that is normally distributed. Since the sample sizes are 170 and 140, respectively, which are considered large enough, the t distribution will provide a good approximation to the sampling distribution of the mean even if the population is not normally distributed.

CHAPTER 10

OBJECTIVES

- To learn how to use hypothesis testing for comparing the difference between the means of two independent populations
- To be able to use hypothesis testing for comparing the difference between the means of two related populations
- To learn how to use hypothesis testing for comparing the difference between the means of two proportions
- To be able to use hypothesis testing for comparing the difference between the variances of two independent populations

OVERVIEW AND KEY CONCEPTS

Z Test for Difference in Two Means $(\mu_1 - \mu_2)$

- **Assumptions:**
    - The two samples are randomly and independently drawn from normal distributions.
    - Population variances are known.
    - If the two populations are not normally distributed, large sample sizes are needed ($n_1 \geq 30$ and $n_2 \geq 30$).
- **Test statistic:**
    - $$Z = \frac{(\bar{X}_1 - \bar{X}_2) - (\mu_1 - \mu_2)}{\sqrt{\dfrac{\sigma_1^2}{n_1} + \dfrac{\sigma_2^2}{n_2}}}$$
    - The alternative hypothesis can be one-tail with a right-tail rejection region, one-tail with a left-tail rejection region or two-tail with both right-tail and left-tail rejection regions.

Pooled-Variance *t* Test for Difference in Two Means $(\mu_1 - \mu_2)$

- **Assumptions:**
    - The two samples are randomly and independently drawn.
    - Both populations are normally distributed.
    - Population variances are unknown but assumed equal.
    - If the two populations are not normally distributed, large sample sizes are needed ($n_1 \geq 30$ and $n_2 \geq 30$).
- **Test statistic:**
    - $$t = \frac{(\bar{X}_1 - \bar{X}_2) - (\mu_1 - \mu_2)}{\sqrt{S_p^2 \left(\dfrac{1}{n_1} + \dfrac{1}{n_2} \right)}} \quad \text{with } n_1 + n_2 - 2 \text{ degrees of freedom}$$

        where $S_p^2 = \dfrac{(n_1 - 1)S_1^2 + (n_2 - 1)S_2^2}{(n_1 - 1) + (n_2 - 1)}$

- The alternative hypothesis can be one-tail with a right-tail rejection region, one-tail with a left-tail rejection region or two-tail with both right-tail and left-tail rejection regions.
- **Confidence interval estimate:** Use the $100(1-\alpha)\%$ confidence interval for the difference in two means.

  - $$\left(\overline{X}_1 - \overline{X}_2\right) \pm t_{\alpha/2, n_1+n_2-2} \sqrt{S_p^2 \left(\frac{1}{n_1} + \frac{1}{n_2}\right)}$$

Separate-Variance t Test for Difference in Two Means $\left(\mu_1 - \mu_2\right)$

- **Assumptions:**
  - The two samples are randomly and independently drawn.
  - Both populations are normally distributed.
  - Both population variances are unknown and assumed not equal.
  - If the two populations are not normally distributed, large sample sizes are needed.
- **Test statistic:**

  - $$t = \frac{\left(\overline{X}_1 - \overline{X}_2\right) - \left(\mu_1 - \mu_2\right)}{\sqrt{\dfrac{S_1^2}{n_1} + \dfrac{S_2^2}{n_2}}}$$ with degrees of freedom ν taken to be the integer

    portion of $\nu = \dfrac{\left(\dfrac{S_1^2}{n_1} + \dfrac{S_2^2}{n_2}\right)^2}{\dfrac{\left(\dfrac{S_1^2}{n_1}\right)^2}{n_1 - 1} + \dfrac{\left(\dfrac{S_2^2}{n_2}\right)^2}{n_2 - 1}}$

  - The alternative hypothesis can be one-tail with a right-tail rejection region, one-tail with a left-tail rejection region or two-tail with both right-tail and left-tail rejection regions.

Z Test for the Mean Difference $\left(\mu_D\right)$ with Known Variance

- **Assumptions:**
  - Both populations are normally distributed.
  - Observations are matched or paired.
  - Variance is known.
  - The test is robust to the normal distribution assumption as long as the sample size is not too small and the population is not highly skewed.
- **Test statistic:**

  - $$Z = \frac{\overline{D} - \mu_D}{\dfrac{\sigma_D}{\sqrt{n}}}$$ where $\overline{D} = \dfrac{\sum\limits_{i=1}^{n} D_i}{n}$

  - The alternative hypothesis can be one-tail with a right-tail rejection region, one-tail with a left-tail rejection region or two-tail with both right-tail and left-tail rejection regions.

Paired t Test for the Mean Difference (μ_D) with Unknown Variance

- **Assumptions:**
  - Both populations are normally distributed.
  - Observations are matched or paired.
  - Variance is unknown.
  - The test is robust to the normal distribution assumption as long as the sample size is not too small and the population is not highly skewed.
- **Test statistic:**
  - $t = \dfrac{\bar{D} - \mu_D}{\dfrac{S_D}{\sqrt{n}}}$ with $n-1$ degrees of freedom

    where $\bar{D} = \dfrac{\displaystyle\sum_{i=1}^{n} D_i}{n}$ and $S_D = \sqrt{\dfrac{\displaystyle\sum_{i=1}^{n}(D_i - \bar{D})^2}{n-1}}$

  - The alternative hypothesis can be one-tail with a right-tail rejection region, one-tail with a left-tail rejection region or two-tail with both right-tail and left-tail rejection regions.
- **Confidence interval estimate:** Use the $100(1-\alpha)\%$ confidence interval for the mean difference.
  - $\bar{D} \pm t_{\alpha/2,n-1} \dfrac{S_D}{\sqrt{n}}$

Z Test for Differences in Two Proportions $(\pi_1 - \pi_2)$

- **Assumptions:**
  - Samples are independently drawn.
  - Populations follow the binomial distribution.
  - Both sample sizes are large enough: $n_1 p_1 \geq 5$, $n_1(1-p_1) \geq 5$, $n_2 p_2 \geq 5$, $n_2(1-p_2) \geq 5$
- **Test statistic:**
  - $Z = \dfrac{(p_1 - p_2) - (\pi_1 - \pi_2)}{\sqrt{\bar{p}(1-\bar{p})\left(\dfrac{1}{n_1} + \dfrac{1}{n_2}\right)}}$ where $\bar{p} = \dfrac{X_1 + X_2}{n_1 + n_2}$ is the pooled estimate of the

    population proportion.
  - The alternative hypothesis can be one-tail with a right-tail rejection region, one-tail with a left-tail rejection region or two-tail with both right-tail and left-tail rejection regions.
- **Confidence interval estimate:** Use the $100(1-\alpha)\%$ confidence interval for the difference in two proportions.
  - $(p_1 - p_2) \pm Z_{\alpha/2} \sqrt{\dfrac{p_1(1-p_1)}{n_1} + \dfrac{p_2(1-p_2)}{n_2}}$

F Test for Difference in Two Variances $\left(\sigma_1^2 - \sigma_2^2\right)$

- **Assumptions:**
    - The two samples are randomly and independently drawn.
    - Both populations are normally distributed.
    - The test is not robust to violation of the normality assumption.
- **Test statistic:**

    - $F = \dfrac{S_1^2}{S_2^2}$ with $n_1 - 1$ numerator degrees of freedom and $n_2 - 1$ denominator degrees of freedom.

    - The upper-tail critical value has $n_1 - 1$ numerator degrees of freedom and $n_2 - 1$ denominator degrees of freedom.

    - The lower-tail critical value can be obtained using $F_L = \dfrac{1}{F_{U^\cdot}}$ where $F_{U^\cdot}$ is the upper-tail critical value with $n_2 - 1$ numerator degrees of freedom and $n_1 - 1$ denominator degrees of freedom.

    - The alternative hypothesis can be one-tail with a right-tail rejection region, one-tail with a left-tail rejection region or two-tail with both right-tail and left-tail rejection regions.

SOLUTIONS TO END OF SECTION
AND CHAPTER REVIEW EVEN PROBLEMS

10.2 H_0: $\mu_1 = \mu_2$ H_1: $\mu_1 \neq \mu_2$
Decision rule: If $Z < -2.58$ or $Z > 2.58$, reject H_0.
Test statistic: $Z = \dfrac{(\bar{X}_1 - \bar{X}_2) - (\mu_1 - \mu_2)}{\sqrt{\dfrac{\sigma_1^2}{n_1} + \dfrac{\sigma_2^2}{n_2}}} = \dfrac{(72-66)-0}{\sqrt{\dfrac{20^2}{40} + \dfrac{10^2}{50}}} = 1.73$

Decision: Since $Z_{calc} = 1.73$ is between the critical bounds of $Z = \pm 2.58$, do not reject H_0.
There is inadequate evidence to conclude the two population means are different.

10.4   (a) $S_p^2 = \dfrac{(n_1-1)\cdot S_1^2 + (n_2-1)\cdot S_2^2}{(n_1-1)+(n_2-1)} = \dfrac{(7)\cdot 4^2 + (14)\cdot 5^2}{7+14} = 22$

$t = \dfrac{(\bar{X}_1 - \bar{X}_2)-(\mu_1-\mu_2)}{\sqrt{S_p^2\left(\dfrac{1}{n_1}+\dfrac{1}{n_2}\right)}} = \dfrac{(42-34)-0}{\sqrt{22\left(\dfrac{1}{8}+\dfrac{1}{15}\right)}} = 3.8959$

(b) $d.f. = (n_1-1)+(n_2-1) = 7+14 = 21$
(c)   Decision rule: $d.f. = 21$. If $t > 2.5177$, reject H_0.
(d)   Decision: Since $t_{calc} = 3.8959$ is greater than the critical bound of $t = 2.5177$, reject H_0. There is enough evidence to conclude that the first population mean is larger than the second population mean.

10.6 $(\bar{X}_1 - \bar{X}_2) \pm t\sqrt{S_p^2\left(\dfrac{1}{n_1}+\dfrac{1}{n_2}\right)} = (42-34) \pm 2.0796\sqrt{22\left(\dfrac{1}{8}+\dfrac{1}{15}\right)}$

$3.7296 \leq \mu_1 - \mu_2 \leq 12.2704$

10.8   (a) H_0: $\mu_1 \leq \mu_2$ where Populations: 1 = new machine, 2 = old machine
The mean breaking strength of parts produced by the new machine is not greater than the mean breaking strength of parts produced by the old machine.
H_1: $\mu_1 > \mu_2$
The mean breaking strength of parts produced by the new machine is greater than the mean breaking strength of parts produced by the old machine.
Decision rule: If $Z > 2.33$, reject H_0.
Test statistic: $Z = \dfrac{(\bar{X}_1 - \bar{X}_2)-(\mu_1-\mu_2)}{\sqrt{\dfrac{\sigma_1^2}{n_1}+\dfrac{\sigma_2^2}{n_2}}} = \dfrac{(72-65)-0}{\sqrt{\dfrac{9^2}{100}+\dfrac{10^2}{100}}} = 5.20$

Decision: Since $Z_{calc} = 5.20$ is greater than the critical bound of 2.33, reject H_0. There is enough evidence to conclude that the mean breaking strength of parts produced by the new machine is greater than the mean breaking strength of parts produced by the old machine.
(b) p-value = virtually zero. The probability of obtaining samples whose means differ by 7 or more units of strength when the null hypothesis is true is virtually zero.

10.10 H_0: $\mu_1 = \mu_2$ H_1: $\mu_1 \neq \mu_2$

(a)   **Age 8:**

PHStat output:

Data	
Hypothesized Difference	0
Level of Significance	0.05
Population 1 Sample	
Sample Size	27
Sample Mean	0.89
Sample Standard Deviation	0.98
Population 2 Sample	
Sample Size	22
Sample Mean	0.86
Sample Standard Deviation	1.07
Intermediate Calculations	
Population 1 Sample Degrees of Freedom	26
Population 2 Sample Degrees of Freedom	21
Total Degrees of Freedom	47
Pooled Variance	1.042836
Difference in Sample Means	0.03
t-Test Statistic	0.102284
Two-Tailed Test	
Lower Critical Value	-2.01174
Upper Critical Value	2.011739
***p*-Value**	0.918966
Do not reject the null hypothesis	

Test statistic: $t = \dfrac{(\overline{X}_1 - \overline{X}_2) - (\mu_1 - \mu_2)}{\sqrt{\dfrac{S_1^2}{n_1} + \dfrac{S_2^2}{n_2}}} = 0.1023$

Decision: Since $t_{calc} = 0.1023$ is between the critical bounds of ± 2.0117, do not reject H_0. There is no evidence of a difference in two means for the Age 8 group.

10.10   (a)   **Age 12:**
cont.   PHStat output:

Data	
Hypothesized Difference	0
Level of Significance	0.05
Population 1 Sample	
Sample Size	39
Sample Mean	0.88
Sample Standard Deviation	1.01
Population 2 Sample	
Sample Size	41
Sample Mean	0.09
Sample Standard Deviation	1.08
Intermediate Calculations	
Population 1 Sample Degrees of Freedom	38
Population 2 Sample Degrees of Freedom	40
Total Degrees of Freedom	78
Pooled Variance	1.095126
Difference in Sample Means	0.79
t-Test Statistic	3.375004
Two-Tailed Test	
Lower Critical Value	-1.99085
Upper Critical Value	1.990848
p-**Value**	0.001153
Reject the null hypothesis	

Test statistic: $t = \dfrac{(\bar{X}_1 - \bar{X}_2) - (\mu_1 - \mu_2)}{\sqrt{\dfrac{S_1^2}{n_1} + \dfrac{S_2^2}{n_2}}} = 3.375$

Decision: Since $t_{calc} = 3.375$ is greater than the upper critical bounds of 2.0117, reject H_0. There is evidence of a difference in two means for the Age 12 group.

10.10   (a)   **Age 16:**
cont.   PHStat output:

Data	
Hypothesized Difference	**0**
Level of Significance	**0.05**
Population 1 Sample	
Sample Size	**35**
Sample Mean	**0.41**
Sample Standard Deviation	**0.81**
Population 2 Sample	
Sample Size	**33**
Sample Mean	**-0.29**
Sample Standard Deviation	**0.92**
Intermediate Calculations	
Population 1 Sample Degrees of Freedom	34
Population 2 Sample Degrees of Freedom	32
Total Degrees of Freedom	66
Pooled Variance	0.748367
Difference in Sample Means	0.7
t-Test Statistic	3.334858
Two-Tailed Test	
Lower Critical Value	**-1.99656**
Upper Critical Value	**1.996564**
p-Value	**0.001403**
Reject the null hypothesis	

Decision: Since $t_{calc} = 3.3349$ is greater than the upper critical bounds of 1.9966, reject H_0. There is evidence of a difference in two means for the Age 16 group.

(b)   The test results show that children in the United States begin to develop preferences for brand name products as early as Age 12.

10.12   (a) H_0: $\mu_1 = \mu_2$ where Populations: 1 = Males, 2 = Females
Mean computer anxiety experienced by males and females is the same.
H_1: $\mu_1 \neq \mu_2$
Mean computer anxiety experienced by males and females is different.
Decision rule: $d.f. = 170$. If $t < -1.974$ or $t > 1.974$, reject H_0.
Test statistic:

$$S_p^2 = \frac{(n_1 - 1) \cdot S_1^2 + (n_2 - 1) \cdot S_2^2}{(n_1 - 1) + (n_2 - 1)} = \frac{(99) \cdot 13.35^2 + (71) \cdot 9.42^2}{99 + 71} = 140.8489$$

$$t = \frac{(\overline{X}_1 - \overline{X}_2) - (\mu_1 - \mu_2)}{\sqrt{S_p^2 \left(\frac{1}{n_1} + \frac{1}{n_2} \right)}} = \frac{(40.26 - 36.85) - 0}{\sqrt{140.8489 \left(\frac{1}{100} + \frac{1}{72} \right)}} = 1.859$$

Decision: Since $t_{calc} = 1.859$ is between the lower and upper critical bound of -1.974 and 1.974, do not reject H_0. There is not enough evidence to conclude that the mean computer anxiety experienced by males and females is different.

(b)   Using PHStat, the p-value = 0.0648.

(c)   In order to use the pooled-variance t test, you need to assume that the populations are normally distributed with equal variances.

10.14   (a) $H_0 : \mu_1 = \mu_2$ Mean waiting times of Bank 1 and Bank 2 are the same.

$H_1 : \mu_1 \neq \mu_2$ Mean waiting times of Bank 1 and Bank 2 are different.

PHStat output:

t Test for Differences in Two Means	
Data	
Hypothesized Difference	0
Level of Significance	0.05
Population 1 Sample	
Sample Size	15
Sample Mean	4.286667
Sample Standard Deviation	1.637985
Population 2 Sample	
Sample Size	15
Sample Mean	7.114667
Sample Standard Deviation	2.082189
Intermediate Calculations	
Population 1 Sample Degrees of Freedom	14
Population 2 Sample Degrees of Freedom	14
Total Degrees of Freedom	28
Pooled Variance	3.509254
Difference in Sample Means	-2.828
t-Test Statistic	-4.13431
Two-Tailed Test	
Lower Critical Value	-2.04841
Upper Critical Value	2.048409
p-Value	0.000293
Reject the null hypothesis	

10.14   (a)   Since the p-value of 0.000293 is less than the 5% level of significance, reject the null
cont.   hypothesis. There is enough evidence to conclude that the mean waiting time is
                     different in the two banks.

(b) p-value = 0.000293. The probability of obtaining a sample that will yield a t test
         statistic more extreme than -4.13431 is 0.000293 if, in fact, the mean waiting times
         of Bank 1 and Bank 2 are the same.

(c)   We need to assume that the two populations are normally distributed.

(d) $$\left(\bar{X}_1 - \bar{X}_2\right) + t\sqrt{S_p^2\left(\frac{1}{n_1} + \frac{1}{n_2}\right)} = \left(4.2867 - 7.1147\right) + 2.0484\sqrt{3.5093\left(\frac{1}{15} + \frac{1}{15}\right)}$$

$$-4.2292 \le \mu_1 - \mu_2 \le -1.4268$$

You are 95% confident that the difference in mean waiting time between Bank 1 and
Bank 2 is between -4.2292 and -1.4268 minutes.

10.16   (a) $H_0 : \mu_1 = \mu_2$ Mean times to clear problems at Office I and Office II are the same.

$H_1 : \mu_1 \ne \mu_2$ Mean times to clear problems at Office I and Office II are different.

PHStat output:

t Test for Differences in Two Means	
Data	
Hypothesized Difference	0
Level of Significance	0.05
Population 1 Sample	
Sample Size	20
Sample Mean	2.214
Sample Standard Deviation	1.718039
Population 2 Sample	
Sample Size	20
Sample Mean	2.0115
Sample Standard Deviation	1.891706
Intermediate Calculations	
Population 1 Sample Degrees of Freedom	19
Population 2 Sample Degrees of Freedom	19
Total Degrees of Freedom	38
Pooled Variance	3.265105
Difference in Sample Means	0.2025
t-Test Statistic	0.354386
Two-Tailed Test	
Lower Critical Value	-2.02439
Upper Critical Value	2.024394
p-Value	0.725009
Do not reject the null hypothesis	

Since the p-value of 0.725 is greater than the 5% level of significance, do not reject
the null hypothesis. There is not enough evidence to conclude that the mean time to
clear problems in the two offices is different.

(b) p-value = 0.725. The probability of obtaining a sample that will yield a t test statistic
         more extreme than 0.3544 is 0.725 if, in fact, the mean waiting times between Office
         1 and Office 2 are the same.

(c)   We need to assume that the two populations are normally distributed.

10.16   (d) $\left(\bar{X}_1 - \bar{X}_2\right) + t\sqrt{S_p^2\left(\dfrac{1}{n_1} + \dfrac{1}{n_2}\right)} = \left(2.214 - 2.0115\right) + 2.0244\sqrt{3.2651\left(\dfrac{1}{20} + \dfrac{1}{20}\right)}$

cont.

$$-0.9543 \le \mu_1 - \mu_2 \le 1.3593$$

10.18   (a) H_0: $\mu_1 = \mu_2$ H_1: $\mu_1 \ne \mu_2$

Excel output:

t-Test: Two-Sample Assuming Equal
Variances

	Untreated	Treated
Mean	165.0948	155.7314
Variance	41.6934168	62.4141
Observations	20	20
Pooled Variance	52.05375826	
Hypothesized Mean Difference	0	
df	38	
t Stat	4.104023608	
P(T<=t) one-tail	0.000103572	
t Critical one-tail	1.685953066	
P(T<=t) two-tail	0.000207144	
t Critical two-tail	2.024394234	

Decision: Since $t_{calc} = 4.104$ is greater than the upper critical bound of 2.024, reject H_0. There is evidence that the mean surface hardness of untreated steel plates is different than the mean surface hardness of treated steel plates.

(b)   p-value = 0.0002. The probability of obtaining two samples with a mean difference of 9.3634 or more is 0.02% if there is evidence that the mean surface hardness of untreated steel plates is different than the mean surface hardness of treated steel plates.

(c)   Since both sample sizes are smaller than 30, you need to assume that the population of hardness of both untreated and treated steel plates is normally distributed.

(d)

$$\left(\bar{X}_1 - \bar{X}_2\right) + t\sqrt{S_p^2\left(\frac{1}{n_1} + \frac{1}{n_2}\right)}$$

$$= \left(165.0948 - 155.7314\right) + 2.0244\sqrt{52.0538\left(\frac{1}{20} + \frac{1}{20}\right)}$$

$$4.7447 \le \mu_1 - \mu_2 \le 13.9821$$

You are 95% confident that the difference in the mean surface hardness between untreated and treated steel plates is between 4.7447 and 13.9821.

10.20 (a) H_0: $\mu_1 = \mu_2$ where Populations: 1 = computer-assisted, individual based;
2 = team-based

Mean assembly times in seconds are the same between employees trained in a computer-assisted, individual-based program and those trained in a team-based program.

H_1: $\mu_1 \neq \mu_2$

Mean assembly times in seconds are different between employees trained in a computer-assisted, individual-based program and those trained in a team-based program.

Decision rule: $d.f. = 40$. If $t < -2.0211$ or $t > 2.0211$, reject H_0.

Test statistic:

$$S_p^{\ 2} = \frac{(n_1 - 1) \cdot S_1^2 + (n_2 - 1) \cdot S_2^2}{(n_1 - 1) + (n_2 - 1)} = \frac{(20) \cdot 1.9333^2 + (20) \cdot 4.5767^2}{20 + 20} = 12.3417$$

$$t = \frac{(\overline{X}_1 - \overline{X}_2) - (\mu_1 - \mu_2)}{\sqrt{S_p^{\ 2}\left(\dfrac{1}{n_1} + \dfrac{1}{n_2}\right)}} = \frac{(17.5571 - 19.8905) - 0}{\sqrt{12.3417\left(\dfrac{1}{21} + \dfrac{1}{21}\right)}} = -2.1522$$

Decision: Since $t_{calc} = -2.1522$ is below the lower critical bound of -2.0211, reject H_0. There is enough evidence to conclude that the mean assembly times in seconds are different between employees trained in a computer-assisted, individual-based program and those trained in a team-based program.

(b) You must assume that each of the two independent populations is normally distributed.

(c) (a) H_0: $\mu_1 = \mu_2$ where Populations: 1 = computer-assisted, individual based;
2 = team-based

Mean assembly times in seconds are the same between employees trained in a computer-assisted, individual-based program and those trained in a team-based program.

H_1: $\mu_1 \neq \mu_2$

Mean assembly times in seconds are different between employees trained in a computer-assisted, individual-based program and those trained in a team-based program.

Decision rule: $d.f. = 26$. If p-value < 0.05, reject H_0.

Excel output:

t-Test: Two-Sample Assuming Unequal Variances

	Computer-Assisted Program	Team-based Program
Mean	17.55714286	19.89047619
Variance	3.737571429	20.94590476
Observations	21	21
Hypothesized Mean Difference	0	
df	27	
t Stat	-2.152203195	
P(T<=t) one-tail	0.020240852	
t Critical one-tail	1.703288035	
P(T<=t) two-tail	0.040481703	
t Critical two-tail	2.051829142	

10.20 (c)   (a)   Since p-value $= 0.041 < 0.05$, reject H_0. There is enough evidence to
cont.   conclude that the mean assembly times in seconds are different between
                                      employees trained in a computer-assisted, individual-based program and
                                      those trained in a team-based program.

          (d)   The results in (a) and (c) are the same.

          (e)   Assuming equal variances:

$$\left(\bar{X}_1 - \bar{X}_2\right) + t\sqrt{S_p^2\left(\frac{1}{n_1} + \frac{1}{n_2}\right)} = \left(17.557 - 19.891\right) + 2.0211\sqrt{12.3417\left(\frac{1}{21} + \frac{1}{21}\right)}$$

$$-4.52 \le \mu_1 - \mu_2 \le -0.14$$

You are 95% confident that the difference between the population means of the two
training methods is between -4.52 and -0.14.

10.22 $d.f. = n - 1 = 20 - 1 = 19$, where $n =$ number of pairs of data

10.24 (a)   Define the difference in hotel rates as the rate in March 2004 minus the rate in
                    June 2002.

$$H_0: \mu_D = 0 \quad \text{vs.} \quad H_1: \mu_D \ne 0$$

Excel output:

t-Test: Paired Two Sample for Means

	Hotel 2004	Hotel 2002
Mean	102.0394444	180.7222
Variance	718.6064173	2473.271
Observations	18	18
Pearson Correlation	0.310844429	
Hypothesized Mean Difference	0	
df	17	
t Stat	-6.867169607	
P(T<=t) one-tail	1.36589E-06	
t Critical one-tail	1.739606432	
P(T<=t) two-tail	2.73178E-06	
t Critical two-tail	2.109818524	

Test statistic: $t = \dfrac{\bar{D} - \mu_D}{\dfrac{S_D}{\sqrt{n}}} = -6.8672$

Decision: Since $t = -6.8672$ is less than the lower critical value of -2.1098, reject
H_0. There is enough evidence to conclude that there is a difference in the mean
daily hotel rates in June 2002 and March 2004.

          (b)   You must assume that the distribution of the differences between the daily hotel rate
                    in June 2002 and March 2004 is approximately normal.

          (c) p-value is virtually zero. The probability of obtaining a mean difference in daily
                    hotel rates that gives rise to a test statistic that deviates from 0 by 6.8672 or more in
                    either direction is virtually zero if there is no difference in the mean daily hotel rate
                    in June 2002 and March 2004.

10.24   (d) $\bar{D} \pm t\dfrac{S_D}{\sqrt{n}} = -78.68 \pm 2.1098 \dfrac{48.6114}{\sqrt{18}}$ $-102.86 \le \mu_D \le -54.51$

cont.   You are 95% confident that the mean difference in hotel rate between March 2004 and June 2002 is somewhere between –$102.86 and –$54.51.

10.26   (a) $H_0: \mu_{\bar{D}} = 0$ There is no difference in the mean price of textbooks between the local bookstore and Amazon.com.

$H_1: \mu_{\bar{D}} \ne 0$ There is a difference in the mean price of textbooks between the local bookstore and Amazon.com.

Decision rule: $d.f. = 14$. If $t < -2.9768$ or $t > 2.9768$, reject H_0.

Test statistic: $t = \dfrac{\bar{D} - \mu_{\bar{D}}}{S_{\bar{D}} / \sqrt{n}} = \dfrac{3.5307 - 0}{13.8493 / \sqrt{15}} = 0.9874$

Decision: Since $t_{calc} = 0.9874$ is between the critical bounds of -2.9768 and 2.9768, do not reject H_0. There is not enough evidence to conclude that there is a difference in the mean price of textbooks between the local bookstore and Amazon.com.

(b)   You must assume that the distribution of the differences between the mean price of business textbooks between on-campus and off-campus stores is approximately normal.

(c) $\bar{D} \pm t\dfrac{S_D}{\sqrt{n}} = 3.5307 \pm 2.9768 \dfrac{13.8493}{\sqrt{15}}$ $-7.1141 \le \mu_D \le 14.1755$

You are 99% confident that the mean difference between the prices is between –7.1141 and 14.1755.

(d)   The results in (a) and (c) are the same. The hypothesized value of 0 for the difference in the mean price of textbooks between the local bookstore and Amazon.com is inside the 99% confidence interval.

10.28   (a)   Define the difference in bone marrow microvessel density as the density before the transplant minus the density after the transplant and assume that the difference in density is normally distributed.

$$H_0: \mu_D \le 0 \quad \text{vs.} \quad H_1: \mu_D > 0$$

Excel output:
t-Test: Paired Two Sample for Means

	Before	After
Mean	312.1429	226
Variance	15513.14	4971
Observations	7	7
Pearson Correlation	0.295069	
Hypothesized Mean Difference	0	
df	6	
t Stat	1.842455	
P(T<=t) one-tail	0.057493	
t Critical one-tail	1.943181	
P(T<=t) two-tail	0.114986	
t Critical two-tail	2.446914	

10.28 (a)
cont.

Test statistic: $t = \dfrac{\overline{D} - \mu_D}{\dfrac{S_D}{\sqrt{n}}} = 1.8425$

Decision: Since $t = 1.8425$ is less than the critical value of 1.943, do not reject H_0.
There is not enough evidence to conclude that the mean bone marrow microvessel density is higher before the stem cell transplant than after the stem cell transplant.

(b) p-value = 0.0575. The probability of obtaining a mean difference in density that gives rise to a test statistic that deviates from 0 by 1.8425 or more is 5.75% if the mean density is not higher before the stem cell transplant than after the stem cell transplant.

(c) $\overline{D} \pm t \dfrac{S_D}{\sqrt{n}} = 86.1429 \pm 2.4469 \dfrac{123.7005}{\sqrt{7}}$ $-28.26 \le \mu_D \le 200.55$

You are 95% confident that the mean difference in bone marrow microvessel density before and after the stem cell transplant is somewhere between -28.26 and 200.55.

10.30 (a) H_0: $\mu_{\overline{D}} \ge 0$

H_1: $\mu_{\overline{D}} < 0$

Decision rule: $d.f. = 39$. If $t < -2.4258$, reject H_0.

Test statistic: $t = \dfrac{\overline{D} - \mu_{\overline{D}}}{S_{\overline{D}} \big/ \sqrt{n}} = -9.372$

Decision: Since $t_{calc} = -9.372$ is less than the critical bound of -2.4258, reject H_0.
There is enough evidence to conclude that the mean strength is less at two days than at seven days.

(b) You must assume that the distribution of the differences between the mean strength of the concrete is approximately normal.

(c) p-value is virtually 0. The probability of obtaining a mean difference that gives rise to a test statistic that is -9.372 or less when the null hypothesis is true is virtually 0.

10.32 (a) $p_1 = \dfrac{X_1}{n_1} = \dfrac{45}{100} = 0.45, \; p_2 = \dfrac{X_2}{n_2} = \dfrac{25}{50} = 0.50,$

and $\overline{p} = \dfrac{X_1 + X_2}{n_1 + n_2} = \dfrac{45 + 25}{100 + 50} = 0.467$

H_0: $\pi_1 = \pi_2$ H_1: $\pi_1 \ne \pi_2$
Decision rule: If $Z < -2.58$ or $Z > 2.58$, reject H_0.

Test statistic: $Z = \dfrac{(p_1 - p_2) - (\pi_1 - \pi_2)}{\sqrt{\overline{p} \cdot (1 - \overline{p}) \left(\dfrac{1}{n_1} + \dfrac{1}{n_2} \right)}} = \dfrac{(0.45 - 0.50) - 0}{\sqrt{0.467 \cdot 0.533 \left(\dfrac{1}{100} + \dfrac{1}{50} \right)}} = -0.58$

Decision: Since $Z_{calc} = -0.58$ is between the critical bound of $Z = \pm 2.58$, do not reject H_0. There is insufficient evidence to conclude that the population proportion of successes differs for group 1 and group 2.

10.32   (b) $(p_1 - p_2) \pm Z \sqrt{\left(\dfrac{p_1(1-p_1)}{n_1} + \dfrac{p_2(1-p_2)}{n_2} \right)} = -0.05 \pm 2.5758 \sqrt{\left(\dfrac{.45(.55)}{100} + \dfrac{.5(.5)}{50} \right)}$

cont.
$$-0.2727 \le \pi_1 - \pi_2 \le 0.1727$$

10.34   (a) H_0: $\pi_1 = \pi_2$ H_1: $\pi_1 \ne \pi_2$ where Populations: 1 = ages 2 to 7, 2 = ages 8 to 18
Decision rule: If $Z < -1.96$ or $Z > 1.96$, reject H_0.
Test statistic:

$$Z = \frac{(p_1 - p_2) - (\pi_1 - \pi_2)}{\sqrt{\overline{p} \cdot (1 - \overline{p}) \left(\dfrac{1}{n_1} + \dfrac{1}{n_2} \right)}} = \frac{(0.2596 - 0.5099) - 0}{\sqrt{0.4235 \cdot (1 - 0.4235) \left(\dfrac{1}{1090} + \dfrac{1}{2065} \right)}} = -13.53$$

Decision: Since $Z_{calc} = -13.53$ is less than the lower critical bound of $Z = -1.96$, reject H_0. There is sufficient evidence to conclude that a significant difference exists in the proportion of children between the ages of 2 and 7, and between the age of 8 and 18 who use a computer each day.

(b) p-value is virtually 0. The probability of obtaining a difference in two sample proportions of -0.2503 or more is virtually 0 when the null hypothesis is true.

(c) $(p_1 - p_2) \pm Z \sqrt{\left(\dfrac{p_1(1-p_1)}{n_1} + \dfrac{p_2(1-p_2)}{n_2} \right)}$ $-0.2841 \le \pi_1 - \pi_2 \le -0.2165$

10.36   (a) H_0: $\pi_1 \ge \pi_2$ H_1: $\pi_1 < \pi_2$ where Populations: 1 = 2002, 2 = 2003
Decision rule: If $Z < -1.645$, reject H_0.
Test statistic:

$$Z = \frac{(p_1 - p_2) - (\pi_1 - \pi_2)}{\sqrt{\overline{p} \cdot (1 - \overline{p}) \left(\dfrac{1}{n_1} + \dfrac{1}{n_2} \right)}} = \frac{(0.25 - 0.4102) - 0}{\sqrt{0.3450 \cdot (1 - 0.3450) \left(\dfrac{1}{500} + \dfrac{1}{729} \right)}} = -5.8019$$

Decision: Since $Z_{calc} = -5.8019$ is less than the critical bound of -1.645, reject H_0. There is sufficient evidence to conclude that the proportion of adults online who use the Internet to gather data about products/services was higher in December 2003 than in 2000.

(b)   Using Excel, the p-value is virtually zero. The probability of obtaining a difference in two sample proportions of -0.16 or smaller is virtually zero when the null hypothesis is true.

10.38 (a) $H_0: \pi_1 \leq \pi_2$ $H_1: \pi_1 > \pi_2$ Population 1 = white workers, 2 = black workers
Decision rule: If $Z > 1.645$, reject H_0.
Test statistic:

$$\bar{p} = \frac{X_1 + X_2}{n_1 + n_2} = \frac{29 + 126}{56 + 407} = 0.3348$$

$$Z = \frac{(p_1 - p_2) - (\pi_1 - \pi_2)}{\sqrt{\bar{p} \cdot (1 - \bar{p})\left(\dfrac{1}{n_1} + \dfrac{1}{n_2}\right)}} = \frac{(0.5179 - 0.3096) - 0}{\sqrt{0.3348 \cdot (1 - 0.3348)\left(\dfrac{1}{56} + \dfrac{1}{407}\right)}} = 3.0965$$

Decision: Since $Z_{calc} = 3.0965$ is greater than the critical bound of 1.645, reject H_0.
There is sufficient evidence to conclude that white workers are more likely to claim
bias than black workers.

(b)   Using Excel, the p-value is 0.00098. The probability of obtaining a difference in two
sample proportions of 0.20828 or larger is 0.00098 when the null hypothesis is true.

10.40 (a) $F_U = 2.20,\ F_L = \dfrac{1}{2.33} = 0.43$

(b) $F_U = 2.57,\ F_L = \dfrac{1}{2.76} = 0.36$

(c) $F_U = 3.09,\ F_L = \dfrac{1}{3.37} = 0.30$

(d) $F_U = 3.50,\ F_L = \dfrac{1}{3.88} = 0.26$

10.42 (a) $F_L = \dfrac{1}{2.33} = 0.429$

(b) $F_L = \dfrac{1}{2.76} = 0.362$

(c) $F_L = \dfrac{1}{3.37} = 0.297$

(d) $F_L = \dfrac{1}{3.88} = 0.258$

10.44 The degrees of freedom for the numerator is 24 and for the denominator is 24.

10.46 Since $F_{calc} = 0.826$ is between the critical bounds of $F_L = 0.441$ and $F_U = 2.27$, do not reject
H_0. There is not enough evidence to conclude that the two population variances are different.

10.48   (a) H_0: $\sigma_1^2 = \sigma_2^2$ The population variances are the same.
H_1: $\sigma_1^2 \neq \sigma_2^2$ The population variances are different.
Decision rule: If $F > 3.18$ or $F < 0.3378$, reject H_0.

Test statistic: $F = \dfrac{S_1^2}{S_2^2} = \dfrac{47.3}{36.4} = 1.2995$

Decision: Since $F_{calc} = 1.2995$ is between the critical bounds of $F_U = 3.18$ and $F_L = 0.3378$, do not reject H_0. There is not enough evidence to conclude that the two population variances are different.

(b) H_0: $\sigma_1^2 \leq \sigma_2^2$ The variance for population 1 is less than or equal to the variance for population 2.
H_1: $\sigma_1^2 > \sigma_2^2$ The variance for population 1 is greater than the variance for population 2.
Decision rule: If $F > 2.62$, reject H_0.

Test statistic: $F = \dfrac{S_1^2}{S_2^2} = \dfrac{47.3}{36.4} = 1.2995$

Decision: Since $F_{calc} = 1.2995$ is less than the critical bound of $F_U = 2.62$, do not reject H_0. There is not enough evidence to conclude that the variance for population 1 is greater than the variance for population 2.

(c) H_0: $\sigma_1^2 \geq \sigma_2^2$ The variance for population 1 is greater than or equal to the variance for population 2.
H_1: $\sigma_1^2 < \sigma_2^2$ The variance for population 1 is less than the variance for population 2.
Decision rule: If $F < 0.4032$, reject H_0.

Test statistic: $F = \dfrac{S_1^2}{S_2^2} = \dfrac{47.3}{36.4} = 1.2995$

Decision: Since $F_{calc} = 1.2995$ is greater than the critical bound of $F_L = 0.4032$, do not reject H_0. There is not enough evidence to conclude that the variance for population 1 is less than the variance for population 2.

10.50   (a) H_0: $\sigma_1^2 = \sigma_2^2$ The population variances are the same.
H_1: $\sigma_1^2 \neq \sigma_2^2$ The population variances are different.
Decision rule: If $F < 0.653$ or $F > 1.556$, reject H_0.

Test statistic: $F = \dfrac{S_1^2}{S_2^2} = \dfrac{13.35^2}{9.42^2} = 2.008$

Decision: Since $F_{calc} = 2.008$ is greater than $F_U = 1.556$, reject H_0. There is enough evidence to conclude that the two population variances are different.

(b) p-value = 0.0022. The probability of obtaining a sample that yields a test statistic more extreme than 2.008 is 0.0022 if the null hypothesis that there is no difference in the two population variances is true.

(c)   The test assumes that the two populations are both normally distributed.

(d)   Based on (a) and (b), a separate variance t test should be used.

10.52   (a) H_0: $\sigma_1^{\,2} = \sigma_2^{\,2}$ The population variances are the same.
H_1: $\sigma_1^{\,2} \neq \sigma_2^{\,2}$ The population variances are different.
Decision rule: If $F < 0.3958$ or $F > 2.5264$, reject H_0.

Test statistic: $F = \dfrac{S_1^2}{S_2^2} = \dfrac{1.718^2}{1.8917^2} = 0.8248$

Decision: Since $F_{calc} = 0.8248$ is between $F_L = 0.3958$ and $F_U = 2.5264$, do not reject H_0. There is not enough evidence to conclude that the two population variances are different.

(b) p-value $= 0.6789$. The probability of obtaining a sample that yields a test statistic more extreme than 0.8248 is 0.6789 if the null hypothesis that there is no difference in the two population variances is true.

(c)   The test assumes that the two populations are both normally distributed.

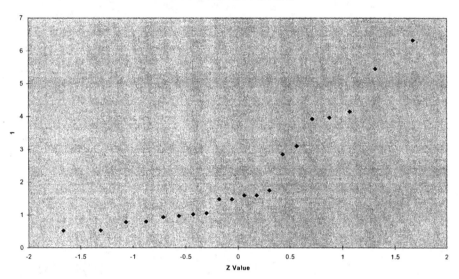

Normal Probability Plot (Office I)

10.52   (c)
cont.

Normal Probability Plot (Office II)

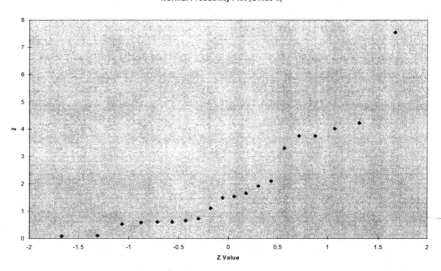

Box-and-whisker Plot

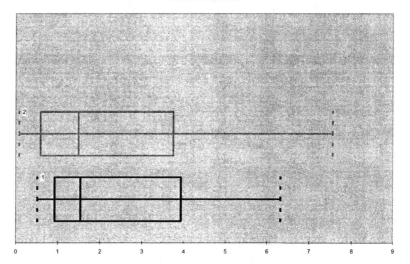

Both the normal probability plots and the box-and-whisker plots suggest that the time to clear problems in both offices does not appear to be normally distributed. Hence, the F test for the difference in variances, which is sensitive to departure from the normality assumption, should not be used to test the equality of two variances. The box-and-whisker plot and the summary statistics suggest that the two samples appear to have about the same amount of dispersion with the exception of a somewhat larger range in Office I. Since the pooled-variance t test is robust to departure from the normality assumption, it can be used to test for the difference in the means.

(d)   Based on the results of (a), it is appropriate to use the pooled-variance t-test to compare the means of the two offices.

10.54 H_0: $\sigma_1^2 \leq \sigma_2^2$ where Populations: 1 = Line A 2 = Line B
H_1: $\sigma_1^2 > \sigma_2^2$
Decision rule: If $F > 2.5437$, reject H_0.

Test statistic: $F = \dfrac{S_1^2}{S_2^2} = \dfrac{0.012^2}{0.005^2} = 5.76$

Decision: Since $F_{calc} = 5.76$ is above the critical bound of $F_U = 2.5437$, reject H_0. There is enough evidence to conclude that the variance in Line A is larger than the variance in Line B.

10.56 The pooled variance t-test should be used when the populations are approximately normally distributed and the variances of the two populations are equal.

10.58 With independent populations, the outcomes in one population do not depend on the outcomes in the second population. With two related populations, either repeated measurements are obtained on the same set of items or individuals, or items or individuals are paired or matched according to some characteristic.

10.60 When you have obtained data from either repeated measurements or paired data.

10.62 (a) $H_0 : \sigma_1^2 \geq \sigma_2^2$ Population: 1 = Internet   2 = brick-and-mortar market
Price variance on the Internet is not less than the price variance in the brick-and-mortar market.
$H_1 : \sigma_1^2 < \sigma_2^2$
Price variance on the Internet is less than the price variance in the brick-and-mortar market

(b)   Type I error: Rejecting the null hypothesis that price variance on the Internet is not less than the price variance in the brick-and-mortar market when the price variance on the Internet is indeed not less than the price variance in the brick-and-mortar market.
Type II error: Failing to reject the null hypothesis that price variance on the Internet is not less than the price variance in the brick-and-mortar market when the price variance on the Internet is indeed less than the price variance in the brick-and-mortar market.

(c)   An F test for differences in two variances can be used.
(d)   You need to assume that the two populations are both normally distributed.
(e)   (a) $H_0 : \mu_1 \geq \mu_2$ Population: 1 = electronic market   2 = physical market
Mean price in electronic markets is not less than the mean price in physical markets.
$H_1 : \mu_1 < \mu_2$
Mean price in electronic markets is less than the mean price in physical markets.

10.62   (e)
cont.

(b)   Type I error: Rejecting the null hypothesis that the mean price in electronic markets is not less than the mean price in physical markets when the mean price in electronic markets is indeed not less than the mean price in physical markets.
Type II error: Failing to reject the null hypothesis that mean price in electronic markets is not less than the mean price in physical markets when the mean price in electronic markets is indeed less than the mean price in physical markets.

(c)   A paired-sample t test for the mean difference can be used.

(d)   You must assume that the distribution of the differences between the mean price in electronic markets and physical markets is approximately normal.

10.64   (a)   The researchers could ask the teenagers, after viewing each ad, to rate the dangers of smoking using a scale from 0 to 10 with 10 representing the most dangerous.

(b) $H_0 : \mu_T \geq \mu_S$ The mean rating on the dangers of smoking for ads produced by Philip Morris is not less than the mean rating on the dangers of smoking for ads produced by the state.

$H_1 : \mu_T < \mu_S$ The mean rating on the dangers of smoking for ads produced by Philip Morris is less than the mean rating on the dangers of smoking for ads produced by the state.

(c)   Type I error is the error made by concluding that ads produced by the state are more effective than those produced by Philip Morris while it is not true. The risk of Type I error here is that teenagers can miss the opportunity from the better ads produced by Philip Morris to recognize the true dangers of smoking and the additional expenses the state will have to incur to produce and run the ads. Type II error is the error made by concluding that ads produced by Philip Morris are no less effective than those produced by the state while ads produced by the state are in fact more effective. The risk of Type II error here is that more teenagers will miss the opportunity to recognize the true dangers of smoking from the ads produced by the state.

(d)   Since both ads are shown to the same group of teenagers, a paired-sample t test for the mean difference is most appropriate.

(e)   Statistically reliable here means the conclusions drawn from the test are reliable because all the assumptions needed for the test to be valid are fulfilled.

10.66   (a) H_0: $\mu_{II} \leq \$80$ The mean monthly electric bill is no more than $80 for single-family homes in county II during the summer season.
H_1: $\mu_{II} > \$80$ The mean monthly electric bill is more than $80 for single-family homes in county II during the summer season.
Decision rule: $d.f. = 20$. If $t > 2.528$, reject H_0.

Test statistic: $t = \dfrac{\bar{X} - \mu}{S/\sqrt{n}} = \dfrac{\$98 - \$80}{\$18/\sqrt{21}} = 4.5826$

Decision: Since $t_{calc} = 4.5826$ is above the critical bound of 2.528, reject H_0. There is sufficient evidence to conclude that the mean monthly electric bill is more than $80 for single-family homes in county II during the summer season.

10.66 (b) H_0: $\sigma_I^2 = \sigma_{II}^2$ The population variances for monthly electric bills in county I and II
cont.   are the same.
            H_1: $\sigma_I^2 \neq \sigma_{II}^2$ The population variances for monthly electric bills in county I and II
            are not the same.
            Decision rule: If $F < 0.3265$ or $F > 3.2220$, reject H_0.

            Test statistic: $F = \dfrac{S_I^2}{S_{II}^2} = \dfrac{30^2}{18^2} = 2.78$

            Decision: Since $F_{calc} = 2.78$ is between the two critical bounds, do not reject H_0.
            There is not enough evidence to conclude that County I and II have different
            population variances for monthly electric bills.

       (c) H_0: $\mu_I \leq \mu_{II}$ The mean monthly electric bill is not higher in County I than
                  in County II.
            H_1: $\mu_I > \mu_{II}$ The mean monthly electric bill is higher in County I than in County II.
            Based on the results in (b) the pooled-variance t-test should be used here.
            Decision: If p-value < 0.01, reject H_0.
            PHStat output:

t Test for Differences in Two Means	
Data	
Hypothesized Difference	0
Level of Significance	0.01
Population 1 Sample	
Sample Size	25
Sample Mean	115
Sample Standard Deviation	30
Population 2 Sample	
Sample Size	21
Sample Mean	98
Sample Standard Deviation	18
Intermediate Calculations	
Population 1 Sample Degrees of Freedom	24
Population 2 Sample Degrees of Freedom	20
Total Degrees of Freedom	44
Pooled Variance	638.1818
Difference in Sample Means	17
t-Test Statistic	2.273408
Upper-Tail Test	
Upper Critical Value	2.414135
p-Value	0.013968
Do not reject the null hypothesis	

            Since p-value $= 0.0140 > 0.01$, do not reject H_0. There is not enough evidence to
            conclude that the mean monthly bill is higher in county I than in county II.

10.66   (d)
cont.

$$\left(\bar{X}_1 - \bar{X}_2\right) + t\sqrt{S_p^2\left(\frac{1}{n_1}+\frac{1}{n_2}\right)} = \left(115-98\right) + 2.6923\sqrt{638.18\left(\frac{1}{25}+\frac{1}{21}\right)}$$

$$-3.1323 \le \mu_1 - \mu_2 \le 37.1323$$

You are 99% confident that the difference between the mean monthly bill in country I and country II is between –$3.13 and $37.13.

10.68   (a) H_0: $\mu \le 10$ minutes. Introductory computer students required no more than a mean of 10 minutes to write and run a program in Visual Basic.
H_1: $\mu > 10$ minutes. Introductory computer students required more than a mean of 10 minutes to write and run a program in Visual Basic.
Decision rule: $d.f. = 8$. If $t > 1.8595$, reject H_0.

Test statistic: $t = \dfrac{\bar{X}-\mu}{S/\sqrt{n}} = \dfrac{12-10}{1.8028/\sqrt{9}} = 3.3282$

Decision: Since $t_{calc} = 3.3282$ is greater than the critical bound of 1.8595, reject H_0. There is enough evidence to conclude that the introductory computer students required more than a mean of 10 minutes to write and run a program in Visual Basic.

(b) H_0: $\mu \le 10$ minutes. Introductory computer students required no more than a mean of 10 minutes to write and run a program in Visual Basic.
H_1: $\mu > 10$ minutes. Introductory computer students required more than a mean of 10 minutes to write and run a program in Visual Basic.
Decision rule: $d.f. = 8$. If $t > 1.8595$, reject H_0.

Test statistic: $t = \dfrac{\bar{X}-\mu}{S/\sqrt{n}} = \dfrac{16-10}{13.2004/\sqrt{9}} = 1.3636$

Decision: Since $t_{calc} = 1.3636$ is less than the critical bound of 1.8595, do not reject H_0. There is not enough evidence to conclude that the introductory computer students required more than a mean of 10 minutes to write and run a program in Visual Basic.

(c)   Although the mean time necessary to complete the assignment increased from 12 to 16 minutes as a result of the increase in one data value, the standard deviation went from 1.8 to 13.2, which in turn brought the t-value down because of the increased denominator.

(d) H_0: $\sigma_{IC}^2 = \sigma_{CS}^2$ The population variances are the same for Introduction to Computers students and computer science majors.
H_1: $\sigma_{IC}^2 \neq \sigma_{CS}^2$ The population variances are different for Introduction to Computers students and computer science majors.
Decision rule: If $F < 0.2328$ or $F > 3.8549$, reject H_0.

Test statistic: $F = \dfrac{S_{IC}^2}{S_{CS}^2} = \dfrac{1.8028^2}{2.0^2} = 0.8125$

10.68 (d)
cont.

Decision: Since $F_{calc} = 0.8125$ is between the critical bounds of 0.2328 and 3.8549, do not reject H_0. There is not enough evidence to conclude that the population variances are different for the Introduction to Computers students and computer majors. Hence, the pooled variance t test is a valid test to see whether computer majors can write a Visual Basic program (on average) in less time than introductory students, assuming that the distributions of the time needed to write a Visual Basic program for both the Introduction to Computers students and the computer majors are approximately normal.

H_0: $\mu_{IC} \leq \mu_{CS}$ The mean amount of time needed by Introduction to Computers students is not greater than the mean amount of time needed by computer majors.

H_1: $\mu_{IC} > \mu_{CS}$ The mean amount of time needed by Introduction to Computers students is greater than the mean amount of time needed by computer majors.

Decision rule: $d.f. = 18$. If $t > 1.7341$, reject H_0.

Test statistic:

$$S_p^2 = \frac{(n_{IC}-1) \cdot S_{IC}^2 + (n_{CS}-1) \cdot S_{CS}^2}{(n_{IC}-1)+(n_{CS}-1)} = \frac{9 \cdot 1.8028^2 + 11 \cdot 2.0^2}{4+5} = 3.6667$$

$$t = \frac{(\bar{X}_{IC} - \bar{X}_{CS}) - (\mu_{IC} - \mu_{CS})}{\sqrt{S_p^2 \left(\frac{1}{n_{IC}} + \frac{1}{n_{CS}}\right)}} = \frac{12.0 - 8.5}{\sqrt{3.6667 \left(\frac{1}{9} + \frac{1}{11}\right)}} = 4.0666$$

Decision: Since $t_{calc} = 4.0666$ is greater than 1.7341, reject H_0. There is enough evidence to support a conclusion that the mean time is higher for Introduction to Computers students than for computer majors.

(e) p-value = 0.000362. If the true population mean amount of time needed for Introduction to Computer students to write a Visual Basic program is indeed no more than 10 minutes, the probability for observing a sample mean greater than the 12 minutes in the current sample is 0.0362%, which means it will be a quite unlikely event. Hence, at a 95% level of confidence, you can conclude that the population mean amount of time needed for Introduction to Computer students to write a Visual Basic program is more than 10 minutes.

As illustrated in part (d) in which there is not enough evidence to conclude that the population variances are different for the Introduction to Computers students and computer majors, the pooled variance t test performed is a valid test to determine whether computer majors can write a Visual Basic program in less time than in introductory students, assuming that the distributions of the time needed to write a Visual Basic program for both the Introduction to Computers students and the computer majors are approximately normal.

10.70   (a) $H_0 : \mu_1 \leq \mu_2$ where Populations: $1 =$ men and $2 =$ women

                $H_1 : \mu_1 > \mu_2$

                Decision rule: $df = 113$. If $t > 2.3598$, reject H_0.

                Test statistic: $t = \dfrac{\bar{D} - \mu_{\bar{D}}}{S_{\bar{D}} / \sqrt{n}} = 7.8735$

                Decision: Since $t_{calc} = 7.8735$ is greater than the critical bound of 2.3598, reject H_0. There is enough evidence to conclude that the mean salary for men is greater than the mean salary for women.

                Excel output:
                t-Test: Paired Two Sample for Means

	Male	Female
Mean	88683.23684	74575.17544
Variance	3834187011	2243135437
Observations	114	114
Pearson Correlation	0.973734531	
Hypothesized Mean Difference	0	
df	113	
t Stat	7.87346338	
P(T<=t) one-tail	1.14975E-12	
t Critical one-tail	2.359802238	
P(T<=t) two-tail	2.29949E-12	
t Critical two-tail	2.620035957	

      (b)   From the Excel output, the p-value is essentially zero.

      (c)

                F-Test Two-Sample for Variances

	Male	Female
Mean	88683.23684	74575.17544
Variance	3834187011	2243135437
Observations	114	114
df	113	113
F	1.709298042	
P(F<=f) one-tail	0.002354401	
F Critical one-tail	1.553353002	

                H_0: $\sigma_1^2 = \sigma_2^2$ The population variances are the same.

                H_1: $\sigma_1^2 \neq \sigma_2^2$ The population variances are different.

                Decision rule: If $F < 0.614$ or $F > 1.629$, reject H_0.

                Test statistic: $F = \dfrac{S_1^2}{S_2^2} = \dfrac{3,834,187,011}{2,243,135,437} = 1.709$

                Decision: Since $F_{calc} = 1.709$ is greater than the upper critical bound of $F_U = 1.629$, reject H_0. There is enough evidence to conclude that the two population variances are different.

10.72

	Manufacturer A	Manufacturer B
Minimum	684	819
First Quartile	852	943
Median	916.5	1015.5
Third Quartile	972	1096
Interquartile Range	120	153
Maximum	1093	1230
Range	409	411
Mean	909.65	1018.35
Median	916.5	1015.5
Mode	926	1077
Standard Deviation	94.3052	96.9014
Sample Variance	8893.4641	9389.8744
Count	40	40

Box-and-whisker Plot

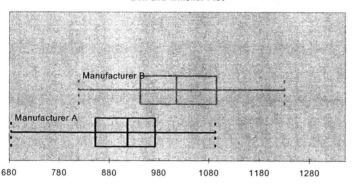

From the box-and-whisker plot and the summary statistics, both data seem to have come from rather symmetrical distributions that are quite normally distributed.

The following F test for any evidence of difference between two population variances suggests that there is insufficient evidence to conclude that the two population variances are significantly different at 5% level of significance.

PHStat output:

F Test for Differences in Two Variances	
Level of Significance	0.05
Population 1 Sample	
Sample Size	40
Sample Standard Deviation	94.30516
Population 2 Sample	
Sample Size	40
Sample Standard Deviation	96.90136
F-Test Statistic	0.947133
Population 1 Sample Degrees of Freedom	39
Population 2 Sample Degrees of Freedom	39
Two-Tailed Test	
Lower Critical Value	0.5289
Upper Critical Value	1.890719
p-Value	0.866186
Do not reject the null hypothesis	

10.72   Since both data are drawn from independent populations, the most appropriate test for any
cont.   difference in the life of the bulbs between the two manufacturers is the pooled-variance t test.

Pooled Variance t Test for Differences in Two Means	
Data	
Hypothesized Difference	0
Level of Significance	0.05
Population 1 Sample	
Sample Size	40
Sample Mean	909.65
Sample Standard Deviation	94.3052
Population 2 Sample	
Sample Size	40
Sample Mean	1018.35
Sample Standard Deviation	96.9014
Intermediate Calculations	
Population 1 Sample Degrees of Freedom	39
Population 2 Sample Degrees of Freedom	39
Total Degrees of Freedom	78
Pooled Variance	9141.676
Difference in Sample Means	-108.7
t-Test Statistic	-5.08431
Two-Tailed Test	
Lower Critical Value	-1.99085
Upper Critical Value	1.990848
p-Value	2.47E-06
Reject the null hypothesis	

Since the p-value is virtually zero, at the 5% level of significance, there is sufficient evidence
to reject the null hypothesis of no difference in the mean life of the bulbs between the two
manufacturers. You can conclude that there is significant difference in the mean life of the
bulbs between the two manufacturers.

Based on the above analyses, you can conclude that there is significant difference in the life
of the bulbs between the two manufacturers.

10.74 From Problem 3.77, you saw that the distribution of all the variables was skewed. The F test for the difference in variances, which is sensitive to departure from the normal distribution assumption, will not be appropriate. You also saw that the variances of all the variables between SUV and non-SUV are also quite different. Hence, you perform a separate variance t tests on the difference of means.

MPG:

$H_0 : \mu_1 = \mu_2$ vs. $H_1 : \mu_1 \neq \mu_2$

t-Test: Two-Sample Assuming Unequal Variances

	MPG	MPG
Mean	22.15556	16.48387
Variance	18.73958	7.258065
Observations	90	31
Hypothesized Mean Difference	0	
df	85	
t Stat	8.527657	
P(T<=t) one-tail	2.44E-13	
t Critical one-tail	1.662979	
P(T<=t) two-tail	4.88E-13	
t Critical two-tail	1.988269	

Since the p-value is essentially zero, reject H_0. There is sufficient evidence to conclude that the mean MPGs are different between SUVs and non-SUVs.

Length:

$H_0 : \mu_1 = \mu_2$ vs. $H_1 : \mu_1 \neq \mu_2$

t-Test: Two-Sample Assuming Unequal Variances

	Length	Length
Mean	187.9778	184.9032
Variance	161.4377	209.557
Observations	90	31
Hypothesized Mean Difference	0	
df	47	
t Stat	1.05125	
P(T<=t) one-tail	0.14926	
t Critical one-tail	1.677927	
P(T<=t) two-tail	0.298519	
t Critical two-tail	2.011739	

Since the p-value = 0.2985 is greater than the 5% level of significance, do not reject H_0.

There is not sufficient evidence to conclude that the mean length is different between SUVs and non-SUVs.

10.74   Width:

cont. $H_0 : \mu_1 = \mu_2$ vs. $H_1 : \mu_1 \neq \mu_2$

t-Test: Two-Sample Assuming Unequal Variances

	Width	Width
Mean	71	72.32258
Variance	9.865169	11.09247
Observations	90	31
Hypothesized Mean Difference	0	
df	50	
t Stat	-1.93447	
P(T<=t) one-tail	0.029362	
t Critical one-tail	1.675905	
P(T<=t) two-tail	0.058724	
t Critical two-tail	2.00856	

Since the *p*-value = 0.0587 is greater than the 5% level of significance, do not reject H_0.

There is not sufficient evidence to conclude that the mean width is different between SUVs and non-SUVs.

Weight:

$H_0 : \mu_1 = \mu_2$ vs. $H_1 : \mu_1 \neq \mu_2$

t-Test: Two-Sample Assuming Unequal Variances

	Weight	Weight
Mean	3391.722	4267.419
Variance	232210.8	783086.5
Observations	90	31
Hypothesized Mean Difference	0	
df	36	
t Stat	-5.24822	
P(T<=t) one-tail	3.51E-06	
t Critical one-tail	1.688297	
P(T<=t) two-tail	7.02E-06	
t Critical two-tail	2.028091	

Since the *p*-value is essentially zero, reject H_0. There is sufficient evidence to conclude that the mean weight is different between SUVs and non-SUVs.

Luggage Capacity:

$H_0 : \mu_1 = \mu_2$ vs. $H_1 : \mu_1 \neq \mu_2$

t-Test: Two-Sample Assuming Unequal Variances

	Cargo Volume	Cargo Volume
Mean	22.39444	42.35484
Variance	323.7837	183.7532
Observations	90	31
Hypothesized Mean Difference	0	
df	69	
t Stat	-6.46746	
P(T<=t) one-tail	6.05E-09	
t Critical one-tail	1.667238	
P(T<=t) two-tail	1.21E-08	
t Critical two-tail	1.994945	

10.74 Since the *p*-value is essentially zero, reject H_0. There is sufficient evidence to conclude
cont. that the mean luggage capacity is different between SUVs and non-SUVs.

Turning Circle:

$H_0 : \mu_1 = \mu_2$ vs. $H_1 : \mu_1 \neq \mu_2$

t-Test: Two-Sample Assuming Unequal Variances

	Turning Circle	Turning Circle
Mean	39.7	40.58065
Variance	6.324719	11.31828
Observations	90	31
Hypothesized Mean Difference	0	
df	42	
t Stat	-1.33465	
P(T<=t) one-tail	0.094591	
t Critical one-tail	1.681951	
P(T<=t) two-tail	0.189182	
t Critical two-tail	2.018082	

Since the *p*-value = 0.1892 is greater than the 5% level of significance, do not reject H_0.

There is not sufficient evidence to conclude that the mean turning circle requirement is
different between SUVs and non-SUVs.

10.76

Prices:

	USA_Price	Imported_Price
Minimum	2.36	4.63
First Quartile	3.71	5.41
Median	4.065	5.68
Third Quartile	6.12	6.39
Maximum	7.79	7.8
Mean	4.7133	5.8627
Median	4.065	5.68
Mode	4.02	#N/A
Standard Deviation	1.4753	0.9030
Sample Variance	2.1766	0.8154
Range	5.43	3.17
Count	54	15
Interquartile Range	2.41	0.98
1.33 (Std. Dev.)	1.9622	1.2010
6 (Std. Dev)	8.8518	5.418

10.76
cont.

Box-and-whisker Plot

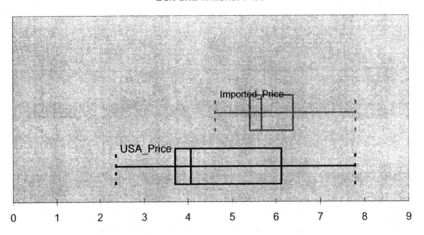

Normal Probability Plot (USA Price)

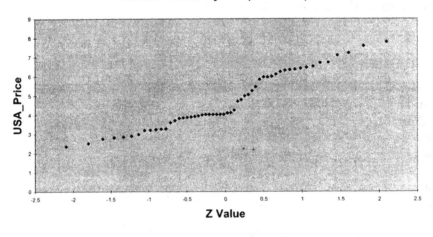

Normal Probability Plot (Imported Price)

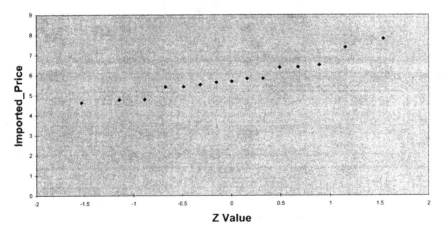

10.76 cont. The box-and-whisker plot, normal probability plot and summary statistics all suggest that the distributions of price of beers brewed in the U.S. and those imported are both skewed to the right. Since both distributions are quite far from being symmetrical, the normality assumption of the population distributions is violated for the price data set so the F test for difference in two variances is not appropriate here. Also the two sample variances suggest that the dispersions in the two populations are quite different. The sample size for beers brewed in the U.S. is quite large at 54 but the sample size for imported beers is only 15. Strictly speaking, neither the pooled-variance t test nor the separate variance t test for difference in the means is appropriate for the analysis of this data set. Nevertheless, the test result for the separate variance t test is reported next.

$H_0 : \mu_I = \mu_{II}$ Mean prices of domestic and imported beers are the same.

$H_1 : \mu_I \neq \mu_{II}$ Mean prices of domestic and imported beers are different.

Excel output:

t-Test: Two-Sample Assuming Unequal Variances

	U.S.	Imported
Mean	4.713333	5.862667
Variance	2.176626	0.815392
Observations	54	15
Hypothesized Mean Difference	0	
df	37	
t Stat	-3.73547	
P(T<=t) one-tail	0.000315	
t Critical one-tail	1.687094	
P(T<=t) two-tail	0.00063	
t Critical two-tail	2.02619	

Since the p-value of 0.00063 is less than the 5% level of significance, there is sufficient evidence to conclude that the mean prices are different between domestic and imported beers.

Calories:

	U.S.	Imported
Mean	143.3889	138.6
Standard Error	4.173844	7.129282
Median	148	148
Mode	143	148
Standard Deviation	30.67137	27.61159
Sample Variance	940.7327	762.4
Kurtosis	1.650411	1.632721
Skewness	-1.2957	-1.67381
Range	143	89
Minimum	58	71
Maximum	201	160
Sum	7743	2079
Count	54	15
First Quartile	142	140
Third Quartile	160	155

10.76
cont.

Normal Probability Plot of Calorie

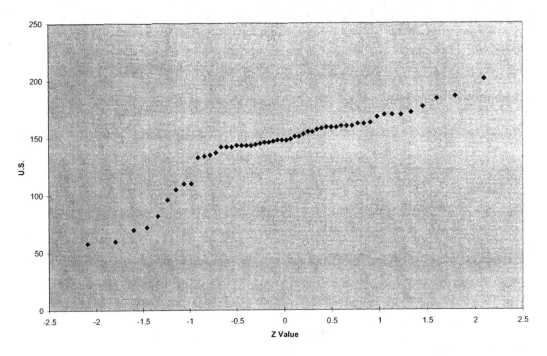

Normal Probability Plot of Calorie

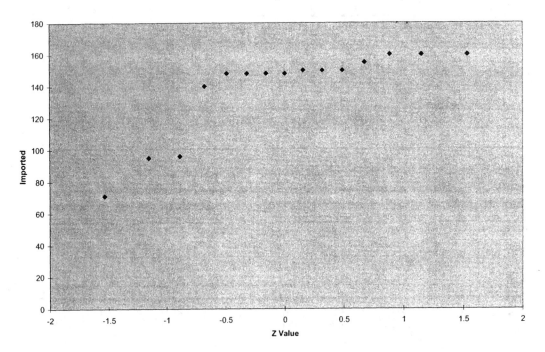

10.76
cont.

Box-and-whisker Plot of Calorie

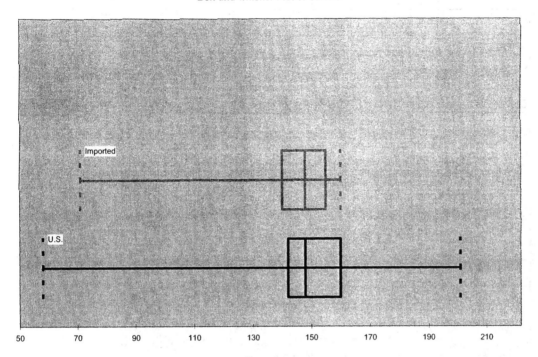

The normal probability plots, box-and-whisker plots and summary statistics all suggest that the distributions of calories of beers brewed in the U.S. and those imported are both skewed to the left. Since both distributions are quite far from being symmetrical, the normality assumption of the population distributions is violated for the calorie data set so the F test for difference in two variances is not appropriate here. The two sample variances, however, suggest that the dispersions in the two populations are not very different. The pooled-variance t test is appropriate for the analysis of this data set.

$H_0 : \mu_I = \mu_{II}$ Mean calories of domestic and imported beers are the same.

$H_1 : \mu_I \neq \mu_{II}$ Mean calories of domestic and imported beers are different.

10.76   Excel output:
cont.

t Test for Differences in Two Means	
Data	
Hypothesized Difference	0
Level of Significance	0.05
Population 1 Sample	
Sample Size	54
Sample Mean	143.3889
Sample Standard Deviation	30.67137
Population 2 Sample	
Sample Size	15
Sample Mean	138.6
Sample Standard Deviation	27.61159
Intermediate Calculations	
Population 1 Sample Degrees of Freedom	53
Population 2 Sample Degrees of Freedom	14
Total Degrees of Freedom	67
Pooled Variance	903.4693
Difference in Sample Means	4.7889
t-Test Statistic	0.54588
Two-Tailed Test	
Lower Critical Value	-1.99601
Upper Critical Value	1.996009
p-Value	0.586962
Do not reject the null hypothesis	

Since the p-value of 0.587 is greater than the 5% level of significance, do not reject the null hypothesis. There is insufficient evidence to conclude that there is any difference in mean calories between domestic beers and imported beers.

Alcohol content:

	U.S.	Imported
Mean	4.5	4.133333
Standard Error	0.208586	0.450256
Median	4.9	4.9
Mode	4.9	5
Standard Deviation	1.532786	1.743833
Sample Variance	2.349434	3.040952
Kurtosis	4.782198	3.274632
Skewness	-2.35183	-2.07045
Range	6	5.6
Minimum	0	0
Maximum	6	5.6
Sum	243	62
Count	54	15
First Quartile	4.5	4.1
Third Quartile	5.3	5

10.76
cont.

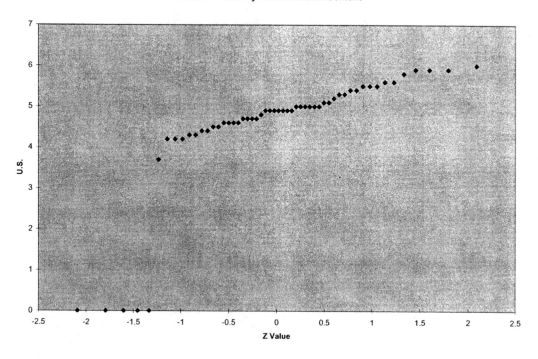

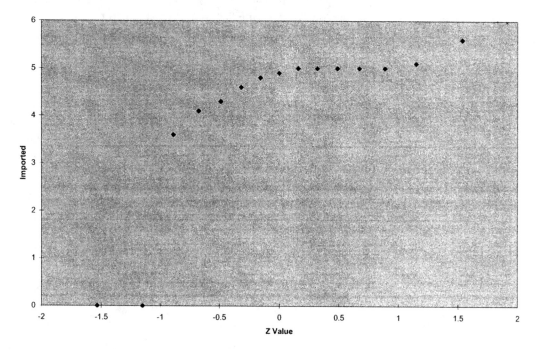

10.76
cont.

Box-and-whisker Plot of Alcohol Content

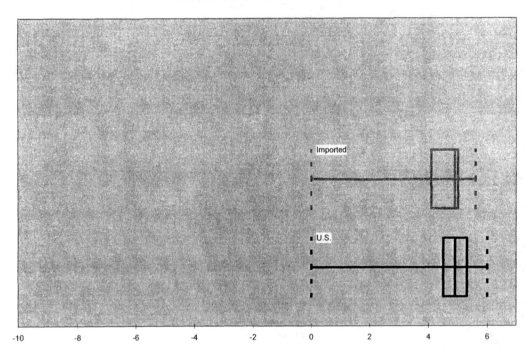

The normal probability plots, box-and-whisker plots and summary statistics all suggest that the distributions of alcohol content of beers brewed in the U.S. and those imported are both skewed to the left. Since both distributions are quite far from being symmetrical, the normality assumption of the population distributions is violated for the alcohol content data set so the F test for difference in two variances is not appropriate here. The two sample variances, however, suggest that the dispersions in the two populations are not very different. The pooled-variance t test is appropriate for the analysis of this data set.

$H_0 : \mu_I = \mu_{II}$ Mean alcohol contents of domestic and imported beers are the same.

$H_1 : \mu_I \neq \mu_{II}$ Mean alcohol contents of domestic and imported beers are different.

10.76 PHStat output:
cont.

t Test for Differences in Two Means	
Data	
Hypothesized Difference	0
Level of Significance	0.05
Population 1 Sample	
Sample Size	54
Sample Mean	4.5
Sample Standard Deviation	1.532786
Population 2 Sample	
Sample Size	15
Sample Mean	4.13333
Sample Standard Deviation	1.743833
Intermediate Calculations	
Population 1 Sample Degrees of Freedom	53
Population 2 Sample Degrees of Freedom	14
Total Degrees of Freedom	67
Pooled Variance	2.49393
Difference in Sample Means	0.36667
t-Test Statistic	0.79552
Two-Tailed Test	
Lower Critical Value	-1.99601
Upper Critical Value	1.996009
p-Value	0.42912
Do not reject the null hypothesis	

Since the p-value of 0.429 is greater than the 5% level of significance, do not reject the null hypothesis. There is insufficient evidence to conclude that there is any difference in mean alcohol content between domestic beers and imported beers.

10.78   (a) $H_0 : \sigma_1^2 = \sigma_2^2$ vs. $H_1 : \sigma_1^2 \neq \sigma_2^2$

F Test for Differences in Two Variances	
Data	
Level of Significance	0.05
Population 1 Sample	
Sample Size	43
Sample Standard Deviation	8109.497
Population 2 Sample	
Sample Size	37
Sample Standard Deviation	4437.92
Intermediate Calculations	
F-Test Statistic	3.339096
Population 1 Sample Degrees of Freedom	42
Population 2 Sample Degrees of Freedom	36
Two-Tailed Test	
Lower Critical Value	0.532047
Upper Critical Value	1.909555
p-Value	0.000361
Reject the null hypothesis	

Since *p*-value = 0.000361 < 0.05, reject H_0. There is evidence of a difference between the variances in the attendance at games with promotions and games without promotions.

(b)   Since the variances cannot assumed to be equal, a separate-variance *t* test for differences in two means should be used.

$H_0 : \mu_I = \mu_{II}$ Mean attendance at games with promotions and games without promotions are the same.

$H_1 : \mu_I \neq \mu_{II}$ Mean attendance at games with promotions and games without promotions are different.

t-Test: Two-Sample Assuming Unequal Variances

	Y	N
Mean	20748.93	13935.7
Variance	65763939	19695135
Observations	43	37
Hypothesized Mean Difference	0	
df	67	
t Stat	4.745049	
P(T<=t) one-tail	5.67E-06	
t Critical one-tail	1.667916	
P(T<=t) two-tail	1.13E-05	
t Critical two-tail	1.996009	

Since the *p*-value is essentially zero, reject H_0.

(c)   There is evidence that there is a difference in the mean attendance at games with promotions and games without promotions at 5% level of significance.

10.80

Normal Probability Plot

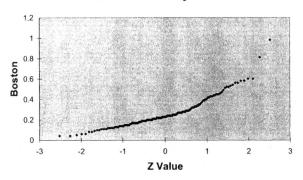

Normal Probability Plot

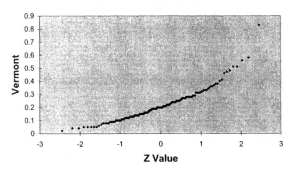

The normal probability plots suggest that the two populations are not normally distributed so an F test is inappropriate for testing the difference in two variances. The sample variances for Boston and Vermont shingles are 0.0203 and 0.015, respectively, which are not very different. It appears that a pooled-variance t test is appropriate for testing the difference in means.

$H_0 : \mu_B = \mu_V$ Mean granule loss of Boston and Vermont shingles are the same.

$H_1 : \mu_B \neq \mu_V$ Mean granule loss of Boston and Vermont shingles are different.

t-Test: Two-Sample Assuming Equal Variances

	Boston	Vermont
Mean	0.264059	0.218
Variance	0.020273	0.015055
Observations	170	140
Pooled Variance	0.017918	
Hypothesized Mean Difference	0	
df	308	
t Stat	3.014921	
P(T<=t) one-tail	0.001392	
t Critical one-tail	1.649817	
P(T<=t) two-tail	0.002784	
t Critical two-tail	1.967696	

Since the p-value = 0.0028 is less than the 5% level of significance, reject H_0. There is sufficient evidence to conclude that there is a difference in the mean granule loss of Boston and Vermont shingles.

CHAPTER 11

OBJECTIVES
- To understand the concepts of experimental design
- To be able to use the one-way ANOVA procedure to test for differences among the means of several groups
- To understand when to use a randomized block design
- To be able to use the two-way analysis of variance and interpret the interaction

OVERVIEW AND KEY CONCEPTS

General Experimental Setting
- Investigators have control over one or more independent variables called treatment variables or factors.
- Each treatment factor has two or more levels.
- Investigators observe the effects on the dependent variable, i.e., the response to the levels of the independent variable(s).
- **Experimental Design:** The plan used to test a hypothesis.

The Completely Randomized Design
- The experimental units (subjects) are assigned randomly to treatments.
- The subjects are assumed to be homogenous.
- There is only one factor or independent variable with two or more treatment levels.
- The completely randomized design will be analyzed by one-way ANOVA.

Some Important Identities in the Completely Randomized Design
- $SST = SSA + SSW$

- $SST = \sum_{j=1}^{c} \sum_{i=1}^{n_j} (X_{ij} - \bar{\bar{X}})^2$

- $SSA = \sum_{j=1}^{c} n_j (\bar{X}_j - \bar{\bar{X}})^2$

- $SSW = \sum_{j=1}^{c} \sum_{i=1}^{n_j} (X_{ij} - \bar{X}_j)^2$

- $MSA = \dfrac{SSA}{c-1}$

- $MSW = \dfrac{SSW}{n-c}$

where n: the total number of observations in the sample

c: the number of groups

n_j: the number of observations in group j

X_{ij} : the ith observation in group j

$$\overline{\overline{X}} = \frac{\sum_{j=1}^{c}\sum_{i=1}^{n_j} X_{ij}}{c} : \text{the overall or grand mean}$$

$\overline{X}_j$: the sample mean of group j

F Test for Differences in More than Two Means

- **Assumptions:**
    - Samples are randomly and independently drawn.
    - Populations are normally distributed. The F test is robust to violation of this assumption.
    - Populations have equal variances. The F test is less sensitive to violation of this assumption when samples are of equal size from each population.
- **The null and alternative hypotheses:**
    - $H_0 : \mu_1 = \mu_2 = \cdots = \mu_c$ There is no treatment effect
    - $H_1 :$ Not all μ_j are the same. There is some treatment effect.
- **Test statistic:**
    - $F = \dfrac{MSA}{MSW}$ with $(c-1)$ numerator degrees of freedom and $(n-c)$ denominator degrees of freedom
    - The F test always has the rejection region in the right tail.

One-way ANOVA Summary Table

Source of Variation	Degrees of Freedom	Sum of Squares	Mean Squares (Variance)	F Statistic
Among (Factor)	$c-1$	SSA	$MSA = SSA/(c-1)$	MSA/MSW
Within (Error)	$n-c$	SSW	$MSW = SSW/(n-c)$	
Total	$n-1$	$SST = SSA + SSW$		

The Tukey-Kramer Procedure for the Completely Randomized Design
- A post hoc (a posteriori) procedure performed after rejection of the null hypothesis of equal means.
- Enables pair-wise comparison to see which pair of means is significantly different.
- **The Tukey-Kramer procedure:**
    1. Compute the absolute difference between any pair of sample means $\left| \overline{X}_j - \overline{X}_{j'} \right|$
    2. Compute the critical range for that pair of sample means using

    $$\text{Critical Range} = Q_{U(c,n-c)} \sqrt{\frac{MSW}{2} \left(\frac{1}{n_j} + \frac{1}{n_{j'}} \right)} \text{ where } Q_{U(c,n-c)} \text{ is the upper-tail critical}$$

    value from the Studentized range distribution with c numerator degrees of freedom and $(n-c)$ denominator degrees of freedom, and n_j and $n_{j'}$ are the two sample sizes for the pair of samples.

    3. The population means of a specific pair are declared significantly different if $\left| \overline{X}_j - \overline{X}_{j'} \right|$ is greater than the critical range.

Levene's Test for Homogeneity of Variance
- Used to test the assumption of equal group variances required in the F test for difference in more than two means.
- **The null and alternative hypotheses:**
    - $H_0 : \sigma_1^2 = \sigma_2^2 = \cdots = \sigma_c^2$ All group variances are the same.
    - H_1 : Not all σ_j^2 are the same. Not all group variances are the same.
- **The Levene's test procedure:**
    - For each observation in each group, obtain the absolute value of the difference between each observation and the median of the group.
    - Carry out a one-way analysis of variance on these absolute differences.

The Randomized Block Design
- Items are divided into blocks by matching individual items in different samples or taking repeated measurement of the same individuals to reduce within group variation (i.e. remove the effect of block before testing).
- Response of each treatment group is obtained.
- **Assumptions:**
    - Samples are randomly and independently drawn.
    - Populations are normally distributed. The F test is robust to violation of this assumption.
    - Populations have equal variances. The F test is less sensitive to violation of this assumption when samples are of equal size from each population.
    - There is no interaction between the levels of treatment and block.

Some Important Identities in the Randomized Block Design

- $SST = SSA + SSBL + SSE$

- $SST = \sum_{j=1}^{c} \sum_{i=1}^{r} \left(X_{ij} - \bar{\bar{X}} \right)^2$

- $SSA = r \sum_{j=1}^{c} \left(\bar{X}_{\bullet j} - \bar{\bar{X}} \right)^2$

- $SSBL = c \sum_{i=1}^{r} \left(\bar{X}_{i \bullet} - \bar{\bar{X}} \right)^2$

- $SSE = \sum_{j=1}^{c} \sum_{i=1}^{r} \left(X_{ij} - \bar{X}_{i \bullet} - \bar{X}_{\bullet j} + \bar{\bar{X}} \right)^2$

- $MSA = \dfrac{SSA}{c-1}$

- $MSBL = \dfrac{SSBL}{r-1}$

- $MSE = \dfrac{SSE}{(r-1)(c-1)}$

    where n: total number of observations $(n = rc)$

    r: the number of blocks

    c: the number of groups or levels

    X_{ij} : the value of the ith block for the jth treatment

$$\bar{X}_{i \bullet} = \frac{\sum_{j=1}^{c} X_{ij}}{c} \quad : \text{the mean of all values in block } i$$

$$\bar{X}_{\bullet j} = \frac{\sum_{i=1}^{r} X_{ij}}{r} : \text{the mean of all values for treatment level } j$$

$$\bar{\bar{X}} = \frac{\sum_{j=1}^{c} \sum_{i=1}^{r} X_{ij}}{rc} : \text{the overall or grand mean}$$

The Randomized Block F Test for Differences in c Means

- **The null and alternative hypotheses:**

    - $H_0 : \mu_{\bullet 1} = \mu_{\bullet 2} = \cdots = \mu_{\bullet c}$ No treatment effect

    - $H_1 :$ Not all $\mu_{\bullet j}$ are equal   There is some treatment effect

- **Test statistic:**

    - $F = \dfrac{MSA}{MSE}$ with $(c-1)$ numerator degrees of freedom and $(r-1)(c-1)$ denominator degrees of freedom.

    - The rejection region is always in the right tail.

The Randomized Block F Test for Block Effect
- **The null and alternative hypotheses:**
    - $H_0 : \mu_{1.} = \mu_{2.} = \cdots = \mu_{r.}$ There is no block effect
    - H_1 : Not all $\mu_{i.}$ are equal   There is some block effect
- **Test statistic:**
    - $F = \dfrac{MSBL}{MSE}$ with $(r-1)$ numerator degrees of freedom and $(r-1)(c-1)$
      denominator degrees of freedom.
    - The rejection region is always in the right tail.

ANOVA Table for the Randomized Block Design

Source of Variation	Degrees of Freedom	Sum of Squares	Mean Squares	F Statistic
Among Treatment	$c-1$	SSA	MSA = SSA/(c − 1)	MSA/ MSE
Among Block	$r-1$	SSBL	MSBL = SSBL/(r − 1)	MSBL/ MSE
Error	$(r-1) \cdot (c-1)$	SSE	MSE = SSE/[(r − 1)•(c− 1)]	
Total	$rc-1$	SST		

The Tukey-Kramer Procedure for the Randomized Block Design
- Similar to the Tukey-Kramer procedure for the completely randomized design except the
  critical range $= Q_{U(c,(r-1)(c-1))}\sqrt{\dfrac{MSE}{r}}$, in which $Q_{U(c,(r-1)(c-1))}$ has c degrees of freedom in
  the numerator and $(r-1)(c-1)$ degrees of freedom in the denominator.

The Two-Factor Factorial Design
- There is one dependent variable and two treatment factors.
- There can be interaction between the two treatment factors.
- **Assumptions:**
    - Populations are normally distributed.
    - Populations have equal variances.
    - Samples are drawn independently and randomly.

Some Important Identities in the Two-Factor Factorial Design

- $SST = SSA + SSB + SSAB + SSE$

- $SST = \sum_{i=1}^{r} \sum_{j=1}^{c} \sum_{k=1}^{n'} \left(X_{ijk} - \bar{\bar{X}} \right)^2$

- $SSA = cn' \sum_{i=1}^{r} \left(\bar{X}_{i..} - \bar{\bar{X}} \right)^2$

- $SSB = rn' \sum_{j=1}^{c} \left(\bar{X}_{.j.} - \bar{\bar{X}} \right)^2$

- $SSAB = n' \sum_{i=1}^{r} \sum_{j=1}^{c} \left(\bar{X}_{ij.} - \bar{X}_{i..} - \bar{X}_{.j.} + \bar{\bar{X}} \right)^2$

- $SSE = \sum_{i=1}^{r} \sum_{j=1}^{c} \sum_{k=1}^{n'} \left(X_{ijk} - \bar{X}_{ij.} \right)^2$

- $MSA = \dfrac{SSA}{r-1}$

- $MSB = \dfrac{SSB}{c-1}$

- $MSAB = \dfrac{SSAB}{(r-1)(c-1)}$

- $MSE = \dfrac{SSE}{rc(n'-1)}$

where n: total number of observations $\left(n = rcn' \right)$

r: the number of level of factor A

c: the number of level of factor B

n': the number of replication in each cell (combination of a particular level of factor A and a particular level of factor B)

X_{ijk}: the value of the kth observation for level i of factor A and level j of factor B

$$\bar{X}_{i..} = \frac{\sum_{j=1}^{c} \sum_{k=1}^{n'} X_{ijk}}{cn'} \quad \text{: the mean of the } i^{th} \text{ level of factor } A$$

$$\bar{X}_{.j.} = \frac{\sum_{i=1}^{r} \sum_{k=1}^{n'} X_{ijk}}{rn'} \quad \text{: the mean of the } j^{th} \text{ level of factor } B$$

$$\bar{X}_{ij.} = \sum_{k=1}^{n'} \frac{X_{ijk}}{n'} \text{: mean of the cell } ij, \text{ the combination of the } i^{th} \text{ level of factor } A \text{ and } j^{th}$$

level of factor B

$$\overline{\overline{X}} = \frac{\sum_{j=1}^{c}\sum_{i=1}^{r}\sum_{k=1}^{n'} X_{ijk}}{rcn'} \text{ : the overall or grand mean}$$

The Two-Factor Factorial Design F Test for Interaction
- **The null and alternative hypotheses:**
  - H_0 : The interaction of A and B is equal to zero
  - H_1 : The interaction of A and B is not equal to zero
- **Test statistic:**
  - $F = \dfrac{MSAB}{MSE}$ with $(r-1)(c-1)$ numerator degrees of freedom and $rc(n'-1)$ denominator degrees of freedom.
  - The rejection region is always in the right tail.
  - In the two-factor factorial design, the test for interaction should be performed prior to the tests for factor A effect and factor B effect.
  - Only when there is no evidence of interaction will the test and interpretation of the main effect be meaningful.

The Two-Factor Factorial Design F Test for Factor A Effect
- **The null and alternative hypotheses:**
  - $H_0 : \mu_{1..} = \mu_{2..} = \cdots = \mu_{r..}$ There is no factor A treatment effect
  - H_1 : Not all $\mu_{i..}$ are equal   There is some factor A treatment effect
- **Test statistic:**
  - $F = \dfrac{MSA}{MSE}$ with $(r-1)$ numerator degrees of freedom and $rc(n'-1)$ denominator degrees of freedom.
  - The rejection region is always in the right tail.
  - This main effect test should be performed only after the test for interaction has concluded that there is insufficient evidence of interaction between factor A and B.

The Two-Factor Factorial Design F Test for Factor B Effect
- **The null and alternative hypotheses:**
  - $H_0 : \mu_{.1.} = \mu_{.2.} = \cdots = \mu_{.c.}$ There is no factor B treatment effect
  - H_1 : Not all $\mu_{.j.}$ are equal   There is some factor B treatment effect
- **Test statistic:**
  - $F = \dfrac{MSB}{MSE}$ with $(c-1)$ numerator degrees of freedom and $rc(n'-1)$ denominator degrees of freedom.
  - The rejection region is always in the right tail.
  - This main effect test should be performed only after the test for interaction has concluded that there is insufficient evidence of interaction between factor A and B.

ANOVA Table for the Two-Factor Factorial Design

Source of Variation	Degrees of Freedom	Sum of Squares	Mean Squares	F Statistic
Factor A (Row)	$r - 1$	SSA	$MSA = SSA/(r - 1)$	MSA/MSE
Factor B (Column)	$c - 1$	SSB	$MSB = SSB/(c - 1)$	MSB/MSE
AB (Interaction)	$(r - 1)(c - 1)$	SSAB	$MSAB = SSAB/[(r - 1)(c - 1)]$	MSAB/MSE
Error	$r \cdot c \cdot (n' - 1)$	SSE	$MSE = SSE/[r \cdot c \cdot (n' - 1)]$	
Total	$r \cdot c \cdot n' - 1$	SST		

The Tukey-Kramer Procedure for the Two-Factor Factorial Design

- **For factor A:** Similar to the Tukey-Kramer procedure for the completely randomized design except the critical range $= Q_{U(r, rc(n'-1))} \sqrt{\dfrac{MSE}{rn'}}$, in which $Q_{U(r, rc(n'-1))}$ has $= r$ degrees of freedom in the numerator and $rc(n' - 1)$ degrees of freedom in the denominator.

- **For factor B:** Similar to the Tukey-Kramer procedure for the completely randomized design except the critical range $= Q_{U(c, rc(n'-1))} \sqrt{\dfrac{MSE}{rn'}}$, in which $Q_{U(c, rc(n'-1))}$ has $= c$ degrees of freedom in the numerator and $rc(n' - 1)$ degrees of freedom in the denominator.

- These multiple comparisons should be performed only after the test for interaction has concluded that there is insufficient evidence of interaction between factor A and B.

SOLUTIONS TO END OF SECTION
AND CHAPTER REVIEW EVEN PROBLEMS

11.2   (a) $SSW = SST - SSA = 210 - 60 = 150$

(b) $MSA = \dfrac{SSA}{c-1} = \dfrac{60}{5-1} = 15$

(c) $MSW = \dfrac{SSW}{n-c} = \dfrac{150}{35-5} = 5$

(d) $F = \dfrac{MSA}{MSW} = \dfrac{15}{5} = 3$

11.4   (a) $df\,A = c - 1 = 3 - 1 = 2$

(b) $df\,W = n - c = 21 - 3 = 18$

(c) $df\,T = n - 1 = 21 - 1 = 20$

11.6   (a)   Decision rule: If $F > 2.95$.

(b)   Since $F_{cal} = 4$ is greater than the critical bound of 2.95, reject H_0.

(c)   There are $c = 4$ degrees of freedom in the numerator and $n - c = 32 - 4 = 28$ degrees of freedom in the denominator. The table does not have 28 degrees of freedom in the denominator so use the next larger critical value, $Q_U = 3.90$.

(d)   To perform the Tukey-Kramer procedure, the critical range is

$$Q_U \sqrt{\frac{MSW}{2}\left(\frac{1}{n_j} + \frac{1}{n_j}\right)} = 3.90\sqrt{\frac{20}{2}\left(\frac{1}{8} + \frac{1}{8}\right)} = 6.166.$$

11.8   (a) $H_0: \mu_1 = \mu_2 = \mu_3$ where 1 = Experts, 2 = Readers, 3 = Darts

$H_1:$ Not all μ_j are equal   where $j = 1, 2, 3$

Decision Rule: If p-value < 0.05, reject H_0.

SPSS output:

	Sum of Squares	df	Mean Square	F	Sig.
Between Groups	9195.435	2	4597.718	10.994	.004
Within Groups	3763.928	9	418.214		
Total	12959.363	11			

Since p-value $= 0.004 < 0.05$, reject the null hypothesis. There is enough evidence to conclude that there is a significant difference in the mean returns for the three categories.

11.8   (b)   To determine which of the means are significantly different from one another, you use

cont.   the Tukey-Kramer procedure to establish the critical range: $Q_{U(c, n-c)} = Q_{U(3, 9)} = 3.95$

SPSS output
Multiple Comparisons
Dependent Variable: RETURNS
Tukey HSD

(I) FACTOR	(J) FACTOR	Mean Difference (I-J)	Std. Error	Sig.	95% Confidence Interval	
					Lower Bound	Upper Bound
1.00	2.00	48.9750	14.4605	.020	8.6008	89.3492
	3.00	-16.1250	14.4605	.529	-56.4992	24.2492
2.00	1.00	-48.9750	14.4605	.020	-89.3492	-8.6008
	3.00	-65.1000	14.4605	.004	-105.4742	-24.7258
3.00	1.00	16.1250	14.4605	.529	-24.2492	56.4992
	2.00	65.1000	14.4605	.004	24.7258	105.4742

* The mean difference is significant at the .05 level.

At 5% level of significance, the Tukey Kramer multiple comparison test shows that there is enough evidence to conclude that Experts and Readers, and Readers and Darts differ in mean return.

(c)   The data collected are the returns of the selected stocks by the 3 categories not the amount of drops compared to the previous returns of the stocks. Even if mean returns are concerned, the experts have the sample mean return of 6.475% while the readers have a sample mean return of –42.5%, and the stocks chosen using the darts have a sample mean return of 22.6%. However, these differences in sample means do not lead to the conclusion of significant differences between the Expert and Darts in population means according to the result of the Tukey-Kramer multiple comparison procedure in part (b).

(d) $H_0: \sigma_1^2 = \sigma_2^2 = \sigma_3^2$ H_1: At least one variance is different.

Minitab output for Levene's test for homogeneity of variance:
Test of Homogeneity of Variances
Levene's Test (any continuous distribution)

Test Statistic: 0.101
P-Value   : 0.905

Since the p-value = 0.905 > 0.05, do not reject H_0. There is not enough evidence to conclude there is a significant difference in the variation in the return for the three categories.

11.10   (a) $H_0: \mu_A = \mu_B = \mu_C = \mu_D$ H_1: At least one mean is different.

$$MSA = \frac{SSA}{c-1} = \frac{1986.475}{3} = 662.1583$$

$$MSW = \frac{SSW}{n-c} = \frac{495.5}{36} = 13.7639$$

$$F = \frac{MSA}{MSW} = \frac{662.1583}{13.76389} = 48.1084$$

$$F_{\alpha,c-1,n-c} = F_{0.05,3,36} = 2.8663$$

ANOVA

Source of Variation	SS	df	MS	F	P-value	F crit
Between Groups	1986.475	3	662.1583	48.10838	1.12E-12	2.866265
Within Groups	495.5	36	13.76389			
Total	2481.975	39				

Since the p-value is essentially zero and $F = 48.1084 > 2.8663$, you can reject H_0. There is sufficient evidence to conclude there is a difference in the mean strength of the four brands of trash bags.

(b)

Tukey Kramer Multiple Comparisons							
Group	Sample Mean	Sample Size	Comparison	Absolute Difference	Std. Error of Difference	Critical Range	Results
1	35.4	10	Group 1 to Group 2	0.9	1.17319601	4.446	Means are not different
2	36.3	10	Group 1 to Group 3	0.5	1.17319601	4.446	Means are not different
3	34.9	10	Group 1 to Group 4	16.1	1.17319601	4.446	Means are different
4	19.3	10	Group 2 to Group 3	1.4	1.17319601	4.446	Means are not different
			Group 2 to Group 4	17	1.17319601	4.446	Means are different
Other Data			Group 3 to Group 4	15.6	1.17319601	4.446	Means are different
Level of significance	0.05						
Numerator d.f.	4						
Denominator d.f.	36						
MSW	13.76389						
Q Statistic	3.79						

$Q_u = 3.79$

$$\text{Critical range} = Q_u \sqrt{\frac{MSW}{2}\left(\frac{1}{n_j} + \frac{1}{n_j}\right)} = 3.79 \sqrt{\frac{13.7639}{2}\left(\frac{1}{10} + \frac{1}{10}\right)} = 4.446$$

From the Tukey-Kramer procedure, there is a difference in mean strength between Kroger and Tuffstuff, Glad and Tuffstuff, and Hefty and Tuffstuff.

11.10   (c) H_0: $\sigma_A^2 = \sigma_B^2 = \sigma_C^2 = \sigma_D^2$ H_1: At least one variance is different.

cont.

	Data			
	KROGER	**GLAD**	**HEFTY**	**TUFFSTUFF**
	34	32	33	26
	30	42	34	18
	40	34	32	20
	38	36	40	15
	36	32	40	20
	30	40	34	20
	30	36	36	17
	42	43	34	18
	36	30	32	19
	38	38	34	20
Median	36	36	34	19.5
	Absolute Difference from the Median			
	KROGER	**GLAD**	**HEFTY**	**TUFFSTUFF**
	2	4	1	6.5
	6	6	0	1.5
	4	2	2	0.5
	2	0	6	4.5
	0	4	6	0.5
	6	4	0	0.5
	6	0	2	2.5
	6	7	0	1.5
	0	6	2	0.5
	2	2	0	0.5

ANOVA output for Levene's test for homogeneity of variance:

ANOVA

Source of Variation	SS	df	MS	F	P-value	F crit
Between Groups	24.075	3	8.025	1.457619	0.242358	2.866265
Within Groups	198.2	36	5.505556			
Total	222.275	39				

$$MSA = \frac{SSA}{c-1} = \frac{24.075}{3} = 8.025$$

$$MSW = \frac{SSW}{n-c} = \frac{198.2}{36} = 5.5056$$

$$F = \frac{MSA}{MSW} = \frac{8.025}{5.5056} = 1.4576$$

$$F_{\alpha,c-1,n-c} = F_{0.05,3,36} = 2.8663$$

Since the p-value = 0.2423 > 0.05 and F = 1.458 < 2.866, do not reject H_0. There is not sufficient evidence to conclude that the variances in strength among the four brands of trash bags are different.

(d)   From the results obtained in (a) and (b), Tuffstuff has the lowest mean strength and should be avoided.

11.12 (a) $H_0: \mu_A = \mu_B = \mu_C = \mu_D = \mu_E$ H_1: At least one mean is different.

ANOVA

Source of Variation	SS	df	MS	F	P-value	F crit
Between Groups	377.8667	4	94.46667	12.56206	9.74E-06	2.758711
Within Groups	188	25	7.52			
Total	565.8667	29				

Since the p-value is essentially zero, reject H_0. There is evidence of a difference in the mean rating of the five advertisements.

(b)

Tukey Kramer Multiple Comparisons							
	Sample	Sample		Absolute	Std. Error	Critical	
Group	Mean	Size	Comparison	Difference	of Difference	Range	Results
1	18	6	Group 1 to Group 2	0.333333	1.11952371	4.668	Means are not different
2	17.66667	6	Group 1 to Group 3	6.666667	1.11952371	4.668	Means are different
3	11.33333	6	Group 1 to Group 4	9	1.11952371	4.668	Means are different
4	9	6	Group 1 to Group 5	2.666667	1.11952371	4.668	Means are not different
5	15.33333	6	Group 2 to Group 3	6.333333	1.11952371	4.668	Means are different
			Group 2 to Group 4	8.666667	1.11952371	4.668	Means are different
Other Data			Group 2 to Group 5	2.333333	1.11952371	4.668	Means are not different
Level of significance	0.05		Group 3 to Group 4	2.333333	1.11952371	4.668	Means are not different
Numerator d.f.	5		Group 3 to Group 5	4	1.11952371	4.668	Means are not different
Denominator d.f.	25		Group 4 to Group 5	6.333333	1.11952371	4.668	Means are different
MSW	7.52						
Q Statistic	4.17						

There is a difference in the mean rating between advertisement A and C, between A and D, between B and C, between B and D and between D and E.

(c) $H_0: \sigma_A^2 = \sigma_B^2 = \sigma_C^2 = \sigma_D^2 = \sigma_E^2$ H_1: At least one variance is different.

ANOVA output for Levene's test for homogeneity of variance:

ANOVA

Source of Variation	SS	df	MS	F	P-value	F crit
Between Groups	14.13333	4	3.533333	1.927273	0.137107	2.758711
Within Groups	45.83333	25	1.833333			
Total	59.96667	29				

Since the p-value = 0.137 > 0.05, do not reject H_0. There is not enough evidence to conclude there is a difference in the variation in rating among the five advertisements.

(d) There is no significant difference between advertisement A and B, and they have the highest mean rating among the five and should be used. There is no significant difference between advertisement C and D, and they are among the lowest in mean rating and should be avoided.

11.14 (a) To test at the 0.05 level of significance whether there is any evidence of a difference in the mean distance traveled by the golf balls differing in design, you conduct an F test:

H_0: $\mu_1 = \mu_2 = \mu_3 = \mu_4$ $\qquad$ H_1: At least one mean is different.

Decision rule: df: 3, 36. If $F > 2.866$, reject H_0.

ANOVA

Source of Variation	SS	df	MS	F	P-value	F crit
Between Groups	2990.99	3	996.9966	53.02982	2.73E-13	2.866265
Within Groups	676.8244	36	18.80068			
Total	3667.814	39				

Since $F_{calc} = 53.03$ is greater than the critical bound of $F = 2.866$, reject H_0. There is enough evidence to conclude that there is significant difference in the mean distance traveled by the golf balls differing in design.

Note: The critical bound of F is obtained using Excel. The critical bound of F using the Table in the text with 3 numerator and 30 denominator degrees of freedom is 2.92.

(b) To determine which of the means are significantly different from one another, you use the Tukey-Kramer procedure to establish the critical range:

$Q_{U(c, n-c)} = Q_{U(4, 36)}$. You use $Q_{U(4, 40)} = 3.79$

critical range $= Q_{U(c,n-c)} \cdot \sqrt{\dfrac{MSW}{2} \cdot \left(\dfrac{1}{n_j} + \dfrac{1}{n_{j'}}\right)} = 3.79 \cdot \sqrt{\dfrac{18.8007}{2} \cdot \left(\dfrac{1}{10} + \dfrac{1}{10}\right)} =$

5.1967

Tukey Kramer Multiple Comparisons					
	Sample	Sample		Absolute	
Group	Mean	Size	Comparison	Difference	Results
1	206.614	10	Group 1 to Group 2	11.902	Means are different
2	218.516	10	Group 1 to Group 3	19.974	Means are different
3	226.588	10	Group 1 to Group 4	22.008	Means are different
4	228.622	10	Group 2 to Group 3	8.072	Means are different
			Group 2 to Group 4	10.106	Means are different
MSW	18.800677		Group 3 to Group 4	2.034	Means are not different

At 5% level of significance, there is enough evidence to conclude that mean traveling distances between all pairs of designs are different with the only exception of the pair between design 3 and design 4.

(c) The assumptions needed in (a) are (i) samples are randomly and independently drawn, (ii) populations are normally distributed, and (iii) populations have equal variances.

11.14   (d)   To test at the 0.05 level of significance whether the variation within the groups is
cont.   similar for all groups, you conduct a Levene's test for homogeneity of variance:

$H_0: \sigma_1^2 = \sigma_2^2 = \sigma_3^2 = \sigma_4^2$ H_1: At least one variance is different.

ANOVA

Source of Variation	SS	df	MS	F	P-value	F crit
Between Groups	40.63675	3	13.54558	2.093228	0.118276	2.866265
Within Groups	232.9613	36	6.471147			
Total	273.598	39				

Since p-value $= 0.1183 > 0.05$, do not reject the null hypothesis. There is not enough
evidence to conclude that there is any difference in the variation of the distance
traveled by the golf balls differing in design.

   (e)   In order to produce golf balls with the farthest traveling distance, either design 3 or 4
can be used.

11.16   (a) $SSE = SST - SSA - SSBL = 210 - 60 - 75 = 75$

   (b) $MSA = \dfrac{SSA}{c-1} = \dfrac{60}{4} = 15$

$MSBL = \dfrac{SSBL}{r-1} = \dfrac{75}{6} = 12.5$

$MSE = \dfrac{SSE}{(r-1)\cdot(c-1)} = \dfrac{75}{6\cdot4} = 3.125$

   (c) $F = \dfrac{MSA}{MSE} = \dfrac{15}{3.125} = 4.80$

   (d) $F = \dfrac{MSBL}{MSE} = \dfrac{12.5}{3.125} = 4.00$

11.18   (a)   There are 5 degrees of freedom in the numerator and 24 degrees of freedom in the
denominator.

   (b) $Q_{U[c,\,(r-1)(c-1)]} = Q_{U(5,\,24)} = 4.17$

   (c)   critical range $= Q_{U[c,\,(r-1)(c-1)]} \cdot \sqrt{\dfrac{MSE}{r}} = 4.17 \cdot \sqrt{\dfrac{3.125}{7}} = 2.786$

11.20   (a) $MSE = \dfrac{MSA}{F} = \dfrac{18}{6} = 3$

$SSE = (MSE)(df\,E) = (3)(12) = 36$

   (b) $SSBL = (F)(MSE)(df\,BL) = (4)(3)(6) = 72$

   (c) $SST = SSA + SSBL + SSE = 36 + 72 + 36 = 144$

   (d)   Since $F = 6 < F_{0.01,2,12} = 6.9266$, do not reject the null hypothesis of no treatment effect.
There is not enough evidence to conclude there is a treatment effect.
Since $F = 4.0 < F_{0.01,6,12} = 4.821$, do not reject the null hypothesis of no block effect.
There is not enough evidence to conclude there is a block effect.

11.22 (a) Decision rule: If $F > 3.07$, reject H_0.
Decision: Since $F_{calc} = 5.185$ is greater than the critical bound $F = 3.07$, reject H_0.
There is enough evidence to conclude that the treatment means are not all equal.

(b) Decision rule: If $F > 2.49$, reject H_0.
Decision: Since $F_{calc} = 5.000$ is greater than the critical bound $F = 2.49$, reject H_0.
There is enough evidence to conclude that the block means are not all equal.

11.24 (a) H_0: $\mu_A = \mu_B = \mu_C = \mu_D$ where A = Bazooka, B = Bubbletape, C = Babblevum, D = Bubblicious
H_1: At least one mean differs.

ANOVA

Source of Variation	SS	df	MS	F	P-value	F crit
Rows (students)	9.28125	3	3.09375	1.072202	0.408518	3.862539
Columns (brands)	16.625	3	5.541667	1.920578	0.196803	3.862539
Error	25.96875	9	2.885417			
Total	51.875	15				

$$MSA = \frac{SSA}{c-1} = \frac{16.625}{3} = 5.5417 \qquad MSE = \frac{SSE}{(r-1)(c-1)} = \frac{25.9688}{9} = 2.8854$$

$$F = \frac{MSA}{MSE} = \frac{5.5417}{2.8854} = 1.9206.$$

Since the p-value = 0.1968 > 0.05, do not reject H_0. There is no evidence of a difference in the mean diameter of the bubbles produced by the different brands.

(b) It is inappropriate to perform the Tukey procedure.

(c) H_0: $\mu_A = \mu_B = \mu_C = \mu_D$ where A = Kyle, B = Sarah, C = Leigh, D = Isaac
H_1: At least one mean differs.

$$MSBL = \frac{SSBL}{r-1} = \frac{9.2813}{3} = 3.0938$$

$$F = \frac{MSBL}{MSE} = \frac{3.0938}{2.8854} = 1.0722$$

Since the p-value = 0.4084 > 0.05, do not reject H_0. There is not enough evidence to conclude there is a difference in the mean diameter of the bubbles across the different students. Hence, there is no significant block effect in this experiment.

(d) From the conclusion in (c), there is not sufficient evidence to conclude that Kyle is the best at blowing big bubbles.

11.26 (a) $H_0: \mu_1 = \mu_2 = \mu_3 = \mu_4 = \mu_5$

where 1 = Itunes, 2 = Wal-Mart, 3 = MusicNow, 4 = Musicmatch, 5 = Napster

H_1: Not all μ_j are equal where $j = 1, 2, 3, 4, 5$

Excel output:

Source of Variation	SS	df	MS	F	P-value	F crit
Blocks	21.93014	4	5.482536	0.227351	0.919062	3.006917
Treatment	20.37742	4	5.094356	0.211254	0.928376	3.006917
Error	385.8375	16	24.11485			
Total	428.1451	24				

$F = 0.2113$. Since the p-value $= 0.9284 > 0.05$, do not reject H_0. There is not evidence of a difference in the mean prices for albums at the five digital music services.

(b) The assumptions needed are: (i) samples are randomly and independently drawn, (ii) populations are normally distributed, (iii) populations have equal variances and (iv) no interaction effect between treatments and blocks.

(c) Since there is not enough evidence of a difference in the mean prices for albums at the five digital music services, it is inappropriate to perform a Tukey procedure to determine which digital music services differ.

(d) $H_0: \mu_{1.} = \mu_{2.} = \cdots = \mu_{5.}$

H_1: Not all $\mu_{i.}$ are equal where $i = 1, 2, \cdots, 5$

$$F = \frac{MSBL}{MSE} = \frac{5.4825}{24.1148} = 0.2274.$$ Since the p-value $= 0.9191 > 0.05$, do not reject H_0. There is not enough evidence of a significant block effect in this experiment. The blocking has not been advantageous in reducing the experimental error.

11.28 (a) $H_0: \mu_1 = \mu_2 = \mu_3$ where 1 = 2 days, 2 = 7 days, 3 = 28 days

H_1: At least one mean differs.

Decision rule: If $F > 3.114$, reject H_0.

ANOVA

Source of Variation	SS	df	MS	F	P-value	F crit
Rows	21.17006	39	0.542822	5.752312	2.92E-11	1.553239
Columns	50.62835	2	25.31417	268.2556	1.09E-35	3.113797
Error	7.360538	78	0.094366			
Total	79.15894	119				

Test statistic: $F = 268.26$

Decision: Since $F_{calc} = 268.26$ is greater than the critical bound $F = 3.114$, reject H_0. There is enough evidence to conclude that there is a difference in the mean compressive strength after 2, 7 and 28 days.

11.28   (b)   From Table E.10, $Q_{U(3, 78)} \Rightarrow Q_{U(3, 60)} = 3.4$.

cont.   critical range $= Q_{U(c,(r-1)(c-1))} \cdot \sqrt{\dfrac{MSE}{r}} = 3.4 \cdot \sqrt{\dfrac{0.0944}{40}} = 0.1651$

$\left| \bar{X}_1 - \bar{X}_2 \right| = 0.5531^*$ $\left| \bar{X}_1 - \bar{X}_3 \right| = 1.5685^*$ $\left| \bar{X}_2 - \bar{X}_3 \right| = 1.0154^*$

At the 0.05 level of significance, all of the comparisons are significant. This is consistent with the results of the F-test indicating that there is significant difference in the mean compressive strength after 2, 7 and 28 days.

(c) $RE = \dfrac{(r-1)MSBL + r(c-1)MSE}{(rc-1)MSE} = \dfrac{39 \cdot 0.5428 + 40 \cdot 2 \cdot 0.0943}{119 \cdot 0.0943} = 2.558$

(d)

Box-and-whisker Plot

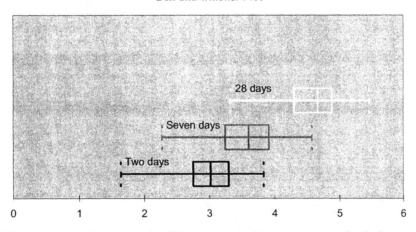

(e)   The compressive strength of the concrete increases over the 3 time periods.

11.30

Source	df	SS	MS	F
Factor A	2	120	(b) $120 \div 2 = 60$	$60 \div 10 = 6$
Factor B	2	110	(b) $110 \div 2 = 55$	$55 \div 10 = 5.5$
Interaction, AB	4	(a) $540-120-110-270=40$	(c) $40 \div 4 = 10$	$10 \div 10 = 1$
Error, E	27	270	(d) $270 \div 27 = 10$	
Total, T	35	540		

11.32 $F_{(2, 27)} = 3.35$ $F_{(4, 27)} = 2.73$

(a)   Decision: Since $F_{calc} = 6.00$ is greater than the critical bound of $F = 3.35$, reject H_0. There is evidence of a difference among factor A means.

(b)   Decision: Since $F_{calc} = 5.50$ is greater than the critical bound of $F = 3.35$, reject H_0. There is evidence of a difference among factor B means.

(c)   Decision: Since $F_{calc} = 1.00$ is less than the critical bound of $F = 2.73$, do not reject H_0. There is insufficient evidence to conclude there is an interaction effect.

11.34

Source	df	SS	MS	F
Factor A	2	$2 \times 80 = 160$	80	$80 \div 5 = 16$
Factor B	$8 \div 2 = 4$	220	$220 \div 4 = 55$	11
Interaction, AB	8	$8 \times 10 = 80$	10	$10 \div 5 = 2$
Error, E	30	$30 \times 5 = 150$	$55 \div 11 = 5$	
Total, T	44	$160 + 220 + 80 + 150 = 610$		

11.36 Two-way ANOVA output from Excel:

ANOVA

Source of Variation	SS	df	MS	F	P-value	F crit
Sample	52.5625	1	52.5625	23.57944	0.000394	4.747221
Columns	1.5625	1	1.5625	0.700935	0.418832	4.747221
Interaction	3.0625	1	3.0625	1.373832	0.2639	4.747221
Within	26.75	12	2.229167			
Total	83.9375	15				

(a) H_0: There is no interaction between development time and developer strength.
H_1: There is an interaction between development time and developer strength.
Decision rule: If $F > 4.747$, reject H_0.   Test statistic: $F = 1.374$.
Decision: Since $F_{calc} = 1.374$ is less than the critical bound of $F = 4.747$, do not reject H_0. There is insufficient evidence to conclude that there is any interaction between development time and developer strength.

(b) H_0: $\mu_1 = \mu_2$ H_1: $\mu_1 \neq \mu_2$
Decision rule: If $F > 4.747$, reject H_0.   Test statistic: $F = 23.58$.
Decision: Since $F_{calc} = 23.58$ is greater than the critical bound of $F = 4.747$, reject H_0. There is sufficient evidence to conclude that developer strength affects the density of the photographic plate film.

(c) H_0: $\mu_{10} = \mu_{14}$ H_1: $\mu_{10} \neq \mu_{14}$
Decision rule: If $F > 4.747$, reject H_0.   Test statistic: $F = 0.701$.
Decision: Since $F_{calc} = 0.701$ is less than the critical bound of $F = 4.747$, do not reject H_0. There is inadequate evidence to conclude that development time affects the density of the photographic plate film.

(d)

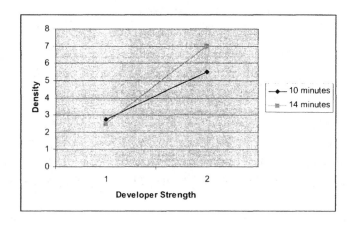

11.36   (e)   At 5% level of significance, developer strength has a positive effect on the density of
cont.   the photographic plate film while the developer time does not have any impact on the
                density. There is no significant interaction between developer time and developer
                strength on the density.

11.38   Two-way ANOVA output from Excel:

Source of Variation	SS	df	MS	F	P-value	F crit
Sample	24274.85	1	24274.85	1986.507	7.07E-20	4.413863
Columns	356.0027	2	178.0014	14.56656	0.000173	3.554561
Interaction	506.3104	2	253.1552	20.7167	2.14E-05	3.554561
Within	219.9576	18	12.21986			
Total	25357.12	23				

(a) H_0: There is no interaction between brand and water temperature.
      H_1: There is an interaction between brand and water temperature.

$$MSAB = \frac{SSAB}{(r-1)(c-1)} = \frac{506.3104}{(1)(2)} = 253.1552$$

$$F = \frac{MSAB}{MSE} = \frac{253.1552}{12.2199} = 20.7167$$

$$F_{0.05,2,18} = 3.555$$

Since $F = 20.7167 > 3.555$ or the p-value $= 2.14E-05 < 0.05$, reject H_0. There is
evidence of interaction between brand of pain-reliever and temperature of the water.

(b)   Since there is interaction between brand and the temperature of the water, it is
      inappropriate to analyze the main effect due to brand.

(c)   Since there is interaction between brand and the temperature of the water, it is
      inappropriate to analyze the main effect due to water temperature.

(d)

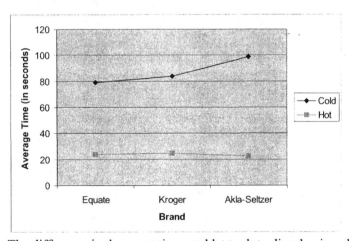

(e)   The difference in the mean time a tablet took to dissolve in cold and hot water
      depends on the brand with Alka-Seltzer having the largest difference and Equate with
      the smallest difference.

11.40   Excel output:

ANOVA

Source of Variation	SS	df	MS	F	P-value	F crit
Sample	0.632813	1	0.632813	0.018939	0.891528	4.195982
Columns	1519.383	1	1519.383	45.47136	2.54E-07	4.195982
Interaction	14.44531	1	14.44531	0.432312	0.516226	4.195982
Within	935.5938	28	33.41406			
Total	2470.055	31				

(a) H_0: There is no interaction between part positioning and tooth size.
H_1: There is an interaction between part positioning and tooth size.
Since $F = 0.4323 < 4.1960$ or the p-value $= 0.5162 > 0.05$, do not reject H_0. There is no evidence of interaction between part positioning and tooth size.

(b) $H_0 : \mu_{\text{Low Tooth Size}} = \mu_{\text{High Tooth Size}}$ H_1: means are different
Since $F = 0.0189 < 4.196$ or the p-value $= 0.8915 > 0.05$, do not reject H_0. There is no evidence of an effect that is due to tooth size.

(c) $H_0 : \mu_{\text{Low Positioning}} = \mu_{\text{High Positioning}}$ H_1: means are different
Since $F = 45.47 > 4.196$ or the p-value $= 2.54\text{E-}07 < 0.05$, reject H_0. There is evidence of an effect that is due to positioning.

(d)

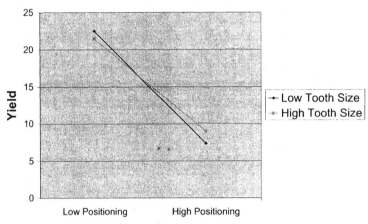

(e)   There is no evidence of interaction between part positioning and tooth size. There is evidence of an effect due to the part partitioning but not the tooth size.

11.42   In a completely randomized design, individual items in different samples are randomly and independently drawn. In a randomized block design, individual items in different samples are matched using common characteristics, or repeated measurements are taken to reduce within group variation.

11.44   The major assumptions of ANOVA are randomness and independence, normality, and homogeneity of variance.

11.46   When the ANOVA has indicated that that at least one of the groups has a different population mean than the others, you should use multiple comparison procedures for evaluating pairwise combinations of the group means. In such cases, the Tukey-Kramer procedure should be used to compare all pairs of means.

11.48   The completely randomized design is used to test for the existence of treatment effect of the treatment variable on the mean level of the dependent variable, while the Levene test is used to test whether the amounts of variation of the dependent variable are the same across the different categories of the treatment variable.

11.50   Interaction measures the difference in the effect of one variable for the different levels of the second factor. If there is no interaction, any difference between levels of one factor will be the same at each level of the second factor.

11.52   (a) H_0: There is no interaction between detergent brand and length of washing cycle.
                H_1: There is an interaction between detergent brand and length of washing cycle.
                Decision rule: If $F > 2.54$, reject H_0.
                Test statistic: $F = 1.49$
                Decision: Since $F_{calc} = 1.49$ is less than the critical bound of $F = 2.54$, do not reject H_0. There is not enough evidence to conclude that there is an interaction between detergent brand and length of washing cycle.

Minitab Output

Two-way Analysis of Variance					
Analysis of Variance for Dirt, Lbs					
Source	DF	SS	MS	F	p
Soap	3	0.000413	0.000138	0.7886	0.5178
Cycle	3	0.027338	0.009113	52.0743	0.0000
Interaction	9	0.002337	0.000260	1.4857	0.2346
Error	16	0.002800	0.000175		
Total	31	0.032888			

        (b) H_0: $\mu_A = \mu_B = \mu_C = \mu_D$ H_1: At least one mean differs.
                Decision rule: If $F > 3.24$, reject H_0.
                Test statistic: $F = 0.79$
                Decision: Since $F_{calc} = 0.79$ is less than the critical bound of $F = 3.24$, do not reject H_0. There is insufficient evidence to conclude that there is any difference in the mean amount of dirt removed from standard household laundry loads across the four detergent brands.

        (c) H_0: $\mu_{18} = \mu_{20} = \mu_{22} = \mu_{24}$ H_1: At least one mean differs.
                Decision rule: If $F > 3.24$, reject H_0.
                Test statistic: $F = 52.07$
                Decision: Since $F_{calc} = 52.07$ is greater than the critical bound of $F = 3.24$, reject H_0. There is adequate evidence to conclude that the mean amount of dirt removed from standard household laundry loads does differ across the four lengths of washing cycle (18, 20, 22, and 24 minutes).

11.52   (d)
cont.

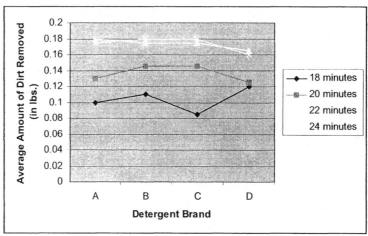

(e)   The Tukey procedure is used for washing cycle times (*F*-test was significant) but not for detergent brands (*F*-test was not significant).

For different lengths of washing cycles, $Q_{U[c,\ rc(n'-1)]} = Q_{U(4,\ 16)} = 4.05$

critical range $= Q_{U[c,\ rc(n'-1)]}\sqrt{\dfrac{MSE}{rn'}} = 4.05\sqrt{\dfrac{0.000175}{8}} = 0.0189$

Pairs of means that differ at the 0.05 level are marked with * below.

$|\overline{X}_{18} - \overline{X}_{20}| = 0.0326*$ $|\overline{X}_{18} - \overline{X}_{22}| = 0.0700*$ $|\overline{X}_{18} - \overline{X}_{24}| = 0.0700*$

$|\overline{X}_{20} - \overline{X}_{22}| = 0.0374*$ $|\overline{X}_{20} - \overline{X}_{24}| = 0.0374*$ $|\overline{X}_{22} - \overline{X}_{24}| = 0$

(f)   Washing cycles for 22 and 24 minutes are not different with respect to dirt removal, but both of these cycles are superior to 18- or 20-minute cycles with respect to dirt removal.

(g)   Excel Output for the one-factor ANOVA:

ANOVA

Source of Variation	SS	df	MS	F	P-value	F crit
Between Groups	0.027338	3	0.009113	45.97297	6.04E-11	2.946685
Within Groups	0.00555	28	0.000198			
Total	0.032888	31				

H_0: $\mu_{18} = \mu_{20} = \mu_{22} = \mu_{24}$ H_1: At least one mean differs.

Decision rule: If $F > 2.95$, reject H_0.

Test statistic: $F = 45.97$

Decision: Since $F_{calc} = 45.97$ is greater than the critical bound of $F = 2.95$, reject H_0. There is adequate evidence to conclude the mean amount of dirt removed from standard household laundry loads does differ across the four lengths of washing cycles (18, 20, 22, and 24 minutes).

The result is consistent with that in (c) where there is adequate evidence to conclude the mean amount of dirt removed from standard household laundry loads does differ across the four lengths of washing cycle.

11.54 (a) To test the homogeneity of variance, you perform a Levene's Test.

H_0: $\sigma_1^2 = \sigma_2^2 = \sigma_3^2$ H_1: Not all σ_j^2 are the same

Excel output:

ANOVA

Source of Variation	SS	df	MS	F	P-value	F crit
Between Groups	0.07	2	0.035	0.07468	0.928383	3.682317
Within Groups	7.03	15	0.468667			
Total	7.1	17				

Since the p-value $= 0.928 > 0.05$, do not reject H_0. There is not enough evidence of a significant difference in the variances of the breaking strengths for the three air-jet pressures.

(b) H_0: $\mu_1 = \mu_2 = \mu_3$ H_1: At least one of the means differs.

Decision rule: If $F > 3.68$, reject H_0.

Minitab Output

One-Way Analysis of Variance

Analysis of Variance on Strength

Source	DF	SS	MS	F	p
Pressure	2	8.074	4.037	4.09	0.038
Error	15	14.815	0.988		
Total	17	22.889			

Test statistic: $F = 4.09$

Decision: Since $F_{calc} = 4.09$ is greater than the critical bound of $F = 3.68$, reject H_0. There is enough evidence to conclude that the mean breaking strengths differ for the three air-jet pressures.

(c) $Q_{(c, n-c)} = Q_{U(3, 15)} = 3.67$

$$\text{critical range} = Q_{U(c,\ n-c)}\sqrt{\frac{MSW}{2}\left(\frac{1}{n_j} + \frac{1}{n_{j'}}\right)} = 3.67\sqrt{\frac{0.988}{2}\left(\frac{1}{6} + \frac{1}{6}\right)} = 1.489$$

The pair of means that differs at the 0.05 level is marked with * below.

$|\bar{X}_{30} - \bar{X}_{40}| = 1.30$ $|\bar{X}_{30} - \bar{X}_{50}| = 1.516*$ $|\bar{X}_{40} - \bar{X}_{50}| = 0.216$

Breaking strength scores under 30 psi are significantly higher than those under 50 psi.

(d) Other things being equal, use 30 psi.

11.56 (a) H_0: There is no interaction between side-to-side aspect and air-jet pressure.
H_1: There is an interaction between side-to-side aspect and air-jet pressure.
Decision rule: If $F > 3.89$, reject H_0.
Minitab Output:

Two-way Analysis of Variance

Analysis of Variance for Strength

Source	DF	SS	MS	F	p
Aspect	1	3.467	3.467	4.8694	0.0476
Pressure	2	8.074	4.037	5.6699	0.0185
Interaction	2	2.808	1.404	1.9719	0.1818
Error	12	8.540	0.712		
Total	17	22.889			

Test statistic: $F = 1.9719$
Decision: Since $F_{calc} = 1.9719$ is less than the critical bound of 3.89, do not reject H_0. There is insufficient evidence to conclude there is an interaction between side-to-side aspect and air-jet pressure.

(b) H_0: $\mu_1 = \mu_2$ H_1: $\mu_1 \neq \mu_2$
Decision rule: If $F > 4.75$, reject H_0.
Test statistic: $F = 4.8694$
Decision: Since $F_{calc} = 4.8694$ is greater than the critical bound of 4.75, reject H_0. There is sufficient evidence to conclude that mean breaking strength does differ between the two levels of side-to-side aspect.

(c) H_0: $\mu_1 = \mu_2 = \mu_3$ H_1: At least one of the means differ.
Decision rule: If $F > 3.89$, reject H_0.
Test statistic: $F = 5.6699$
Decision: Since $F_{calc} = 5.6699$ is greater than the critical bound of 3.89, reject H_0. There is enough evidence to conclude that the mean breaking strengths differ for the three air-jet pressures.

(d)

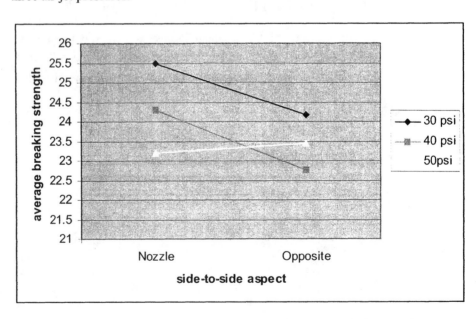

11.56 (e) $Q_{U[c,\ rc(n'-1)]} = Q_{U(3,\ 12)} = 3.77$

cont.   critical range $= Q_{U[c,\ rc(n'-1)]} \cdot \sqrt{\dfrac{MSE}{rn'}} = 3.77 \cdot \sqrt{\dfrac{0.712}{2 \cdot 3}} = 1.30$

Pairs of means that differ at the 0.05 level are marked with * below.

$\left|\overline{X}_{30} - \overline{X}_{40}\right| = 1.30^{*}$ $\left|\overline{X}_{30} - \overline{X}_{50}\right| = 1.51^{*}$ $\left|\overline{X}_{40} - \overline{X}_{50}\right| = 0.21$

Mean breaking strengths under 30 psi are higher than those under 40 psi or 50 psi.

(f)   The mean breaking strength is highest under 30 psi.

(g)   The two-factor experiment gave a more complete, refined set of results than the one-factor experiment. Not only was the side-to-side aspect factor significant, the application of the Tukey procedure on the air-jet pressure factor determined that breaking strength scores are highest under 30 psi.

11.58 (a) H_0: There is no interaction between buffer size and data file size.
H_1: There is an interaction between buffer size and data file size.
Decision rule: If $F > 3.55$, reject H_0.
Test statistic: $F = 4.0835$
Decision: Since $F_{calc} = 4.0835$ is greater than the critical bound of 3.55, reject H_0. There is sufficient evidence to conclude there is an interaction between buffer size and data file size.
Minitab Output

Two-way Analysis of Variance					
Analysis of Variance for ReadTime					
Source	DF	SS	MS	F	p
Buffer	1	0.93220	0.93220	131.8529	0.0000
FileSize	2	0.27630	0.13815	19.5403	0.0000
Interaction	2	0.05773	0.02887	4.0835	0.0345
Error	18	0.12723	0.00707		
Total	23	1.39346			

(b) H_0: $\mu_1 = \mu_2$ H_1: $\mu_1 \neq \mu_2$
Decision rule: If $F > 4.41$, reject H_0.
Test statistic: $F = 131.8529$
Decision: Since $F_{calc} = 131.8529$ is well greater than the critical bound of 4.41, reject H_0. However, you cannot directly conclude that there is a significant difference in mean read times due to buffer size (main effects) because the mean read times for different buffer sizes are different for different sizes.

(c) H_0: $\mu_{Sm} = \mu_{Med} = \mu_{Lrg}$ H_1: At least one of the means differ.
Decision rule: If $F > 3.55$, reject H_0.
Test statistic: $F = 19.5403$
Decision: Since $F_{calc} = 19.5403$ is greater than the critical bound of 3.55, reject H_0. However, you cannot directly conclude that there is a significant difference in mean read times due to file size (main effects) because the mean read times for different buffer sizes are different for different sizes.

11.58   (d)
cont.

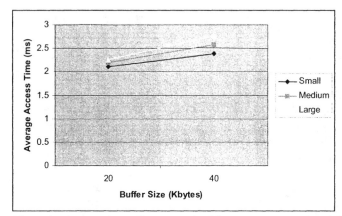

Given the interaction effect was significant, some levels of file size work better with one of the buffer sizes than the other. You cannot directly conclude that there is a significant difference in mean read times due to buffer size or file size (main effects) because the mean read times for different buffer sizes are different for different sizes of files.

(e)   Conclusions about the relative speed of the buffers or file sizes cannot be drawn because buffers and file sizes interact.

(f)   In the completely randomized design, there is not enough evidence of a difference between mean access read times for the three file sizes. In the two-factor factorial design, there is significant interaction between buffer size and data file size. Taking the interaction affect into consideration, there is enough evidence of both buffer size effect and data file size effect on access read times.

11.60   PHStat output of two-way ANOVA
ANOVA

Source of Variation	SS	df	MS	F	P-value	F crit
Sample	8192	1	8192	41.75787	5.33E-07	4.195982
Columns	133644.5	1	133644.5	681.239	3.4E-21	4.195982
Interaction	9800	1	9800	49.95449	1.09E-07	4.195982
Within	5493	28	196.1786			
Total	157129.5	31				

H_0: There is no interaction between browser and computer.
H_1: There is an interaction between browser and computer.
Decision rule: If p-value > 0.05, reject H_0.
Test statistic: $F = 49.95$
Decision: Since p-value is virtually zero, reject H_0. There is sufficient evidence to conclude there is an interaction between browser and the type of computer.

11.60
cont.

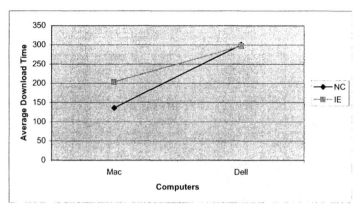

The existence of interaction effect complicates the interpretation of the main effects. You cannot directly conclude that there is a significant difference between mean download time of different browsers because the difference is not the same over all the computers. Likewise, you cannot directly conclude that there is a significant difference between mean download time of different computers because the difference is not the same over the two browsers. From the graph, it appears that Dell performs the same regardless of browser type and the Mac performs faster with Netscape than it does with IE.

11.62   (a) H_0: $\mu_1 = ... = \mu_8$ H_1: Not all μ_j are the same.

Decision rule: If $F > 2.95$, reject H_0.

Note: Since the F-table does not include a value for 7 and 88 degrees of freedom, use 7 and 60 degrees of freedom.

Test statistic: $F = 4.81$

Decision: Since $F_{calc} = 4.81$ is greater than the critical bound of 2.95, reject H_0. There is sufficient evidence to show a difference in the mean rating scores among the wines.

11.62 (a)   Minitab Output:
cont.

```
One-Way Analysis of Variance

Analysis of Variance on Rating
Source   DF     SS     MS     F      p
Wine      7   440.3   62.9   4.81  0.000
Error    88  1151.7   13.1
Total    95  1592.0
                          Individual 95% CIs For Mean
                          Based on Pooled StDev
 Level   N    Mean    StDev ---------+---------+---------+-------
   1    12   10.417   3.059      (------*------)
   2    12   14.667   2.995                 (------*------)
   3    12   11.167   3.040        (------*------)
   4    12    9.333   2.774   (------*------)
   5    12   14.417   4.209                (------*------)
   6    12    8.417   4.502 (------*------)
   7    12   11.833   4.469             (-----*------)
   8    12    9.750   3.388       (-----*------)
                           ---------+---------+---------+-------
Pooled StDev =   3.618              9.0      12.0    15.0
```

(b)   The "within wines" term in (a) is SSW. It is comprised of the among blocks ($SSBL$)
         and "error" term (SSE) in (a).

(c)   In this study, the mean rating scores among the eight wines are so significantly
         different that employing the wrong procedure did not affect the overall conclusion --
         there is evidence of a difference among the wines. However, by not taking advantage
         of the actual blocking, the experimental error was inflated in SSW, and this could
         have led to an erroneous decision. Here the conclusions from the pairwise
         comparisons are much weaker. Using the Tukey-Kramer procedure, Wine #2 and
         Wine #5 are no longer significantly preferred over Wine #8. In addition, Wine #5
         now differs from Wine #4 only by chance.

CHAPTER 12

OBJECTIVES

- To understand how to use and when to use the Chi-Square test for contingency tables
- To understand how to use the Marascuilo procedure for determining pairwise differences when evaluating more than two proportions
- To understand how to use the Chi-Square test to evaluate the goodness of fit of a set of data to a specific probability distribution
- To learn how and when to use nonparametric tests

OVERVIEW AND KEY CONCEPTS

χ^2 Test for Differences in Two Proportions (Independent Samples)

- **Assumptions:**
    - Independent samples
    - Large sample sizes: All expected frequencies ≥ 5.
- **Test statistic:**
    - $$\chi^2 = \sum_{\text{All Cells}} \frac{(f_0 - f_e)^2}{f_e} \text{ with 1 degree of freedom}$$

    where

    f_o : observed frequency in a cell

    f_e = [(row total)(column total)]/n : expected frequency in a cell

    - The rejection region is always in the right tail.

χ^2 Test for Differences among More Than Two Proportions

- **Assumptions:**
    - Independent samples
    - Large sample sizes: All expected frequencies ≥ 1.
- **Test statistic:**
    - $$\chi^2 = \sum_{\text{All Cells}} \frac{(f_0 - f_e)^2}{f_e} \text{ with } (c-1) \text{ degree of freedom}$$

    where

    f_o : observed frequency in a cell

    f_e = [(row total)(column total)]/n: expected frequency in a cell.

    - The rejection region is always in the right tail.

Marascuilo Procedure
- Enable one to make comparison between all pairs of groups.
- **The Marascuilo multiple comparison procedure:**
    1. Compute the absolute differences $\left| p_j - p_{j'} \right|$ among all pairs of groups.

    2. The critical range for a pair where $j \neq j'$ is $\sqrt{\chi_U^2} \sqrt{\dfrac{p_j(1-p_j)}{n_j} + \dfrac{p_{j'}(1-p_{j'})}{n_{j'}}}$ where

       χ_U^2 is the upper-tail critical value from a χ^2 distribution with $(c-1)$ degrees of freedom.

    3. A specific pair is considered significantly different if $\left| p_j - p_{j'} \right| >$ critical range.

χ^2 Test of Independence
- **Assumptions:**
    - One sample is drawn with two factors; each factor has two or more levels (categories) of responses.
    - Large sample sizes: All expected frequencies ≥ 1.
- **Test statistic:**
    - $\chi^2 = \sum_{\text{All Cells}} \dfrac{(f_0 - f_e)^2}{f_e}$ with $(r-1)(c-1)$ degree of freedom

      where

      f_o : observed frequency in a cell

      f_e = [(row total)(column total)]/n: expected frequency in a cell

      r: the number of rows in the contingency table.

      c: the number of columns in the contingency table.
    - The rejection region is always in the right tail.
    - The χ^2 test does not show the nature of any relationship nor causality.

McNemar Test for the Difference between Two Proportions (Related Samples)
- **Assumptions:**
    - Related samples; repeated measurements on the same set of respondents
- **Test statistic:**
    - $Z = \dfrac{B-C}{\sqrt{B+C}}$

      where

      B: number of respondents that answer yes to condition 1 and no to condition 2

      C: number of respondents that answer no to condition 1 and yes to condition 2
    - The test statistic Z is approximately distributed as a standardized normal distribution.
    - The alternative hypothesis can be one-tail with a right-tail rejection region, one-tail with a left-tail rejection region or two-tail with both right-tail and left-tail rejection regions.

χ^2 Test for the Population Variance $\left(\sigma^2\right)$ or Standard Deviation $\left(\sigma\right)$

- **Assumption:**
  - Population is normally distributed.
- **Test statistic:**
  - $\chi^2 = \dfrac{(n-1)S^2}{\sigma^2}$ with $(n-1)$ degrees of freedom.
  - The alternative hypothesis can be one-tail with a right-tail rejection region, one-tail with a left-tail rejection region or two-tail with both right-tail and left-tail rejection regions.

χ^2 Goodness of Fit Test for Probability Distributions

- **The χ^2 goodness of fit test procedure:**
  1. Determine the specific probability distribution to be fitted to the data.
  2. Hypothesize or estimate from the data the values of each parameter of the selected probability distribution.
  3. Determine the theoretical probability in each category using the selected probability distribution.
  4. Compute the χ^2 test statistic:

  $$\chi^2_{k-p-1} = \sum_k \frac{\left(f_0 - f_e\right)^2}{f_e}$$

  where f_0 = observed frequency

  f_e = theoretical or expected frequency = $nP(X)$

  k = number of categories or classes remaining after combining classes

  p = number of parameters estimated from the data

  n = sample size

  $P(X)$ = theoretical probability

  5. The χ^2_{k-p-1} test statistic can be approximated by a Chi-square distribution with $(k-p-1)$ degrees of freedom.
  6. The rejection region is always in the right tail.

Wilcoxon Rank Sum Test for Difference in Two Medians $\left(M_1 - M_2\right)$

- **Assumptions:**
  - Both populations do not need to be normally distributed. It is a distribution free procedure.
  - The two samples are randomly and independently drawn.
  - The test is also appropriate when only ordinal data is available.
- **Test procedure:**
  1. Assign ranks, $R_1, R_2, \cdots, R_{n_1+n_2}$, to each of the $n_1 + n_2$ sample observations.
     - If sample sizes are not the same, let n_1 refer to the smaller sample size.
     - Assign average rank for any ties.
  2. Compute the sum of the ranks, T_1 and T_2, for each of the two samples.

3. Test statistic: The sum of ranks of the smaller sample, T_1.
4. Obtain the critical value(s), T_{1L}, T_{1U} or both, from a table.
5. Compare the test statistic T_1 to the critical value(s).

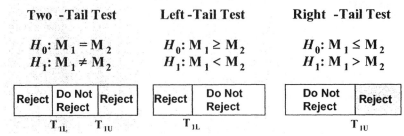

Two -Tail Test	Left -Tail Test	Right -Tail Test
H_0: $M_1 = M_2$	H_0: $M_1 \geq M_2$	H_0: $M_1 \leq M_2$
H_1: $M_1 \neq M_2$	H_1: $M_1 < M_2$	H_1: $M_1 > M_2$

6. Make a statistical decision.
7. Draw a conclusion.

Wilcoxon Rank Sum Test for Difference in Two Medians $(M_1 - M_2)$, Large Sample

- **Test statistic:**
    - For large sample (at least one sample size > 10), the test statistic T_1 is approximately normally distributed with mean $\mu_{T_1} = \dfrac{n_1(n+1)}{2}$ and standard deviation

      $\sigma_{T_1} = \sqrt{\dfrac{n_1 n_2 (n+1)}{12}}$ where $n_1 \leq n_2$ and $n = n_1 + n_2$

    - $Z = \dfrac{T_1 - \mu_{T_1}}{\sigma_{T_1}}$ has a standard normal distribution.

Wilcoxon Signed-ranks Test for the Median Difference (M_D)

- **Assumptions:**
    - The observed data either constitute a random sample of n independent items or individuals, each with two measurements, one taken before and the other taken after the presentation of some treatment or the observed data constitute a random sample of n independent pairs of items or individuals with values for each member of the match pair ($i = 1, 2, \ldots, n$).
    - The underlying variable of interest is continuous.
    - The observed data are measured at interval or ratio level.
    - The distribution of the population of difference scores between repeated measurements or between matched items or individuals is approximately symmetric.
- **Test procedure:**
    1. For each item in a sample of n items obtain a difference score D_i between two measurements.
    2. Obtain a set of n absolute differences $|D_i|$.
    3. Drop any absolute difference score of zero, thereby yielding a set of $n' \leq n$.
    4. Assign ranks R_i from 1 to n' to each of the $|D_i|$ such that the smallest $|D_i|$ gets rank 1 and the largest gets rank n'. If two or more $|D_i|$ are equal, they are each assigned

the average rank of the ranks they would have been assigned individually had ties in the data not occurred.

5. Obtain the signed ranks $R_i^{(+)}$ and $R_i^{(-)}$ from each of the n' ranks R_i where the "+" or " – " sign is determined depending on whether D_i was originally positive or negative.

6. **Test statistic:** The Wilcoxon test statistic is $W = \sum_{i=1}^{n'} R_i^{(+)}$ where $R_i^{(+)}$ are the positive signed ranks.

7. If $n' \le 20$, use Table E.9 to obtain the critical value(s) of the test statistic W. Perform the test with a one-tail (two-tail) alternative hypothesis with rejection region(s) similar to the rejection region(s) of a typical Z test.

8. If $n' > 20$, W is approximately normally distributed with mean $\mu_W = \dfrac{n'(n'+1)}{4}$ and standard deviation $\sigma_W = \sqrt{\dfrac{n'(n'+1)(2n'+1)}{24}}$. Obtain the critical value(s) from a standardized normal distribution for a one-tail (two-tail) alternative hypothesis. Perform a Z test with $Z = \dfrac{W - \mu_W}{\sigma_W}$.

The Kruskal-Wallis Rank Test: Nonparametric Analysis for the One-Way ANOVA

- It is used to analyze the completely randomized design.
- This is an extension of Wilcoxon rank sum test for difference in two medians.
- It is a distribution free test procedure without any distribution assumption on the population.
- **The null and alternative hypotheses:**
    - $H_0 : M_1 = M_2 = \cdots = M_c$
    - $H_1 :$ Not all M_j are the same.

- **Assumptions:**
    - Samples are randomly and independently drawn.
    - The dependent variable is a continuous variable.
    - Data may be ranked both within and among samples.
    - Each sample group size is greater than five.
    - The populations have the same variation and shape.
    - The test is robust to the same variation and shape assumption.
- **The Kruskal-Wallis rank test procedure:**
1. Obtain the ranks of the observations.
2. Add the ranks for each of the c groups.
3. Compute the H statistic: $H = \left[\dfrac{12}{n(n+1)} \sum_{j=1}^{c} \dfrac{T_j^2}{n_j} \right] - 3(n+1)$ where $n = n_1 + n_2 + \cdots + n_c$.
4. The distribution of the H test statistic can be approximated by a χ^2 distribution with $(c-1)$ degrees of freedom if each sample group size is greater than 5
5. The rejection region is in the right tail.

Friedman Rank Test: Nonparametric Analysis for the Randomized Block Design

- It is used to analyze a randomized block design.
- It is a distribution free test procedure without any distribution assumption on the population.
- It can be used when the data collected are only in rank form within each block.
- **The null and alternative hypotheses:**
  - $H_0 : M_{.1} = M_{.2} = \cdots = M_{.c}$
  - $H_1 :$ Not all $M_{.j}$ are the same.

- **Assumptions:**
  - The r blocks are independent.
  - The underlying random variable of interest is continuous.
  - The observed data constitute at least an ordinal scale of measurement within each of the r blocks.
  - There is no interaction between the r blocks and the c treatment levels.
  - The c populations have the same variability.
  - The c populations have the same shape.

- **The Friedman rank test procedure:**
  1. In each of the r independent blocks, the c observations are replaced by their corresponding ranks such that rank 1 is given to the smallest observation in the block and rank c to the largest. If any values in a block are tied, they are assigned the average of the ranks that they would otherwise have been given.

  2. **Test statistic:** $F_R = \dfrac{12}{rc(c+1)} \sum_{j=1}^{c} R_{.j}^2 - 3r(c+1)$

     where $R_{.j}^2$ is the square of the rank total for group j ($j = 1, 2, \ldots, c$)

     r is the number of independent blocks

     c is the number of groups or treatment levels

  3. F_R can be approximated by the chi-square distribution with $(c-1)$ degrees of freedom when $r > 5$.

  4. The rejection region is in the right tail.

SOLUTIONS TO END OF SECTION
AND CHAPTER REVIEW EVEN PROBLEMS

12.2   (a)   For $df = 1$ and $\alpha = 0.95$, $\chi^2 = 0.0039$.

(b)   For $df = 1$ and $\alpha = 0.975$, $\chi^2 = 0.00098$.

(c)   For $df = 1$ and $\alpha = 0.99$, $\chi^2 = 0.000157$.

12.4   (a)

Observed Freq	Expected Freq	Observed Freq	Expected Freq	Total Obs, Row 1
20	25	30	25	50
chi-sq contrib= 1.00		chi-sq contrib= 1.00		
Observed Freq	Expected Freq	Observed Freq	Expected Freq	Total Obs, Row 2
30	25	20	25	50
chi-sq contrib= 1.00		chi-sq contrib= 1.00		
Total Obs, Col 1		Total Obs, Col 2		GRAND TOTAL
50		50		100

(b)   Decision rule: If $\chi^2 > 3.841$, reject H_0.

Test statistic: $\chi^2 = \sum \dfrac{(f_0 - f_e)^2}{f_e} = 1.00 + 1.00 + 1.00 + 1.00 = 4$

Decision: Since $\chi^2_{calc} = 4$ is greater than the critical value of 3.841, it is significant at the 5% level of significance.

12.6   (a) H_0: $\pi_1 = \pi_2$ H_1: $\pi_1 \neq \pi_2$

Decision rule: $df = 1$. If $\chi^2 > 3.841$, reject H_0.

Test statistic: $\chi^2 = 1$

Decision: Since $\chi^2 = 1$ is less than the upper critical bound of 3.841, do not reject H_0. There is not enough evidence to conclude that there is a significant difference between males and females in the proportion who make gas mileage a priority.

(b) H_0: $\pi_1 = \pi_2$ H_1: $\pi_1 \neq \pi_2$

Decision rule: $df = 1$. If $\chi^2 > 3.841$, reject H_0.

Test statistic: $\chi^2 = 10$

Decision: Since $\chi^2 = 10$ is greater than the upper critical bound of 3.841, reject H_0. There is enough evidence to conclude that there is a significant difference between males and females in the proportion who make gas mileage a priority.

(c)   The larger sample size in (b) increases the difference between the observed and expected frequencies and, hence, results in a larger test statistic value.

12.8   (a) $H_0: \pi_1 = \pi_2$ $H_1: \pi_1 \neq \pi_2$

PHStat output with computation:

Observed Frequencies					Calculations	
	Column variable					
Row variable	African Americans	Whites	Total		fo-fe	
Own Stocks	370	420	790		-25	25
Do Not Own Stocks	130	80	210		25	-25
Total	500	500	1000			
Expected Frequencies						
	Column variable					
Row variable	African Americans	Whites	Total		(fo-fe)^2/fe	
Own Stocks	395	395	790		1.58227	1.58227
Do Not Own Stocks	105	105	210		5.95238	5.95238
Total	500	500	1000			
Data						
Level of Significance	0.05					
Number of Rows	2					
Number of Columns	2					
Degrees of Freedom	1					
Results						
Critical Value	3.841455					
Chi-Square Test Statistic	15.06932					
p-Value	0.000104					
Reject the null hypothesis						

Decision rule: $df = 1$. If $\chi^2 > 3.841$, reject H_0.

Test statistic: $\chi^2 = \sum_{\text{all cells}} \frac{(f_0 - f_e)^2}{f_e} = 15.0693$

Decision: Since $\chi^2_{calc} = 15.0693$ is greater than the upper critical bound of 3.841, reject H_0. There is enough evidence to conclude that there is a significant difference in the proportion of African American and whites who invest in stocks.

(b)   p-value is 0.0001. The probability of obtaining a test statistic of 15.0693 or larger when the null hypothesis is true is 0.0001.

(c)   The results of (a) and (b) are exactly the same as those of Problem 10.39. The χ^2_{calc} in (a) and the Z_{calc} in Problem 10.39 (a) satisfy the relationship that $\chi^2_{calc} = 15.0693 = (Z_{calc})^2 = (-3.8819)^2$ and the p-value in Problem 10.39 (b) is exactly the same as the p-value obtained in (b).

12.10   (a) H_0: $\pi_1 = \pi_2$ H_1: $\pi_1 \neq \pi_2$

Decision rule: $df = 1$. If $\chi^2 > 3.841$, reject H_0.

Test statistic: $\chi^2 = 33.333$

Decision: Since $\chi^2_{calc} = 33.333$ is greater than the upper critical bound of 3.841, reject H_0. There is enough evidence to conclude that there is a significant difference between the proportion of males and females who place more importance on brand names today than a few years ago.

(b) p-value is virtually 0. The probability of obtaining a test statistic of 33.333 or larger when the null hypothesis is true is virtually 0.

12.12   (a)   The expected frequencies in the first row are 20, 30, and 40.
The expected frequencies in the second row are 30, 45, and 60.

(b) $\chi^2 = 12.500$. The critical value with 2 degrees of freedom and $\alpha = 0.05$ is 5.991. The result is deemed significant.

(c)   Pairs of proportions that differ at the 0.05 level are marked with * below:

Pairwise Comparisons	Critical Range	$\left\| p_j - p_{j'} \right\|$
A to B	0.19582	0.2*
A to C	0.1848	0.3*
B to C	0.1848	0.1

There are two (2) pairs of proportions that differ significantly.

12.14 PHStat output:

Observed Frequencies						
	Column variable					
Row variable	**German y**	**France**	**UK**	**Greece**	**US**	**Total**
Yes	100	120	280	390	570	1460
No	900	880	720	610	430	3540
Total	1000	1000	1000	1000	1000	5000

Expected Frequencies						
	Column variable					
Row variable	Germany	France	UK	Greece	US	Total
Yes	292	292	292	292	292	1460
No	708	708	708	708	708	3540
Total	1000	1000	1000	1000	1000	5000

Data	
Level of Significance	0.05
Number of Rows	2
Number of Columns	5
Degrees of Freedom	4

Results	
Critical Value	9.487728
Chi-Square Test Statistic	742.3961
p-Value	2.3E-159
Reject the null hypothesis	

(a) $H_0 : \pi_1 = \pi_2 = \pi_3 = \pi_4 = \pi_5$ H_1 : Not all π_j are equal.

where population 1 = Germany, 2 = France, 3 = UK, 4 = Greece, 5 = US

Test statistic: $\chi^2 = \sum_{\text{All cells}} \dfrac{\left(f_o - f_e\right)^2}{f_e} = 742.3961$

Decision: Since the calculated test statistic 742.3961 is greater than the critical value of 9.4877, you reject H_0 and conclude that there is a difference in the proportion of people who eat out at least once a week in the various countries.

(b)   p-value is virtually zero. The probability of obtaining a data set which gives rise to a test statistic of 742.3961 or more is virtually zero if there is no difference in the proportion of people who eat out at least once a week in the various countries.

12.14   (c)   Excel output of the Marascuilo procedure:
cont.

Group	Sample Proportion	Sample Size		
1	0.10	1000		
2	0.12	1000		
3	0.28	1000		
4	0.39	1000		
5	0.57	1000		
Other Data				
Level of significance	0.05			
d.f	4			
Sqrt(chi-square)	3.0802			
Comparison	Absolute Difference	Std. Error of Difference	Critical Range	Results
Group 1 to Group 2	0.02	0.01399	0.04308	Means are not different
Group 1 to Group 3	0.18	0.01708	0.05260	Means are different
Group 1 to Group 4	0.29	0.01811	0.05578	Means are different
Group 1 to Group 5	0.47	0.01831	0.05639	Means are different
Group 2 to Group 3	0.16	0.01753	0.05399	Means are different
Group 2 to Group 4	0.27	0.01853	0.05709	Means are different
Group 2 to Group 5	0.45	0.01873	0.05768	Means are different
Group 3 to Group 4	0.11	0.02096	0.06457	Means are different
Group 3 to Group 5	0.29	0.02114	0.06510	Means are different
Group 4 to Group 5	0.18	0.02198	0.06769	Means are different

At 5% level of significance, there is no significant difference between the proportions of Germany and France while there is significant difference between all the remaining pair of countries.

12.16 (a) $H_0 : \pi_1 = \pi_2 = \pi_3$ H_1: at least one proportion differs

where population 1 = under 35, 2 = 35-54, 3 = over 54

PHStat output:

Observed Frequencies						Calculations		
	Column variable							
Row variable	Under 35	35-54	Over 54	Total		fo-fe		
Saturday	48	56	24	128		5.333	13.333	-18.667
A Day other than Saturday	152	144	176	472		-5.333	-13.333	18.667
Total	200	200	200	600				
Expected Frequencies								
	Column variable							
Row variable	Under 35	35-54	Over 54	Total		(fo-fe)^2/fe		
Saturday	42.667	42.667	42.667	128		0.667	4.167	8.167
A Day other than Saturday	157.333	157.333	157.333	472		0.181	1.130	2.215
Total	200	200	200	600				
Data								
Level of Significance	0.05							
Number of Rows	2							
Number of Columns	3							
Degrees of Freedom	2							
Results								
Critical Value	5.9915							
Chi-Square Test Statistic	16.5254							
p-Value	0.0003							
Reject the null hypothesis								

Decision rule: $df = (c - 1) = (3 - 1) = 2$. If $\chi^2 > 5.9915$, reject H_0.

Test statistic: $\chi^2 = \sum_{\text{all cells}} \frac{(f_0 - f_e)^2}{f_e} = 16.5254$

Decision: Since $\chi^2_{calc} = 16.5254$ is greater than the upper critical bound of 5.9915, reject H_0. There is enough evidence to conclude that there is a significant relationship between age and major grocery shopping day.

(b)   p-value = 0.0003. The probability of obtaining a sample that gives rise to a test statistic that is equal to or more than 16.5254 is 0.03% if the null hypothesis is true.

12.16 (c)
cont.

Pairwise Comparisons	Critical Range	$\lvert p_j - p_{j'} \rvert$
1 to 2	0.1073	0.04
2 to 3	0.0959	0.16*
1 to 3	0.0929	0.12*

There is a significance difference between the 35-54 and over 54 groups, and between the under 35 and over 54 groups.

(d)   The stores can use this information to target their marketing on the specific group of shoppers on Saturday and the days other than Saturday.

12.18 (a) $H_0: \pi_1 = \pi_2 = \pi_3$ H_1: at least one proportion differs

where population 1 = insurance companies, 2 = pharmacies, 3 = medical researchers
Decision rule: $df = (c - 1) = (3 - 1) = 2$. If $\chi^2 > 5.9915$, reject H_0.

Test statistic: $\chi^2 = 128.24$

Decision: Since $\chi^2_{calc} = 128.24$ is greater than the upper critical bound of 5.9915, reject H_0. There is enough evidence to show that there is a significant difference in the proportion of people who object to their medical records being shared.

(b)

Pairwise Comparisons	Critical Range	$\lvert p_j - p_{j'} \rvert$
1 to 2	0.0483	0.23*
2 to 3	0.0527	0.08*
1 to 3	0.0470	0.15*

There is a significance difference between any pair of the organizations.

12.20 (a) $H_0: \pi_1 = \pi_2 = \pi_3$ H_1: Not all π_j are equal.

Observed Frequencies:

	City			
Minibar Charges Posted	Hong Kong	New York	Paris	Total
Yes	86	76	78	240
No	14	24	22	60
Total	100	100	100	300

Expected Frequencies:

	City			
Minibar Charges Posted	Hong Kong	New York	Paris	Total
Yes	80	80	80	240
No	20	20	20	60
Total	100	100	100	300

Level of Significance	0.05
Number of Rows	2
Number of Columns	3
Degrees of Freedom	2
Critical Value	5.991476
Chi-Square Test Statistic	3.499998
p-Value	0.173774
Do not reject the null hypothesis	

Test statistic: $\chi^2 = \sum_{\text{All cells}} \dfrac{(f_o - f_e)^2}{f_e} = 3.50$

12.20 (a)   Decision: Since the calculated test statistic of 3.50 is smaller than the critical value of
cont.   5.991, you do not reject the null hypothesis. There is not sufficient evidence to conclude
               that there is a difference in the proportion of hotels that correctly post minibar charges
               among the three cities.

       (b)   The p-value is 0.174. The probability of obtaining a sample that gives rise to a test
               statistic equal to or more extreme than 3.5 is 0.174 if the null hypothesis is true.

12.22   Since the null hypotheses are not rejected for all the 3 items, it is not necessary to
               perform the Marascuilo procedure.

12.24 $df = (r - 1)(c - 1) = (3 - 1)(4 - 1) = 6$

12.26 (a) H_0: There is no relationship between the quarter of the year and the numbers
               assigned.
               H_1: There is a relationship between the quarter of the year and the numbers assigned.
               Decision rule: If $\chi^2 > 12.592$, reject H_0.

	A	B	C	D	E	F	G	H
1	Lottery Fairness							
2								
3	Observed Frequencies:			Quarter of Year				
4			Number Set	Jan-Mar	Apr-June	Jul-Sept	Oct-Dec	Total
5			Low	21	28	35	38	122
6			Medium	34	22	29	37	122
7			High	36	41	28	17	122
8			Total	91	91	92	92	366
9								
10	Expected Frequencies:			Quarter of Year				
11			Number Set	Jan-Mar	Apr-June	Jul-Sept	Oct-Dec	Total
12			Low	30.333333	30.333333	30.666667	30.666667	122
13			Medium	30.333333	30.333333	30.666667	30.666667	122
14			High	30.333333	30.333333	30.666667	30.666667	122
15			Total	91	91	92	92	366
16								
17								
18	Level of Significance	0.05						
19	Number of Rows	3						
20	Number of Columns	4						
21	Degrees of Freedom	6						
22	Critical Value	12.5916						
23	Chi-Square Test Statistic	20.6802						
24	p -Value	0.00209						
25	Reject the null hypothesis							

               Test statistic: $\chi^2 = 20.680$

               Decision: Since the $\chi^2_{calc} = 20.680$ is greater than the critical bound of 12.592, reject H_0.
               There is evidence of a relationship between the quarter of the year in which draftable-
               aged men were born and the numbers assigned as their draft eligibilities during the
               Vietnam War.

       (b)   It appears that the results of the lottery drawing are different from what would be
               expected if the lottery were random.

12.26 (c) (a) H_0: There is no relationship between the quarter of the year in which
cont.   draftable-aged men were born and the numbers assigned as their draft
        eligibilities during the Vietnam War.
        H_1: There is a relationship between the quarter of the year in which draftable-
        aged men were born and the numbers assigned as their draft eligibilities.
        Decision rule: If $\chi^2 > 12.592$, reject H_0.

        Test statistic: $\chi^2 = 9.803$

        Decision: Since $\chi^2_{calc} = 9.803$ is less than the critical bound of 12.592, do not
        reject H_0. There is not enough evidence to conclude there is any relationship
        between the quarter of the year in which draftable-aged men were born and the
        numbers assigned as their draft eligibilities during the Vietnam War.

      (b)   It appears that the results of the lottery drawing are consistent with what would
        be expected if the lottery were random.

12.28 (a) H_0: There is no relationship between the commuting time of company employees and
        the level of stress-related problems observed on the job.
        H_1: There is a relationship between the commuting time of company employees and
        the level of stress-related problems observed on the job.
        PHStat output:

Observed Frequencies								
		Stress				Calculations		
Commuting Time	High	Moderate	Low	Total		fo-fe		
Under 15 min.	9	5	18	32		-3.1379	-0.2414	3.3793
15-45 min.	17	8	28	53		-3.1034	-0.6810	3.7845
Over 45 min.	18	6	7	31		6.2414	0.9224	-7.1638
Total	44	19	53	116				
Expected Frequencies								
		Stress						
Commuting Time	High	Moderate	Low	Total		(fo-fe)^2/fe		
Under 15 min.	12.1379	5.2414	14.6207	32		0.8112	0.0111	0.7811
15-45 min.	20.1034	8.6810	24.2155	53		0.4791	0.0534	0.5915
Over 45 min.	11.7586	5.0776	14.1638	31		3.3129	0.1676	3.6233
Total	44	19	53	116				
Level of Significance	0.01							
Number of Rows	3							
Number of Columns	3							
Degrees of Freedom	4							
Results								
Critical Value	13.2767		Chi-Square Test Statistic	9.8311		p-Value	0.04337	

12.28   (a)   Decision rule: If $\chi^2 > 13.277$, reject H_0.

cont.   Test statistic: $\chi^2 = \sum\limits_{\text{all cells}} \dfrac{(f_0 - f_e)^2}{f_e} = 9.831$

Decision: Since $\chi^2_{\text{calc}} = 9.831$ is less than the critical bound of 13.277, do not reject H_0. There is not enough evidence to conclude there is any relationship between the commuting time of company employees and the level of stress-related problems observed on the job.

(b)   Decision rule: If $\chi^2 > 9.488$, reject H_0.

Test statistic: $\chi^2 = 9.831$

Decision: Since the $\chi^2_{\text{calc}} = 9.831$ is greater than the critical bound of 9.488, reject H_0. There is enough evidence at the 0.05 level to conclude there is a relationship between the commuting time of company employees and the level of stress-related problems observed on the job.

12.30 H_0: There is no relationship between when the decision is made of what to have for dinner and the type of household.

H_1: There is a relationship between when the decision is made of what to have for dinner and the type of household.

Decision rule: $d.f. = 12$. If $\chi^2 > 21.026$, reject H_0.   Test statistic: $\chi^2 = 129.520$

Decision: Since the $\chi^2_{\text{calc}} = 129.520$ is greater than the critical bound of 21.026, reject H_0. There is enough evidence to conclude there is a relationship between when the decision is made of what to have for dinner and the type of household.

12.32   (a) $H_0 : \pi_1 \geq \pi_2$ $H_1 : \pi_1 < \pi_2$ where 1 = beginning, 2 = end

Decision rule: If $Z < -1.645$, reject H_0.

Test statistic: $Z = \dfrac{B - C}{\sqrt{B + C}} = \dfrac{9 - 22}{\sqrt{9 + 22}} = -2.3349$

Decision: Since $Z = -2.3349 < -1.645$, reject H_0. There is enough evidence to conclude that the proportion of coffee drinkers who prefer Brand A is lower at the beginning of the advertising campaign than at the end of the advertising campaign.

(b) p-value = 0.0098. The probability of obtaining a data set which gives rise to a test statistic smaller than -2.3349 is 0.98% if the proportion of coffee drinkers who prefer Brand A is not lower at the beginning of the advertising campaign than at the end of the advertising campaign.

12.34   (a) $H_0 : \pi_1 \geq \pi_2$ $H_1 : \pi_1 < \pi_2$ where 1 = before, 2 = after

Decision rule: If $Z < -1.645$, reject H_0.

Test statistic: $Z = \dfrac{B - C}{\sqrt{B + C}} = \dfrac{5 - 15}{\sqrt{5 + 15}} = -2.2361$

Decision: Since $Z = -2.2361 < -1.645$, reject H_0. There is enough evidence to conclude that the proportion who prefer Brand A is lower before the advertising than after the advertising.

(b) p-value = 0.0127. The probability of obtaining a data set which gives rise to a test statistic smaller than -2.2361 is 1.27% if the proportion who prefer Brand A is not lower before the advertising than after the advertising.

12.36   (a) $H_0 : \pi_1 \geq \pi_2$ $H_1 : \pi_1 < \pi_2$ where 1 = year 1, 2 = year 2
Decision rule: If $Z < -1.645$, reject H_0.

Test statistic: $Z = \dfrac{B - C}{\sqrt{B + C}} = \dfrac{4 - 25}{\sqrt{4 + 25}} = -3.8996$

Decision: Since $Z = -3.8996 < -1.645$, reject H_0. There is enough evidence to conclude that the proportion of employees absent less than 5 days was lower in year 1 than in year 2.

(b) p-value is virtually zero. The probability of obtaining a data set which gives rise to a test statistic smaller than -3.8996 is virtually zero if the proportion of employees absent less than 5 years was not lower in year 1 than in year 2.

12.38   (a)   For $df = 23$ and $\alpha = 0.01$, $\chi_L^2 = 9.2604$ and $\chi_U^2 = 44.1814$.
(b)   For $df = 19$ and $\alpha = 0.05$, $\chi_L^2 = 8.9065$ and $\chi_U^2 = 32.8523$.
(c)   For $df = 15$ and $\alpha = 0.10$, $\chi_L^2 = 7.2609$ and $\chi_U^2 = 24.9958$.

12.40 $\chi^2 = \dfrac{(n-1) \cdot S^2}{\sigma^2} = \dfrac{15 \cdot 10^2}{12^2} = 10.417$

12.42   (a)   For $df = 15$ and $\alpha = 0.05$, $\chi_L^2 = 6.262$ and $\chi_U^2 = 27.488$.
(b)   For $df = 15$ and $\alpha = 0.05$, $\chi^2 = 7.261$.

12.44   You must assume that the data in the population are normally distributed to be able to use the chi-square test of a population variance or standard deviation. If the data selected do not come from an approximately normally distributed population, particularly for small sample sizes, the accuracy of the test can be seriously affected.

12.46   (a) H_0: $\sigma = \$200$. The standard deviation of the amount of auto repairs is equal to $200.
H_1: $\sigma \neq \$200$. The standard deviation of the amount of auto repairs is not equal to $200.
Decision rule: $df = 24$. If $\chi^2 < 12.401$ or $\chi^2 > 39.364$, reject H_0.

Test statistic: $\chi^2 = \dfrac{(n-1) \cdot S^2}{\sigma^2} = \dfrac{24 \cdot 237.52^2}{200^2} = 33.849$

Decision: Since the test statistic of $\chi_{calc}^2 = 33.849$ is between the critical boundaries of 12.401 and 39.364, do not reject H_0. There is insufficient evidence to conclude that the standard deviation of the amount of auto repairs is not equal to $200.

(b)   You must assume that the data in the population are normally distributed to be able to use the chi-square test of a population variance or standard deviation.

(c) p-value = 2(0.0874) = 0.1748. The probability of obtaining a sample whose standard deviation will give rise to a test statistic equal to or more extreme than 33.849 is 0.1748 when the null hypothesis is true.
Note: The p-value was found using Excel.

12.48 (a) H_0: $\sigma \geq 0.035$ inch. The standard deviation of the diameter of doorknobs is greater
             than or equal to 0.035 inch in the redesigned production process.
             H_1: $\sigma < 0.035$ inch. The standard deviation of the diameter of doorknobs is less than
             0.035 inch in the redesigned production process.
             Decision rule: $df = 24$. If $\chi^2 < 13.848$, reject H_0.

             Test statistic: $\chi^2 = \dfrac{(n-1) \cdot S^2}{\sigma^2} = \dfrac{24 \cdot 0.025^2}{0.035^2} = 12.245$

             Decision: Since the test statistic of $\chi^2_{calc} = 12.245$ is less than the critical boundary of
             13.848, reject H_0. There is sufficient evidence to conclude that the standard deviation
             of the diameter of doorknobs is less than 0.035 inch in the redesigned production
             process.

       (b)   You must assume that the data in the population are normally distributed to
             be able to use the chi-square test of a population variance or standard deviation.

       (c) p-value = $(1 - 0.9770) = 0.0230$. The probability of obtaining a test statistic equal to
             or more extreme than the result obtained from this sample data is 0.0230 if the
             population standard deviation is indeed no less than 0.035 inch.

12.50 (a) H_0: $\sigma \leq 2.5$ ampere-hours. The standard deviation in the capacity of the battery is
             equal to 2.5 ampere-hours.
             H_1: $\sigma > 2.5$ ampere-hours. The standard deviation in the capacity of the battery
             differs from 2.5 ampere-hours.
             Decision rule: $df = 19$. If $\chi^2 > 30.144$, reject H_0.

             Test statistic: $\chi^2 = \dfrac{(n-1) \cdot S^2}{\sigma^2} = \dfrac{19 \cdot 2.6589^2}{2.5^2} = 21.492$

             Decision: Since the test statistic of $\chi^2_{calc} = 21.492$ is less than the critical
             boundary of 30.144, do not reject H_0. There is not sufficient evidence to conclude
             that the standard deviation in the capacity of a certain type of battery differs from 2.5
             ampere-hours.

       (b)   You must assume that the data in the population are normally distributed to be able to
             use the chi-square test of a population variance or standard deviation.

       (c) p-value = 0.3103. The probability of obtaining a test statistic equal to or more
             extreme than the result obtained from this sample data is 0.3103 if the population
             standard deviation is indeed no greater than 2.5 ampere-hours.

12.52 $\lambda = 1.5$

H_0 : The number of service interruptions per day follows a Poison distribution.
H_1 : The number of service interruptions per day does not follow a Poison distribution.

Interruptions Per Day	f_0	$m_j f_j$	$P(X)$
0	160	0	0.223130
1	175	175	0.334695
2	86	172	0.251021
3	41	123	0.125511
4	18	72	0.047067
5	12	60	0.014120
6	8	48	0.003530
7 or more	0	0	0.000926
Total	500	650	

Combine the last two categories:

Interruptions Per Day	f_0	f_e	$(f_0 - f_e)^2 / f_e$
0	160	111.5651	21.02756048
1	175	167.3476	0.349923817
2	86	125.5107	12.43795484
3	41	62.75536	7.54191515
4	18	23.53326	1.301007902
5	12	7.059978	3.456642648
6 or more	8	2.22799	14.9534285
Total	500	500	61.06843334

$$\chi^2_{k-p-1} = \sum_k \frac{(f_0 - f_e)^2}{f_e} = 61.0684 \qquad \chi^2_{crit} = \chi^2_{6,0.01} = 16.8119$$

Since 61.0684 > 16.8119, reject H_0. There is sufficient evidence to conclude that the distribution of service interruptions does not follow a Poisson distribution with a population mean of 1.5 at the 1% level of significance.

12.54 H_0 : Battery life follows a normal distribution.
H_1 : Battery life does not follow a normal distribution.

Life	$P(X)$	f_e
under 0	0.001938	0.968776928
0 - under 1	0.029741	14.87047242
1 - under 2	0.172953	86.47668571
2 - under 3	0.377089	188.5444078
3 - under 4	0.310381	155.1906456
4 - under 5	0.096272	48.13607992
5 - under 6	0.011144	5.571843365
6 or more	0.0005	0.241088258
Total	1.000000	500

12.54   Combine the first two and the last two classes:
cont.

Life	f_0	f_e	$(f_0 - f_e)^2 / f_e$
under 1	12	15.83925	0.930589
1 - under 2	94	86.47669	0.654515
2 - under 3	170	188.5444	1.823947
3 - under 4	188	155.1906	6.936331
4 - under 5	28	48.13608	8.423239
5 or more	8	5.812932	0.822867
Total	500	500	19.59149

$$\chi^2_{k-p-1} = \sum_k \frac{(f_0 - f_e)^2}{f_e} = 19.5915 \qquad \chi^2_{crit} = \chi^2_{3,0.05} = 7.8147$$

Since $19.5915 > 7.8147$, reject H_0. There is sufficient evidence to conclude that the distribution of battery life does not follow a normal distribution.

12.56   (a)   The lower and upper critical values are 31 and 59, respectively.
    (b)   The lower and upper critical values are 29 and 61, respectively.
    (c)   The lower and upper critical values are 25 and 65, respectively.
    (d)   As the level of significance α gets smaller, the width of the nonrejection region gets wider.

12.58   (a)   The lower critical value is 31.
    (b)   The lower critical value is 29.
    (c)   The lower critical value is 27.
    (d)   The lower critical value is 25.

12.60   The lower and upper critical values are 40 and 79, respectively.

12.62   (a)   The ranks for Sample 1 are 1, 2, 4, 5, and 10, respectively.
           The ranks for Sample 2 are 3, 6.5, 6.5, 8, 9, and 11, respectively.
    (b) $T_1 = 1 + 2 + 4 + 5 + 10 = 22$
    (c) $T_2 = 3 + 6.5 + 6.5 + 8 + 9 + 11 = 44$
    (d) $T_1 + T_2 = \dfrac{n(n+1)}{2} = \dfrac{11(12)}{2} = 66 \qquad T_1 + T_2 = 22 + 44 = 66$

12.64   Decision: Since $T_1 = 22$ is greater than the lower critical bound of 20, do not reject H_0.

12.66   (a) $H_0: M_1 = M_2$ where Populations: 1 = LIRR,   2 = NJT
                    $H_1: M_1 \neq M_2$

PHStat output:

Data	
Level of Significance	**0.05**
Population 1 Sample	
Sample Size	10
Sum of Ranks	141
Population 2 Sample	
Sample Size	12
Sum of Ranks	112
Intermediate Calculations	
Total Sample Size n	22
$T1$ Test Statistic	141
$T1$ Mean	115
Standard Error of $T1$	15.16575
Z Test Statistic	1.714389
Two-Tailed Test	
Lower Critical Value	-2.57583
Upper Critical Value	2.575835
***p*-value**	0.086457
Do not reject the null hypothesis	

$$\mu_{T_1} = \frac{n_1(n+1)}{2} = \frac{10(22+1)}{2} = 115$$

$$\sigma_{T_1} = \sqrt{\frac{n_1 n_2 (n+1)}{12}} = \sqrt{\frac{(10)(12)(22+1)}{12}} = 15.1658$$

$$Z = \frac{T_1 - \mu_{T_1}}{\sigma_{T_1}} = 1.714$$

Decision: Since $Z = 1.714$ is between the critical bounds of -2.58 and 2.58, do not reject H_0. There is not enough evidence to conclude that there is any difference in the median tendencies to be late.

(b)   You must assume approximately equal variability in the two populations.

(c)   There is insufficient evidence to conclude that there is any significant difference in the median tendencies of the railroads to be late.

12.68   (a) $H_0: M_1 \geq M_2$ where Populations: 1 = unflawed

                                                                      2 = flawed

$H_1: M_1 < M_2$

Decision rule: If $Z < -1.645$, reject H_0.

Test statistic: $T_1 = 286$

$$\mu_{T_1} = \frac{n_1 \cdot (n+1)}{2} = \frac{18 \cdot (59)}{2} = 531; \quad \sigma_{T_1} = \sqrt{\frac{n_1 \cdot n_2 \cdot (n+1)}{12}} = \sqrt{\frac{18 \cdot 40 \cdot 59}{12}} = 59.498$$

$$Z = \frac{T_1 - \mu_{T_1}}{\sigma_{T_1}} = \frac{286 - 531}{59.498} = -4.118$$

Decision: Since $Z_{calc} = -4.118$ is less than the lower critical bound of -1.645, reject H_0. There is enough evidence to conclude that the median crack size is less for the unflawed sample than for the flawed sample.

    (b)   You must assume approximately equal variability in the two populations.

    (c)   Using both the pooled-variance t-test and the separate-variance t-test allowed you to reject the null hypothesis and conclude in Problem 10.21 that the mean crack size is less for the unflawed sample than for the flawed sample. In this test using the Wilcoxon rank sum test with large-sample Z-approximation also allowed you to reject the null hypothesis and conclude that the median crack size is less for the unflawed sample than for the flawed sample.

12.70   (a) $H_0: M_1 = M_2$ where Populations: 1 = Office I   2 = Office II

            $H_1: M_1 \neq M_2$

PHStat Output:

Wilcoxon Rank Sum Test	
Data	
Level of Significance	**0.05**
Population 1 Sample	
Sample Size	20
Sum of Ranks	434.5
Population 2 Sample	
Sample Size	20
Sum of Ranks	385.5
Intermediate Calculations	
Total Sample Size n	40
$T1$ Test Statistic	434.5
$T1$ Mean	410
Standard Error of $T1$	36.96846
Z Test Statistic	0.662727
Two-Tailed Test	
Lower Critical Value	**-1.95996**
Upper Critical Value	**1.959961**
p-value	**0.507505**
Do not reject the null hypothesis	

12.70 (a)   Decision rule: If $Z < -1.96$ or $Z > 1.96$, reject H_0.

cont.   Decision: Since $Z_{calc} = 0.6627$ is between the lower and upper critical bounds of ± 1.96, do not reject H_0. There is not enough evidence to conclude that the median time to clear the problems between the two offices is different.

(b)   You must assume approximately equal variability in the two populations.

(c)   Using both the pooled-variance t-test and the separate-variance t-test in Problem 10.16, you do not reject the null hypothesis; you conclude that there is not enough evidence to show that the mean waiting time between the two branches is different. In this test using the Wilcoxon rank sum test with large-sample Z-approximation, you also do not reject the null hypothesis; you conclude that there is not enough evidence to show that the median waiting time between the two branches is different.

12.72 (a) $W_U = 53$ (b) $W_U = 56$ (c) $W_U = 59$ (d) $W_U = 61$

12.74

Observation	D_i	abs(D_i)	Sign of D_i	R	signed R	R(+)
1	3.2	3.2 +		6	6	6
2	1.7	1.7 +		2.5	2.5	2.5
3	4.5	4.5 +		7	7	7
4	0	0 Discard		-	-	-
5	11.1	11.1 +		9	9	9
6	-0.8	0.8 -		1	-1	0
7	2.3	2.3 +		5	5	5
8	-2	2 -		4	-4	0
9	0	0 Discard		-	-	-
10	14.8	14.8 +		10	10	10
11	5.6	5.6 +		8	8	8
12	1.7	1.7 +		2.5	2.5	2.5

$W = \Sigma_{i=1}^{n'} R_i^{(+)} = 50$

12.76   Since $W = 50 > W_U = 47$, reject H_0.

12.78 $n' = 12$, $\alpha = 0.05$, $W_U = 61$

12.80 (a) $H_0: M_D = 0$ $H_1: M_D \neq 0$
              where Populations: $1 = 2004$, $2 = 2002$
              Minitab output:

```
Wilcoxon Signed Rank Test: Differences

Test of median = 0.000000 versus median not = 0.000000

                      N for   Wilcoxon              Estimated
               N      Test    Statistic      P      Median
Differen       18      18         3.0     0.000      -80.91
```

Since the p-value is virtually zero, reject H_0. There is sufficient evidence of a difference in the median daily hotel rate in June 2002 and March 2004.

12.80   (b)   The *t* test for the mean difference in Problem 10.24 concludes that there is a
cont.   difference in the mean daily hotel rate between June 2002 and March 2004, and the
              Wilcoxon signed-ranks test concludes that there is a difference in the median daily
              hotel rate between June 2002 and March 2004.

12.82   (a) H_0: $M_D = 0$ where Populations: 1 = In-line 2 = Analytical lab
              H_1: $M_D \neq 0$
              Minitab Output:

```
┌─────────────────────────────────────────────────────────────────────┐
│ Wilcoxon Signed Rank Test: Differences                                │
│                                                                       │
│ Test of median = 0.000000 versus median not = 0.000000                │
│                                                                       │
│                     N for    Wilcoxon              Estimated          │
│                N    Test    Statistic        P      Median            │
│ Differen      24     23        128.5      0.784   -0.005000           │
└─────────────────────────────────────────────────────────────────────┘
```

Since the *p*-value = 0.784 is greater than the 0.05 level of significance, do not reject
H_0. There is insufficient evidence of a difference in the median measurements in-
line and from an analytical lab.

        (b)   Using the paired-sample *t*-test in Problem 10.25, you do not reject the null
              hypothesis; you conclude that there is not enough evidence of a difference in the
              mean measurements in-line and from an analytical lab. Using the Wilcoxon signed
              rank test, you do not reject the null hypothesis; you conclude that there is not enough
              evidence of a difference in the median measurements in-line and from an analytical
              lab.

12.84   (a) H_0: $M_D = 0$ where Populations: 1 = Before 2 = After
              H_1: $M_D \neq 0$
              Minitab Output:

```
┌─────────────────────────────────────────────────────────────────────┐
│ Wilcoxon Signed Rank Test: Differences                                │
│                                                                       │
│ Test of median = 0.000000 versus median not = 0.000000                │
│                                                                       │
│                     N for    Wilcoxon              Estimated          │
│                N    Test    Statistic        P      Median            │
│ Differen      35     35        156.0      0.009    -5.500             │
└─────────────────────────────────────────────────────────────────────┘
```

Since the *p*-value = 0.009 is smaller than the 0.01 level of significance, reject H_0.

There is sufficient evidence of a difference in the median performance ratings
between the two programs.

        (b)   Using the paired-sample *t*-test in Problem 10.29, you reject the null hypothesis and
              conclude that there is enough evidence of a difference in the mean performance
              ratings between the two programs. Using the Wilcoxon signed rank test, you reject
              the null hypothesis and conclude that there is enough evidence of a difference in the
              median performance ratings between the two programs.

12.86   For the 0.01 level of significance and 5 degrees of freedom, $\chi_U^2 = 15.086$.

12.88 $H_0: M_A = M_B = M_C$ H_1: At least one of the medians differs.
Decision rule: If $H > \chi_U^2 = 9.210$, reject H_0.   Test statistic: $H = 0.64$

Decision: Since $H_{calc} = 0.64$ is less than the critical bound of 9.210, do not reject H_0. There is insufficient evidence to show any real difference in the median reaction times for the three learning methods.

Minitab Output

Kruskal-Wallis Test				
LEVEL	NOBS	MEDIAN	AVE. RANK	Z VALUE
1	9	10.00	11.6	-0.74
2	8	15.50	13.3	0.12
3	8	12.50	14.4	0.64
OVERALL	25		13.0	
H = 0.64 d.f. = 2 p = 0.728				

12.90   (a) $H_0: M_{Front} = M_{Middle} = M_{Rear}$ H_1: At least one of the medians differs.
Decision rule: If $H > \chi_U^2 = 5.991$, reject H_0.

Sample	Value	Rank			Front	Middle	Rear
Middle	1.4	1					
Middle	1.6	2		Tj	88.5	25	57.5
Middle	1.8	3		Tj^2	7832.25	625	3306.25
Middle	2	4		nj	6	6	6
Rear	2.2	5		Tj^2/nj	1305.375	104.1667	551.0417
Middle	2.4	6					
Rear	2.8	7.5					
Rear	2.8	7.5					
Middle	3.2	9					
Front	4	10.5					
Rear	4	10.5					
Rear	4.6	12					
Front	5	13					
Front	5.4	14					
Rear	6	15					
Front	6.2	16					
Front	7.2	17					
Front	8.6	18					

Decision: Reject H_0 if $H > \chi_{.05,2}^2 = 5.991$.

Test statistic: $H = 11.82$ (adjusted for ties by Minitab)

Note: The test statistic

$$H = \left[\frac{12}{n(n+1)} \sum_{j=1}^{c} \frac{T_j^2}{n_j} \right] - 3(n+1) = \left[\frac{12}{18(19)} (1960.5833) \right] - 3(19) = 11.79 \text{ is}$$

computed by hand and unadjusted for ties.

12.90   (a)   Decision: Since $H_{calc} = 11.82$ is greater than the critical bound of 5.991, reject H_0.
cont.   There is sufficient evidence to show there is a difference in the median sales of pet
               toys among the three store aisle locations.

        (b)   In problem 11.13, you concluded that there was a difference in mean sales volumes
               in thousands of dollars across the three store aisle locations. The results are
               consistent.

Minitab Output

Kruskal-Wallis Test

LEVEL	NOBS	MEDIAN	AVE. RANK	Z VALUE
1	6	5.800	14.8	2.95
2	6	1.900	4.2	-3.00
3	6	3.400	9.6	0.05
OVERALL	18		9.5	

H = 11.79 d.f. = 2 p = 0.003
H = 11.82 d.f. = 2 p = 0.003 (adjusted for ties)

12.92   PHStat output:

Kruskal-Wallis Rank Test	
Data	
Level of Significance	0.05
Group 1	
Sum of Ranks	254
Sample Size	10
Group 2	
Sum of Ranks	270
Sample Size	10
Group 3	
Sum of Ranks	241
Sample Size	10
Group 4	
Sum of Ranks	55
Sample Size	10
Intermediate Calculations	
Sum of Squared Ranks/Sample Size	19852.2
Sum of Sample Sizes	40
Number of groups	4
H Test Statistic	22.26
Test Result	
Critical Value	7.814725
p-Value	5.76E-05
Reject the null hypothesis	

        (a) H_0: $M_{Kroger} = M_{Glad} = M_{Hefty} = M_{Tuffstuff}$ H_1: At least one of the medians differs.
               Since the p-value is virtually zero, reject H_0. There is sufficient evidence of a
               difference in the median strength of the four brands of trash bags.

        (b)   In (a), you conclude that there is evidence of a difference in the median strength of
               the four brands of trash bags, while in problem 11.10, you conclude that there is
               evidence of a difference in the mean strength of the four brands.

12.94 (a) H_0: $M_1 = M_2 = M_3 = M_4 = M_5 = M_6$ H_1: At least one of the medians differs.
           Reject H_0 if $F_R > 9.2363$.

     (b)   Since $F_R = 11.56 > 9.2363$, reject H_0. There is enough evidence that the medians are different.

12.96   Minitab output:

Friedman Test: Diameter versus Brand, Student

```
Friedman test for Diameter by Brand blocked by Student

S = 3.90   DF = 3   P = 0.272
S = 4.11   DF = 3   P = 0.250 (adjusted for ties)

                 Est     Sum of
Brand        N   Median  Ranks
Bazooka      4   9.500   13.0
Bubbleta     4   7.313    8.0
Bubbleyu     4   8.000    7.0
Bubblici     4   9.313   12.0

Grand median  =   8.531
```

     (a) $H_0 : M_A = M_B = M_C = M_D$ $H_1 :$ Not all medians are equal.

	Rank			
	Bazooka	**Bubbletape**	**Bubbleyum**	**Bubblicious**
	2	3	1	4
	3	1	2	4
	4	1	2.5	2.5
	4	3	1.5	1.5
R.j	13	8	7	12
(R.j)^2	169	64	49	144

Test statistic: $F_R = \dfrac{12}{rc(c+1)}\sum_{j=1}^{c} R_{.j}^2 - 3r(c+1) = \dfrac{12}{(4)(4)(5)}(426) - 3(4)(5) = 3.9$

Upper critical value: $\chi_U^2 = \chi_{0.05,3}^2 = 7.8147$ p-value $= 0.272$

Since the p-value $= 0.272 > 0.05$ and $F_R = 3.9 < 7.81$, do not reject H_0. There is insufficient evidence of a difference in the median diameter of the bubbles produced by the different brands.

     (b)   In (a), you conclude that there is no evidence of a difference in the median diameter of the bubbles produced by the different brands while in problem 11.24(a), you conclude that there is no evidence of a difference in the mean diameter of the bubbles produced by the different brands.

12.98   Minitab output:
Friedman Test: Thickness versus Position, Batch1

```
Friedman test for Thickness by Position blocked by Batch1

S = 97.97   DF = 4   P = 0.000
S = 99.63   DF = 4   P = 0.000 (adjusted for ties)

                      Est     Sum of
Position       N    Median    Ranks
   1          30    240.45    32.0
   2          30    242.55    64.0
  18          30    245.25    97.5
  19          30    249.15    141.0
  28          30    246.85    115.5

Grand median  =   244.85
```

(a) $H_0 : M_1 = M_2 = M_{18} = M_{19} = M_{28}$ H_1 : Not all medians are equal.

Since the p-value is virtually zero, reject H_0 at 0.05 level of significance. There is evidence of a difference in the median thickness of the wafers for the five positions.

(b)   In (a), you conclude that there is evidence of a difference in the median thickness of the wafers for the five positions, and in problem 11.27, you conclude that there is evidence of a difference in the mean thickness of the wafers for the five positions.

12.100   The Chi-square test for the difference between two proportions can be used only when the alternative hypothesis is two-tailed.

12.102   The Chi-square test for independence can be used as long as all expected frequencies are at least one.

12.104   The Wilcoxon rank sum test should be used when you are unable to assume that each of two independent populations are normally distributed.

12.106   The Kruskal-Wallis test should be used if you cannot assume that the populations are normally distributed.

12.108   (a) H_0: There is no relationship between a student's gender and his/her pizzeria selection.
H_1: There is a relationship between a student's gender and his/her pizzeria selection.
Decision rule: $d.f. = 1$. If $\chi^2 > 3.841$, reject H_0.   Test statistic: $\chi^2 = 0.412$
Decision: Since the $\chi^2_{calc} = 0.412$ is smaller than the critical bound of 3.841, do not reject H_0. There is not enough evidence to conclude that there is a relationship between a student's gender and his/her pizzeria selection.

(b)   Test statistic: $\chi^2 = 2.624$
Decision: Since the $\chi^2_{calc} = 2.624$ is less than the critical bound of 3.841, do not reject H_0. There is not enough evidence to conclude that there is a relationship between a student's gender and his/her pizzeria selection.

12.108 (c) H_0: There is no relationship between price and pizzeria selection.
cont. H_1: There is a relationship between price and pizzeria selection.
            Decision rule: $d.f. = 2$. If $\chi^2 > 5.991$, reject H_0.   Test statistic: $\chi^2 = 4.956$
            Decision: Since the $\chi^2_{calc} = 4.956$ is smaller than the critical bound of 5.991, do not
            reject H_0. There is not enough evidence to conclude that there is a relationship
            between price and pizzeria selection.
       (d) p-value = 0.0839. The probability of obtaining a sample that gives a test statistic
            equal to or greater than 4.956 is 8.39% if the null hypothesis of no relationship
            between price and pizzeria selection is true.
       (e) Since there is no evidence that price and pizzeria selection are related, it is
            inappropriate to determine which prices are different in terms of pizzeria preference.

12.110 (a) $H_0: \pi_1 = \pi_2$ $H_1: \pi_1 \neq \pi_2$
            where population 1 = boys, 2 = girls

            Test statistic: $\chi^2 = \sum_{\text{All cells}} \frac{(f_o - f_e)^2}{f_e} = 3.3084$

            Decision: Since the calculated test statistic 3.3084 is less than the critical value of
            3.8415, you do not reject H_0; you conclude that there is not a significant difference
            between the proportion of boys and girls who worry about having enough money.
       (b) p-value = 0.0689. The probability of obtaining a data set which gives rise to a test
            statistic larger than 3.3084 is 6.89% if there is no difference between the proportion of
            boys and girls who worry about having enough money.

12.112 (a) H_0: There is no relationship between type of user and the seriousness of concern over
               the first statement.
            H_1: There is a relationship between type of user and the seriousness of concern over
               the first statement.
            Decision rule: If $\chi^2 > 3.841$, reject H_0.   Test statistic: $\chi^2 = 12.026$
            Decision: Since the $\chi^2_{calc} = 12.026$ is greater than the critical bound of 3.841, reject H_0.
            There is enough evidence to conclude there is a relationship between type of user and
            the seriousness of concern over the first statement.
       (b) The p-value = 0.000525. The probability of obtaining a sample that gives rise to a test
            statistic of 12.026 or larger is 0.000525 if there is in fact no relationship between type of
            user and the seriousness of concern over the first statement.
       (c) H_0: There is no relationship between type of user and the seriousness of concern over
               the second statement.
            H_1: There is a relationship between type of user and the seriousness of concern over
               the first statement.
            Decision rule: If $\chi^2 > 3.841$, reject H_0.   Test statistic: $\chi^2 = 7.297$
            Decision: Since the $\chi^2_{calc} = 7.297$ is greater than the critical bound of 3.841, reject H_0.
            There is enough evidence to conclude there is a relationship between type of user and
            the seriousness of concern over the second statement.
       (d) The p-value = 0.00691. The probability of obtaining a sample that gives rise to a test
            statistic of 7.297 or larger is 0.00691 if there is in fact no relationship between type of
            user and the seriousness of concern over the second statement.

12.114 (a) H_0: There is no relationship between the attitudes of employees toward the use of self-managed work teams and employee job classification.

H_1: There is a relationship between the attitudes of employees toward the use of self-managed work teams and employee job classification.

Decision rule: If $\chi^2 > 12.592$, reject H_0.

Test statistic: $\chi^2 = 11.895$

Decision: Since $\chi^2_{calc} = 11.895$ is less than the critical bound 12.592, do not reject H_0. There is not enough evidence to conclude that there is a relationship between the attitudes of employees toward the use of self-managed work teams and employee job classification.

(b) H_0: There is no relationship between the attitudes of employees toward vacation time without pay and employee job classification.

H_1: There is a relationship between the attitudes of employees toward vacation time without pay and employee job classification.

Decision rule: If $\chi^2 > 12.592$, reject H_0.

Test statistic: $\chi^2 = 3.294$

Decision: Since $\chi^2_{calc} = 3.294$ is less than the critical bound 12.592, do not reject H_0. There is not enough evidence to conclude that there is a relationship between the attitudes of employees toward vacation time without pay and employee job classification.

12.116 H_0: There is no relationship between type of incident and type of model.

H_1: There is a relationship between type of incident and type of model.

Test statistic: $\chi^2 = \sum_{\text{All cells}} \dfrac{\left(f_o - f_e\right)^2}{f_e} = 160.38$

Decision rule: If $\chi^2 > 5.991$, reject H_0.

Decision: Since $\chi^2_{calc} = 160.38$ is greater than the critical bound 5.991, reject H_0. There is enough evidence to conclude that there is a relationship between type of incident and type of model.

12.118 (a) $H_0 : \pi_1 = \pi_2$ $H_1 : \pi_1 \neq \pi_2$ where 1 = before, 2 = after

Decision rule: If $Z < -1.645$ or $Z > 1.645$, reject H_0.

Test statistic: $Z = \dfrac{B - C}{\sqrt{B + C}} = \dfrac{6 - 14}{\sqrt{6 + 14}} = -1.7889$

Decision: Since $Z = -1.7889$ is smaller than the lower critical bound of -1.645, reject H_0. There is enough evidence of a difference in the proportion of respondents who prefer Coca-Cola before and after viewing the ads.

(b) p-value = 0.0736. The probability of obtaining a data set which gives rise to a test statistic equal to or more extreme than -1.7889 is 7.36% if there is not a difference in the proportion of respondents who prefer Coca-Cola before and after viewing the ads.

(c)   The numbers in the second table are obtained from the row and column totals of the first table.

12.118 (d) $H_0: \pi_1 = \pi_2$ $H_1: \pi_1 \neq \pi_2$ where 1 = before, 2 = after

cont.

Test statistic: $\chi^2 = \sum\limits_{\text{All cells}} \dfrac{(f_o - f_e)^2}{f_e} = 0.6528$

Decision: Since the calculated test statistic 0.6528 is smaller than the critical value of 3.8415, you do not reject H_0; you conclude that there is not a significant difference in preference for Coca-Cola before and after viewing the ads.

(e) p-value = 0.4191. The probability of obtaining a data set which gives rise to a test statistic larger than 0.6528 is 41.91% if there is not a significant difference in preference for Coca-Cola before and after viewing the ads.

(f)   The McNemar test performed using the information in the first table takes into consideration the fact that the same set of respondents are surveyed before and after viewing the ads while the chi-square test performed using the information in the second table ignores this fact. The McNemar test should be used because of the related samples (before-after comparison).

CHAPTER 13

OBJECTIVES

- To use regression analysis to predict the value of a dependent variable based on an independent variable
- To understand the meaning of the regression coefficient b_0 and b_1
- To be familiar with the assumptions of regression analysis, how to evaluate the assumptions, and what to do if the assumptions are violated
- To be able to make inferences about the slope and correlation coefficient
- To be able to estimate mean values and predict individual values

OVERVIEW AND KEY CONCEPTS

Purpose of Regression Analysis

- Regression analysis is used for predicting the values of a dependent (response) variable based on the value of at least one independent (explanatory) variable.

The Simple Linear Regression Model

- The relationship between the dependent variable (Y) and the explanatory variable (X) is described by a linear function.
- The change of the explanatory variable causes the explained (dependent) variable to change.
- The value of the explained variable depends on the explanatory variable.
- The population linear regression: $Y_i = \beta_0 + \beta_1 X_i + \varepsilon_i$ where β_0 is the intercept and β_1 is the slope of the population regression line $\mu_{Y|X} = \beta_0 + \beta_1 X_i$ and ε_i is called the error term.

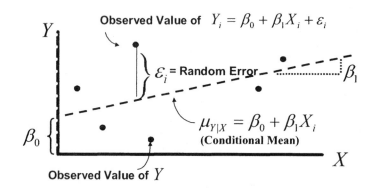

- The parameters β_0 and β_1 are unknown and need to be estimated.
- The least squares estimates for β_0 and β_1 are b_0 and b_1, respectively, obtained by minimizing the sum of squared residuals, $\sum_{i=1}^{n} \left(Y_i - \left(b_0 + b_1 X_i \right) \right)^2 = \sum_{i=1}^{n} e_i^2$.

- The sample linear regression: $Y_i = b_0 + b_1 X_i + e_i$ where b_0 is the intercept and b_1 is the slope of the simple linear regression equation $\hat{Y} = b_0 + b_1 X_i$ and e_i is called the residual.

- The simple linear regression equation (sample regression line) $\hat{Y} = b_0 + b_1 X_i$ can be used to predict the value of the dependent variable for a given value of the independent variable X.

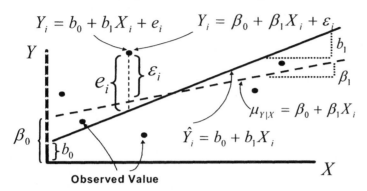

Interpretations of β_0, β_1, b_0 and b_1

- $\beta_0 = E(Y \mid X = 0) = \mu_{Y|X=0}$ is the average value of Y when the value of X is zero.

- $b_0 = \hat{E}(Y \mid X = 0) = \hat{Y}(X = 0)$ is the *estimated* average value of Y when the value of X is zero.

- $\beta_1 = \dfrac{\text{change in } E(Y \mid X)}{\text{change in } X} = \dfrac{\text{change in } \mu_{Y|X}}{\text{change in } X}$ measures the change in the average value of Y as a result of a one-unit change in X.

- $b_1 = \dfrac{\text{change in } \hat{E}(Y \mid X)}{\text{change in } X} = \dfrac{\text{change in } \hat{Y}}{\text{change in } X}$ measures the *estimated* change in the average value of Y as a result of a one-unit change in X.

Some Important Identities in the Simple Linear Regression Model

- $Y_i = \beta_0 + \beta_1 X_i + \varepsilon_i = \mu_{Y|X} + \varepsilon_i$. The value of the dependent variable is decomposed into the value on the population regression line and the error term.

- $Y_i = b_0 + b_1 X_i + e_i = \hat{Y}_i + e_i$. The value of the dependent variable is decomposed into the value on the sample regression line (fitted regression line) and the residual term.

- $\mu_{Y|X} = \beta_0 + \beta_1 X_i = E(Y \mid X)$ is the population regression line, which measures the average value of the dependent variable Y for a particular value of the independent variable X. Hence, it is also sometimes called the conditional mean regression line.

- $\hat{Y}_i = b_0 + b_1 X_i$ is the sample regression line (simple linear regression equation), which measures the *estimated* average value of the dependent variable Y for a particular value of the independent variable X. It also provides prediction for the value of Y for a given value of X.

- $\varepsilon_i = Y_i - \mu_{Y|X} = Y_i - (\beta_0 + \beta_1 X_i)$ is the error.

- $e_i = Y_i - \hat{Y}_i = Y_i - (b_0 + b_1 X_i)$ is the residual.

- $SST = \sum_{i=1}^{n} \left(Y_i - \bar{Y}\right)^2$ is the total sum of squares.

- $SSR = \sum_{i=1}^{n} \left(\hat{Y}_i - \bar{Y}\right)^2$ is the regression (explained) sum of squares.

- $SSE = \sum_{i=1}^{n} \left(Y_i - \hat{Y}_i\right)^2 = \sum_{i=1}^{n} e_i^2$ is the error (residual) sum of squares.

- $MSR = \dfrac{SSR}{k} = \dfrac{SSR}{1}$ where k is the number of the independent variable, which is 1 in the simple linear regression model.

- $MSE = \dfrac{SSE}{n-k-1} = \dfrac{SSE}{n-2}$

- The coefficient of determination

    - $r^2 = \dfrac{SSR}{SST} = \dfrac{\text{Regression Sum of Squares}}{\text{Total Sum of Squares}}$

    - The coefficient of determination measures the proportion of variation in Y that is explained by the independent variable X in the regression model.

- Standard error of estimate

    - $S_{YX} = \sqrt{\dfrac{SSE}{n-2}} = \sqrt{\dfrac{\sum_{i=1}^{n}\left(Y - \hat{Y}_i\right)^2}{n-2}}$

    - The standard error of estimate is the standard deviation of the variation of observations around the sample regression line $\hat{Y}_i = b_0 + b_1 X_i$.

The ANOVA Table for the Simple Linear Regression Model as Presented in Excel

ANOVA					
	df	SS	MS	F	Significance F
Regression	k	SSR	MSR=SSR/k	MSR/MSE	p-value of the F Test
Residuals	n-k-1	SSE	MSE=SSE/(n-k-1)		
Total	n-1	SST			

Assumptions Needed for the Simple Linear Regression Model

- Normality of error: The errors around the population regression line are normally distributed at each X value. This also implies that the dependent variable is normally distributed at each value of the independent variable.
- Homoscedasticity: The variance (amount of variation) of the errors around the population regression line is the same at each X value.
- Independence of errors: The errors around the population regression line are independent for each value of X.

Residual Analysis

- Residual analysis is used to evaluate whether the regression model that has been fitted to the data is an appropriate model.
- **Residual analysis for linearity:**

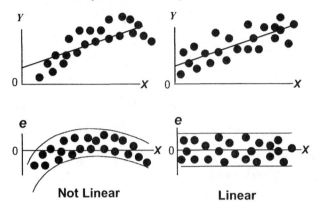

- **Residual analysis for homoscedasticity:**

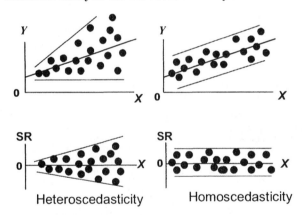

- **Residual analysis for independence:**

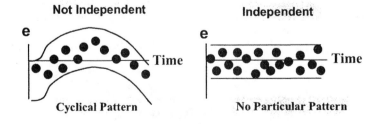

Residual Is Plotted Against Time to Detect Any Autocorrelation

- **Residual analysis for independence using Durbin-Watson statistic:**
    1. H_0: No autocorrelation (error terms are independent)

       H_1: There is autocorrelation (error terms are not independent)

    2. Compute the Durbin-Watson statistic $D = \dfrac{\sum\limits_{i=2}^{n}(e_i - e_{i-1})^2}{\sum\limits_{i=1}^{n}e_i^2}$

    3. Obtain the critical values d_L and d_U from a table.
    4. Compare the Durbin-Watson statistic with the critical values.

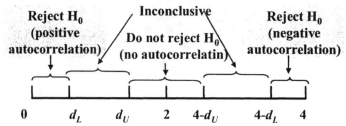

    5. Make a statistical decision.
    6. Draw a conclusion.

t Test for the Slope Parameter β_1

- $H_0 : \beta_1 = 0$ (Y does not depend on X)

  $H_1 : \beta_1 \neq 0$ (Y depends linearly on X)

- **Test statistic:**
    - $t = \dfrac{b_1 - \beta_1}{S_{b_1}}$ with $(n-2)$ degrees of freedom, where $S_{b_1} = \dfrac{S_{YX}}{\sqrt{\sum\limits_{i=1}^{n}(X_i - \bar{X})^2}}$

    - The t test can also be a one-tail test for a one-tail alternative.
- **Confidence interval estimate:** Use the $100(1-\alpha)\%$ confidence interval for the slope parameter β_1.
    - $b_1 \pm t_{\alpha/2, n-2} S_{b_1}$

F Test for the Slope Parameter β_1

- $H_0: \beta_1 = 0$ (*Y* does not depend on *X*)

  $H_1: \beta_1 \neq 0$ (*Y* depends linearly on *X*)

- **Test statistic:**

  - $F = \dfrac{\dfrac{SSR}{1}}{\dfrac{SSE}{(n-2)}}$ with 1 numerator degrees of freedom and $(n-2)$ denominator

    degrees of freedom.
  - The *F* test always has a right-tail rejection region and can only be used for the two-tail alternative.

The Relationship between the *t* Test and *F* Test for the Slope Parameter β_1

- For $H_0: \beta_1 = 0$ vs $H_1: \beta_1 \neq 0$, $t^2 = F$ and the *p*-value of the *t* test is identical to the *p*-value of the *F* test.

Correlation Analysis

- Correlation analysis is concerned with the strength of any linear relationship between 2 quantitative variables.
- There is no causal effect implied in a correlation analysis.
- The population correlation coefficient ρ is used to measure the strength of the linear relationship between the variables while the sample correlation coefficient r provides an estimate of the strength.
- **Features of ρ and r :**
  - They are unit free.
  - Their values range between –1 and 1.
  - The close is the value to –1, the stronger is the negative linear relationship.
  - The close is the value to +1, the stronger is the positive linear relationship.
  - The close is the value to 0, the weaker is any linear relationship.

t Test for a Linear Relationship

- **Hypotheses:**
  - $H_0: \rho = 0$ (There is no linear relationship)
  - $H_1: \rho \neq 0$ (There is some linear relationship)
- **Test statistic:**

  - $t = \dfrac{r - \rho}{\sqrt{\dfrac{1 - r^2}{n - 2}}}$ with $(n-2)$ degrees of freedom, where

    $r = \sqrt{r^2} = \dfrac{\displaystyle\sum_{i=1}^{n}(X_i - \bar{X})(Y_i - \bar{Y})}{\sqrt{\displaystyle\sum_{i=1}^{n}(X_i - \bar{X})^2 \sum_{i=1}^{n}(Y_i - \bar{Y})^2}}$.

  - The *t* test can be a one-tail test for a one-tail alternative.

Confidence Interval Estimate for the Mean of Y $\left(\mu_{Y|X} \right)$

- The point estimate for $\mu_{Y|X=X_i}$ is $\hat{Y}_i$

- The confidence interval estimate for $\mu_{Y|X}$ is $\hat{Y}_i \pm t_{\alpha/2, n-2} S_{YX} \sqrt{\dfrac{1}{n} + \dfrac{(X_i - \bar{X})^2}{\displaystyle\sum_{i=1}^{n}(X_i - \bar{X})^2}}$

Prediction Interval for an Individual Response Y

- The point prediction for an individual response Y_i at a particular X_i, denoted as $Y_{X=X_i}$ is

$$\hat{Y}_i = b_0 + b_1 X_i$$

- The prediction interval for an individual response Y_i is

$$\hat{Y}_i \pm t_{\alpha/2, n-2} S_{YX} \sqrt{1 + \dfrac{1}{n} + \dfrac{(X_i - \bar{X})^2}{\displaystyle\sum_{i=1}^{n}(X_i - \bar{X})^2}}$$

Common Pitfalls in Regression Analysis

- Lacking an awareness of the assumptions underlying least-squares regression
- Not knowing how to evaluate the assumptions
- Not knowing what the alternatives to least-squares regression are if a particular assumption is violated
- Using a regression model without knowledge of the subject matter
- Extrapolating outside the relevant range
- Concluding that a significant relationship identified in an observational study is due to a cause-and-effect relationship

Strategy for Avoiding the Pitfalls in Regression

- Always start with a scatter plot to observe the possible relationship between X and Y
- Check the assumptions of the regression after the regression model has been fit, before moving on to using the results of the model
- Plot the residuals versus the independent variable to determine whether the model fit to the data is appropriate and check visually for violations of the homoscedasticity assumption
- Use a histogram, stem-and-leaf display, box-and-whisker plot, or normal probability plot of the residuals to graphically evaluate whether the normality assumption has been seriously violated
- If the evaluations indicate violations in the assumptions, use alternative methods to least-squares regression or alternative least-squares models (quadratic or multiple regression) depending on what the evaluation has indicated
- If the evaluations do not indicate violations in the assumptions, then the inferential aspects of the regression analysis can be undertaken, tests for the significance of the regression coefficients can be done, and confidence and prediction intervals can be developed
- Avoid making predictions and forecasts outside the relevant range of the independent variable

- Always note that the relationships identified in observational studies may or may not be due to a cause-and-effect relationship, and remember that while causation implies correlation, correlation does not imply causation

SOLUTIONS TO END OF SECTION
AND CHAPTER REVIEW EVEN PROBLEMS

13.2   (a)   yes,   (b) no,   (c) no,   (d) yes

13.4   (a)

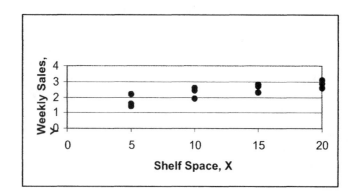

(b)   For each increase in shelf space of an additional foot, there is an expected increase in weekly sales of an estimated 0.074 hundreds of dollars, or \$7.40.

(c) $\hat{Y} = 1.45 + 0.074X = 1.45 + 0.074(8) = 2.042$, or \$204.20

13.6   (a)

Scatter Diagram

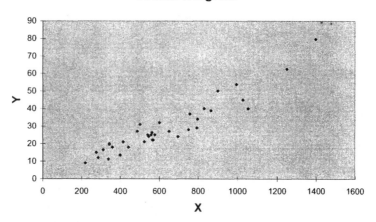

(b)   Partial Excel output:

	Coefficients	Standard Error	t Stat	P-value
Intercept	-2.3697	2.0733	-1.1430	0.2610
Feet	0.0501	0.0030	16.5223	0.0000

(c)   The estimated mean amount of labor will increase by 0.05 hour for each additional cubic foot moved.

(d) $\hat{Y} = -2.3697 + 0.0501(500) = 22.6705$

13.8   (a)

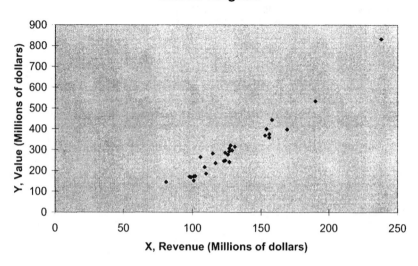

Scatter Diagram

(b) $b_0 = -246.2599$, $b_1 = 4.1897$

(c)   For each additional million dollars increase in revenue, the mean annual value will increase by an estimated 4.1897 million dollars.

(d) $\hat{Y} = -246.2599 + 4.1897(150) = 382.2005$ million dollars.

13.10   (a)

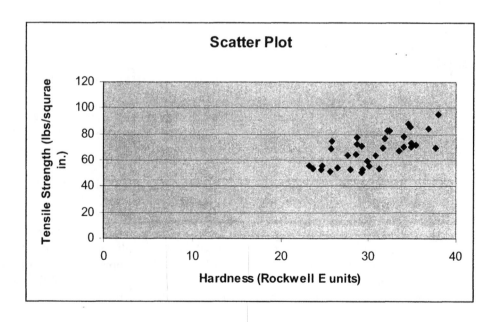

13.10 (b) $\hat{Y} = 6.0483 + 2.0191X$

cont. (c)   For each increase of one additional Rockwell E unit in hardness, the estimated mean tensile strength will increase by 2.0191 thousand pounds per square inch.

       (d) $\hat{Y} = 6.0483 + 2.0191(30) = 66.620$ thousand pounds per square inch.

13.12 $SST = 40$ and $r^2 = 0.90$. So, 90% of the variation in the dependent variable can be explained by the variation in the independent variable.

13.14 $r^2 = 0.75$. So, 75% of the variation in the dependent variable can be explained by the variation in the independent variable.

13.16 (a) $r^2 = \dfrac{SSR}{SST} = \dfrac{2.0535}{3.0025} = 0.684$. So, 68.4% of the variation in the dependent variable can be explained by the variation in the independent variable.

       (b) $s_{YX} = \sqrt{\dfrac{SSE}{n-2}} = \sqrt{\dfrac{\sum\limits_{i=1}^{n}\left(Y_i - \hat{Y}_i\right)^2}{n-2}} = \sqrt{\dfrac{0.949}{10}} = 0.308$

       (c)   Based on (a) and (b), the model should be very useful for predicting sales.

13.18 (a) $r^2 = 0.8892$. So, 88.92% of the variation in the dependent variable can be explained by the variation in the independent variable.

       (b) $s_{YX} = 5.0314$

       (c)   Based on (a) and (b), the model should be very useful for predicting labor hours.

13.20 (a) $r^2 = 0.9424$. So, 94.24% of the variation in value of a baseball franchise can be explained by the variation in its annual revenue.

       (b) $s_{YX} = 33.7876$

       (c)   Based on (a) and (b), the model should be very useful for predicting the value of a baseball franchise.

13.22 (a) $r^2 = 0.4613$. So, 46.13% of the variation in the dependent variable can be explained by the variation in the independent variable.

       (b) $s_{YX} = 9.0616$

       (c)   Based on (a) and (b), the model is only marginally useful for predicting tensile strength.

13.24   A residual analysis of the data indicates a pattern, with sizeable clusters of consecutive residuals that are either all positive or all negative. If the data is cross-sectional, this pattern indicates a violation of the assumption of linearity and a quadratic model should be investigated. If the data is time-series, the pattern indicates a violation of the assumption of independence of errors.

13.26   (a)

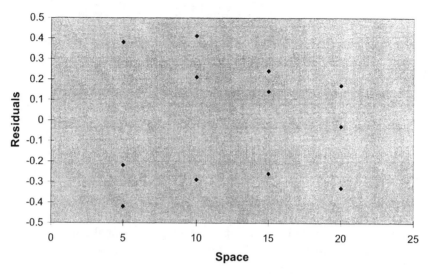

Based on the residual plot, there does not appear to be a pattern in the residual plot.

(b)

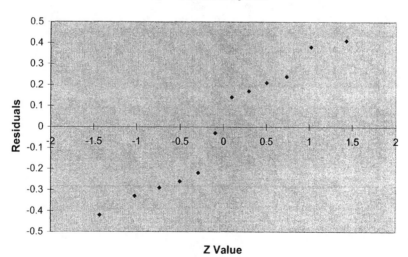

Based on the residual plot, there is not apparent heteroskedasticity effect. The normal probability plot of the residuals indicates a departure from the normality assumption.

13.28   (a)

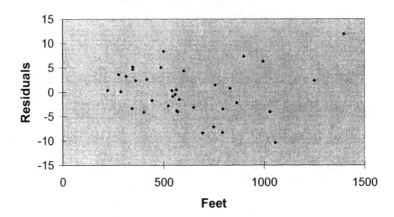

Based on the residual plot, there appears to be a nonlinear pattern in the residuals. A quadratic model should be investigated.

(b)

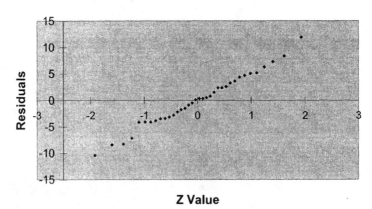

The assumptions of normality and equal variance do not appear to be seriously violated.

13.30 (a)

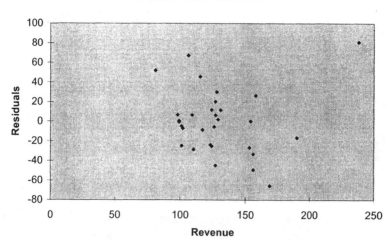

Based on the residual plot, there appears to be a nonlinear pattern in the residuals. A quadratic model should be investigated.

(b)

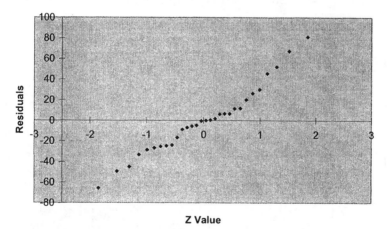

The normal probability plot of the residuals does not reveal significant departure from the normality assumption. The assumption of equal variance does not appear to be seriously violated.

13.32   (a)

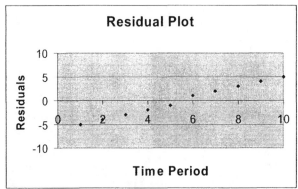

An increasing linear relationship exists.

(b)   There appears to be strong positive autocorrelation among the residuals.

13.34   (a)   No, it is not necessary to compute the Durbin-Watson statistic since the data have been collected for a single period for a set of stores.

(b)   If a single store was studied over a period of time and the amount of shelf space varied over time, computation of the Durbin-Watson statistic would be necessary.

13.36   (a) $b_1 = \dfrac{SSXY}{SSX} = \dfrac{201399.05}{12495626} = 0.0161$

$b_0 = \overline{Y} - b_1 \overline{X} = 71.2621 - 0.0161(4393) = 0.458$

(b) $\hat{Y} = 0.458 + 0.0161X = 0.458 + 0.0161(4500) = 72.908$ or $72,908

(c)

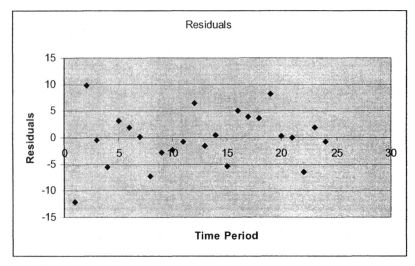

(d) $D = \dfrac{\sum_{i=2}^{n}\left(e_i - e_{i-1}\right)^2}{\sum_{i=1}^{n} e_i^2} = \dfrac{1243.2244}{599.0683} = 2.08 > 1.45$. There is no evidence of positive

autocorrelation among the residuals.

(e)   Based on a residual analysis, the model appears to be adequate.

13.38   (a) $b_0 = -2.535, b_1 = 0.060728$

(b) $\hat{Y} = -2.535 + 0.060728X = -2.535 + 0.060728(83) = 2.5054$ or $\$2505.40$

(c)

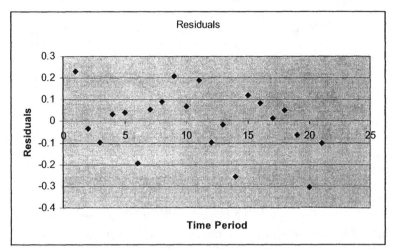

(d) $D = 1.64 > 1.42$. There is no evidence of positive autocorrelation among the residuals.

(e)   The plot of the residuals versus time period shows some clustering of positive and negative residuals for intervals in the domain, suggesting a nonlinear model might be better. Otherwise, the model appears to be adequate.

13.40   (a) $H_0 : \beta_1 = 0 \qquad H_1 : \beta_1 \neq 0$

Test statistic: $t = (b_1 - 0)/s_{b_1} = 4.5/1.5 = 3.00$

(b)   With n = 18, df = 18 – 2 =16, $t_{16} = \pm 2.1199$.

(c)   Reject H_0. There is evidence that the fitted linear regression model is useful.

(d) $b_1 - t_{16}s_{b_1} \leq \beta_1 \leq b_1 + t_{16}s_{b_1}$

$4.5 - 2.1199(1.5) \leq \beta_1 \leq 4.5 + 2.1199(1.5)$

$1.32 \leq \beta_1 \leq 7.68$

13.42   (a) $H_0 : \beta_1 = 0 \qquad H_1 : \beta_1 \neq 0$

$t = \dfrac{b_1 - \beta_1}{S_{b_1}} = \dfrac{0.074}{0.0159} = 4.65 > t_{10} = 2.2281$ with 10 degrees of freedom for

$\alpha = 0.05$. Reject H_0. There is enough evidence to conclude that the fitted linear regression model is useful.

(b) $b_1 \pm t_{n-2}S_{b_1} = 0.074 \pm 2.2281(0.0159)$ $\qquad\qquad\qquad$ $0.0386 \leq \beta_1 \leq 0.1094$

13.44   (a) $t = 16.5223 > t_{34} = 2.0322$ for $\alpha = 0.05$. Reject H_0. There is evidence that the fitted linear regression model is useful.

(b) $0.0439 \leq \beta_1 \leq 0.0562$

13.46 (a) $H_0 : \beta_1 = 0$ $\qquad\qquad$ $H_1 : \beta_1 \neq 0$

PHStat output:

	Coefficients	Standard Error	t Stat	P-value	Lower 95%	Upper 95%
Intercept	-246.2599	26.0405	-9.4568	0.0000	-299.6015	-192.9183
Revenue	4.1897	0.1957	21.4075	0.0000	3.7888	4.5906

Since the *p*-value is essentially zero, reject H_0 at 5% level of significance. There is evidence of a linear relationship between annual revenue sales and franchise value.

(b) $3.7888 \leq \beta_1 \leq 4.5906$

13.48 (a) *p*-value = 7.26497E-06 < 0.05. Reject H_0. There is evidence that the fitted linear regression model is useful.

(b) $1.2463 \leq \beta_1 \leq 2.7918$

13.50 (a) $(\% \text{ daily change in ULPIX}) = b_0 + 2.00(\% \text{ daily change in S\&P 500 Index})$

(b) If the S&P gains 30% in a year, the ULPIX is expected to gain an estimated 60%.

(c) If the S&P loses 35% in a year, the ULPIX is expected to lose an estimated 70%.

(d) Since the leverage funds have higher volatility and, hence, higher risk than the market, risk averse investors should stay away from these funds. Risk takers, on the other hand, will benefit from the higher potential gain from these funds.

13.52 (a) $r = -0.4014$.

(b) $t = -1.8071$, *p*-value = 0.089 > 0.05. Do not reject H_0. At the 0.05 level of significance, there is no linear relationship between the turnover rate of pre-boarding screeners and the security violations detected.

(c) There is not sufficient evidence to conclude that there is a linear relationship between the turnover rate of pre-boarding screeners and the security violations detected.

13.54 (a) $r = 0.4838$

(b) $t = 2.5926$, *p*-value = 0.0166 < 0.05. Reject H_0. At the 0.05 level of significance, there is a linear relationship between the cold-cranking amps and the price.

(c) The higher the price of a battery is, the higher is its cold-cranking amps.

(d) Yes, the expectation that batteries with higher cranking amps to have a higher price is borne out by the data.

13.56 (a) When $X = 4$, $\hat{Y} = 5 + 3X = 5 + 3(4) = 17$

$$h = \frac{1}{n} + \frac{(X_i - \overline{X})^2}{\sum_{i=1}^{n}(X_i - \overline{X})^2} = \frac{1}{20} + \frac{(4-2)^2}{20} = 0.25$$

95% confidence interval: $\hat{Y} \pm t_{18} s_{YX} \sqrt{h} = 17 \pm 2.1009 \cdot 1 \cdot \sqrt{0.25}$

$$15.95 \leq \mu_{Y|X=4} \leq 18.05$$

(b) 95% prediction interval: $\hat{Y} \pm t_{18} s_{YX} \sqrt{1+h} = 17 \pm 2.1009 \cdot 1 \cdot \sqrt{1.25}$

$$14.651 \leq Y_{X=4} \leq 19.349$$

(c) The intervals in this problem are wider because the value of X is farther from $\overline{X}$.

13.58 (a) $\hat{Y}_i \pm t_{n-2} S_{YX} \sqrt{h_i} = 2.042 \pm 2.2281(0.3081)\sqrt{0.1373}$

$$1.7876 \le \mu_{Y|X=8} \le 2.2964$$

(b) $\hat{Y}_i \pm t_{n-2} S_{YX} \sqrt{1+h_i} = 2.042 \pm 2.2281(0.3081)\sqrt{1+0.1373}$

$$1.3100 \le Y_{X=8} \le 2.7740$$

(c)   Part (b) provides an interval prediction for the individual response given a specific value of the independent variable, and part (a) provides an interval estimate for the mean value given a specific value of the independent variable. Since there is much more variation in predicting an individual value than in estimating a mean value, a prediction interval is wider than a confidence interval estimate holding everything else fixed.

13.60 (a) $20.7990 \le \mu_{Y|X=500} \le 24.5419$

(b) $12.2755 \le Y_{X=500} \le 33.0654$

(c)   Part (b) provides an interval prediction for the individual response given a specific value of the independent variable, and part (a) provides an interval estimate for the mean value given a specific value of the independent variable. Since there is much more variation in predicting an individual value than in estimating a mean value, a prediction interval is wider than a confidence interval estimate holding everything else fixed.

13.62 (a) $367.0757 \le \mu_{Y|X=150} \le 397.3254$

(b) $311.3562 \le Y_{X=150} \le 453.0448$

(c)   Part (b) provides an interval prediction for the individual response given a specific value of the independent variable, and part (a) provides an interval estimate for the mean value given a specific value of the independent variable. Since there is much more variation in predicting an individual value than in estimating a mean value, a prediction interval is wider than a confidence interval estimate holding everything else fixed.

13.64   The slope of the line, b_1, represents the estimated expected change in Y per unit change in X. It represents the estimated mean amount that Y changes (either positively or negatively) for a particular unit change in X. The Y intercept b_0 represents the estimated mean value of Y when X equals 0.

13.66   The unexplained variation or error sum of squares (SSE) will be equal to zero only when the regression line fits the data perfectly and the coefficient of determination equals 1.

13.68   Unless a residual analysis is undertaken, you will not know whether the model fit is appropriate for the data. In addition, residual analysis can be used to check whether the assumptions of regression have been seriously violated.

13.70　The normality of error assumption can be evaluated by obtaining a histogram, box-and-whisker plot, and/or normal probability plot of the residuals. The homoscedasticity assumption can be evaluated by plotting the residuals on the vertical axis and the X variable on the horizontal axis. The independence of errors assumption can be evaluated by plotting the residuals on the vertical axis and the time order variable on the horizontal axis. This assumption can also be evaluated by computing the Durbin-Watson statistic.

13.72　The confidence interval for the mean response estimates the mean response for a given X value. The prediction interval estimates the value for a single item or individual.

13.74　(a)　　$b_0 = 24.84$, $b_1 = 0.14$

(b)　　24.84 is the portion of estimated mean delivery time that is not affected by the number of cases delivered. For each additional case, the estimated mean delivery time increases by 0.14 minutes.

(c)　　$\hat{Y} = 24.84 + 0.14X = 24.84 + 0.14(150) = 45.84$

(d)　　No, 500 cases is outside the relevant range of the data used to fit the regression equation.

(e)　　$r^2 = 0.972$. So, 97.2% of the variation in delivery time can be explained by the variation in the number of cases.

(f)　　Based on a visual inspection of the graphs of the distribution of residuals and the residuals versus the number of cases, there is no pattern. The model appears to be adequate.

(g)　　$t = 24.88 > t_{18} = 2.1009$ with 18 degrees of freedom for $\alpha = 0.05$. Reject H_0. There is evidence that the fitted linear regression model is useful.

(h)　　$44.88 \leq \mu_{Y|X=150} \leq 46.80$

(i)　　$41.56 \leq Y_{X=150} \leq 50.12$

(j)　　$0.1282 \leq \beta_1 \leq 0.1518$

13.76　(a)

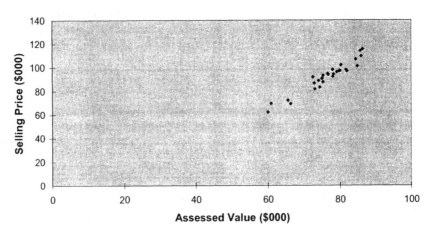

Scatter Diagram

$b_0 = -44.172$, $b_1 = 1.78171$

13.76 (b)   Since the assessed value of a home cannot be zero, the intercept has no practical
cont.   interpretation. -44.172 is the portion of estimated mean selling price that is not
             affected by the assessed value. For each additional dollar in assessed value, the
             estimated mean selling price increases by $1.78.

(c) $\hat{Y} = -44.172 + 1.78171X = -44.172 + 1.78171(70) = 80.458$ or $80,458

(d) $r^2 = 0.926$. 92.6% of the variation in selling price can be explained by the variation
      in the assessed value.

(e)   Based on a visual inspection of the graphs of the distribution of residuals and the
      residuals versus the assessed value, there is no pattern. The model appears to be
      adequate.

(f) $t = 18.66 > t_{28} = 2.0484$ with 28 degrees of freedom for $\alpha = 0.05$. Reject H_0.

      There is evidence that the fitted linear regression model is useful.

(g) $78.707 \le \mu_{Y|X=70} \le 82.388$

(h) $73.195 \le Y_{X=70} \le 87.900$

(i) $1.5862 \le \beta_1 \le 1.9772$

13.78 (a)

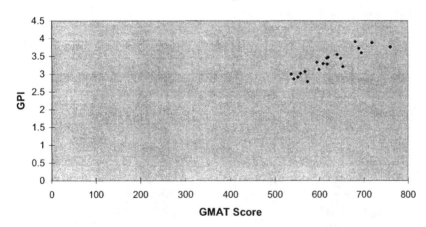

Scatter Diagram

$b_0 = 0.30$, $b_1 = 0.00487$

(b)   0.30 is the portion of estimated mean GPI index that is not affected by the GMAT
      score. The mean GPI index of a student with a zero GMAT score is estimated to be
      0.30. For each additional point on the GMAT score, the estimated GPI increases by
      an average of 0.00487.

(c) $\hat{Y} = 0.30 + 0.00487X = 0.30 + 0.00487(600) = 3.222$

(d) $r^2 = 0.7978$. 79.78% of the variation in the GPI can be explained by the
      variation in the GMAT score.

(e)   Based on a visual inspection of the graphs of the distribution of residuals and the
      residuals versus the GMAT score, there is no pattern. The model appears to be
      adequate.

(f) $t = 8.428 > t_{18} = 2.1009$ with 18 degrees of freedom for $\alpha = 0.05$. Reject H_0.

      There is evidence that the fitted linear regression model is useful.

(g) $3.144 \le \mu_{Y|X=600} \le 3.301$

13.78 (h) $2.886 \le Y_{X=600} \le 3.559$

cont. (i) $0.00366 \le \beta_1 \le 0.00608$

13.80 (a)

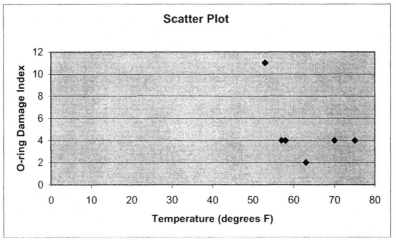

There is not any clear relationship between atmospheric temperature and O-ring damage from the scatter plot.

(b),(f)

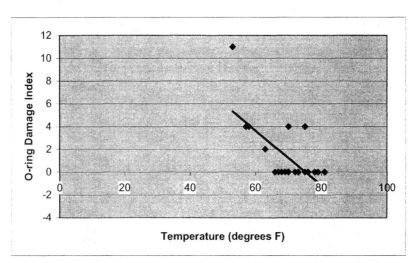

(c)   In (b), there are 16 observations with an O-ring damage index of 0 for a variety of temperatures. If one concentrates on these observations with no O-ring damage, there is obviously no relationship between O-ring damage index and temperature. If all observations are used, the observations with no O-ring damage will bias the estimated relationship. If the intention is to investigate the relationship between the degrees of O-ring damage and atmospheric temperature, it makes sense to focus only on the flights in which there was O-ring damage.

(d)   Prediction should not be made for an atmospheric temperature of 31 ^{0}F because it is outside the range of the temperature variable in the data. Such prediction will involve extrapolation, which assumes that any relationship between two variables will continue to hold outside the domain of the temperature variable.

(e) $\hat{Y} = 18.036 - 0.240X$

13.80 (g)   A nonlinear model is more appropriate for these data.
cont. (h)

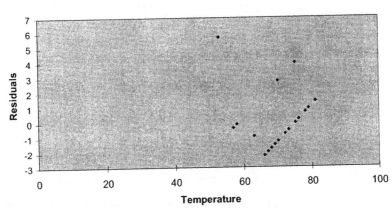

Temperature Residual Plot

The string of negative residuals and positive residuals that lie on a straight line with a positive slope in the lower-right corner of the plot is a strong indication that a nonlinear model should be used if all 23 observations are to be used in the fit.

13.82 (a)

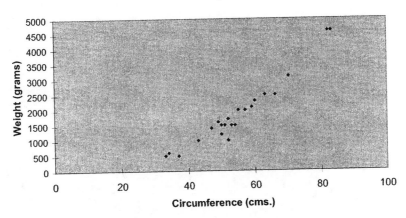

Scatter Diagram

$\hat{Y} = -2629.222 + 82.4717X$

(b)   For each increase of one centimeter in circumference, the estimated mean weight of a pumpkin will increase by 82.4717 grams.

(c) $\hat{Y} = -2629.222 + 82.4717(60) = 2319.080$ grams.

(d)   There appears to be a positive relationship between weight and circumference of a pumpkin. It is a good idea for the farmer to sell pumpkins by circumference instead of weight for circumference is a good predictor of weight, and it is much easier to measure the circumference of a pumpkin than its weight.

(e) $r^2 = 0.9373$.   93.73% of the variation in pumpkin weight can be explained by the variation in circumference.

13.82   (f)
cont.

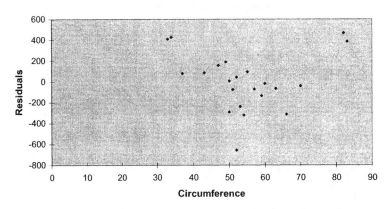

There appears to be a nonlinear relationship between circumference and weight.

(g) p-value is virtually 0. Reject H_0. There is sufficient evidence to conclude that there is a linear relationship between the circumference and the weight of a pumpkin.

(h) $72.7875 < \beta_1 < 92.1559$

(i) $2186.9589 < \mu_{Y|X=60} < 2451.2020$

(j) $1726.5508 < Y_{X=60} < 2911.6101$

13.84   (a)

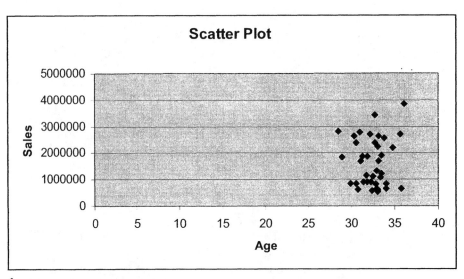

(b) $\hat{Y} = 931626.16 + 21782.76X$

(c)   Since median age of customer base cannot be 0, b_0 just captures the portion of the latest one-month sales total that varies with factors other than median age.

$b_1 = 21782.76$ means that as the median age of customer base increases by one year, the estimated mean latest one-month sales total will increase by \$21782.76.

(d) $r^2 = 0.0017$. Only 0.17% of the total variation in the franchise's latest one-month sales total can be explained by using the median age of customer base.

13.84 (e)
cont.

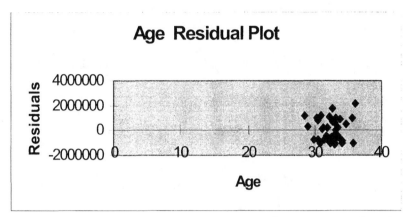

The residuals are very evenly spread out across different range of median age.

(f) $H_0 : \rho = 0$ $H_1 : \rho \neq 0$

Test statistic: $t = \dfrac{r}{\sqrt{\dfrac{1-r^2}{n-2}}} = 0.2482$

Decision rule: Reject H_0 when $|t| > 2.0289$.

Decision: Since $t = 0.2482$ is less than the upper critical bound 2.4926, do not reject H_0. There is not enough evidence to conclude that there is a linear relationship between one-month sales total and median age of customer base.

(g) $b_1 \pm t_{n-2} S_{b_1} = 21782.76354 \pm 2.0281 (87749.63)$

$$-156181.50 \leq \beta_1 \leq 199747.02$$

13.86 (a)

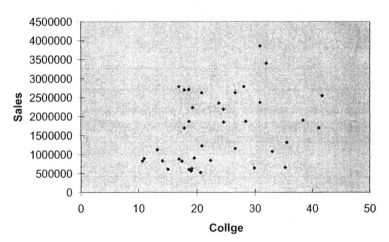

There is a positive linear relationship between total sales and percentage of customer base with a college diploma.

13.86   (b) $\hat{Y} = 789847.38 + 35854.15X$

cont.   (c) $b_1 = 35854.15$ means that as the percent of customer base with a college diploma increases by one, the estimated mean latest one-month sales total will increase by $35854.15.

(d) $r^2 = 0.1036$. 10.36% of the total variation in the franchise's latest one-month sales total can be explained by the percentage of customer base with a college diploma.

(e)

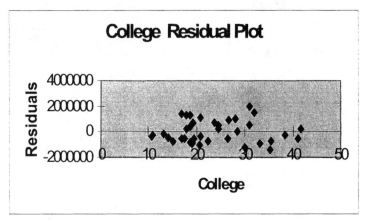

The residuals are quite evenly spread out around zero even though there might be a slight tendency for the variance to increase as the percentage of customer base with a college diploma increases.

(f) $H_0: \rho = 0$ $H_1: \rho \neq 0$

Test statistic: $t = \dfrac{r}{\sqrt{\dfrac{1-r^2}{n-2}}} = 2.0392$

Decision rule: Reject H_0 when $|t|>2.0289$.

Decision: Since $t = 2.0392$ is greater than the upper critical bound 2.4926, reject H_0.

There is enough evidence to conclude that there is a linear relationship between one-month sales total and percentage of customer base with a college diploma.

(g) $b_1 \pm t_{n-2} S_{b_1} = 35854.15 \pm 2.0281(17582.269)$

$$195.75 \leq \beta_1 \leq 71512.60$$

13.88   (a)

Scatter Diagram

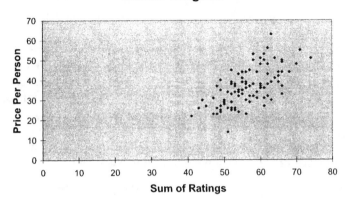

$$\hat{Y} = -13.6561 + 0.8932X$$

(b)   Since no restaurant will receive a summated rating of 0, it is not meaningful to interpret b_0. For each additional unit of increase in summated rating, the estimated mean price per person will increase by \$0.8932.

(c) $\hat{Y} = -13.6561 + 0.8932(50) = \$31.01$

(d) $r^2 = 0.4246.$ 42.46% of the variation in price per person can be explained by the variation in summated rating.

(e)

Summated rating Residual Plot

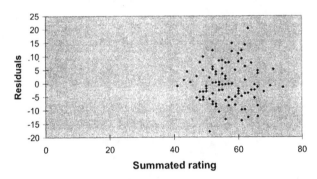

Based on a visual inspection of the residual plot of summated rating, there may be a violation of the homoscedasticity assumption.

(f) p-value is virtually 0. Reject H_0. There is very strong evidence to conclude that there is a linear relationship between price per person and summated rating.

(g) $\$29.07 \le \mu_{Y|X=50} \le \$32.94$

(h) $\$16.95 \le Y_{X=50} \le \$45.06$

(i) $0.6848 \le \beta_1 \le 1.1017$

(j)   The linear regression model appears to have provided an adequate fit and shown a significant linear relationship between price per person and summated rating. Since 42.46% of the variation in price per person can be explained by the variation in summated rating, price per person is moderately useful in predicting the price.

13.90   (a)

	MSFT	FORD	GM	IAL
MSFT	1	0.167371	0.156788	-0.23227
FORD		1	0.866746	0.696919
GM			1	0.628925
IAL				1

(b)   There is a strongly positive linear relationship between the stock price of Ford and GM, a moderately strong positive linear relationship between the stock price of Ford and IAL and between GM and IAL, a very weak positive linear relationship between the stock price of Ford and Microsoft, and between GM and Microsoft, and a rather weak negative linear relationship between Microsoft and IAL.

(c)   It is not a good idea to have all the stocks in an individual's portfolio be strongly, positively correlated among each other because the portfolio risk can be reduced when a pair of stock prices is negatively related in a two-stock portfolio.

CHAPTER 14

OBJECTIVES

- To learn how to develop a multiple regression model
- To know how to interpret the regression coefficients
- To learn how to determine which independent variables to include in the regression model
- To know how to determine which independent variables are more important in predicting a dependent variable
- To be able to use categorical variable in regression models
- To learn how to predict a categorical dependent variable using logistic regression

OVERVIEW AND KEY CONCEPTS

The Multiple Regression Model

- The multiple regression model describes the relationship between one dependent variable and 2 or more independent variables in a linear function.

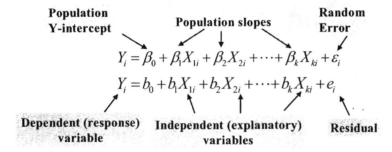

The Simple Linear Regression and Multiple Regression Compared

- Coefficients in a simple regression pick up the impact of that variable plus the impacts of other variables that are correlated with it and the dependent variable.
- Coefficients in a multiple regression net out the impacts of other variables in the equation. Hence, they are called *net regression coefficients*.

Interpretation of the Estimated Coefficients

- **The Y intercept (b_0):** The estimated average value of Y_i when all $X_i = 0$.

- **Slope (b_i):** Estimated that the average value of Y changes by b_i for each one-unit increase in X_i holding constant the effect of all other independent variables.

Predicting the Dependent Variable Y

- Use the estimated sample regression equation (multiple linear regression equation):

$$\hat{Y}_i = b_0 + b_1 X_{1i} + \cdots + b_k X_{ki}$$

The Venn Diagram and Explanatory Power of the Multiple Regression Model

Variations in X_1 not used in explaining variation in Y

Variations in Y not explained by X_1 (SSE)

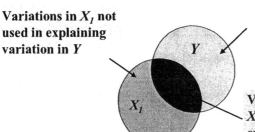

Variations in Y explained by X_1 or variations in X_1 used in explaining variation in Y (SSR)

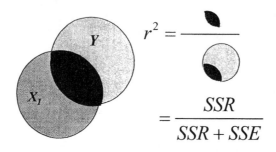

$$r^2 = \frac{\text{(dark overlap)}}{\text{(Y circle)}} = \frac{SSR}{SSR + SSE}$$

Variation *NOT* explained by X_1 nor X_2 (SSE)

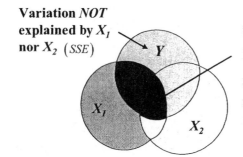

***Overlapping* variation in both X_1 and X_2 are used in explaining the *variation* in Y but *NOT* in the *estimation* of β_1 nor β_2**

Coefficient of Multiple Determination

- Coefficient of multiple determination measures the proportion of total variation in Y explained by all X variables taken together.

- $r^2_{Y \cdot 12 \cdots k} = \dfrac{SSR}{SST} = \dfrac{\text{Explained Variation}}{\text{Total Variation}}$

- It never decreases when an additional X variable is added to the model, which is a disadvantage when comparing among models.

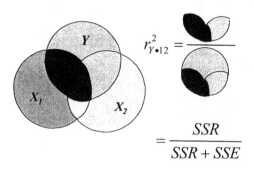

$$r^2_{Y \cdot 12} = \frac{}{}$$

$$= \frac{SSR}{SSR + SSE}$$

Adjusted Coefficient of Multiple Determination

- It measures the proportion of variation in Y explained by all X variables adjusted for the number of X variables used.

- $r^2_{adj} = 1 - \left[\left(1 - r^2_{Y \cdot 12 \cdots k} \right) \dfrac{n-1}{n-k-1} \right]$

- It penalizes excessive use of independent variables.

- It is smaller than $r^2_{Y \cdot 12 \cdots k}$.

- It is useful in comparing among models.

- It can have a negative value.

- Its value can decrease when an additional explanatory variable is added to the existing model.

Interpretation of Coefficient of Multiple Determination

- $r^2_{Y \cdot 12 \cdots k}$ measures the proportion of total variation in Y that can be explained by all X variables.

- r^2_{adj} measures the proportion of total variation in Y that can be explained by all X variables after adjusting for the number of independent variables and sample size.

F Test for the Significance of the Entire Multiple Regression Model
- **The hypotheses:**
    - $H_0 : \beta_1 = \beta_2 = \cdots = \beta_k = 0$ (There is no linear relationship)
    - $H_1 :$ At least one $\beta_i \neq 0$ (At least one independent variable affects Y)
- **Test statistic:**
    - $F = \dfrac{MSR}{MSE} = \dfrac{SSR(\text{all})/k}{SSE(\text{all})/(n-k-1)}$ with k numerator degrees of freedom and $(n-k-1)$ denominator degrees of freedom.
    - The rejection region is always in the right tail.

t Test for the Significance of Individual Variables
- **The hypotheses:**
    - $H_0 : \beta_i = 0$ (X_i does not affect Y)
    - $H_1 : \beta_i \neq 0$ (X_i affects Y)
- **Test statistic:**
    - $t = \dfrac{b_j - \beta_j}{S_{b_j}}$ with $(n-k-1)$ degrees of freedom.
    - The t test can also be a one-tail test for a one-tail alternative.
- Confidence interval estimate for β_j: Use the $100(1-\alpha)\%$ confidence interval for β_j.
    - $b_j \pm t_{\alpha/2, n-k-1} S_{b_j}$

Contribution of a Single Independent Variable X_j
- The contribution of an independent variable X_j to the regression model is measured by

$SSR(X_j \mid \text{all variables except } X_j)$
$= SSR(\text{all variables including } X_j) - SSR(\text{all variables except } X_j)$

The Partial F Test for Determining the Contribution of an Independent Variable

- **The hypotheses:**
    - H_0: Variable X_j does not significantly improve the model after all the other X have been included
    - H_1: Variable X_j significantly improve the model once all the other X have been included
- **Test statistic:**
    - $F = \dfrac{SSR\left(X_j \mid \text{all variables except } X_j\right)}{MSE(\text{all})}$ with 1 and $\left(n - k - 1\right)$ degrees of freedom.
    - The rejection region is always in the right tail.
    - This partial F test statistic $F_{1,n-k-1}$ always equals to the squared of the t test statistic for the significance of X_j, i.e., $\left(t_{n-k-1}\right)^2 = F_{1,n-k-1}$.

Coefficient of Partial Determination

- It measures the proportion of variation in the dependent variable that is explained by X_j while controlling for (holding constant) the other independent variables.

- $r^2_{Yj\bullet \text{ all variables except } X_j} = \dfrac{SSR\left(X_j \mid \text{all variables except } X_j\right)}{SST - SSR\left(\text{all variables including } X_j\right) + SSR\left(X_j \mid \text{all variables except } X_j\right)}$

Two independent variables model

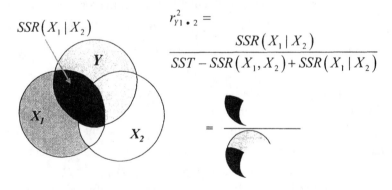

$$r^2_{Y1\bullet 2} = \frac{SSR\left(X_1 \mid X_2\right)}{SST - SSR\left(X_1, X_2\right) + SSR\left(X_1 \mid X_2\right)}$$

Dummy-Variable Model and Interactions

- Dummy variables are used to represent categorical explanatory variables with two or more levels.
- A dummy variable is always coded as 0 and 1.
- The number of dummy variables needed is equal to the number of levels minus 1.
- **Interpretation of the estimated slope coefficient of a dummy variable:** The slope coefficient of a dummy variable measures the estimated average incremental effect of the presence of the characteristic captured by the dummy variable holding constant the effect of all other independent variables.
- In the dummy-variable model, it is assumed that the slope of the dependent variable Y with an independent variable X is the same for each of the two levels of the dummy variable.
- To test whether the slope of the dependent variable Y with an independent variable X is the same for each of the two levels of the dummy variable, we can introduce the interaction term and test for the significance of this interaction term.

  E.g., Let X_1 and X_2 be two numerical independent variables, and X_3 be a dummy variable.

  To test whether the slopes of Y with X_1 and/or X_2 are the same for each of the two levels of X_3, the regression model is $Y_i = \beta_0 + \beta_1 X_{1i} + \beta_2 X_{2i} + \beta_3 X_{3i} + \beta_4 X_{1i} X_{3i} + \beta_5 X_{2i} X_{3i} + \varepsilon_i$

    - **The hypotheses:**

      $H_0 : \beta_4 = \beta_5 = 0$ (no interaction of X_1 with X_3 or X_2 with X_3)

      $H_1 : \beta_4$ and/or $\beta_5 \neq 0$ (X_1 and/or X_2 interacts with X_3)

    - **Partial F test statistic:** $F = \dfrac{\left(SSR(X_1, X_2, X_3, X_4, X_5) - SSR(X_1, X_2, X_3) \right) / 2}{MSE(X_1, X_2, X_3, X_4, X_5)}$

      with 2 and $(n - 6)$ degrees of freedom.

- To test only whether the slope of Y with X_1 is the same for each of the two level of X_3, we can perform a t test on $H_0 : \beta_4 = 0$ vs. $H_1 : \beta_4 \neq 0$. Likewise, to test only whether the slope of Y with just X_2 along is the same for each of the two level of X_3, one can perform a t test on $H_0 : \beta_5 = 0$ vs. $H_1 : \beta_5 \neq 0$.

- If all the independent variables are numerical variables, the above analysis can be extended to test for whether the independent variables interact with each other.

  E.g., Let X_1, X_2 and X_3 be three numerical independent variables. To evaluate possible interaction between the independent variables, the regression model to use is

  $Y_i = \beta_0 + \beta_1 X_{1i} + \beta_2 X_{2i} + \beta_3 X_{3i} + \beta_4 X_{1i} X_{2i} + \beta_5 X_{1i} X_{3i} + \beta_6 X_{2i} X_{3i} + \varepsilon_i$

    - To test whether the three interaction terms significantly improve the regression model:
        - **The hypotheses:**

          $H_0 : \beta_4 = \beta_5 = \beta_6 = 0$ (There are no interaction among X_1, X_2 and X_3)

          $H_1 : \beta_4 \neq 0$ and/or $\beta_5 \neq 0$ and/or $\beta_6 \neq 0$ (X_1 interact with X_2, and/or X_1 interacts with X_3, and/or X_2 interacts with X_3)

❑ **Partial *F* test statistic:**

$$F = \frac{\left(SSR(X_1,X_2,X_3,X_4,X_5,X_6) - SSR(X_1,X_2,X_3)\right)/3}{MSE(X_1,X_2,X_3,X_4,X_5,X_6)} \text{ with 3 and}$$

$(n-7)$ degrees of freedom.

- To test the contribution of each interaction separately to determine which interaction terms should be included in the model, we can perform separate *t* test.

Logistic Regression

- **Odds ratio:** Odds ratio $= \dfrac{\text{probability of success}}{1 - \text{probability of success}}$

- **Logistic regression model:** $\ln(\text{odds ratio}) = \beta_0 + \beta_1 X_{1i} + \beta_2 X_{2i} + \cdots + \beta_k X_{ki} + \varepsilon_i$

- **Logistic regression equation:** $\ln(\text{estimated odds ratio}) = b_0 + b_1 X_{1i} + b_2 X_{2i} + \cdots + b_k X_{ki}$

- **Estimated odds ratio:** $e^{\ln(\text{estimated odds ratio})}$

- **Estimated probability of success:** $\dfrac{\text{estimated odds ratio}}{1 + \text{estimated odds ratio}}$

- **Interpretation of the estimated slope coefficient** b_j: b_j measures the estimated change in the natural logarithm of the odds ratio as a result of a one unit change in X_j holding constant the effects of all the other independent variables.

Testing whether the Logistic Regression is a Good-Fitting Model

- **The hypotheses:**
  - H_0: The model is a good-fitting model
  - H_1: The model is not a good-fitting model
- **Test statistic:**
  - The *deviance statistic* has a χ^2 distribution with $(n-k-1)$ degrees of freedom.
  - The rejection region is always in the right tail.

Testing whether an Independent Variable Makes a Significant Contribution to a Logistic Model

- **The hypotheses:**
  - $H_0: \beta_j = 0$ (X_j does not make a significant contribution to the logistic model)
  - $H_1: \beta_j \neq 0$ (X_j makes a significant contribution to the logistic model)
- **Test statistic:**
  - The *Wald statistic* is normally distributed.
  - This is a two-tail test with left and right-tail rejection regions.

SOLUTIONS TO END OF SECTION
AND CHAPTER REVIEW EVEN PROBLEMS

14.2 (a) Holding constant the effect of X_2, for each increase of one unit in X_1, the response variable Y is estimated to increase an average of 2 units. Holding constant the effect of X_1, for each increase of one unit in X_2, the response variable Y is estimated to increase an average of 7 units.

(b) The Y-intercept 50 is the estimate of the mean value of Y if X_1 and X_2 are both 0.

14.4 (a) $\hat{Y} = -2.72825 + 0.047114 X_1 + 0.011947 X_2$

(b) For a given number of orders, each increase of $1,000 in sales is estimated to result in a mean increase in distribution cost of $47.114. For a given amount of sales, each increase of one order is estimated to result in a mean increase in distribution cost of $11.95.

(c) The interpretation of b_0 has no practical meaning here because it would have been the estimated mean distribution cost when there were no sales and no orders.

(d) $\hat{Y}_i = -2.72825 + 0.047114(400) + 0.011947(4500) = 69.878$ or $69,878

(e) $66,419.93 \le \mu_{Y|X} \le 73,337.01$

(f) $59,380.61 \le Y_X \le 80,376.33$

14.6 (a) $\hat{Y} = 156.4 + 13.081 X_1 + 16.795 X_2$

(b) For a given amount of newspaper advertising, each increase of $1000 in radio advertising is estimated to result in a mean increase in sales of $13,081. For a given amount of radio advertising, each increase of $1000 in newspaper advertising is estimated to result in the mean increase in sales of $16,795.

(c) When there is no money spent on radio advertising and newspaper advertising, the estimated mean amount of sales is $156,430.44.

(d) $\hat{Y}_i = 156.4 + 13.081(20) + 16.795(20) = 753.95$ or $753,950

(e) $623,038.31 \le \mu_{Y|X} \le 884,860.93$

(f) $396,522.63 \le Y_X \le 1,111,376.60$

14.8 (a) $\hat{Y} = 400.8057 + 456.4485 X_1 - 2.4708 X_2$ where X_1 = Land, X_2 = Age

(b) For a given age, each increase by one acre in land area is estimated to result in a mean increase in appraised value of $456.45 thousands. For a given acreage, each increase of one year in age is estimated to result in the mean decrease in appraised value of $2.47 thousands.

(c) The interpretation of b_0 has no practical meaning here because it would have meant the estimated mean appraised value of a new house that has no land area.

(d) $\hat{Y} = 400.8057 + 456.4485(0.25) - 2.4708(45) = 403.73$ thousands.

(e) $372.7370 \le \mu_{Y|X} \le 434.7243$

(f) $235.1964 \le Y_X \le 572.2649$

14.10   (a) $MSR = SSR / k = 30 / 2 = 15$
$MSE = SSE / (n - k - 1) = 120 / 10 = 12$

(b) $F = MSR / MSE = 15 / 12 = 1.25$

(c) $F = 1.25 < F_{U(2, 13-2-1)} = 4.103$. Do not reject H_0. There is not sufficient evidence of a significant linear relationship.

(d) $r^2 = \dfrac{SSR}{SST} = \dfrac{30}{150} = 0.2$

(e) $r_{adj}^2 = 1 - \left[\left(1 - r_{Y.12}^2 \right) \dfrac{n-1}{n-k-1} \right] = 0.04$

14.12   (a) $F = 97.69 > F_{U(2, 15-2-1)} = 3.89$. Reject H_0. There is evidence of a significant linear relationship with at least one of the independent variables.

(b) p-value = virtually zero. The probability of obtaining an F test statistic of 97.69 or larger is virtually zero if H_0 is true.

(c) $r_{Y.12}^2 = SSR / SST = 12.6102 / 13.38473 = 0.9421$. So, 94.21% of the variation in the long-term ability to absorb shock can be explained by variation in forefoot absorbing capability and variation in midsole impact.

(d) $r_{adj}^2 = 1 - \left[\left(1 - r_{Y.12}^2 \right) \dfrac{n-1}{n-k-1} \right] = 1 - \left[(1 - 0.9421) \dfrac{15-1}{15-2-1} \right] = 0.93245$

14.14   (a) $MSR = SSR / k = 3368.087 / 2 = 1684.04$
$MSE = SSE / (n - k - 1) = 477.043 / 21 = 22.72$
$F = MSR / MSE = 1684 / 22.7 = 74.13$
$F = 74.13 > F_{U(2, 24-2-1)} = 3.467$. Reject H_0. There is evidence of a significant linear relationship.

(b) p-value = virtually zero. The probability of obtaining an F test statistic of 74.13 or larger is virtually zero if H_0 is true.

(c) $r_{Y.12}^2 = SSR / SST = 3368.087 / 3845.13 = 0.8759$. So, 87.59% of the variation in distribution cost can be explained by variation in sales and variation in number of orders.

(d) $r_{adj}^2 = 1 - \left[\left(1 - r_{Y.12}^2 \right) \dfrac{n-1}{n-k-1} \right] = 1 - \left[(1 - 0.8759) \dfrac{24-1}{24-2-1} \right] = 0.8641$

14.16   (a) $MSR = SSR / k = 2,028,033 / 2 = 1,014,016$
$MSE = SSE / (n - k - 1) = 479,759.9 / 19 = 25,251$
$F = MSR / MSE = 1,014,016 / 25,251 = 40.16$
$F = 40.16 > F_{U(2, 22-2-1)} = 3.522$. Reject H_0. There is evidence of a significant linear relationship.

(b) p-value < 0.001. The probability of obtaining an F test statistic of 40.16 or larger is less than 0.001 if H_0 is true.

14.16 (c) $r_{Y.12}^2 = SSR / SST = 2,028,033 / 2,507,793 = 0.8087$. So, 80.87% of the variation
cont.   in sales can be explained by variation in radio advertising and variation in newspaper
          advertising.

       (d) $r_{adj}^2 = 1 - \left[(1 - r_{Y.12}^2) \dfrac{n-1}{n-k-1} \right] = 1 - \left[(1 - 0.8087) \dfrac{22-1}{22-2-1} \right] = 0.7886$

14.18 (a)   Based upon a residual analysis the model appears adequate.

       (b)   There is no evidence of a pattern in the residuals versus time.

       (c) $D = \dfrac{\displaystyle\sum_{i=2}^{n} (e_i - e_{i-1})^2}{\displaystyle\sum_{i=1}^{n} e_i^2} = \dfrac{1077.0956}{477.0430} = 2.26$

       (d) $D = 2.26 > 1.55$. There is no evidence of positive autocorrelation in the residuals.

14.20   There appears to be a quadratic relationship in the plot of the residuals against both radio and
       newspaper advertising. Thus, quadratic terms for each of these explanatory models should be
       considered for inclusion in the model.

14.22

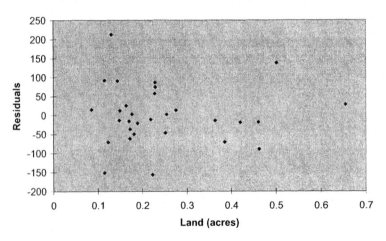

14.22
cont.

Age Residual Plot

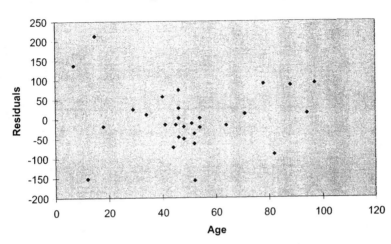

There is no particular pattern in the residual plots and the model appears to be adequate.

14.24 (a) The slope of X_2 in terms of the t statistic is 3.75 which is larger than the slope of X_1 in terms of the t statistic which is 3.33.

(b) 95% confidence interval on β_1: $b_1 \pm t_{n-k-1}s_{b_1}$, $4 \pm 2.1098(1.2)$

$$1.46824 \le \beta_1 \le 6.53176$$

(c) For X_1: $t = b_1 / s_{b_1} = 4/1.2 = 3.33 > t_{17} = 2.1098$ with 17 degrees of freedom for α = 0.05. Reject H_0. There is evidence that the variable X_1 contributes to a model already containing X_2.

For X_2: $t = b_2 / s_{b_2} = 3/0.8 = 3.75 > t_{17} = 2.1098$ with 17 degrees of freedom for α = 0.05. Reject H_0. There is evidence that the variable X_2 contributes to a model already containing X_1.

Both variables X_1 and X_2 should be included in the model.

14.26 (a) 95% confidence interval on β_1: $b_1 \pm t_{n-k-1}s_{b_1}$, $0.0471 \pm 2.0796(0.0203)$

$$0.00488 \le \beta_1 \le 0.08932$$

(b) For X_1: $t = b_1 / s_{b_1} = 0.0471/0.0203 = 2.32 > t_{21} = 2.0796$ with 21 degrees of freedom for α = 0.05. Reject H_0. There is evidence that the variable X_1 contributes to a model already containing X_2.

For X_2: $t = b_2 / s_{b_2} = 0.01195/0.00225 = 5.31 > t_{21} = 2.0796$ with 21 degrees of freedom for α = 0.05. Reject H_0. There is evidence that the variable X_2 contributes to a model already containing X_1.

Both variables X_1 and X_2 should be included in the model.

14.28   (a)   95% confidence interval on β_1: $b_1 \pm t_{n-k-1}s_{b_1}$, $13.0807 \pm 2.093(1.7594)$

$$9.398 \leq \beta_1 \leq 16.763$$

(b)   For X_1: $t = b_1 / s_{b_1} = 13.0807 / 1.7594 = 7.43 > t_{19} = 2.093$ with 19 degrees of freedom for $\alpha = 0.05$. Reject H_0. There is evidence that the variable X_1 contributes to a model already containing X_2.

For X_2: $t = b_2 / s_{b_2} = 16.7953 / 2.9634 = 5.67 > t_{19} = 2.093$ with 19 degrees of freedom for $\alpha = 0.05$. Reject H_0. There is evidence that the variable X_2 contributes to a model already containing X_1.

Both variables X_1 and X_2 should be included in the model.

14.30   (a) $227.5865 \leq \beta_1 \leq 685.3104$

(b)   For X_1: $t = b_1 / s_{b_1} = 456.4485 / 111.5405 = 4.0922$ and p-value = 0.0003. Since p-value < 0.05, reject H_0. There is evidence that the variable X_1 contributes to a model already containing X_2.

For X_2: $t = b_2 / s_{b_2} = -2.4708 / 0.6808 = -3.6295$ and p-value = 0.0012. Since p-value < 0.05, reject H_0. There is evidence that the variable X_2 contributes to a model already containing X_1.

Both variables X_1 and X_2 should be included in the model.

14.32   (a)   For X_1: $SSR(X_1 | X_2) = SSR(X_1 \ and \ X_2) - SSR(X_2) = 30 - 15 = 15$

$$F = \frac{SSR(X_1 | X_2)}{MSE} = \frac{15}{120 / 10} = 1.25 < F_{U(1,10)} = 4.965$$ with 1 and 10 degrees of freedom and $\alpha = 0.05$. Do not reject H_0. There is not sufficient evidence that the variable X_1 contributes to a model already containing X_2.

For X_2: $SSR(X_2 | X_1) = SSR(X_1 \ and \ X_2) - SSR(X_1) = 30 - 20 = 10$

$$F = \frac{SSR(X_2 | X_1)}{MSE} = \frac{10}{120 / 10} = 0.833 < F_{U(1,10)} = 4.965$$ with 1 and 10 degrees of freedom and $\alpha = 0.05$. Do not reject H_0. There is not sufficient evidence that the variable X_2 contributes to a model already containing X_1.

Neither independent variable X_1 nor X_2 makes a significant contribution to the model in the presence of the other variable. Also the overall regression equation involving both independent variables is not significant:

$$F = \frac{MSR}{MSE} = \frac{30 / 2}{120 / 10} = 1.25 < F_{U(2,10)} = 4.103$$

Neither variable should be included in the model and other variables should be investigated.

14.32   (b) $r_{Y1.2}^2 = \dfrac{SSR(X_1|X_2)}{SST - SSR(X_1 \ and \ X_2) + SSR(X_1|X_2)} = \dfrac{15}{150 - 30 + 15}$

cont.

= 0.1111. Holding constant the effect of variable X_2, 11.11% of the variation in Y can be explained by the variation in variable X_1.

$r_{Y2.1}^2 = \dfrac{SSR(X_2|X_1)}{SST - SSR(X_1 \ and \ X_2) + SSR(X_2|X_1)} = \dfrac{10}{150 - 30 + 10}$

= 0.0769. Holding constant the effect of variable X_1, 7.69% of the variation in Y can be explained by the variation in variable X_2.

14.34   (a)   For X_1:

$SSR(X_1|X_2) = SSR(X_1 \ and \ X_2) - SSR(X_2) = 3368.087 - 3246.062 = 122.025$

$F = \dfrac{SSR(X_1|X_2)}{MSE} = \dfrac{122.025}{477.043/21} = 5.37 > F_{U(1,21)} = 4.325$ with 1 and 21 degrees

of freedom and $\alpha = 0.05$. Reject H_0. There is evidence that the variable X_1 contributes to a model already containing X_2.

For X_2:

$SSR(X_2|X_1) = SSR(X_1 \ and \ X_2) - SSR(X_1) = 3368.087 - 2726.822 = 641.265$

$F = \dfrac{SSR(X_2|X_1)}{MSE} = \dfrac{641.265}{477.043/21} = 28.23 > F_{U(1,21)} = 4.325$ with 1 and 21 degrees

of freedom and $\alpha = 0.05$. Reject H_0. There is evidence that the variable X_2 contributes to a model already containing X_1.

Since each independent variable, X_1 and X_2, makes a significant contribution to the model in the presence of the other variable, the most appropriate regression model for this data set should include both variables.

(b) $r_{Y1.2}^2 = \dfrac{SSR(X_1|X_2)}{SST - SSR(X_1 \ and \ X_2) + SSR(X_1|X_2)}$

$= \dfrac{122.025}{3845.13 - 3368.087 + 122.025} = 0.2037$. Holding constant the effect of the

number of orders, 20.37% of the variation in Y can be explained by the variation in sales.

$r_{Y2.1}^2 = \dfrac{SSR(X_2|X_1)}{SST - SSR(X_1 \ and \ X_2) + SSR(X_2|X_1)}$

$= \dfrac{641.265}{3845.13 - 3368.087 + 641.265} = 0.5734$. Holding constant the effect of sales,

57.34% of the variation in Y can be explained by the variation in the number of orders.

14.36 (a) For X_1:
$$SSR(X_1|X_2) = SSR(X_1 \text{ and } X_2) - SSR(X_2) = 2,028,033 - 632,259.4 = 1,395,773.6$$
$$F = \frac{SSR(X_1|X_2)}{MSE} = \frac{1,395,773.6}{479,759.9/19} = 55.28 > F_{U(1,19)} = 4.381 \text{ with 1 and 19}$$
degrees of freedom and $\alpha = 0.05$. Reject H_0. There is evidence that the variable X_1 contributes to a model already containing X_2.
For X_2:
$$SSR(X_2|X_1) = SSR(X_1 \text{ and } X_2) - SSR(X_1) = 2028033 - 1216940 = 811093$$
$$F = \frac{SSR(X_2|X_1)}{MSE} = \frac{811,093}{479,759.9/19} = 32.12 > F_{U(1,19)} = 4.381 \text{ with 1 and 19 degrees}$$
of freedom and $\alpha = 0.05$. Reject H_0. There is evidence that the variable X_2 contributes to a model already containing X_1.
Since each independent variable, X_1 and X_2, makes a significant contribution to the model in the presence of the other variable, the most appropriate regression model for this data set should include both variables.

(b) $$r^2_{Y1.2} = \frac{SSR(X_1|X_2)}{SST - SSR(X_1 \text{ and } X_2) + SSR(X_1|X_2)}$$
$$= \frac{1,395,773.6}{2,507,793 - 2,028,033 + 1,395,773.6} = 0.7442. \text{ Holding constant the effect of}$$
newspaper advertising, 74.42% of the variation in Y can be explained by the variation in radio and television advertising.
$$r^2_{Y2.1} = \frac{SSR(X_2|X_1)}{SST - SSR(X_1 \text{ and } X_2) + SSR(X_2|X_1)}$$
$$= \frac{811,093}{2,507,793 - 2,028,033 + 811,093} = 0.6283. \text{ Holding constant the effect of radio}$$
and television advertising, 62.83% of the variation in Y can be explained by the variation in newspaper advertising.

14.38 (a) Holding constant the effect of X_2, the estimated mean value of the dependent variable will increase by 4 units for each increase of one unit of X_1.

(b) Holding constant the effects of X_1, the presence of the condition represented by $X_2 = 1$ is estimated to increase the mean value of the dependent variable by 2 units.

(c) $t = 3.27 > t_{17} = 2.1098$. Reject H_0. The presence of X_2 makes a significant contribution to the model.

14.40 (a) $\hat{Y} = 43.737 + 9.219X_1 + 12.697X_2$, where X_1 = number of rooms and X_2 = neighborhood (east = 0).

(b) Holding constant the effect of neighborhood, for each additional room, the selling price is estimated to increase by a mean of 9.219 thousands of dollars, or $9219. For a given number of rooms, a west neighborhood is estimated to increase average selling price over an east neighborhood by 12.697 thousands of dollars, or $12,697.

(c) $\hat{Y} = 43.737 + 9.219(9) + 12.697(0) = 126.71$ or $126,710

$109.5600 \le Y_{X=X_i} \le 143.8551$ $\qquad$ $121.4714 \le \mu_{Y|X=X_i} \le 131.9437$

(d) Based on a residual analysis, the model appears adequate.

(e) $F = 55.39 > F_{2,17} = 3.5915$. Reject H_0. There is evidence of a relationship between selling price and the two dependent variables.

(f) For X_1: $t = 8.95 > t_{17} = 2.1098$. Reject H_0. Number of rooms makes a significant contribution and should be included in the model.

For X_2: $t = 3.59 > t_{17} = 2.1098$. Reject H_0. Neighborhood makes a significant contribution and should be included in the model.

Based on these results, the regression model with the two independent variables should be used.

(g) $7.0466 \le \beta_1 \le 11.3913$, $5.2377 \le \beta_2 \le 20.1557$

(h) $r^2_{Y.12} = 0.867$. 86.7% of the variation in selling price can be explained by variation in number of rooms and variation in neighborhood.

(i) $r^2_{adj} = 0.851$

(j) $r^2_{Y1.2} = 0.825$. Holding constant the effect of neighborhood, 82.5% of the variation in selling price can be explained by variation in number of rooms. $r^2_{Y2.1} = 0.431$.

Holding constant the effect of number of rooms, 43.1% of the variation in selling price can be explained by variation in neighborhood.

(k) The slope of selling price with number of rooms is the same regardless of whether the house is located in an east or west neighborhood.

(l) $\hat{Y} = 53.95 + 8.032X_1 - 5.90X_2 + 2.089X_1X_2$.

For $X_1 X_2$: the p-value is 0.330. Do not reject H_0. There is no evidence that the interaction term makes a contribution to the model.

(m) The two-variable model in (a) should be used.

14.42 (a) $\hat{Y} = 8.0100 + 0.0052X_1 - 2.1052X_2$, where X_1 = depth (in feet) and X_2 = type of drilling (wet = 0, dry = 1).

(b) Holding constant the effect of type of drilling, for each foot increase in depth of the hole, the additional drilling time is estimated to increase by a mean of 0.0052 minutes. For a given depth, a dry drilling is estimated to reduce mean additional drilling time over wet drilling by 2.1052 minutes.

(c) Dry drilling: $\hat{Y} = 8.0101 + 0.0052(100) - 2.1052 = 6.4276$ minutes.

$6.2096 \le \mu_{Y|X=X_i} \le 6.6457$, $\quad$ $4.92304 \le Y_{X=X_i} \le 7.9322$

14.42 (d)
cont.

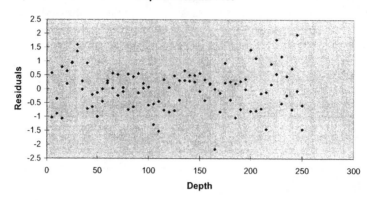

Depth Residual Plot

Based on a residual analysis, the model appears adequate.

(e) $F = 111.109$ with 2 and 97 degrees of freedom, $F_{2,97} = 3.09$ using Excel. p-value is virtually 0. Reject H_0 at 5% level of significance. There is evidence of a relationship between additional drilling time and the two dependent variables.

(f) For X_1: $t = 5.0289 > t_{97} = 1.9847$. Reject H_0. Depth of the hole makes

a significant contribution and should be included in the model.

For X_2: $t = -14.0331 < t_{97} = -1.9847$. Reject H_0. Type of drilling makes a

significant contribution and should be included in the model.

Based on these results, the regression model with the two independent variables should be used.

(g) $0.0032 \le \beta_1 \le 0.0073$, $-2.4029 \le \beta_2 \le -1.8075$

(h) $r_{Y.12}^2 = 0.6961$. 69.61% of the variation in additional drilling time can be explained

by the depth of the hole and variation in type of drilling.

(i) $r_{adj}^2 = 0.6899$

(j) $r_{Y1.2}^2 = 0.2068$. Holding constant the effect of type of drilling, 20.68% of the

variation in additional drilling time can be explained by variation in depth of the hole.

$r_{Y2.1}^2 = 0.6700$. Holding constant the effect of the depth of the hole, 67% of the

variation in additional drilling time can be explained by variation in type of drilling.

(k) The slope of additional drilling time with depth of the hole is the same regardless of whether it is a dry drilling hole or a wet drilling hole.

(l) $\hat{Y} = 7.9120 + 0.0060X_1 - 1.9091X_2 - 0.0015X_1X_2$.

For X_1X_2: the p-value is $0.4624 > 0.05$. Do not reject H_0. There is not evidence that the interaction term makes a contribution to the model.

(m) The two-variable model in (a) should be used.

14.44 (a) $\hat{Y} = 31.5594 + 0.0296X_1 + 0.0041X_2 + 1.7159 \times 10^{-5} X_3$.

where X_1 = sales, X_2 = orders, $X_3 = X_1 X_2$
For X_1X_2: the p-value is $0.3249 > 0.05$. Do not reject H_0. There is not enough evidence that the interaction term makes a contribution to the model.

(b) Since there is not enough evidence of any interaction effect between sales and orders, the model in problem 14.4 should be used.

14.46 (a) $\hat{Y} = -1293.3105 + 43.6600X_1 + 56.9335X_2 - 0.8430X_3$.

where X_1 = radio advertisement, X_2 = newspaper advertisement, $X_3 = X_1 X_2$
For X_1X_2: the p-value is $0.0018 < 0.05$. Reject H_0. There is enough evidence that the interaction term makes a contribution to the model.

(b) Since there is enough evidence of an interaction effect between radio and newspaper advertisement, the model in this problem should be used.

14.48 (a) $\hat{Y} = 250.4237 + 0.0127X_1 - 1.4785X_2 + 0.004X_3$.

where X_1 = staff present, X_2 = remote hours, $X_3 = X_1 X_2$
For X_1X_2: the p-value is $0.2353 > 0.05$. Do not reject H_0. There is not enough evidence that the interaction term makes a contribution to the model.

(b) Since there is not enough evidence of an interaction effect between total staff present and remote hours, the model in problem 14.7 should be used.

14.50 Holding constant the effect of other variables, the natural logarithm of the estimated odds ratio for the dependent categorical response will increase by a mean of 2.2 for each unit increase in the independent variable to which the coefficient corresponds.

14.52 Estimated Probability of Success = Odds Ratio / (1 + Odds Ratio) = 0.75/(1 + 0.75) = 0.4286

14.54 (a) ln(estimated odds ratio) = $-6.94 + 0.13947X_1 + 2.774X_2$
= $-6.94 + 0.13947(36) + 2.774(0) = -1.91908$
Estimated odds ratio = $e^{-1.91908} = 0.1467$
Estimated Probability of Success = Odds Ratio / (1 + Odds Ratio)
= 0.1467/(1 + 0.1467) = 0.1280

(b) From the text discussion of the example, 70.16% of the individuals who charge $36,000 per annum and possess additional cards can be expected to purchase the premium card. Only 12.80% of the individuals who charge $36,000 per annum and do not possess additional cards can be expected to purchase the premium card. For a given amount of money charged per annum, the likelihood of purchasing a premium card is substantially higher among individuals who already possess additional cards than for those who do not possess additional cards.

(c) ln(estimated odds ratio) = $-6.94 + 0.13947X_1 + 2.774X_2$
= $-6.94 + 0.13947(18) + 2.774(0) = -4.42954$
Estimated odds ratio = $e^{-4.42954} = 0.0119$
Estimated Probability of Success = Odds Ratio / (1 + Odds Ratio)
= 0.0119/(1 + 0.0119) = 0.01178

(d) Among individuals who do not purchase additional cards, the likelihood of purchasing a premium card diminishes dramatically with a substantial decrease in the amount charged per annum.

14.56 (a)   Let X_1 = grade point average and X_2 = GMAT score.
ln(estimated odds) = $-121.95 + 8.053\ X_1 + 0.15729\ X_2$

(b)   Holding constant the effects of GMAT score, for each increase of one point in GPA, ln(odds) increases by an estimate of 8.053. Holding constant the effects of GPA, for each increase of one point in GMAT score, ln(odds) increases by an estimate of 0.15729.

(c)   ln(estimated odds ratio) = $-121.95 + 8.053\ (3.25) + 0.15729\ (600) = -1.40375$
Estimated odds ratio = $e^{-1.04375} = 0.246$
Estimated Probability of Success = Odds Ratio / (1 + Odds Ratio)
$= 0.246/(1 + 0.246) = 0.197$

(d)   The deviance statistic is 8.122, which is less than the critical value of 40.113 and which has a p-value of virtually 1.000. Do not reject H_0. The model is a good fitting model.

(e)   For GPA variable: $Z = 1.60 < 1.96$. Do not reject H_0. There is not sufficient evidence that undergraduate grade point average makes a significant contribution to the model. For GMAT: $Z = 2.07 > 1.96$. Reject H_0. There is sufficient evidence that GMAT score makes a significant contribution to the model.

(f)   ln(estimated odds) = $-2.765 + 1.02\ X_1$
Deviance statistic = 29.172, p-value = 0.257
Z-value for β_1: 0.83, p-value = 0.406

(g)   ln(estimated odds) = $-60.15 + 0.09904\ X_2$
Deviance statistic = 9.545, p-value = 0.998
Z-value for β_2: 2.3, p-value = 0.021

(h)   Based on the p-values corresponding to the Z-values for the variable coefficients in the logistic regression equation and corresponding to the deviance statistics, the model in part (a) is a better fit than the model in part (f). However, the model in part (g) appears to be about as good a fit as the model in part (a).

14.58 (a)   Let X_1 = price of the pizza.
ln(estimated odds) = $1.243 - 0.25034\ X_1$
For X_1: $Z = -2.68 < -1.96$. Reject H_0. There is sufficient evidence that price of the pizza makes a significant contribution to the model.

(b)   Let X_1 = price of the pizza, X_2 = gender.
ln(estimated odds) = $1.220 - 0.25019\ X_1 + 0.0377\ X_2$
For X_1: $Z = -2.68 < -1.96$. Reject H_0. There is sufficient evidence that price of the pizza makes a significant contribution to the model.
For X_2: $Z = 0.10 < 1.96$. Do not reject H_0. There is not sufficient evidence to conclude that gender makes a significant contribution to the model.

(c)   Model (a): Deviance statistic = 0.258. p-value = 0.998 > 0.05. Do not reject H_0. There is insufficient evidence to conclude that model (a) is not a good fit.
Model (b): Deviance statistic = 7.804. p-value = 0.731 > 0.05. Do not reject H_0. There is insufficient evidence to conclude that model (a) is not a good fit. However, the Z test in (b) suggests that there is not sufficient evidence to conclude that gender makes a significant contribution to the model. Using the parsimony principle, the model in (a) is preferred to the model in (b).

(d)   ln(estimated odds ratio) = $1.243 - 0.25034\ X_1 = 1.243 - 0.25034\ (8.99) = -1.0076$
Estimated odds ratio = $e^{-1.0076} = 0.3651$
Estimated Probability of Success = estimated odds ratio / (1 + estimated odds ratio)
$= 0.3651/(1 + 0.3651) = 0.2675$

14.58   (e)   ln(estimated odds ratio) = 1.243 -0.25034 X_1 = 1.243 -0.25034 (11.49) = -1.6334
cont.   Estimated odds ratio = $e^{-1.6334}$ = 0.1953
                 Estimated Probability of Success
                 = estimated odds ratio / (1 + estimated odds ratio)
                 = 0.1953/(1 + 0.1953) = 0.1634
         (f)   ln(estimated odds ratio) = 1.243 -0.25034 X_1 = 1.243 -0.25034 (13.99) = -2.2593
                 Estimated odds ratio = $e^{-2.2593}$ = 0.1044
                 Estimated Probability of Success
                 = estimated odds ratio / (1 + estimated odds ratio)
                 = 0.1044/(1 + 0.1044) = 0.0946

14.60   Testing the significance of the entire regression model involves a simultaneous test of
        whether any of the independent variables are significant. Testing the contribution of each
        independent variable tests the contribution of that independent variable after accounting for
        the effect of the other independent variables in the model.

14.62   The coefficients in a least squares regression are obtained by minimizing the sum of the
        squared differences between the actual values and the fitted values of the dependent variable.
        In logistic regression, the coefficients are obtained by maximizing a likelihood function. The
        dependent variable in a least squares regression is numerical while the dependent variable in
        a logistic regression is categorical coded into 0 and 1 for failure and success, respectively.

14.64   You test whether the interaction of the dummy variable and each of the independent variables
        in the model make a significant contribution to the regression model.

14.66   It is assumed that the slope of the dependent variable Y with an independent variable X is the
        same for each of the two levels of the dummy variable.

14.68   (a) $\hat{Y} = -44.988 + 1.7506 X_1 + 0.368 X_2$, where X_1 = assessed value (in thousands of
                dollars) and X_2 = time period (in months).
        (b)   Holding constant the effects of time period, for each additional thousand dollars in
                assessed value the selling price of the house is estimated to increase on the average
                by 1.7506 thousands of dollars, or $1,750.60. Holding constant the effects of assessed
                value, for each additional month the selling price of the house is estimated to increase
                on the average by 0.368 thousands of dollars, or $368.
        (c) $\hat{Y} = -44.988 + 1.7506(70) + 0.368(12) = 81.969$ or $81,969
        (d)   All four residual plots indicate that the fitted model appears to be adequate.
        (e) $F = 223.46 > F_{U(2,27)} = 3.35$ with 2 and 27 degrees of freedom. Reject H_0. At
                least one of the independent variables is linearly related to the dependent variable.
        (f)   The p-value is less than 0.001. This means that the probability of obtaining an F test
                statistic of 223.46 or greater if there were not relationship between the dependent
                variable and independent variables is less than 0.001.
        (g) $r^2_{Y.12} = 0.943$. So, 94.3% of the variation in selling price can be explained
                by the variation in assessed value and the variation in time period.
        (h) $r^2_{adj} = 0.939$

14.68   (i)   For X_1: $t = 20.41 > t_{27} = 2.0518$ with 27 degrees of freedom. Reject H_0. There is
cont.   enough evidence that X_1 significantly contributes to a model already containing X_2.
               For X_2: $t = 2.873 > t_{27} = 2.0518$ with 27 degrees of freedom. Reject H_0. There is
               enough evidence that X_2 significantly contributes to a model already containing X_1.
               Therefore, each independent variable makes a significant contribution in the presence
               of the other variable, and both variables should be included in the model.

        (j)   For X_1, the p-value is less than 0.001. This means the probability of obtaining a t-test
               statistic which differs from zero by 20.41 or more (positively or negatively) when β_1
               $= 0$ is less than 0.001. For X_2, the p-value is 0.008. This means the probability of
               obtaining a t-test statistic which differs from zero by 2.873 or more (positively or
               negatively) when $\beta_2 = 0$ is 0.008.

        (k) $1.575 \le \beta_1 \le 1.927$. This is a net regression coefficient. That is, taking into account
               the time period, this coefficient measures the expected increase in selling price for
               each additional thousand dollars in assessed value. In Problem 13.76, the coefficient
               did not take into account (and hold constant) the effects of the time period.

        (l) $r_{Y1.2}^2 = 0.9392$. For a given time period, 93.92% of the variation in selling price can
               be explained by variation in assessed value. $r_{Y2.1}^2 = 0.2342$. For a given assessed
               value, 23.42% of the variation in selling price can be explained by variation in time
               period.

14.70   (a) $\hat{Y} = 63.7751 + 10.7252X_1 - 0.2843X_2$, where X_1 = size (in thousands of square
               feet) and X_2 = age (in years).

        (b)   Holding constant the effects of age, for each additional thousand square feet the
               assessed value of the house is estimated to increase by a mean of 10.7252 thousands
               of dollars, or $10,725.20. Holding constant the effects of size, for each year of age
               the assessed value of the house is estimated to decrease by a mean of 0.2843
               thousands of dollars, or $284.30.

        (c) $\hat{Y} = 63.7751 + 10.7252(1.75) - 0.2843(10) = 79.702$ or $79,702

        (d)   The residual plot against age indicates a potential pattern that may require the
               addition of nonlinear terms. One value appears to be an outlier in all four plots.

        (e) $F = 28.58 > F_{U(2,12)} = 3.89$ with 2 and 12 degrees of freedom. Reject H_0. At least
               one of the independent variables is linearly related to the dependent variable.

        (f)   The p-value is less than 0.001. This means that the probability of obtaining an F test
               statistic of 28.58 or greater if there were not relationship between the dependent
               variable and independent variables is less than 0.001.

        (g) $r_{Y.12}^2 = 0.8265$. 82.65% of the variation in assessed value can be explained by the
               variation in size and the variation in age.

        (h) $r_{adj}^2 = 0.7976$

        (i)   For X_1: $t = 3.558 > t_{12} = 2.1788$ with 12 degrees of freedom. Reject H_0. There is
               evidence that X_1 significantly contributes to a model already containing X_2. For X_2:
               $t = -3.400 < -t_{12} = -2.1788$ with 12 degrees of freedom. Reject H_0. There is
               evidence that X_2 significantly contributes to a model already containing X_1.
               Therefore, each independent variable makes a significant contribution in the presence
               of the other variable, and both variables should be included in the model.

14.70   (j)   For X_1, the p-value is 0.004. This means the probability of obtaining a t-test statistic
cont.   which differs from zero by 3.558 or more (positively or negatively) when $\beta_1 = 0$ is
                 0.004. For X_2, the p-value is 0.005. This means the probability of obtaining a t-test
                 statistic which differs from zero by 3.4 or more (positively or negatively) when $\beta_2 =$
                 0 is 0.005.

        (k) $4.158 \le \beta_1 \le 17.293$. This is a net regression coefficient. That is, taking into
                 account the age of the house, this coefficient measures the expected increase in
                 assessed value for each additional thousand square feet of size. In Problem 13.77, the
                 coefficient did not take into account (and hold constant) the effects of age.

        (l) $r_{Y1.2}^2 = 0.5134$. For a given age of the house, 51.34% of the variation in assessed
                 value can be explained by variation in size. $r_{Y2.1}^2 = 0.4907$. For a given amount of
                 size in square feet, 49.07% of the variation in assessed value can be explained by
                 variation in age.

        (m)   No. The age of the house does have a significant bearing on its assessed value.

14.72   (a) $\hat{Y} = 40.8765 - 0.0121 \text{ length} - 0.0050 \text{ weight}$

        (b) $b_1 = -0.0121$: Holding weight fixed, the estimated mean mileage of a car will
                 decrease by 0.0121 miles per gallon as the length of the car increases by one inch.
                 $b_2 = -.0050$: Holding length fixed, the estimate mean mileage of a car will
                 decrease by .0050 miles per gallon as the weight of the car increases by one pound.

        (c)   23.6603 miles per gallon.

        (d)

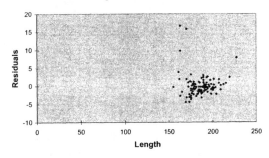

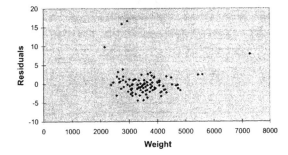

14.72   (d)   According to the residual plot of length, the homoscedasticity assumption seems to
cont.   have been violated. From the residual plot of weight, there seems to be a quadratic
                         relationship between mileage and weight.

(e)   Yes, there is a significant relationship between gasoline mileage and the two
          explanatory variables at the 0.05 level of significance because the p-value of the F
          test is essentially zero.

(f)   The p-value is essentially zero. It is almost impossible to have observed data which
          will give rise to an F test statistic equal to or more extreme than 92.9287 if there is
          really no significant relationship between gasoline mileage and the two explanatory
          variables.

(g)   61.17% of the total variation in gasoline mileage can be explained by length and
          weight of a car.

(h) $r^2_{adj} = 0.6051$

(i)   PHStat output:

	Coefficients	Standard Error	t Stat	P-value
Intercept	40.87650495	4.059910501	10.06832661	1.3805E-17
Length	-0.012071414	0.02632727	-0.458513689	0.647426793
Weight	-0.004954095	0.000483677	-10.24256569	5.32269E-18

At 0.05 level of significance, only weight makes a significant contribution to the
regression model. The model should include only weight as the explanatory variable.

(j)   The p-value for length is 0.6474. The probability of observing a data set which
          yields a t-test statistic for length equal to or more extreme than -0.4585 is 64.74%.
          The p-value for weight is essentially zero. The probability of observing a data set
          which yields a t test statistic for weight more extreme than -10.2426 is essentially
          zero.

(k) $-0.0059 \le \beta_2 \le -0.0040$

(l) $r^2_{Y1 \bullet 2} = 0.0018$, $r^2_{Y2 \bullet 1} = 0.4706$. Holding weight constant, 0.18% of the variation in
          mileage can be explained by length. Holding length constant, 47.06% of the
          variation in mileage can be explained by weight.

14.74   (a) $\hat{Y} = 152.0316 - 2.4587X_1 - 15.8687X_2$, where X_1 = league dummy (0 = American,
                         1 = National) and X_2 = ERA.

(b)   Holding constant the effect of ERA, the estimated mean number of wins for a team in
          the American league is 2.4587 above that of the National league.   Holding constant
          the effect of league, for each unit increase in ERA, the estimated mean number of
          wins is estimated to decrease by 15.8687.

(c) $\hat{Y} = 152.0316 - 2.4587(0) - 15.8687(4.5) \cong 81 \text{wins}$.

14.74   (d)
cont.

E.R.A. Residual Plot

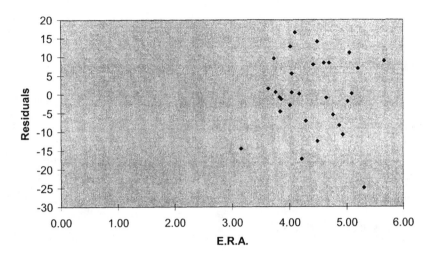

Based on the residual analysis, the model appears adequate.

(e) $F = 11.4784$ with 2 and 27 degrees of freedom.
p-value = 0.00025< 0.05. Reject H_0. There is evidence of a relationship between number of wins and the two dependent variables.

(f)   For X_1: $t = -0.6447$. p-value = 0.5246 > 0.05. Do not reject H_0. Which league the team is in does not make a significant contribution and should not be included in the model.
For X_2: $t = -4.7763$. p-value is virtually zero < 0.05. Reject H_0. ERA makes a significant contribution and should be included in the model.
The model should include ERA but not the league dummy.

(g) $-10.2842 \le \beta_1 \le 5.3668$, $-22.6856 \le \beta_2 \le -9.0518$

(h) $r^2_{Y.12} = 0.4595$. 45.95% of the variation in number of wins can be explained by variation in type of league and variation in ERA.

(i) $r^2_{adj} = 0.4195$

(j) $r^2_{Y1.2} = 0.0152$. Holding constant the effect of ERA, 1.52% of the variation in number of wins can be explained by variation in the type of league.
$r^2_{Y2.1} = 0.4580$. Holding constant the effect of league, 45.80% of the variation in number of wins can be explained by variation in ERA.

(k)   The slope of number of wins with ERA is the same regardless of whether the team is in the American or National league.

(l) $\hat{Y} = 162.6777 - 21.8842X_1 - 18.2211X_2 + 4.4027X_1X_2$.
For X_1X_2: the p-value is 0.5189. Do not reject H_0. There is not evidence that the interaction term makes a contribution to the model.

(m)   The model with only ERA should be used.

CHAPTER 15

OBJECTIVES

- To be able to use quadratic terms in a regression model
- To be able to use transformed variables in a regression model
- To examine the effect of each observation on the regression model
- To be able to measure the correlation among the independent variables
- To build a regression model using either the stepwise or best-subsets approach
- To understand the pitfalls involved in developing a multiple regression model

OVERVIEW AND KEY CONCEPTS

The Quadratic Regression Model

- In a quadratic regression model, the relationship between the dependent variable and one or more independent variable is a quadratic polynomial function.
- The quadratic regression model is useful when the residual plot reveals nonlinear relationship.
- The quadratic regression model:
    - $Y_i = \beta_0 + \beta_1 X_{1i} + \beta_2 X_{1i}^2 + \varepsilon_i$
    - The quadratic relationship can be between Y and more than one X variable as well.
- **Testing for the overall significance of the quadratic regression model:**
    - The test for the overall significance of the quadratic regression model is exactly the same as testing for the overall significance of any multiple regression model.
    - **Test statistic:** $F = \dfrac{MSR}{MSE}$.
- **Testing for quadratic effect:**
    - **The hypotheses:** $H_0 : \beta_2 = 0$ (no quadratic effect) vs. $H_1 : \beta_2 \neq 0$ (the quadratic term is needed)
    - **Test statistic:** $t = \dfrac{b_2 - \beta_2}{S_{b_2}}$.
    - This is a two-tail test with a left tail and a right-tail rejection region.

Using Transformation in Regression Models

- The following three transformation models are often used to overcome violations of the homoscedasticity assumption, as well as to transform a model that is not linear in form into one that is linear.
- **Square-root transformation:**
  - $Y_i = \beta_0 + \beta_1 \sqrt{X_{1i}} + \varepsilon_i$
  - The dependent variable is Y_i and the independent variable is $\sqrt{X_{1i}}$.
- **Transformed multiplicative model:**
  - $\log Y_i = \log \beta_0 + \beta_1 \log X_{1i} + \cdots + \beta_k \log X_{ki} + \log \varepsilon_i$
  - The dependent variable is $\log Y_i$ and the independent variables are $\log X_{1i}$, $\log X_{2i}$, etc.
- **Transformed exponential model:**
  - $\ln Y_i = \beta_0 + \beta_1 X_{1i} + \cdots + \beta_k X_{ki} + \ln \varepsilon_i$
  - The dependent variable is $\ln Y_i$ and the independent variables are X_{1i}, X_{2i}, etc.

Influential Analysis

- Influential analysis is performed to determined observations that have influential effect on the fitted model.
- Potentially influential points become candidate for removal from the model
- Criteria used are
  - **The hat matrix elements h_i:** If $h_i > 2(k+1)/n$, X_i is an influential point.
  - **The Studentized deleted residuals t_i^* :** X_i is influential if $\left| t_i^* \right| > t_{0.05, n-k-2}$ where $t_{0.05, n-k-2}$ is the critical value of a two-tail test at a 10% level of significance.
  - **Cooks' distance statistic D_i :** X_i is considered influential if $D_i > F_{k+1, n-k-1}$ where $F_{k+1, n-k-1}$ is the critical value of an F distribution with $k+1$ and $n-k-1$ degrees of freedom at a 0.50 level of significance.
- All three criteria are complementary. Only when all 3 criteria provide consistent result should an observation be removed.

Collinearity

- Some of the explanatory variables are highly correlated with each other.
- The collinear variables do not provide new information and it becomes difficult to separate the effect of such variables on the dependent variable.

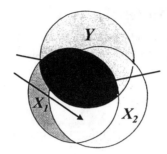

Large *Overlap* reflects collinearity between X_1 and X_2

Large *Overlap* in variation of X_1 and X_2 is used in explaining the variation in Y but *NOT* in estimating β_1 and β_2

- The values of the regression coefficient for the correlated variables may fluctuate drastically depending on which independent variables are included in the model.
- Variance inflationary factor (VIF) is used to measure collinearity.
  - $VIF_j = \dfrac{1}{\left(1 - R_j^2\right)}$ where R_j^2 is the coefficient determination of regressing X_j on all the other explanatory variables.
  - If $VIF_j > 5$, X_j is considered highly correlated with the other explanatory variables.

Model Building

- The goal is to develop a good model with the fewest explanatory variables that is easier to interpret and has lower probability of collinearity.
- **Stepwise regression procedure:** Provides limited evaluation of alternative models.
- **Best-subsets approach:** Uses the Mallow's C_p and selects the models with small C_p near $k+1$.
- **Model building flowchart:**

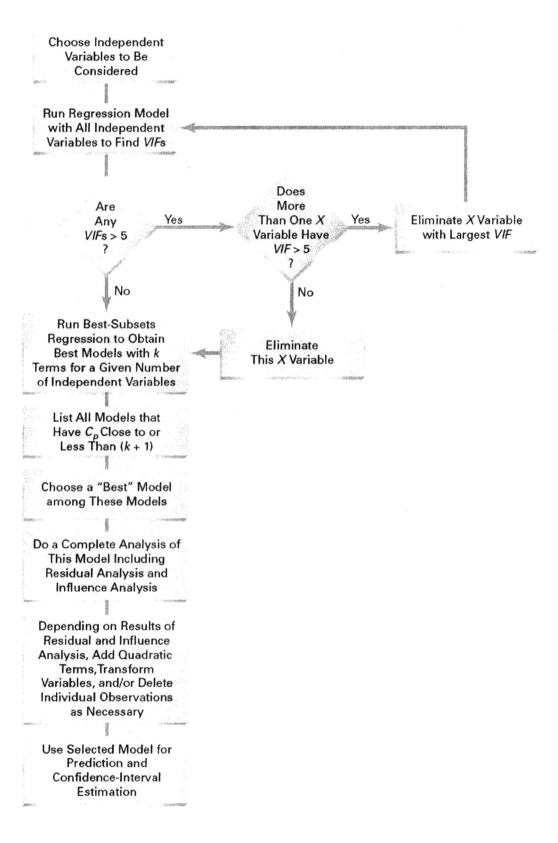

SOLUTIONS TO END OF SECTION AND CHAPTER REVIEW EVEN PROBLEMS

15.2   (a)

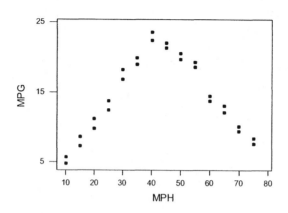

     (b) $\hat{Y} = -7.556 + 1.2717X - 0.0145X^2$

     (c) $\hat{Y} = -7.556 + 1.2717(55) - 0.0145(55^2) = 18.52$

     (d)   Based on residual analysis, there are patterns in the residuals vs. highway speed, vs. the quadratic variable (speed squared), and vs. the fitted values.

     (e) $F = 141.46 > F_{2,25} = 3.39$. Reject H_0. The overall model is significant. The p-value < 0.001.

     (f)   The p-value < 0.001. $t = -16.63 < -t_{25} = -2.0595$. Reject H_0. The quadratic effect is significant. Therefore, the quadratic model is a better fit than the linear regression model.

     (g) $r_{Y.12}^2 = 0.919$. 91.9% of the variation in miles per gallon can be explained by the quadratic relationship between miles per gallon and highway speed.

     (h) $r_{adj}^2 = 0.912$

15.4   (a)

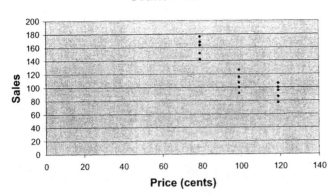

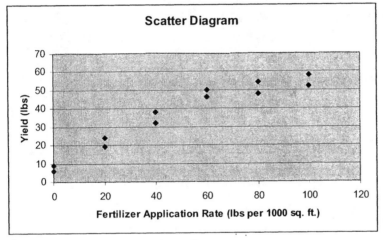

(b) $\hat{Y} = 6.643 + 0.895X - 0.0041X^2$

(c) $\hat{Y} = 6.643 + 0.895(70) - 0.0041(70^2) = 49.17$

15.4 **(d)**
cont.

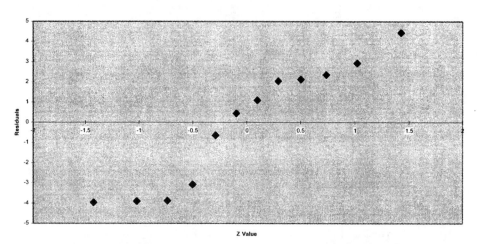

A residual analysis indicates no strong patterns. However, the distribution of residuals appears to deviate from a normal distribution according to the normal probability plot.

(e) $F = 157.32 > F_{2,9} = 4.26$. Reject H_0. The overall model is significant.

(f) The p-value < 0.001 indicates that the probability of having an F-test statistic of at least 157.32 when $\beta_1 = 0$ and $\beta_2 = 0$ is less than 0.001.

(g) $t = -4.27 < -t_9 = -2.2622$. Reject H_0. The quadratic effect is significant.

(h) The p-value $= 0.002$ indicates that the probability of having a t-test statistic with an absolute value of at least 4.27 is equal to 0.002 when $\beta_2 = 0$.

(i) $r^2_{Y.12} = 0.972$. So, 97.2% of the variation in yield can be explained by the quadratic relationship between yield and fertilizer application rate.

(j) $r^2_{adj} = 0.966$

15.6 **(a)** $\log \hat{Y} = \log(3.07) + 0.9\log(8.5) + 1.41\log(5.2) = 2.33318$
$\hat{Y} = 10^{2.33318} = 215.37$

(b) Holding constant the effects of X_2, for each additional unit of the logarithm of X_1, the logarithm of Y is estimated to increase by a mean of 0.9. Holding constant the effects of X_1, for each additional unit of the logarithm of X_2, the logarithm of Y is estimated to increase by a mean of 1.41.

15.8   (a) $\hat{Y} = 9.04 + 0.852\sqrt{X_1}$

(b) $\hat{Y} = 9.04 + 0.852\sqrt{55} = 15.36$ miles per gallon

(c)   The residual analysis indicates a clear quadratic pattern. The model does not adequately fit the data.

(d) $t = 1.35 < t_{26} = 2.0555$. Do not reject H_0. The model does not provide a significant relationship.

(e) $r^2 = 0.066$. Only 6.6% of the variation in miles per gallon can be explained by variation in the square root of highway speed.

(f) $r^2_{adj} = 0.030$

(g)   The quadratic regression model in Problem 15.2 is far superior to the inadequate model here. The square root of highway speed did virtually nothing to enhance the fit.

15.10   (a) $\ln\hat{Y} = 2.475 + 0.018546X_1$

(b) $\ln\hat{Y} = 2.475 + 0.018546(55) = 3.495$ $\hat{Y} = e^{3.495} = 32.95$ pounds.

(c)   The residual analysis indicates a clear quadratic pattern. The model does not adequately fit the data.

(d) $t = 6.11 > t_{10} = 2.2281$. Reject H_0. The model provides a significant relationship.

(e) $r^2 = 0.789$. So, 78.9% of the variation in the natural logarithm of Yield can be explained by variation in the amount of fertilizer applied.

(f) $r^2_{adj} = 0.768$

(g)   The quadratic regression model in Problem 15.4 is superior to the model here.

15.12   Observations 14 ($h_i = 0.3568$) and 19 ($h_i = 0.2828$) are influential as they have $h_i > 2(2+1)/24 = 0.25$.

Observations 1, 2, and 14 had an effect on the model: $\left|t_1^*\right| = 2.5783$, $\left|t_2^*\right| = 1.8465$, and $\left|t_{14}^*\right| = 1.8429$. All of these values exceed $t_{24-2-2,.05} = 1.7247$.

The largest value for Cook's D_i is 0.5637, which is less than $F_{.50,2+1,24-2-1} = 0.8149$. Thus, there is insufficient evidence to delete any observations in the model.

15.14   Observations 1 ($h_i = 0.2924$), 2 ($h_i = 0.2924$), 13 ($h_i = 0.3564$) and 14 ($h_i = 0.3564$) are influential as they have $h_i > 2(2+1)/22 = 0.2727$.

Observations 2, 4, 7, and 13 had an effect on the model: $\left|t_2^*\right| = 2.44$, $\left|t_4^*\right| = 1.98$, $\left|t_7^*\right| = 1.87$, and $\left|t_{13}^*\right| = 1.96$. All of these values exceed $t_{22-2-2,.05} = 1.7341$.

The largest value for Cook's D_i is 0.652 for Observation 2, which is less than $F_{.50,2+1,22-2-1} = 0.8177$. Since this value and the D_i value for Observation 13 were substantially above the D_i values for the other observations and were also found to have had an effect on the model and to be influential, a model was studied with Observations 2 and 13 deleted. In this model, $b_0 = -24.7$, $b_1 = 14.932$ and $b_2 = 19.107$, with $r^2_{Y.12} = 0.88$.

15.16   Observations 8 ($h_i = 0.2370$), 18 ($h_i = 0.3449$), and 26 ($h_i = 0.2285$) are influential as they have $h_i > 2(2+1)/30 = 0.2$.

Observations 8, 9, 10, and 14 had an effect on the model: $\left|t_8^*\right| = 2.06$, $\left|t_9^*\right| = 2.09$, $\left|t_{10}^*\right| = 3.40$, and $\left|t_{14}^*\right| = 2.24$. All of these values exceed $t_{30-2-2,.05} = 1.7056$.

The largest value for Cook's D_i is 0.5475 for Observation 10, which is less than $F_{.50,2+1,30-2-1} = 0.8089$. Using the 3 criteria, there is insufficient evidence for removal of any observation from the model.

15.18 $VIF = \dfrac{1}{1-0.2} = 1.25$

15.20 $R_1^2 = 0.64$, $VIF_1 = \dfrac{1}{1-0.64} = 2.778$

$R_2^2 = 0.64$, $VIF_2 = \dfrac{1}{1-0.64} = 2.778$

There is no reason to suspect the existence of collinearity.

15.22 $R_1^2 = 0.008464$, $VIF_1 = \dfrac{1}{1-0.008464} = 1.009$

$R_2^2 = 0.008464$, $VIF_2 = \dfrac{1}{1-0.008464} = 1.009$

There is no reason to suspect the existence of collinearity.

15.24 $VIF = \dfrac{1}{1-0.0411} = 1.0428$. There is no reason to suspect the existence of collinearity.

15.26   (a) $C_p = \dfrac{(1-R_k^2)(n-T)}{1-R_T^2} - [n - 2(k+1)] = \dfrac{(1-0.274)(40-7)}{1-0.653} - [40 - 2(2+1)]$

$= 35.04$

(b) C_p overwhelmingly exceeds $k + 1 = 3$, the number of parameters (including the Y-intercept), so this model does not meet the criterion for further consideration as the best model.

15.28   Let Y = selling price, X_1 = assessed value, X_2 = time period, and X_3 = whether house was new ($0 = $ no, $1 = $ yes).
Based on a full regression model involving all of the variables, all of the VIF values (1.3, 1.0, and 1.3, respectively) are less than 5. There is no reason to suspect the existence of collinearity.
Based on a best subsets regression and examination of the resulting C_p values, the models that should be considered further appear to be a model with variables X_1 and X_2, which has $C_p = 2.8$, and the full regression model, which has $C_p = 4.0$. Based on a regression analysis with all original variables, variable X_3 fails to make a significant contribution to the model at the 0.05 level. Thus, the best model is the model using assessed value (X_1) and time (X_2) as the independent variables.

15.28   A residual analysis shows no strong patterns.

cont.   The final model is: $\hat{Y} = -44.9882 + 1.7506X_1 + 0.3680X_2$

$r_{Y.12}^2 = 0.9430$, $r_{adj}^2 = 0.9388$

Overall significance of the model: $F = 223.4575$, p-value < 0.001.
Each independent variable is significant at the 0.05 level.
A stepwise regression in Minitab yields the same model.

15.30   Let Y = gasoline mileage, X_1 = weight, X_2 = width, X_3 = length, and X_4 = 1 if SUV; 0
otherwise.
Based on a full regression model involving all of the variables:
$VIF_1 = 5.1$, $VIF_2 = 4.8$, $VIF_3 = 4.6$, $VIF_4 = 2.6$
Variable X_1 should be dropped from the model.
Minitab output:

Best Subsets Regression: MPG versus Width, Length, SUV1
Response is MPG

					W	L e	S
					i	n	S
					d	g	U
					t	t	V
Vars	R-Sq	R-Sq(adj)	C-p	S	h	h	1
1	39.3	38.8	69.5	3.6603	X		
1	28.2	27.6	103.6	3.9806			X
1	26.6	26.0	108.5	4.0245		X	
2	61.1	60.5	4.5	2.9424		X	X
2	57.4	56.7	15.8	3.0785	X		X
2	39.3	38.3	71.5	3.6758	X	X	
3	61.9	61.0	4.0	2.9235	X	X	X

Based on regression model for remaining variables, all VIF values are less than 5. The best-
subsets output reveals only one model with X_2, X_3, and X_4 has $C_p \leq k + 1$. Influential analysis
using hat matrix diagonal elements, residuals and Cook's distance statistic reveals that none
of the observations should be removed from the regression model.

15.30
cont.

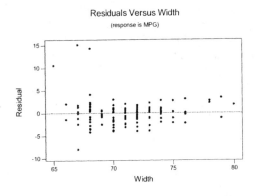

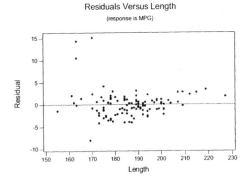

Analysis of the residual plots indicates that the homoscedasticity assumption is violated. There also appears to be quadratic effect of length and width on MPG.

Minitab Output:

```
The regression equation is
MPG = 236 - 0.207 Width - 2.00 Length - 4.05 SUV1 + 0.00508 Length(SQ)
         -0.000000 Width(SQ)


Predictor          Coef     SE Coef          T        P      VIF
Constant         236.01       36.31       6.50    0.000
Width           -0.2072      0.1573      -1.32    0.190      4.4
Length          -2.0024      0.3810      -5.26    0.000    432.0
SUV1            -4.0526      0.8467      -4.79    0.000      2.4
Length(S       0.005080 ·   0.001026      4.95    0.000    448.0
Width(SQ  -0.00000026  0.00000008      -3.20    0.002      4.2


S = 2.648       R-Sq = 69.3%     R-Sq(adj) = 68.0%


Analysis of Variance


Source             DF          SS         MS        F        P
Regression          5     1820.68     364.14    51.92    0.000
Residual Error    115      806.61       7.01
Total             120     2627.29
```

The small p-values of the square of length and square of width from the above regression output show that the quadratic effect of both length and width is significant at the 0.05 level of significance.

15.30   The resulting model:

cont. $\hat{Y} = 236.01 - 0.2072X_2 - 2.0024X_3 - 4.0526X_4 - 0.00000026X_2^2 + 0.0051X_3^2$

$r^2 = 69.3\%$, $r_{adj}^2 = 68\%$

Overall significance of the model: $F = 51.92$, p-value is essentially zero.

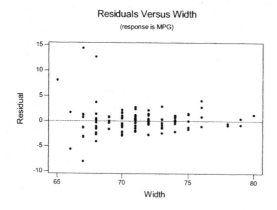

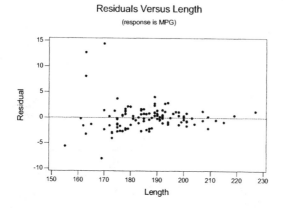

Residual analysis reveals that there is still a problem of the lack of homoscedasticity.

15.32   Let Y = price, X_1 = text speed, X_2 = text cost, X_3 = color photo time, X_4 = color photo cost. Based on a full regression model involving all of the variables:
All *VIF*s are less than 5. So there is no reason to suspect collinearity between any pair of variables.
The best-subset approach yields the following models to be considered:
Partial PHStat output from the best-subsets selection:

Model	Cp	k	R Square	Adj. R Square	Std. Error	Consider This Model?
X1X2X3	3.063595	4	0.524353	0.394630984	59.53637	Yes
X1X2X3X4	5	5	0.527359	0.338302174	62.24466	Yes
X1X3	2.592803	3	0.452076	0.360755595	61.17948	Yes

Partial PHStat output of the full regression model:

	Coefficients	Standard Error	t Stat	P-value
Intercept	335.3080897	65.84754648	5.092188056	0.00046935
Text Speed	-23.46745075	14.06190177	-1.668867492	0.126103211
Text Cost	-6.429188147	5.698538218	-1.12821708	0.285568543
Color Photo Time	-7.470425481	4.683317933	-1.595113889	0.141770953
Color Photo Cost	13.82312558	54.81425163	0.252181233	0.806008407

Since the *p*-values of X_2 and X_4 are both greater than 0.05, they should be dropped from the model.
PHStat output of the model with only X_1 and X_3:

Regression Statistics	
Multiple R	0.672366138
R Square	0.452076224
Adjusted R Square	0.360755595
Standard Error	61.17947528
Observations	15

ANOVA

	df	SS	MS	F	Significance F
Regression	2	37058.19499	18529.0975	4.950428256	0.027059569
Residual	12	44915.13834	3742.928195		
Total	14	81973.33333			

	Coefficients	Standard Error	t Stat	P-value
Intercept	326.8080104	56.60295611	5.773691568	8.82928E-05
Text Speed	-23.85700143	12.91282757	-1.847542786	0.089456849
Color Photo Time	-10.23438315	3.963094482	-2.582422194	0.023990486

The most appropriate model:

$$\hat{Y} = 326.8080 - 23.8570X_1 - 10.2344X_3$$

Analysis of the residual plots does not reveal any specific pattern.

15.34   Stepwise regression attempts to find the best regression model without examining all possible regressions by adding and subtracting X variables at each step of the process. Best-subsets regression examines each possible regression model and uses the C_p statistic to determine which models can be considered to be good fitting models.

15.36   A hat matrix element h_i measures the possible influence of each X_i on the fitted regression model while a deleted residual measures the difference of an observation Y_i from the value predicted by a model that includes all other observations.

15.38   (a)   Let Y = wins, X_1 = game receipts, X_2 = local TV and radio revenue, X_3 = other local revenue, X_4 = player compensation.

Based on a full regression model involving all of the variables:

The VIF for X_1, X_2, X_3, and X_4 are, respectively, 4.53, 2.50, 2.63, 3.33, and are all less than 5. So there is no reason to suspect collinearity between any pair of variables.

The best-subsets approach does not yield a clear best model with the following result:

Model	Cp	k	R Square	Adj. R Square	Std. Error	Consider This Model?
X1	0.0897	2	0.2020	0.1735	11.8243	Yes
X1X2	1.5826	3	0.2175	0.1596	11.9236	Yes
X1X2X3	3.0004	4	0.2353	0.1471	12.0117	Yes
X1X2X3X4	5.0000	5	0.2354	0.1130	12.2495	Yes
X1X2X4	3.5694	4	0.2179	0.1277	12.1476	Yes
X1X3	1.5395	3	0.2189	0.1610	11.9136	Yes
X1X3X4	3.4831	4	0.2206	0.1306	12.1271	Yes
X1X4	1.9674	3	0.2058	0.1469	12.0130	Yes
X2	1.0472	2	0.1727	0.1432	12.0393	Yes
X2X3	1.1758	3	0.2300	0.1729	11.8284	Yes
X2X3X4	3.1539	4	0.2306	0.1419	12.0485	Yes
X2X4	2.4146	3	0.1921	0.1322	12.1160	Yes
X3	0.6063	2	0.1862	0.1572	11.9407	Yes
X3X4	1.9563	3	0.2061	0.1473	12.0104	Yes
X4	1.5018	2	0.1588	0.1288	12.1400	Yes

The stepwise approach recommends that regular season game receipts (X_1) is the only variable needed with the following result:

Stepwise
Analysis
Table of Results for General Stepwise

Regular season game receipts ($millions) entered.

	df	SS	MS	F	Significance F
Regression	1	991.10488	991.10488	7.08879	0.01271
Residual	28	3914.76178	139.81292		
Total	29	4905.86667			

	Coefficients	Standard Error	t Stat	P-value	Lower 95%
Intercept	69.0198	4.9682	13.8924	0.0000	58.8430
game receipts	0.2582	0.0970	2.6625	0.0127	0.0596

No other variables could be entered into the model. Stepwise ends.

15.38   (a)   PHStat output of the best model:
cont.

Regression Statistics	
Multiple R	0.4495
R Square	0.2020
Adjusted R Square	0.1735
Standard Error	11.8243
Observations	30

ANOVA

	df	SS	MS	F	Significance F
Regression	1	991.1049	991.1049	7.0888	0.0127
Residual	28	3914.7618	139.8129		
Total	29	4905.8667			

	Coefficients	Standard Error	t Stat	P-value
Intercept	69.0198	4.9682	13.8924	0.0000
Regular season game receipts ($millions)	0.2582	0.0970	2.6625	0.0127

The p-value of game receipts is $0.013 < 0.05$ and, hence, game receipts is a significant independent variable.

Regular season game receipts ($millions)
Residual Plot

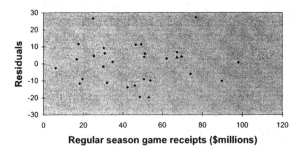

The residual plot does not reveal any obvious pattern.

Normal Probability Plot

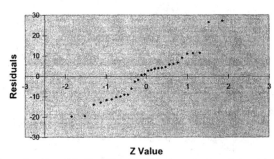

The normal probability plot shows sign of violation from the normality assumption.

(b)   The r^2 in (a) is 0.2020, which is much smaller than the r^2 of 0.9430 in problem 15.35(a). The four on-field team statistics have higher explanatory power than the variables used in (a).

15.40-15.42

Let Y = appraised value, X_1 = land area, X_2 = interior size, X_3 = age, X_4 = number of rooms, X_5 = number of bathrooms, X_6 = garage size.

(a)

Glencove:

Based on a full regression model involving all of the variables:

All *VIF*s are less than 5. So there is no reason to suspect collinearity between any pair of variables.

The best-subset approach yielded the following models to be considered:

Model	Cp	k	R Square	Adj. R Square	Std. Error	Consider This Model?
X1X2X3	3.650863	4	0.829632	0.809974373	52.47949	Yes
X1X2X3X4	4.149255	5	0.839606	0.813942457	51.92867	Yes
X1X2X3X4X5	5.908748	6	0.841203	0.808120255	52.7349	Yes
X1X2X3X4X5X6	7	7	0.847239	0.807387908	52.83544	Yes
X1X2X3X4X6	5.115483	6	0.846472	0.814486602	51.85268	Yes

The stepwise regression approach reveals the following best model:

	Coefficients	Standard Error	t Stat	P-value
Intercept	136.7940357	53.82963694	2.54124017	0.017353728
House Size(sq ft)	0.128818369	0.020923194	6.156725888	1.64543E-06
Land (acres)	276.0876372	78.19612858	3.530707239	0.001568793
Age	-1.398931849	0.475516859	-2.941918512	0.006773518

Combining the results of both approaches, the most appropriate multiple regression model for predicting appraised value in Glencove is

$$\hat{Y} = 136.7940 + 276.0876X_1 + 0.1288X_2 - 1.3989X_3$$

Roslyn:

Based on a full regression model involving all of the variables:

All *VIF*s are less than 5. So there is no reason to suspect collinearity between any pair of variables.

The best-subset approach yielded the following models to be considered:

Model	Cp	k	R Square	Adj. R Square	Std. Error	This Model?
X1X2	2.4059	3	0.8374	0.8252	72.1055	Yes
X1X2X3X4X5	5.0427	6	0.8580	0.8284	71.4432	Yes
X1X2X3X4X5X6	7	7	0.8582	0.8213	72.9122	Yes
X1X2X3X5	4.5556	5	0.8487	0.8244	72.2612	Yes
X1X2X4	3.5674	4	0.8424	0.8242	72.3031	Yes
X1X2X4X5	3.0773	5	0.8578	0.8350	70.0523	Yes
X1X2X4X5X6	5.0021	6	0.8582	0.8287	71.3803	Yes
X1X2X5	2.5851	4	0.8485	0.8310	70.9006	Yes
X1X2X5X6	4.4102	5	0.8496	0.8255	72.0470	Yes

15.40-15.42   The stepwise regression approach reveals the following best model:
cont.

	Coefficients	Standard Error	t Stat	P-value
Intercept	93.1310	44.5718	2.0895	0.0462
House Size(sq ft)	0.1428	0.0196	7.2842	0.0000
Land	660.0916	141.5133	4.6645	0.0001

The p-value of X_3, X_4, X_5, X_6 are all greater than 0.05 in the regression model with X_1, X_2, X_3, X_4, X_5, and X_6. Combing the results of both approaches, the most appropriate multiple regression model for predicting appraised value in Roslyn is

$$\hat{Y} = 93.1310 + 660.0916X_1 + 0.1428X_2$$

Freeport:

Based on a full regression model involving all of the variables:
All *VIF*s are less than 5. So there is no reason to suspect collinearity between any pair of variables.
The best-subset approach yielded the following models to be considered:

Model	Cp	k	R Square	Adj. R Square	Std. Error	This Model?
X1X2X3X4	3.834689	5	0.873698	0.853489619	21.04431	Yes
X1X2X3X4X5	5.632946	6	0.874767	0.84867679	21.38716	Yes
X1X2X3X4X5X6	7	7	0.878121	0.846326523	21.55261	Yes
X1X2X3X4X6	5.028879	6	0.877968	0.85254467	21.11206	Yes
X1X2X4X5X6	5.631183	6	0.874776	0.848688081	21.38637	Yes
X1X2X4X6	3.702829	5	0.874397	0.854300154	20.98601	Yes
X1X2X5X6	4.901186	5	0.868046	0.846933926	21.50997	Yes
X1X2X6	3.084531	4	0.867075	0.851737417	21.16977	Yes
X2X3X4	2.339328	4	0.871024	0.856141953	20.85295	Yes
X2X3X4X5	4.272654	5	0.871377	0.850797473	21.23677	Yes
X2X3X4X5X6	5.626606	6	0.874801	0.848717389	21.38429	Yes
X2X3X4X6	3.626999	5	0.874799	0.854766276	20.95242	Yes
X2X3X6	3.887328	4	0.862821	0.846992473	21.50586	Yes
X2X4X5X6	4.225896	5	0.871625	0.851084891	21.21631	Yes
X2X4X6	2.232616	4	0.871589	0.85677268	20.80719	Yes
X2X5X6	3.858479	4	0.862974	0.847162986	21.49387	Yes
X2X6	1.903766	3	0.862734	0.852565858	21.11055	Yes

The stepwise regression approach reveals that the following best model:

	Coefficients	Standard Error	t Stat	P-value
Intercept	110.2676327	12.26077283	8.993530367	9.48178E-10
House Size(sq ft)	0.08210861	0.006673054	12.30450334	8.22931E-13

Combining the results of both approaches, the most appropriate multiple regression model for predicting appraised value in Freeport is

$$\hat{Y} = 110.2676 + 0.0821X_2$$

(b)   The adjusted r^2 for the best model in 15.38(a), 15.39(a), and 15.40(a) are, respectively, 0.81, 0.8117 and 0.8383. The model in 15.40(a) has the highest explanatory power after adjusting for the number of independent variables and sample size.

15.44   Let Y = appraised value, X_1 = land area, X_2 = interior size, X_3 = age, X_4 = number of rooms, X_5 = number of bathrooms, X_6 = garage size, X_7 = 1 if Glencove and 0 otherwise, X_8 = 1 if Roslyn and 0 otherwise.

(a)   Based on a full regression model involving all of the variables:
        All *VIF*s are less than 5. So there is no reason to suspect collinearity between any pair of variables.
        Minitab best-subset approach yielded the following models to be considered:
        Best Subsets Regression: Appraised Value versus Land (acres), House Size(s, ...
        Response is Appraised Value

					L a n d e (a c	H o u s e A S i	 R o o g e	 R B a t m s	 G e a r a h e	G l G n C g o s	 e R a o r s C l o y v n
Vars	R-Sq	R-Sq(adj)	C-p	S	c	i	e	s	s	e	v n
1	58.7	58.3	251.1	121.23	X						
1	47.3	46.7	344.7	137.04							X
1	44.0	43.4	371.5	141.23					X		
2	80.0	79.6	79.1	84.805	X						X
2	71.3	70.6	150.6	101.72	X						X
2	67.5	66.8	181.2	108.15					X		X
3	85.2	84.7	39.0	73.480	X	X					X
3	84.7	84.1	43.3	74.771	X						X X
3	83.2	82.6	55.3	78.251	X	X					X
4	87.8	87.2	19.5	67.018	X	X	X				X
4	87.8	87.2	19.8	67.120	X	X					X X
4	87.0	86.4	26.0	69.176	X	X		X			X
5	89.2	88.6	10.3	63.506	X	X	X				X X
5	89.1	88.4	11.3	63.883	X	X		X			X X
5	88.6	87.9	15.3	65.293	X	X				X	X X
6	89.8	89.0	7.7	62.192	X	X	X		X		X X
6	89.6	88.9	8.7	62.572	X	X		X X			X X
6	89.5	88.7	10.2	63.118	X	X	X	X			X X
7	90.1	89.2	7.1	61.610	X	X	X	X X			X X
7	89.8	88.9	9.3	62.413	X	X		X X X		X	X
7	89.8	88.9	9.5	62.490	X	X	X		X X		X X
8	90.1	89.1	9.0	61.941	X	X	X	X X X		X	X X

Following is the Minitab output for the multiple regression model that has the smallest C_p and the highest adjusted r-square:
The regression equation is
Appraised Value = 49.4 + 343 Land (acres) + 0.115 House Size(sq ft) – 0.585 Age – 8.24 Rooms + 26.9 Baths + 5.0 Garage + 56.4 Glencove + 210 Roslyn

Predictor	Coef	SE Coef	T	P	VIF
Constant	49.43	40.12	1.23	0.221	
Land (ac	342.96	68.73	4.99	0.000	1.5
House Si	0.11480	0.01545	7.43	0.000	2.7
Age	-0.5853	0.3898	-1.50	0.137	1.8
Rooms	-8.236	5.252	-1.57	0.121	1.5
Baths	26.92	12.46	2.16	0.034	2.1
Garage	5.01	14.10	0.36	0.723	2.1
Glen Cov	56.44	17.69	3.19	0.002	1.6
Roslyn	210.40	18.19	11.57	0.000	1.7

15.44 (a)
cont.

The individual t test for the significance of each independent variable at 5% level of significance concludes that only X_1, X_2, X_5, X_7, X_8, are significant individually. This subset, however, is not chosen when the C_p criterion is used.

Mintab stepwise regression analysis yields the following:
Stepwise Regression: Appraised Value versus Land (acres), House Size(s,...

```
Alpha-to-Enter: 0.05  Alpha-to-Remove: 0.05

Response is Appraise on  8 predictors, with N =    90
```

	Step	1	2	3	4	5	6
	Constant	-6.398	16.754	2.581	96.031	57.460	23.397
House Si		0.207	0.164	0.125	0.120	0.121	0.106
T-Value		11.19	11.95	8.98	9.46	10.07	7.70
P-Value		0.000	0.000	0.000	0.000	0.000	0.000
Roslyn			193	191	186	220	213
T-Value			9.63	11.01	11.71	12.05	11.76
P-Value			0.000	0.000	0.000	0.000	0.000
Land (ac				427	406	348	347
T-Value				5.47	5.68	4.97	5.06
P-Value				0.000	0.000	0.000	0.000
Age					-1.37	-1.05	-0.79
T-Value					-4.29	-3.31	-2.37
P-Value					0.000	0.001	0.020
Glen Cov						59	58
T-Value						3.27	3.26
P-Value						0.002	0.002
Baths							26
T-Value							2.14
P-Value							0.035
S		121	84.8	73.5	67.0	63.5	62.2
R-Sq		58.75	80.04	85.19	87.82	89.19	89.76
R-Sq(adj)		58.28	79.58	84.67	87.25	88.55	89.02
C-p		251.1	79.1	39.0	19.5	10.3	7.7

Following is the multiple regression output for the model chosen by stepwise regression:

15.44   (a)   **Regression Analysis: Appraised Va versus Land (acres), House Size(s,**
cont.   ...
```
The regression equation is
Appraised Value = 23.4 + 347 Land (acres) + 0.106 House Size(sq ft) -
0.792 Age  + 26.4 Baths + 57.7 Glencove + 213 Roslyn

Predictor         Coef      SE Coef          T         P        VIF
Constant         23.40        34.85       0.67     0.504
Land (ac        347.02        68.55       5.06     0.000        1.5
House Si        0.10614      0.01379       7.70     0.000        2.1
Age             -0.7921       0.3338      -2.37     0.020        1.3
Baths            26.38        12.32       2.14     0.035        2.0
Glen Cov         57.74        17.69       3.26     0.002        1.6
Roslyn          213.46        18.15      11.76     0.000        1.7
S = 62.19      R-Sq = 89.8%      R-Sq(adj) = 89.0%
```

This model has a C_p value of 7.7 and an adjusted r-square of 89.0. All the variables
are significant individually at 5% level of significance. Combining the stepwise
regression and the best subset regression results along with the individual t test
results, the most appropriate multiple regression model for predicting the appraised
value is

$$\hat{Y} = 23.40 + 347.02\, X_1 + 0.10614\, X_2 - 0.7921\, X_3 + 26.38\, X_5 + 57.74\, X_7$$
$$+ 213.46\, X_8$$

(b)   The estimated average appraised value in Glencove is 57.74 above Freeport for two
otherwise identical properties. The estimated average appraised value in Roslyn is
213.46 above Freeport for two otherwise identical properties. The estimated average
appraised value in Glen Cov is 213.45 − 57.74 = 155.72 below Roslyn for two
otherwise identical properties.

15.46   Denote X_1 = weight, X_2 = width, X_3 = length, X_4 = cargo volume, X_5 = turning circle,
X_6 = horsepower, and X_7 = 1 if SUV and 0 otherwise.

An analysis of the linear regression model using PHStat with all possible independent
variables reveals that two of the variables, X_1 and X_3, have *VIF* values in excess of 5.0.

Based on the procedure recommended in the text, variables were deleted one at time from the
model, selecting the variable with the largest *VIF* value, until there were no variables with
VIF > 5. Repetitions of this step resulted in the removal of weight and length from the model.

An analysis of the linear regression model with the remaining independent variables indicates
that none of the remaining variables have a *VIF* value that is 5.0 or larger.

Renaming: X_1 = width, X_2 = cargo, X_3 = turning circle, X_4 = horsepower , and X_5 = 1 if
SUV and 0 otherwise.

The best-subsets approach reveals that the model with all the 5 remaining variables is the
most appropriate multiple regression model.

Influence analysis using the hat matrix elements, the deleted residuals and Cook's distance
statistic does not reveal any observation that needs to be removed.

15.46
cont.

Residuals Versus Width
(response is MPG)

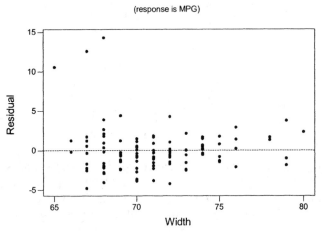

Residuals Versus Turning
(response is MPG)

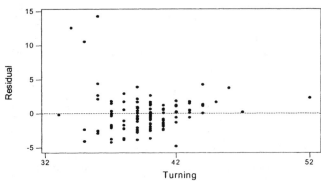

Residuals Versus Cargo Vo
(response is MPG)

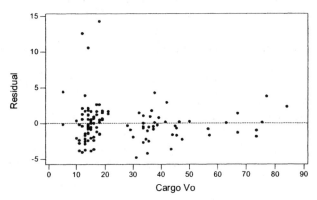

15.46   The residual plots reveal the violations of homoscedasticity assumption. Also there appears
cont.   to be a quadratic relationship between MPG and horsepower. Letting $X_7 = X_4^2$, the Minitab
output of the multiple regression model follows:
Regression Analysis: MPG versus Width, Cargo Volume, ...

```
The regression equation is
MPG = 75.7 - 0.242 Width - 0.0258 Cargo Volume - 0.304 Turning Circle
         - 0.243 Horsepower - 4.41 SUV Dummy +0.000581 Horsepower SQ

Predictor         Coef      SE Coef          T        P      VIF
Constant        75.652        6.981      10.84    0.000
Width          -0.2420       0.1106      -2.19    0.031      2.8
Cargo Vo      -0.02584      0.01556      -1.66    0.100      1.9
Turning        -0.3042       0.1067      -2.85    0.005      1.9
Horsepow      -0.24323      0.03176      -7.66    0.000     46.8
SUV Dumm       -4.4063       0.5639      -7.81    0.000      1.3
Horsepow    0.00058078   0.00008417       6.90    0.000     45.3

S = 2.355      R-Sq = 75.9%     R-Sq(adj) = 74.7%

Analysis of Variance

Source             DF           SS          MS        F        P
Regression          6      1995.26      332.54    59.98    0.000
Residual Error    114       632.03        5.54
Total             120      2627.29
```

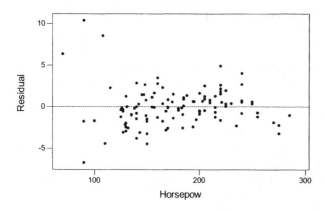

The new residual plot for horsepower indicates that the quadratic term has captured the nonlinear relationship between MPG and horsepower. The full model F test statistic has a p-
value that is virtually 0. There is sufficient evidence to conclude that all the variables
together significantly explain gas mileage. The individual t test statistic for each of the
explanatory variables also has p-value smaller than 0.05 with the exception of cargo volume,
which has a p-value of 0.0997.

15.46
cont.   The new Minitab output with cargo volume removed:
   Regression Analysis: MPG versus Width, Turning Circle, ...

```
The regression equation is
MPG = 81.3 - 0.309 Width - 0.344 Turning Circle - 0.243 Horsepower
        - 4.83 SUV Dummy +0.000586 Horsepower SQ

Predictor        Coef      SE Coef         T        P      VIF
Constant       81.254        6.158     13.20    0.000
Width         -0.3086        0.1038     -2.97    0.004      2.4
Turning       -0.3442        0.1048     -3.29    0.001      1.8
Horsepow     -0.24344       0.03201     -7.61    0.000     46.8
SUV Dumm      -4.8314        0.5062     -9.54    0.000      1.0
Horsepow   0.00058613    0.00008475      6.92    0.000     45.2

S = 2.372       R-Sq = 75.4%     R-Sq(adj) = 74.3%

Analysis of Variance

Source           DF           SS          MS        F        P
Regression        5      1979.99      396.00    70.35    0.000
Residual Error  115       647.30        5.63
Total           120      2627.29
```

The r^2 does not decrease substantially after the removal of cargo volume and the p-values of the t tests for the significance of individual slope coefficients are essentially zero.
The final model is:

$$\hat{Y} = 81.254 - 0.3086 \text{ Width} - 0.3442 \text{ Turning Circle} - 0.2434 \text{ Horsepower}$$

$$+ 5.8613 \times 10^{-4} \text{ Horsepower}^2 - 4.8314 \text{ SUV}$$

Residual analysis on the final model still shows signs of violation of the homoscedasticity assumption.

15.48   In the multiple regression model with solar radiation, soil temperature, vapor pressure, wind speed, relative humidity, dew point, and ambient air temperature, the highest *VIF* value of 739.18 belonged to vapor pressure. After dropping vapor pressure from the multiple regression model, the highest *VIF* value of 90.00 in the remaining multiple regression belonged to air temperature. After air temperature was removed from the model, soil radiation had the highest *VIF* of 18.84 in the remaining multiple regression. Soil radiation was dropped from the multiple regression model next. The highest *VIF* of 7.36 in the remaining model belonged to wind speed. Wind speed was dropped from the model next and all the *VIF* values in the remaining multiple regression of X_1 = soil temperature, X_2 = relative humidity, and X_3 = dew point were smaller than 5.
C_p statistic was computed for all subsets and the subsets that were not recommended by the C_p statistic were simple regression with soil temperature, simple regression with relative humidity, and multiple regression with both soil temperature and relative humidity.
Using a 0.05 level of significance and performing t tests on the significance of soil temperature, dew point and relative humidity individually led to the conclusion that only dew point was significant individually. The partial F test on the significance of soil temperature and relative humidity as a group yielded a p-value of 0.627, hence, led to the conclusion that both soil temperature and relative humidity were insignificant as a group as well. The residual plot in the simple regression of radon concentration on dew point indicated some possible nonlinear relationship. A logarithmic transformation on dew point was performed.

15.48   The residual plot in the linear-log model did not reveal any more nonlinear relationship and
cont.   the p-value of the t test was 0.046, which was smaller than the 5% level of significance. The
        coefficient of determination was pretty low at 0.10. Only 10% of the variation in radon
        concentration could be explained by using dew point.
        The normal probability plot suggests that the error distribution is very close to a normal
        distribution.

15.50   (a)   Let $X_1 = $ Temp $X_2 = $ Win% $X_3 = $ OpWin% $X_4 = $ Weekend $X_5 = $ Promotion

Regression Statistics	
Multiple R	0.548682487
R Square	0.301052472
Adjusted R Square	0.253826288
Standard Error	6442.445556
Observations	80

ANOVA

	df	SS	MS	F	Significance F
Regression	5	1322911703	264582340.6	6.374693962	5.64724E-05
Residual	74	3071377751	41505104.74		
Total	79	4394289454			

	Coefficients	Standard Error	t Stat	P-value	Lower 95%	Upper 95%
Intercept	-3862.480824	6180.945239	-0.624901318	0.533958024	-16178.2845	8453.322857
Temp	51.70312897	62.94392766	0.821415677	0.414048121	-73.71539943	177.1216574
Win%	21.10849307	16.23380374	1.300280169	0.19754021	-11.23807078	53.45505692
OpWin%	11.34534827	6.461665194	1.755793272	0.083261605	-1.529802193	24.22049874
Weekend	367.5377188	2786.263932	0.13191059	0.895413015	-5184.215009	5919.290446
Promotion	6927.882029	2784.344175	2.488155771	0.015091308	1379.954501	12475.80956

        (b) $\hat{Y} = -3862.481 + 51.703X_1 + 21.108X_2 + 11.345X_3 + 367.538X_4 + 6927.882X_5$

        (c)   Intercept:
                 Since all the non-dummy independent variables cannot have zero values, the
                 intercept should be interpreted as the portion of paid attendance that varies with
                 factors other than those already included in the model.
                 Temp:
                 As the high temperature increases by one degree, the estimated mean paid attendance
                 will increase by 51.70 taking into consideration all the other independent variables
                 included in the model.
                 Win%:
                 As the winning percentage of the team improves by 1%, the estimated mean paid
                 attendance will increase by 21.11 taking into consideration all the other independent
                 variables included in the model.
                 OpWin%:
                 As the opponent team's winning percentage at the time of the game improves by 1%,
                 the estimated mean paid attendance will increase by 11.35 taking into consideration
                 all the other independent variables included in the model.
                 Weekend:
                 The estimated mean paid attendance of a game played on a weekend will be 367.54
                 higher than when the game is played on a weekday taking into consideration all the
                 other independent variables included in the model.
                 Promotion:
                 The estimated mean paid attendance on promotion day will be 6927.88 higher than
                 when there is no promotion taking into consideration all the other independent
                 variables included in the model.

15.50   (d) $H_0 : \beta_j = 0$ $H_1 : \beta_j \neq 0$ for j = 1, 2, 3, 4, or 5

cont.   At a 0.05 level of significance, the only independent variable that makes a significant contribution to the regression model individually is the promotion dummy variable.

  (e)   Adjusted $r^2 = 0.2538$. 25.38% of the variation in attendance can be explained by the 5 independent variables after adjusting for the number of independent variables and the sample size.

  (f)

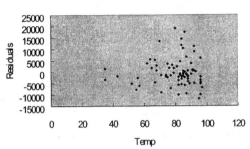

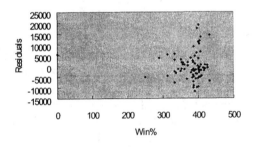

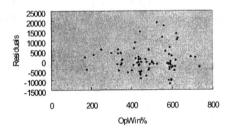

15.50 (f)
cont.

Normal Probability Plot

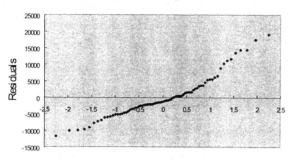

Z Value

The residual plots of temperature, team's winning percentage and opponent team's winning percentage reveal potential violation of the homoscedasticity assumption. The normal probability plot also reveals non-normality in the residuals.

(g)   With all the 5 independent variables in the model:
 – None of the VIF is > 5.

Model	Cp	k	R Square	Adj. R Square	Std. Error	Consider This Model?
X1X2X3X4X5	6	6	0.301052	0.253826288	6442.446	Yes
X1X2X3X5	4.0174	5	0.300888	0.263602154	6400.104	Yes
X1X3X5	3.703162	4	0.284966	0.256740664	6429.852	Yes
X2X3X4X5	4.674724	5	0.29468	0.257062456	6428.46	Yes
X2X3X5	2.680286	4	0.294627	0.26678334	6386.265	Yes

Based on the smallest C_p value and the highest adjusted R-square, the best model is the following:

	Coefficients	Standard Error	t Stat	P-value	Lower 95%	Upper 95%
Intercept	-1669.988177	5531.248104	-0.30191887	0.763538564	-12686.43764	9346.46129
Win%	27.4932005	14.0652218	1.954693705	0.054297102	-0.520152407	55.50655341
OpWin%	10.53699651	6.324477812	1.666065851	0.099817096	-2.059308864	23.13330188
Promotion	7089.212249	1455.76966	4.869734852	5.9398E-06	4189.791975	9988.632523

Since only X_5 makes significant contribution to the regression model at 5% level of significance, the more parsimonious model includes only X_5.

(b) $\hat{Y} = 13{,}935.703 + 6{,}813.228 X_5$

	Coefficients	Standard Error	t Stat	P-value
Intercept	13935.7027	1096.695459	12.70699408	1.09284E-20
Promotion	6813.22753	1495.880191	4.554661244	1.90736E-05

(c)   Intercept:
The estimated mean paid attendance on non-promotion day is 13,935.70.
Promotion:
The estimated mean paid attendance on promotion day will be 6,813.23 higher than when there is no promotion.

15.50   (g)

cont.

(d) $H_0 : \beta_j = 0$ $H_1 : \beta_j \neq 0$ for $j = 5$

At the 0.05 level of significance, promotion makes a significant contribution to the regression model.

(e) $r^2 = 0.2101$. 21.02% of the variation in attendance can be explained by promotion.

(f)   Since the independent variable is a dummy variable, the usual residual analysis is not meaningful here. The residual plot reveals non-normality in the residuals.

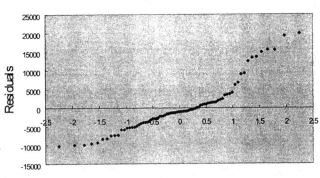

Normal Probability Plot

15.52   (a)   Let $X_1 = \text{Temp}$ $X_2 = \text{Win\%}$ $X_3 = \text{OpWin\%}$ $X_4 = \text{Weekend}$ $X_5 = \text{Promotion}$

Regression Statistics	
Multiple R	0.625289536
R Square	0.390987004
Adjusted R Square	0.350386138
Standard Error	4320.381297
Observations	81

ANOVA

	df	SS	MS	F	Significance F
Regression	5	898754711.7	179750942.3	9.630016278	3.94963E-07
Residual	75	1399927091	18665694.55		
Total	80	2298681803			

	Coefficients	Standard Error	t Stat	P-value	Lower 95%	Upper 95%
Intercept	10682.45521	6013.474857	1.776419701	0.079719211	-1297.003842	22661.91425
Temp	82.20546833	38.59788228	2.129792192	0.036469445	5.314525708	159.096411
Win%	26.26250802	12.37716144	2.121852263	0.037152917	1.60593222	50.91908383
OpWin%	7.367011607	5.929542741	1.24242491	0.217950544	-4.445246053	19.17926927
Weekend	3369.907577	1026.248391	3.283715332	0.001558126	1325.515463	5414.299691
Promotion	3129.013192	1030.12174	3.037517868	0.003280737	1076.904969	5181.121414

(b) $\hat{Y} = 10{,}682.455 + 82.205 X_1 + 26.263 X_2 + 7.367 X_3 + 3{,}369.908 X_4 + 3{,}129.013 X_5$

15.52   (c)   Intercept:
cont.
> Since all the non-dummy independent variables cannot have zero values, the intercept should be interpreted as the portion of paid attendance that varies with factors other than those already included in the model.

Temp:
> As the high temperature increases by one degree, the estimated mean paid attendance will increase by 82.21 taking into consideration all the other independent variables included in the model.

Win%:
> As the winning percentage of the team improves by 1%, the estimated mean paid attendance will increase by 26.26 taking into consideration all the other independent variables included in the model.

OpWin%:
> As the opponent team's winning percentage at the time of the game improves by 1%, the estimated mean paid attendance will increase by 7.37 taking into consideration all the other independent variables included in the model.

Weekend:
> The estimated mean paid attendance of a game played on a weekend will be 3,369.91 higher than when the game is played on a weekday taking into consideration all the other independent variables included in the model.

Promotion:
> The estimated mean paid attendance on promotion day will be 3,129.01 higher than when there is no promotion taking into consideration all the other independent variables included in the model.

(d) $H_0 : \beta_j = 0$ $H_1 : \beta_j \neq 0$ for $j = 1, 2, 3, 4,$ or 5

At the 0.05 level of significance, the independent variables that make a significant contribution to the regression model individually are temperature, team's winning percentage, the weekend and promotion dummy variables.

(e)   Adjusted $r^2 = 0.3504$. 35.04% of the variation in attendance can be explained by the 5 independent variables after adjusting for the number of independent variables and the sample size.

(f)

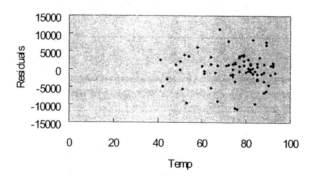

Temp Residual Plot

15.52   (f)
cont.

Win% Residual Plot

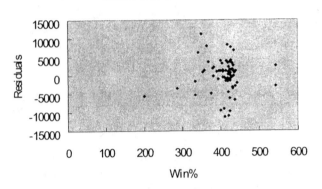

OpWin% Residual Plot

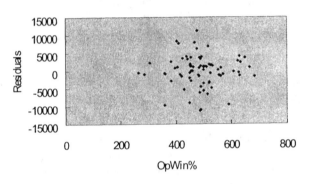

Normal Probability Plot

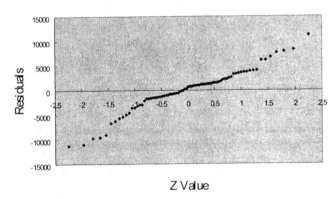

The residual plots do not reveal any obvious pattern. The normal probability plot does not reveal departure from the normality assumption.

15.52 (g)   With all the 5 independent variables in the model:
   None of the *VIF* is > 5.

Model	Cp	k	R Square	Adj. R Square	Std. Error	Consider This Model?
X1X2X3X4X5	6	6	0.390987	0.350386138	4320.381	Yes

Based on the smallest C_p value and the highest adjusted R-square, the best model is the full model that includes all the independent variables.

Since X_3 does not make significant contribution to the regression model at 5% level of significance, the more parsimonious model includes X_1, X_2, X_4 and X_5.

(b) $\hat{Y} = 14{,}965.626 + 88.888X_1 + 23.269X_2 + 3{,}562.425X_4 + 3{,}029.087X_5$

	Coefficients	Standard Error	t Stat	P-value
Intercept	14965.62623	4944.771809	3.026555483	0.003375413
Temp	88.88797075	38.35774548	2.317340856	0.023179453
Win%	23.26917677	12.1837526	1.909853026	0.059925592
Weekend	3562.425371	1018.104525	3.499076257	0.000784145
Promotion	3029.087074	1030.643544	2.939024935	0.004358397

(c)   Intercept:
   Since all the non-dummy independent variables cannot have zero values, the intercept should be interpreted as the portion of paid attendance that varies with factors other than those already included in the model.
   Temp:
   As the high temperature increases by one degree, the estimated mean paid attendance will increase by 88.89 taking into consideration all the other independent variables included in the model.
   Win%:
   As the winning percentage of the team improves by 1%, the estimated mean paid attendance will increase by 23.27 taking into consideration all the other independent variables included in the model.
   Weekend:
   The estimated mean paid attendance of a game played on a weekend will be 3,562.53 higher than when the game is played on a weekday taking into consideration all the other independent variables included in the model.
   Promotion:
   The estimated mean paid attendance on promotion day will be 3,029.09 higher than when there is no promotion taking into consideration all the other independent variables included in the model.

(d) $H_0 : \beta_j = 0$ $H_1 : \beta_j \neq 0$ for $j = 5$

   At the 0.05 level of significance, temperature, and the weekend and promotion dummy variables make a significant contribution to the regression model individually.

15.52   (g)   (e)   Adjusted $r^2 = 0.3457$. 34.57% of the variation in attendance can be explained by the 4 independent variables after adjusting for the number of independent variables and the sample size.

(f)

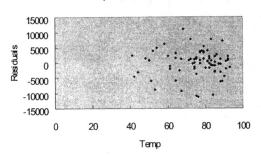

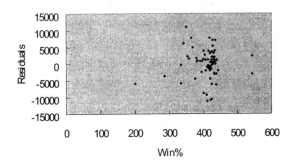

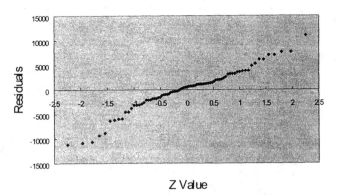

The residual plots do not reveal any obvious pattern. The normal probability plot does not reveal departure from the normality assumption.

15.54   The Philadelphia Phillies ran the most effective promotions in 2002 that generated an additional 11,184.54 attendance on days when a promotion was held.

CHAPTER 16

OBJECTIVES

- To learn about eight different forecasting models: moving averages, exponential smoothing, linear trend, quadratic trend, exponential trend, Holt-Winters, autoregressive, and least-squares model for seasonal data
- To be able to choose the most appropriate time series forecasting model
- To understand price indexes and the difference between aggregated and unaggregated indexes

OVERVIEW AND KEY CONCEPTS

Time series: A set of numerical data obtained at a regular interval.

Component factors of the classical multiplicative time series model

- **Trend:** Overall or persistent, long-term upward or downward pattern of movement. It is usually caused by changes in technology, growth in population, wealth and value, the duration of which is several years.
- **Seasonal:** Fairly regular periodic fluctuations that occurs within each 12-month period year after year. It is caused by weather conditions, social customs, or religion customs and the duration of which is within 12 months.
- **Cyclical:** Repeating up-and-down swings or movements through four phases: from peak (prosperity) to contraction (recession) to trough (depression) to expansion (recovery or growth). It is usually caused by the interactions of numerous combinations of factors that influence the economy. Its duration is usually two to ten years.
- **Irregular:** The erratic, or "residual" fluctuations in a series that exist after taking into account all the other three components. It is usually caused by random variations in data or due to unforeseen events, such as strikes or natural disasters.
- $Y_i = T_i \times C_i \times S_i \times I_i$ where T_i, C_i, I_i are value of trend, cyclical and irregular components in time period i, and S_i is the value of the seasonal component in time period i. There is no seasonal component for annual data.

Smoothing the Annual Time Series

- **Moving averages for a chosen period of length L:**
    - A series of arithmetic means computed over time such that each mean is calculated for a sequence of observed values having that particular length L.
    - It is denoted as $MA(L)$.
    - It is easy to compute.

- **Exponential smoothing:**
  - $E_1 = Y_1$

    $E_i = WY_i + (1 - W)E_{i-1}$ where

    E_i = value of the exponentially smoothed series in time period i

    E_{i-1} = value of the exponentially smoothed series already computed in time period i-1

    Y_i = observed value of the time series in period i

    W = subjectively assigned weight or smoothing coefficient $(0 < W < 1)$
  - **Forecasting with exponentially smoothed series:** $\hat{Y}_{i+1} = E_i$
  - Exponential smoothing can only be used to perform one period ahead forecast.
  - Use a W close to 0 for smoothing out unwanted cyclical and irregular component; use a W close to 1 for forecasting.

Least-Squares Trend Fitting and Forecasting

- The least-squares trend fitting is used for intermediate and long-range forecast using the trend component of a time series.
- **Linear trend model:**
  - $Y_i = \beta_0 + \beta_1 X_i + \varepsilon_i$ where X_i is the coded year with a value of 0 for the first observation, a value of 1 for the second observation, etc.
  - **Linear trend forecasting equation:** $\hat{Y}_i = b_0 + b_1 X_i$
  - b_0 is interpreted as the predicted mean value of the time series for the 1st year.
  - b_1 measures the predicted change per year in the mean value of the time series.
- **Quadratic trend model:**
  - $Y_i = \beta_0 + \beta_1 X_i + \beta_2 X_i^2 + \varepsilon_i$
  - **Quadratic trend forecasting equation:** $\hat{Y}_i = b_0 + b_1 X_i + b_2 X_i^2$
- **Exponential trend model:**
  - $Y_i = \beta_0 \beta_1^{X_i} \varepsilon_i$ or $\log Y_i = \log \beta_0 + (\log \beta_1) X_i + \log \varepsilon_i$ where $(\beta_1 - 1) \times 100\%$ is the annual compound growth rate (in %).
  - **Exponential trend forecasting equation:** $\log \hat{Y}_i = b_0 + b_1 X_i$ or

    $\hat{Y}_i = 10^{(b_0 + b_1 X_i)} = \left(10^{b_0}\right)\left(10^{b_1}\right)^{X_i} = \hat{\beta}_0 \hat{\beta}_1^{X_i}$ where $10^{b_0} = \hat{\beta}_0$, $10^{b_1} = \hat{\beta}_1$ and

    $\left(\hat{\beta}_1 - 1\right) \times 100\%$ is the estimated annual compound growth rate in %.
- **Selecting the appropriate least-squares trend model:**
  - Use the linear trend model if the first differences are more or less constant

    $Y_2 - Y_1 = Y_3 - Y_2 = \cdots = Y_n - Y_{n-1}$
  - Use the quadratic trend model if the second differences are more or less constant

    $\left[(Y_3 - Y_2) - (Y_2 - Y_1)\right] = \cdots = \left[(Y_n - Y_{n-1}) - (Y_{n-1} - Y_{n-2})\right]$

- Use the exponential trend model if the percentage differences are more or less constant

$$\left(\frac{Y_2 - Y_1}{Y_1}\right)100\% = \left(\frac{Y_3 - Y_2}{Y_2}\right)100\% = \cdots = \left(\frac{Y_n - Y_{n-1}}{Y_{n-1}}\right)100\%$$

The Holt-Winters Method

- It is an extension of the exponential smoothing and has the ability to detect future trend and overall movement.
- It can provide intermediate and/or long-term forecast.
- Level: $E_i = U\left(E_{i-1} + T_{i-1}\right) + \left(1 - U\right)Y_i$

  Trend: $T_i = VT_{i-1} + \left(1 - V\right)\left(E_i - E_{i-1}\right)$

  E_i : level of smoothed series in time period i

  E_{i-1} : level of smoothed series in time period $i - 1$

  T_i : value of trend component in time period i

  T_{i-1} : value of trend component in time period $i - 1$

  Y_i : observed value of the time series in period i

  U : smoothing constant (where $0 < U < 1$)

  V : smoothing constant (where $0 < V < 1$)

  $E_2 = Y_2$ and $T_2 = Y_2 - Y_1$

- The Holt-Winters forecast:
    - $\hat{Y}_{n+j} = E_n + j\left(T_n\right)$

        where $\hat{Y}_{n+j}$: forecasted value j years into the future

        E_n : level of smoothed series in period n

        T_n : value of trend component in period n

        j : number of years into the future

The Autoregressive Model

- The autoregressive model is appropriate for forecasting.
- It takes advantage of autocorrelation in the time series, i.e. the fact that the values of a series of data at particular points in time are highly correlated with the values that precede and succeed them.
- p^{th} **order autoregressive model:**
    - $Y_i = A_0 + A_1 Y_{i-1} + A_2 Y_{i-2} + \cdots + A_p Y_{i-p} + \delta_i$
- p^{th} **order autoregressive equation:**
    - $\hat{Y}_i = a_0 + a_1 Y_{i-1} + a_2 Y_{i-2} + \cdots + a_p Y_{i-p}$

- p^{th} order autoregressive forecasting equation:

    - $\hat{Y}_{n+j} = a_0 + a_1\hat{Y}_{n+j-1} + a_2\hat{Y}_{n+j-2} + \cdots + a_p\hat{Y}_{n+j-p}$

      where

      $j =$ the number of years into the future

      $\hat{Y}_{n+j-p} =$ forecast of Y_{n+j-p} from the current time period for $j - p > 0$

      $\hat{Y}_{n+j-p} =$ the observed value for Y_{n+j-p} from the current time period for $j - p \leq 0$

- t **test for significance of the highest-order autoregressive parameter A_p:**

    - **The hypotheses:** $H_0 : A_p = 0$ vs. $H_1 : A_p \neq 0$.

    - **Test statistic:** $t = \dfrac{a_p - A_p}{S_{a_p}}$

    - This is a two-tail test with right-tail and left-tail rejection regions.

- **Autoregressive modeling steps:**

    1. Choose p: Note that the degree of freedom is $(n - 2p - 1)$.

    2. Form a series of "lag predictors" variables $Y_{i-1}, Y_{i-2}, \cdots, Y_{i-p}$.

    3. Estimate the autoregressive equation.

    4. Test the significance of the highest-order autoregressive parameter A_p : If the null hypothesis is rejected, this model is selected. Otherwise, decrease p by 1 and repeat steps 3-4.

Selecting a Forecasting Model

- **Perform a residual analysis:**

    - Obtain the residual plots and look for pattern.

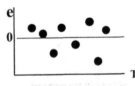

Random errors

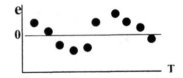

Cyclical effects not accounted for

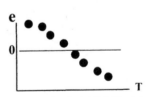

Trend not accounted for

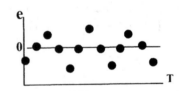

Seasonal effects not accounted for

- **Measure Errors:**
    - Choose the model that gives the smallest measuring errors.
    - S_{YX} or $SSE = \sum_{i=1}^{n}\left(Y_i - \hat{Y}_i\right)^2$ is sensitive to outliers
    - Mean absolute deviation $MAD = \dfrac{\sum_{i=1}^{n}\left|Y_i - \hat{Y}_i\right|}{n}$ is not sensitive to extreme observations.
- **Principle of parsimony:**
    - When two or more models provide good fit to the data, select the simplest model.
    - Simplest model types: least-squares linear trend model, least-squares quadratic trend model, 1st order autoregressive model.
    - More complex types: 2nd or 3rd order autoregressive model, least-squares exponential trend model.

Forecasting with Seasonal Data

- Use categorical predictor variables with least-squares trend fitting.
- **Exponential model with quarterly data:**
    - $Y_i = \beta_0 \beta_1^{X_i} \beta_2^{Q_1} \beta_3^{Q_2} \beta_4^{Q_3} \varepsilon_i$
      where

      X = coded quarter values

      Q_1 = 1 if first quarter, 0 otherwise

      Q_2 = 1 if second quarter, 0 otherwise

      Q_3 = 1 if third quarter, 0 otherwise

      $\beta_0 = Y$ intercept

      $(\beta_1 - 1)100\%$ = quarterly compound growth rate (in %)

      β_2 = multiplier for first quarter relative to fourth quarter

      β_3 = multiplier for second quarter relative to fourth quarter

      β_4 = multiplier for third quarter relative to fourth quarter

      ε_i = value of the irregular component for time period i
- **The exponential growth with quarterly data forecasting equation:**
    - $\log(\hat{Y}) = b_0 + b_1 X_i + b_2 Q_1 + b_3 Q_2 + b_4 Q_3 + b_5 Q_4$
    - $\hat{Y}_i = \hat{\beta}_0 \hat{\beta}_1^{X_i} \hat{\beta}_2^{Q_1} \hat{\beta}_3^{Q_2} \hat{\beta}_4^{Q_3}$ where $\hat{\beta}_0 = 10^{b_0}$, $\hat{\beta}_1 = 10^{b_1}$, $\hat{\beta}_2 = 10^{b_2}$, $\hat{\beta}_3 = 10^{b_3}$, and $\hat{\beta}_4 = 10^{b_4}$
- Similarly for monthly data.

Index Numbers

- **Index numbers** measure the value of an item (or group of items) at a particular point in time as a percentage of the item's (or group of items') value at another point in time.
- A **price index** reflects the percentage change in the price of a commodity (or group of commodities) in a given period of time over the price paid for that commodity (or group of commodities) at a particular point of time in the past.
- **Simple price index:** $I_i = \left(\dfrac{P_i}{P_{base}}\right)100$

    where I_i = price index for year I
      P_i = price for year I
      P_{base} = price for the base year

- Shifting the base for a simple price index: $I_{new} = \left(\dfrac{I_{old}}{I_{new\,base}}\right)100$

    where I_{new} = new price index
      I_{old} = old price index
      $I_{new\,base}$ = value of the old price index for the new base year

- An **aggregate price index** reflects the percentage change in the price of a group of commodities (often referred to as a market basket) in a given period of time over the price paid for that group of commodities at a particular point of time in the past.
- An **unweighted aggregate price index** places equal weight on all the items in the market basket.

    - $I_U^{(t)} = \left(\dfrac{\sum_{i=1}^{n} P_i^{(t)}}{\sum_{i=1}^{n} P_i^{(0)}}\right)100$

    where t = time period $(0, 1, 2, \ldots)$
      i = item $(1, 2, \ldots, n)$
      n = total number of items under consideration
      $\sum_{i=1}^{n} P_i^{(t)}$ = sum of the prices paid for each of the n commodities at time period t
      $\sum_{i=1}^{n} P_i^{(0)}$ = sum of the prices paid for each of the n commodities at time period 0
      $I_U^{(t)}$ = value of the unweighted price index at time t

- A **weighted aggregate price index** allows for the differences in the consumption levels associated with the different items comprising the market basket by attaching a weight to each item to reflect the consumption quantity of that item.
- The **Laspeyres price index** is a weighted aggregate price index that uses the consumption quantities associated with the base year in the calculation of all price indexes in the series.

    - $I_L^{(t)} = \left(\dfrac{\sum_{i=1}^{n} P_i^{(t)} Q_i^{(0)}}{\sum_{i=1}^{n} P_i^{(0)} Q_i^{(0)}}\right)100$

    where t = time period $(0, 1, 2, \ldots)$
      i = item $(1, 2, \ldots, n)$
      n = total number of items under consideration
      $Q_i^{(0)}$ = quantity of item i at time period 0
      $I_L^{(t)}$ = value of the Laspeyres price index at time t

- The **Paasche Price Index** uses the consumption quantities experienced in the year of interest instead of using the initial quantities.

  - $$I_P^{(t)} = \left(\frac{\sum_{i=1}^{n} P_i^{(t)} Q_i^{(t)}}{\sum_{i=1}^{n} P_i^{(0)} Q_i^{(t)}} \right) 100$$

  where t = time period (0, 1, 2, ...)

         i = item (1, 2, ..., n)

         n = total number of items under consideration

         $Q_i^{(t)}$ = quantity of item i at time period t

         $I_P^{(t)}$ = value of the Paasche price index at time t

  - Is a more accurate reflection of total consumption costs at time t.
  - Accurate consumption values for current purchases are often hard to obtain.
  - If a particular product increases greatly in price compared to the other items in the market basket, consumers will avoid the high-priced item out of necessity, not because of changes in what they might prefer to purchase.

SOLUTIONS TO END OF SECTION AND CHAPTER REVIEW EVEN PROBLEMS

16.2 (a) Since you need data from four prior years to obtain the centered 9-year moving average for any given year and since the first recorded value is for 1955, the first centered moving average value you can calculate is for 1959.

(b) You would lose four years for the period 1955-1958 since you do not have enough past values to compute a centered moving average. You will also lose the final four years of recorded time series since you do not have enough later values to compute a centered moving average. Therefore, you will lose a total of eight years in computing a series of 9-year moving averages.

16.4 (a),(b),(c),(d)

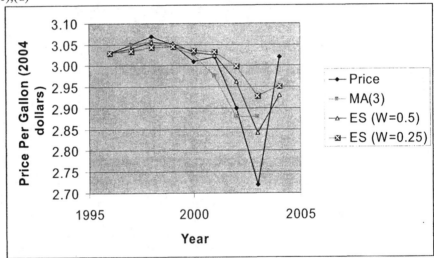

(b),(c),(d)

Year	Price	MA(3)	ES (*W*=0.5)	ES (*W*=0.25)
1996	3.03		3.0300	3.0300
1997	3.05	3.0500	3.0400	3.0350
1998	3.07	3.0567	3.0550	3.0438
1999	3.05	3.0433	3.0525	3.0453
2000	3.01	3.0267	3.0313	3.0365
2001	3.02	2.9767	3.0256	3.0324
2002	2.90	2.8800	2.9628	2.9993
2003	2.72	2.8800	2.8414	2.9295
2004	3.02		2.9307	2.9521

(e) The exponentially smoothed series with $W = 0.5$ is generally lower than that with $W = 0.25$ in the more recent years. The exponential smoothing with $W = 0.5$ assigns more weight to the more recent values and is better for forecasting, while the exponential smoothing with $W = 0.25$ which assigns more weight to more distance values is better suited for eliminating unwanted cyclical and irregular variations.

16.6   (a),(b),(c),(d)

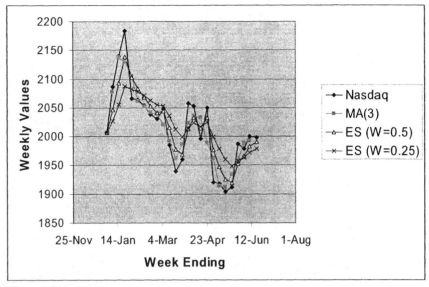

(b),(c),(d)

Week	Nasdaq	MA(3)	ES (*W*=0.5)	ES (*W*=0.25)
2-Jan	2007		2007.00	2007.00
9-Jan	2087	2078.00	2047.00	2027.00
16-Jan	2140	2137.00	2093.50	2055.25
23-Jan	2184	2130.00	2138.75	2087.44
30-Jan	2066	2104.67	2102.38	2082.08
6-Feb	2064	2061.33	2083.19	2077.56
13-Feb	2054	2052.00	2068.59	2071.67
20-Feb	2038	2040.67	2053.30	2063.25
27-Feb	2030	2038.67	2041.65	2054.94
5-Mar	2048	2021.00	2044.82	2053.20
12-Mar	1985	1991.00	2014.91	2036.15
19-Mar	1940	1961.67	1977.46	2012.11
26-Mar	1960	1985.67	1968.73	1999.09
2-Apr	2057	2023.33	2012.86	2013.56
8-Apr	2053	2035.33	2032.93	2023.42
16-Apr	1996	2033.00	2014.47	2016.57
23-Apr	2050	1988.67	2032.23	2024.93
30-Apr	1920	1962.67	1976.12	1998.69
7-May	1918	1914.00	1947.06	1978.52
14-May	1904	1911.33	1925.53	1959.89
21-May	1912	1934.33	1918.76	1947.92
28-May	1987	1959.33	1952.88	1957.69
4-Jun	1979	1988.67	1965.94	1963.02
10-Jun	2000	1992.33	1982.97	1972.26
18-Jun	1998		1990.49	1978.70

(e)   There is a general downward trend after January 23, 2004, with a tendency to recover after May 21, 2004.

16.8   (a),(b),(c),(e)

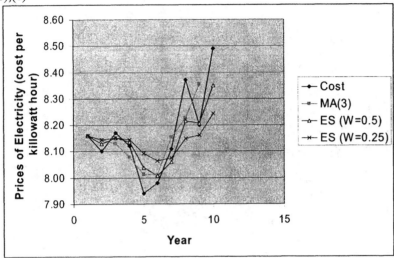

(b),(c),(e)

Year	Cost	MA(3)	ES (W=0.5)	ES (W=0.25)
1994-1995	8.16		8.16	8.16
1995-1996	8.10	8.14	8.13	8.15
1996-1997	8.17	8.13	8.15	8.15
1997-1998	8.12	8.08	8.14	8.14
1998-1999	7.94	8.01	8.04	8.09
1999-2000	7.98	8.01	8.01	8.06
2000-2001	8.11	8.15	8.06	8.08
2001-2002	8.37	8.23	8.21	8.15
2002-2003	8.20	8.35	8.21	8.16
2003-2004	8.49		8.35	8.24

(d) $W = 0.5$: $\hat{Y}_{2004-2005} = E_{2003-2004} = 8.35$

(e) $W = 0.25$: $\hat{Y}_{2004-2005} = E_{2003-2004} = 8.24$

(f)   The exponentially smoothed forecast for 2003-2004 with $W = 0.5$ is higher than that with $W = 0.25$. The exponential smoothing with $W = 0.5$ assigns more weight to the more recent values and is better for forecasting, while the exponential smoothing with $W = 0.25$ which assigns more weight to more distance values is better suited for eliminating unwanted cyclical and irregular variations.

16.10   (a)   The Y-intercept $b_0 = 4.0$ is the fitted trend value reflecting the real total revenues (in millions of real constant 1995 dollars) during the origin or base year 1985.

(b)   The slope $b_1 = 1.5$ indicates that the real total revenues are increasing at a rate of 1.5 million dollars per year.

(c)   Year is 1989, $X = 1989 - 1985 = 4$

$\hat{Y}_5 = 4.0 + 1.5(4) = 10.0$ million dollars

(d)   Year is 2004, $X = 2004 - 1985 = 19$,

$\hat{Y}_{20} = 4.0 + 1.5(19) = 32.5$ million dollars

(e)   Year is 2007, $X = 2007 - 1985 = 22$

$\hat{Y}_{23} = 4.0 + 1.5(22) = 37.0$ million dollars

16.12   (a)

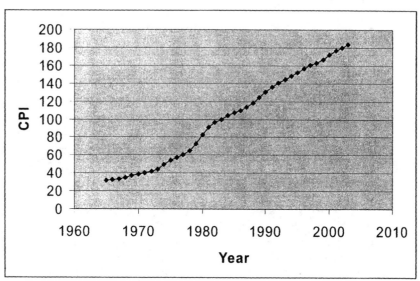

(b)   There has been an upward trend in the CPI in the United States over the 39-year
         period. The rate of increase became faster in the late 70's and mid 80's but the rate of
         increase tapered off in the early 80's and early 90's.

16.14   (a)

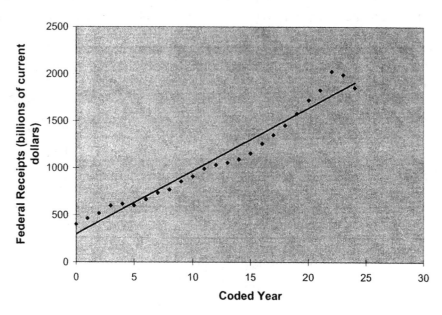

(b) $\hat{Y} = 296.1348 + 67.0448X$

(c) $\hat{Y} = 296.1348 + 67.0448X$, where X = years relative to 1978

         $X = 2003 - 1978 = 25$, $\hat{Y} = 296.1348 + 67.0448(25) = \$1972.254$ billion

         $X = 2004 - 1978 = 26$, $\hat{Y} = 296.1348 + 67.0448(26) = \$2039.299$ billion

(d)   There is an upward trend in federal receipts between 1978 and 2002. The trend
         appears to be non-linear. Either a quadratic trend or exponential trend model could
         be explored.

16.16   (a), (b), (c), (d)

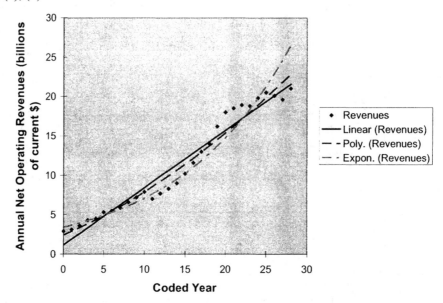

(b)   Linear trend: $\hat{Y} = 1.1414 + 0.7288X$ where X is relative to 1975.

(c)   Quadratic trend: $\hat{Y} = 2.4098 + 0.4469X + 0.0101X^2$ where X is relative to 1975.

(d)   Exponential trend: $\log_{10} \hat{Y} = 0.5319 + 0.0318X$ where X is relative to 1975.

(e)   Linear trend: $\hat{Y}_{2004} = 1.1414 + 0.7288(29) = \$22.2771$ billion

$\hat{Y}_{2005} = 1.1414 + 0.7288(30) = \$23.0059$ billion

Quadratic trend: $\hat{Y}_{2004} = 2.4098 + 0.4469(29) + 0.0101(29)^2 = \$23.8374$ billion

$\hat{Y}_{2005} = 2.4098 + 0.4469(30) + 0.0101(30)^2 = \$24.8783$ billion

Exponential trend: $\hat{Y}_{2004} = 10^{0.5319+0.0318(29)} = \$28.5329$ billion

$\hat{Y}_{2005} = 10^{0.5319+0.0318(30)} = \$30.7036$ billion

16.18   (a),(b),(c),(d)

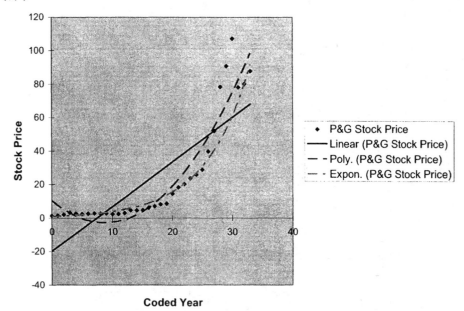

Coded Year

(b)   Linear trend: $\hat{Y} = -19.8639 + 2.6699X$ where X is relative to 1970

(c)   Quadratic trend: $\hat{Y} = 10.4629 - 3.0164X + 0.1723X^2$ where X is relative to 1970

(d)   Exponential trend: $\log_{10} \hat{Y} = 0.0075 + 0.0592X$ where X is relative to 1970

16.18   (e)
cont.

1st Difference	2nd Difference	% Difference
0.15		10.56338
0.6	0.45	38.21656
0.97	0.37	44.70046
-0.51	-1.48	-16.242
-0.25	0.26	-9.5057
0.28	0.53	11.76471
0.2	-0.08	7.518797
-0.15	-0.35	-5.24476
0.19	0.34	7.01107
-0.37	-0.56	-12.7586
-0.07	0.3	-2.7668
0.57	0.64	23.17073
1.65	1.08	54.45545
-0.01	-1.66	-0.21368
0.24	0.25	5.139186
1.38	1.14	28.10591
0.86	-0.52	13.6725
1.09	0.23	15.24476
0.46	-0.63	5.582524
5.81	5.35	66.78161
3.82	-1.99	26.32667
2.02	-1.8	11.02019
3.41	1.39	16.75676
2.09	-1.32	8.796296
2.93	0.84	11.33462
10.86	7.93	37.73454
12.39	1.53	31.25631
26.27	13.88	50.4901
12.44	-13.83	15.88761
16.45	4.01	18.12872
-29.13	-45.58	-27.176
1.94	31.07	2.485268
7.81	5.87	9.7625

Investigating the 1st, 2nd and percentage differences does not suggest any particular trend model is more appropriate than the others. The exponential trend model does seem to fit the data better especially in the early years.

(f) $X = 2004 - 1970 = 34$. Using the exponential trend model,

$\hat{Y}_{2004} = 10^{0.0075+0.0592(34)} = \$105.07$

16.20 (a)   For Time Series I, the graph of Y vs. X appears to be more linear than the graph of log Y vs. X, so a linear model appears to be more appropriate. For Time Series II, the graph of log Y vs. X appears to be more linear than the graph of Y vs. X, so an exponential model appears to be more appropriate.

   (b)   Time Series I: $\hat{Y} = 100.082 + 14.9752X$, where X = years relative to 1995

   Time Series II: $\hat{Y} = 99.704(1.1501)^X$, where X = years relative to 1995

   (c) $X = 10$ for year 2005 in all models. Forecasts for the year 2005:

   Time Series I: $\hat{Y} = 100.082 + 14.9752(10) = 249.834$

   Time Series II: $\hat{Y} = 99.704(1.1501)^{10} = 403.709$

16.22 (a)

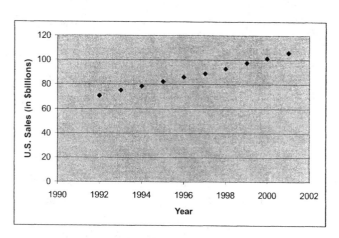

   (b)

Year	Sales	Adjusted Sales	CPI
1992	70.6	50.32	140.3
1993	74.9	51.83	144.5
1994	78.5	52.97	148.2
1995	82.5	54.13	152.4
1996	85.9	54.75	156.9
1997	88.8	55.33	160.5
1998	92.5	56.75	163
1999	97.5	58.52	166.6
2000	101.4	58.89	172.2
2001	105.5	59.57	177.1

16.22   (c), (d), (e), (f)
cont.

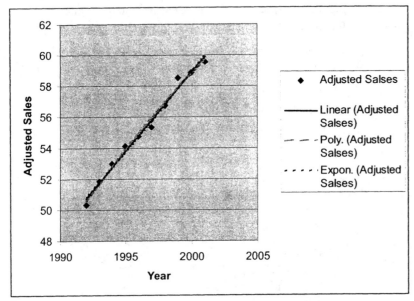

Linear trend: $\hat{Y} = 70.6964 + 3.8030X$, where X is relative to 1992

Quadratic trend: $\hat{Y} = 50.5363 + 1.1476X - 0.0138X^2$, where X is relative to 1992

Exponential trend: $\log_{10} \hat{Y} = 1.7059 + 0.0081X$, where X is relative to 1992

(g)

Year	Forecasts of adjusted sales Based on Models		
	Linear	Quadratic	Exponential
2002	60.9329	60.6284	61.1614
2003	61.9559	61.4854	62.3071

16.24 $E_{15} = 25.30$, $T_{15} = 2.13$

$\hat{Y}_{16} = E_{15} + T_{15} = 25.30 + 2.13 = 25.30$

$\hat{Y}_{17} = E_{15} + 2T_{15} = 25.30 + (2)2.13 = 27.43$

$\hat{Y}_{18} = E_{15} + 3T_{15} = 25.30 + (3)2.13 = 29.57$

$\hat{Y}_{19} = E_{15} + 4T_{15} = 25.30 + (4)2.13 = 31.70$

$\hat{Y}_{20} = E_{15} + 5T_{15} = 25.30 + (5)2.13 = 33.83$

16.26   (a) $U = 0.3, V = 0.3$

YEAR	GDP	E	T		YEAR	GDP	E	T
1980	2789.5				1992	6337.7	6331.602	282.508
1981	3128.4	3128.4	338.9		1993	6657.4	6644.413	303.7204
1982	3255	3318.69	234.873		1994	7072.2	7034.98	364.5131
1983	3536.7	3541.759	226.6101		1995	7397.7	7398.238	363.6345
1984	3933.2	3883.751	307.3773		1996	7816.9	7800.392	390.598
1985	4220.3	4211.548	321.6716		1997	8304.3	8270.307	446.12
1986	4462.8	4483.926	287.1658		1998	8747	8737.828	461.1008
1987	4739.5	4748.978	271.6858		1999	9268.4	9247.559	495.1417
1988	5103.8	5078.859	312.4228		2000	9817	9794.71	531.5485
1989	5484.4	5456.465	358.0507		2001	10100.8	10168.44	421.0738
1990	5803.1	5806.525	352.4572		2002	10480.8	10513.41	367.8052
1991	5995.9	6044.825	272.5472		2003	10987.9	10955.9	420.0791

$$\hat{Y}_{2004} = E_{2003} + 1T_{2003} = 10{,}955.8956 + (1)(420.0791) = \$11{,}375.9747 \text{ billion}$$

$$\hat{Y}_{2005} = E_{2003} + 2T_{2003} = 10{,}955.8956 + (2)(420.0791) = \$11{,}796.0538 \text{ billion.}$$

(b) $U = 0.7, V = 0.7$

YEAR	GDP	E	T		YEAR	GDP	E	T
1980	2789.5				1992	6337.7	6329.39	303.3685
1981	3128.4	3128.4	338.9		1993	6657.4	6640.151	305.5862
1982	3255	3403.61	319.793		1994	7072.2	6983.676	316.9679
1983	3536.7	3667.392	302.9897		1995	7397.7	7329.761	325.7029
1984	3933.2	3959.227	299.6434		1996	7816.9	7703.895	340.2322
1985	4220.3	4247.299	296.172		1997	8304.3	8122.179	363.6478
1986	4462.8	4519.27	288.9116		1998	8747	8564.179	387.1534
1987	4739.5	4787.577	282.7302		1999	9268.4	9046.452	415.6895
1988	5103.8	5080.355	285.7446		2000	9817	9568.599	447.6268
1989	5484.4	5401.59	296.3916		2001	10100.8	10041.6	455.2384
1990	5803.1	5729.517	305.8523		2002	10480.8	10492.03	453.7951
1991	5995.9	6023.528	302.3		2003	10987.9	10958.44	457.5822

$$\hat{Y}_{2004} = E_{2003} + 1T_{2003} = 10{,}958.4446 + (1)(457.5822) = \$11{,}416.0268 \text{ billion}$$

$$\hat{Y}_{2005} = E_{2003} + 2T_{2003} = 10{,}958.4446 + (2)(457.5822) = \$11{,}873.6090 \text{ billion.}$$

16.26   (c) $U = 0.3, V = 0.7$
cont.

YEAR	GDP	E	T		YEAR	GDP	E	T
1980	2789.5				1992	6337.7	6336.577	301.2423
1981	3128.4	3128.4	338.9		1993	6657.4	6651.526	305.3541
1982	3255	3318.69	294.317		1994	7072.2	7037.604	329.5713
1983	3536.7	3559.592	278.2925		1995	7397.7	7388.543	335.9815
1984	3933.2	3904.605	298.3088		1996	7816.9	7789.187	355.3804
1985	4220.3	4215.084	301.9598		1997	8304.3	8256.38	388.9242
1986	4462.8	4479.073	290.5685		1998	8747	8716.491	410.2803
1987	4739.5	4748.543	284.2388		1999	9268.4	9225.911	440.0222
1988	5103.8	5082.494	299.1527		2000	9817	9771.68	471.7462
1989	5484.4	5453.574	320.7308		2001	10100.8	10143.59	441.7946
1990	5803.1	5794.461	326.7778		2002	10480.8	10512.17	419.8323
1991	5995.9	6033.502	300.4565		2003	10987.9	10971.13	431.5698

$$\hat{Y}_{2004} = E_{2003} + 1T_{2003} = 10971.1321 + (1)(431.5698) = \$11402.7019 \text{ billion}$$

$$\hat{Y}_{2005} = E_{2003} + 2T_{2003} = 10971.1321 + (2)(431.5698) = \$11834.2718 \text{ billion.}$$

(d)   Given the historical movement of the time series, which suggests that there is a cyclical component in addition to the upward trend, a better projection model will be to give more weight to the more recent levels and trends. As a result, any recent changes in the level or trend of the time series that are caused by the cyclical component will be readily picked up in the projection. Hence, the projection in model (a) will be a better choice.

(e)   The forecasts in (a)-(c) are higher than those of Problem 16.13 (c). The GDP has been expanding since 1992. This is being captured and reflected in the Holt-Winters method with $U = 0.3$ and $V = 0.3$, which gives more weight to recent levels and trends of the time series, but not in the linear trend, which is very much constrained by the model specification. The linear trend model will be more appropriate if the forecasts are more long run than the immediate short-run forecasts.

16.28   (a) $U = 0.3$, $V = 0.3$

Year	Revenues	E	T		Year	Revenues	E	T
1975	2.9				1990	10.2	9.983102	0.982191
1976	3.1	3.1	0.2		1991	11.6	11.40959	1.293198
1977	3.6	3.51	0.347		1992	13	12.91084	1.438833
1978	4.3	4.1671	0.56407		1993	14	14.1049	1.267495
1979	4.5	4.569351	0.450797		1994	16.2	15.95172	1.673021
1980	5.3	5.216044	0.587924		1995	18	17.88742	1.856899
1981	5.5	5.591191	0.43898		1996	18.5	18.8733	1.247182
1982	5.9	5.939051	0.375196		1997	18.9	19.26614	0.649147
1983	6.6	6.514274	0.515215		1998	18.8	19.13459	0.102655
1984	7.2	7.148847	0.598765		1999	19.8	19.63117	0.378406
1985	7.9	7.854284	0.673435		2000	20.5	20.35287	0.618713
1986	7	7.458316	-0.07515		2001	20.1	20.36148	0.191635
1987	7.7	7.604951	0.0801		2002	19.6	19.88593	-0.27539
1988	8.3	8.115515	0.381425		2003	21	20.58316	0.405444
1989	9	8.849082	0.627924		2004			

$\hat{Y}_{2004} = E_{2003} + 1T_{2003} = 20.5832 + (1)(0.4054) = 20.9886$ billions of constant 1982-1984 dollars.

$\hat{Y}_{2005} = E_{2003} + 2T_{2003} = 20.5832 + (2)(0.4054) = 21.3941$ billions of constant 1982-1984 dollars.

    (b) $U = 0.7$, $V = 0.7$

Year	Revenues	E	T		Year	Revenues	E	T
1975	2.9				1990	10.2	9.555528	0.488476
1976	3.1	3.1	0.2		1991	11.6	10.5108	0.628516
1977	3.6	3.39	0.227		1992	13	11.69752	0.795977
1978	4.3	3.8219	0.28847		1993	14	12.94545	0.931562
1979	4.5	4.227259	0.323537		1994	16.2	14.57391	1.140631
1980	5.3	4.775557	0.390965		1995	18	16.40018	1.346322
1981	5.5	5.266565	0.420978		1996	18.5	17.97255	1.414137
1982	5.9	5.75128	0.440099		1997	18.9	19.24068	1.370336
1983	6.6	6.313966	0.476875		1998	18.8	20.06771	1.207344
1984	7.2	6.913589	0.513699		1999	19.8	20.83254	1.074589
1985	7.9	7.569102	0.556243		2000	20.5	21.48499	0.947948
1986	7	7.787741	0.454962		2001	20.1	21.73306	0.737983
1987	7.7	8.079893	0.406119		2002	19.6	21.60973	0.47959
1988	8.3	8.430208	0.389378		2003	21	21.76252	0.381551
1989	9	8.87371	0.405615		2004			

$\hat{Y}_{2004} = E_{2003} + 1T_{2003} = 21.7625 + (1)(0.3816) = 22.1441$ billions of constant 1982-1984 dollars.

$\hat{Y}_{2004} = E_{2003} + 2T_{2003} = 21.7625 + (2)(0.3816) = 22.5256$ billions of constant 1982-1984 dollars.

16.28   (c) $U = 0.3$, $V = 0.7$
cont.

Year	Revenues	E	T	Year	Revenues	E	T
1975	2.9			1990	10.2	9.931143	0.627984
1976	3.1	3.1	0.2	1991	11.6	11.28774	0.846567
1977	3.6	3.51	0.263	1992	13	12.74029	1.028363
1978	4.3	4.1419	0.37367	1993	14	13.9306	1.076946
1979	4.5	4.504671	0.3704	1994	16.2	15.84226	1.327362
1980	5.3	5.172521	0.459635	1995	18	17.75089	1.501741
1981	5.5	5.539647	0.431882	1996	18.5	18.72579	1.343689
1982	5.9	5.921459	0.416861	1997	18.9	19.25084	1.098099
1983	6.6	6.521496	0.471814	1998	18.8	19.26468	0.772821
1984	7.2	7.137993	0.515219	1999	19.8	19.87125	0.722945
1985	7.9	7.825964	0.567044	2000	20.5	20.52826	0.703164
1986	7	7.417902	0.274513	2001	20.1	20.43943	0.465565
1987	7.7	7.697725	0.276106	2002	19.6	19.9915	0.191517
1988	8.3	8.202149	0.344601	2003	21	20.7549	0.363084
1989	9	8.864025	0.439784	2004			

$\hat{Y}_{2004} = E_{2003} + 1T_{2003} = 20.7549 + (1)(0.3631) = 21.1180$ billions of constant 1982-1984 dollars.

$\hat{Y}_{2005} = E_{2003} + 2T_{2003} = 20.7549 + (2)(0.3631) = 21.4811$ billions of constant 1982-1984 dollars.

(d)   Given the historical movement of the time series, which suggests that there is a cyclical component in addition to the upward trend, a better projection model will be to give more weight to the more recent levels and trends. As a result, any recent changes in the level or trend of the time series that are caused by the cyclical component will be readily picked up in the projection. Hence, the projection in model (a) will be a better choice.

(e)

Year	Linear	Quadratic	Exponential	HW ($U = 0.3$, $V = 0.3$)	HW ($U = 0.7$, $V = 0.7$)	HW ($U = 0.3$, $V = 0.7$)
2004	22.2771	23.8374	28.5329	20.9886	22.1441	21.1180
2005	23.0059	24.8783	30.7036	21.3941	22.5256	21.4811

The real operating revenue of Coca Cola has experienced contraction since 1996. This is being captured and reflected in the Holt-Winters method with $U = 0.3$ and $V = 0.3$, which gives more weight to recent levels and trends of the time series, but not in the 3 trend models in Problem 16.15(e), which are very much constrained by the model specifications. The Holt-Winters method with $U = 0.7$ and $V = 0.7$, and $U = 0.3$ and $V = 0.7$, which gives more weight to past trends behaves more like the trend models.

16.30 (a) $U = 0.3, V = 0.3$

Year	P&G Stock Price	E	T		Year	P&G Stock Price	E	T
1970	1.42				1987	7.15	7.06294	0.937614
1971	1.57	1.57	0.15		1988	8.24	8.168166	1.054943
1972	2.17	2.035	0.3705		1989	8.7	8.856933	0.798619
1973	3.14	2.91965	0.730405		1990	14.51	13.05367	3.177299
1974	2.63	2.936017	0.230578		1991	18.33	17.70029	4.205826
1975	2.38	2.615978	-0.15485		1992	20.35	20.81683	3.44333
1976	2.66	2.600338	-0.0574		1993	23.76	23.91005	3.198249
1977	2.86	2.76488	0.097958		1994	25.85	26.22749	2.581683
1978	2.71	2.755851	0.023068		1995	28.78	28.78875	2.567388
1979	2.9	2.863676	0.082397		1996	39.64	37.15484	6.62648
1980	2.53	2.654822	-0.12148		1997	52.03	49.5554	10.66833
1981	2.46	2.482003	-0.15742		1998	78.3	72.87712	19.52571
1982	3.03	2.818376	0.188236		1999	90.74	91.23885	18.71092
1983	4.68	4.177984	1.008196		2000	107.19	108.0179	17.35863
1984	4.67	4.824854	0.755268		2001	78.06	92.25497	-5.82648
1985	4.91	5.111037	0.426908		2002	80	81.92855	-8.97644
1986	6.29	6.064383	0.795415		2003	87.81	83.35263	-1.69607

$$\hat{Y}_{2004} = E_{2003} + (1)T_{2003} = 83.3526 + (1)(-1.6961) = 81.6566$$

(b) $U = 0.7, V = 0.7$

Year	P&G Stock Price	E	T		Year	P&G Stock Price	E	T
1970	1.42				1987	7.15	6.110177	0.598039
1971	1.57	1.57	0.15		1988	8.24	7.167751	0.735899
1972	2.17	1.855	0.1905		1989	8.7	8.142555	0.807571
1973	3.14	2.37385	0.289005		1990	14.51	10.61809	1.30796
1974	2.63	2.652999	0.286048		1991	18.33	13.84723	1.884315
1975	2.38	2.771333	0.235734		1992	20.35	17.11708	2.299976
1976	2.66	2.902947	0.204498		1993	23.76	20.71994	2.69084
1977	2.86	3.033211	0.182228		1994	25.85	24.14255	2.91037
1978	2.71	3.063807	0.136738		1995	28.78	27.57104	3.065807
1979	2.9	3.110382	0.109689		1996	39.64	33.33779	3.876091
1980	2.53	3.01305	0.047583		1997	52.03	41.65872	5.209541
1981	2.46	2.880443	-0.00647		1998	78.3	56.29778	8.038398
1982	3.03	2.920778	0.007569		1999	90.74	72.25733	10.41474
1983	4.68	3.453843	0.165218		2000	107.19	90.02745	12.62136
1984	4.67	3.934342	0.259802		2001	78.06	95.27216	10.40836
1985	4.91	4.408901	0.324229		2002	80	97.97637	8.097116
1986	6.29	5.200191	0.464347		2003	87.81	100.5944	6.453402
					2004			

$$\hat{Y}_{2004} = E_{2003} + (1)T_{2003} = 100.5944 + (1)(6.4534) = 107.0478$$

16.30 (c) $U = 0.3, V = 0.7$

cont.

Year	P&G Stock Price	E	T		Year	P&G Stock Price	E	T
1970	1.42				1987	7.15	6.991194	0.715096
1971	1.57	1.57	0.15		1988	8.24	8.079887	0.827175
1972	2.17	2.035	0.2445		1989	8.7	8.762119	0.783692
1973	3.14	2.88185	0.425205		1990	14.51	13.02074	1.826172
1974	2.63	2.833117	0.283023		1991	18.33	17.28507	2.55762
1975	2.38	2.600842	0.128434		1992	20.35	20.19781	2.664154
1976	2.66	2.680783	0.113886		1993	23.76	23.49059	2.852742
1977	2.86	2.840401	0.127606		1994	25.85	25.998	2.749142
1978	2.71	2.787402	0.073424		1995	28.78	28.77014	2.756043
1979	2.9	2.888248	0.081651		1996	39.64	37.20586	4.459944
1980	2.53	2.66197	-0.01073		1997	52.03	48.92074	6.636426
1981	2.46	2.517373	-0.05089		1998	78.3	71.47715	11.41242
1982	3.03	2.860945	0.06745		1999	90.74	88.38487	13.06101
1983	4.68	4.154518	0.435287		2000	107.19	105.4668	14.26728
1984	4.67	4.645942	0.452128		2001	78.06	90.56221	5.515727
1985	4.91	4.966421	0.412633		2002	80	84.82338	2.13936
1986	6.29	6.016716	0.603932		2003	87.81	87.55582	2.317284

$$\hat{Y}_{2004} = E_{2003} + (1)T_{2003} = 87.5558 + (1)(2.3173) = 89.8731$$

(d)   Given the historical movement of the time series, which suggests that the stock price had been gaining values at an increasing rate up until 1999, experienced a drastic decline in values in 2000 and has since shown signs of recovery, a better projection model will be to give more weight to the more recent levels and past trend. Since there is strong evidence from the last two years of a likely recovery back to the level prior to the decline in 1999, a Holt-Winters method with $U = 0.3$ and $V = 0.7$ that assigns more weight to the recent values and past trend should be used.

(e)   The forecasts in (a) and (c) are lower and the forecast in (b) is higher than that in the exponential trend model of Problem 16.18 (f). This reflects the fact that the exponential trend model is very much restricted by its model specification while the Holt-Winters method with $U = 0.3$ and $V = 0.3$ is more capable of capturing the more recent drop in price and downward adjustment in trend. The Holt-Winters method with $U = 0.3$ and $V = 0.7$ is more capable of capturing the more recent drop in price but a potential recovery back to the past trend before the downturn in 2000.

16.32 $t = \dfrac{a_3}{S_{a_2}} = \dfrac{0.24}{0.10} = 2.4 > t_{10, 0.025} = 2.2281$. Reject H_0. There is sufficient evidence that the third-order regression parameter is significantly different than zero. A third-order autoregressive model is appropriate.

16.34 (a) $t = \dfrac{a_3}{S_{a_2}} = \dfrac{0.24}{0.15} = 1.6 < t_{10, 0.025} = 2.2281$. Do not reject H_0. . There is not sufficient evidence that the third-order regression parameter is significantly different than zero. A third-order autoregressive model is not appropriate.

(b)   Fit a second-order autoregressive model and test to see if it is appropriate.

16.36   (a)

	Coefficients	Standard Error	t Stat	P-value
Intercept	0.507324828	0.328088403	1.546305275	0.136295922
YLag1	1.324054626	0.230152736	5.752938894	8.69803E-06
YLag2	-0.377257993	0.398220921	-0.947358546	0.353746749
YLag3	0.052375007	0.247364273	0.211732301	0.834265125

Since p-value = 0.83 > 0.05, do not reject H_0 that $A_3 = 0$. Third-order term can be deleted.

(b)

	Coefficients	Standard Error	t Stat	P-value
Intercept	0.491754829	0.294238824	1.671277849	0.107657271
YLag1	1.305343547	0.197863376	6.597196381	7.9982E-07
YLag2	-0.306996174	0.198756006	-1.544588168	0.13553086

Since p-value = 0.14 > 0.05, do not reject H_0 that $A_2 = 0$. Second-order term can be deleted.

(c)

	Coefficients	Standard Error	t Stat	P-value
Intercept	0.590485192	0.267056187	2.211089726	0.036028545
YLag1	1.005085762	0.021250029	47.29808935	9.46432E-27

Since p-value is essentially zero, reject H_0 that $A_1 = 0$. A first-order autoregressive model is appropriate.

(d) $\hat{Y}_i = 0.5905 + 1.0051 Y_{i-1}$

Year	Forecasts
2004	21.6973
2005	22.3981

16.38   (a)

	Coefficients	Standard Error	t Stat	P-value
Intercept	2.165260706	1.997834745	1.083803708	0.288035545
YLag1	1.149028187	0.193078394	5.951096668	2.40687E-06
YLag2	-0.075699255	0.294810826	-0.256772305	0.79930113
YLag3	-0.071232591	0.205502555	-0.346626302	0.731559051

Since p-value = 0.73 > 0.05, do not reject H_0 that $A_3 = 0$. Third-order term can be deleted.

(b)

	Coefficients	Standard Error	t Stat	P-value
Intercept	2.090603156	1.887259991	1.107745179	0.277075376
YLag1	1.161012214	0.184340222	6.298203408	7.05204E-07
YLag2	-0.150795363	0.194558577	-0.775064074	0.444576094

Since p-value = 0.44 > 0.05, do not reject H_0 that $A_2 = 0$. Second-order term can be deleted.

(c)

	Coefficients	Standard Error	t Stat	P-value
Intercept	2.06439653	1.802051783	1.145581136	0.260735509
YLag1	1.024862401	0.048248505	21.2413295	4.92554E-20

Since p-value is essentially zero, reject H_0 that $A_1 = 0$. A first-order autoregressive model is appropriate.

16.38   (d) $\hat{Y}_i = 2.0644 + 1.0249Y_{i-1}$

cont.

Year	Forecasts
2004	92.0576
2005	96.4107

16.40   (a) $S_{YX} = \sqrt{\dfrac{\sum\limits_{i=1}^{n}(Y_i - \hat{Y}_i)^2}{n - p - 1}} = \sqrt{\dfrac{45}{12 - 1 - 1}} = 2.121$. The standard error of the estimate is

2.121.

   (b) $MAD = \dfrac{\sum\limits_{i=1}^{n}|Y_i - \hat{Y}_i|}{n} = \dfrac{18}{12} = 1.5$. The mean absolute deviation is 1.5.

16.42   (a)

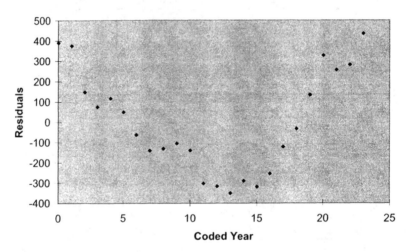

Coded Year Residual Plot

The residuals in the linear trend model show strings of consecutive positive and negative values.

   (b) $S_{YX} = 256.6194$

   (c) $MAD = 214.9249$

   (d)   The residuals in the linear trend model show strings of consecutive positive and negative values. The linear trend model is inadequate in capturing the non-linear trend.

16.44   (a)

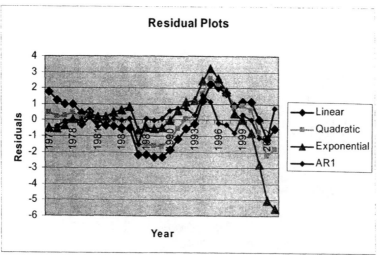

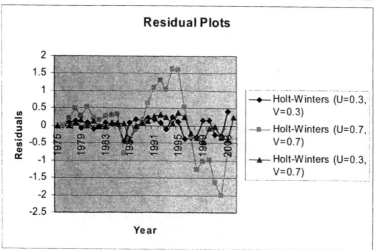

(b),(c)

	Linear	Quadratic	Exponential	Holt-Winters (U=0.3, V=0.3)	Holt-Winters (U=0.7, V=0.7)	Holt-Winters (U=0.3, V=0.7)	AR1
SSE	52.5259	41.0468	98.1693	1.2714	22.7087	1.4261	12.1429
Syx	1.3948	1.2565	1.9068	0.2211	0.9346	0.2342	0.6834
MAD	1.1311	0.8981	1.1808	0.1748	0.7168	0.1766	0.4775
k	1	2	1	1	1	1	1

(d)   The residuals in the three trend models show strings of consecutive positive and negative values. The Holt-Winters method with $U = 0.7$, $V = 0.7$ and $U = 0.3$, $V = 0.7$ also shows consecutive positive and negative values. The Holt-Winters method with $U = 0.3$, $V = 0.3$ and the autoregressive model perform well for the historical data and has a fairly random pattern of residuals. The Holt-Winters method with $U = 0.3$, $V = 0.3$ also has the smallest values in MAD and S_{YX}. Based on the principle of parsimony, the Holt-Winters method with $U = 0.3$, $V = 0.3$ would probably be the best model for forecasting.

16.46 (a)

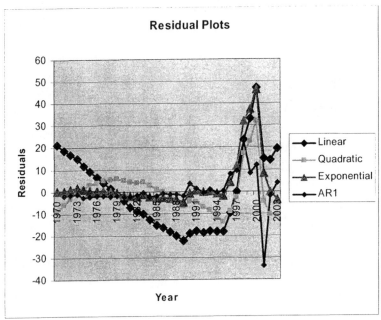

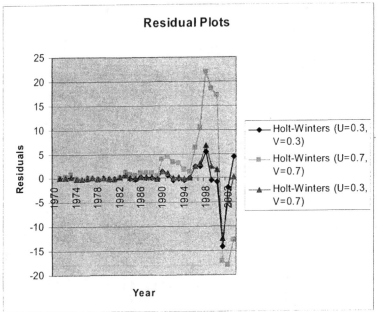

(b),(c)

	Linear	Quadratic	Exponential	Holt-Winters (U=0.3, V=0.3)	Holt-Winters (U=0.7, V=0.7)	Holt-Winters (U=0.3, V=0.7)	AR1
SSE	10522.16	3059.93	4908.52	271.32	2117.25	254.36	2141.86
Syx	18.13	9.94	12.39	2.96	8.26	2.86	8.31
MAD	15.11	6.93	5.34	1.16	4.53	1.20	4.28
k	1	2	1	1	1	1	1

16.46 (d)
cont.

The residuals in the three trend models show strings of consecutive positive and negative values. The Holt-Winters method with $U = 0.7$, $V = 0.7$ also shows strings of consecutive positive and negative values, in particular in the right tail. The Holt-Winters method with $U = 0.3$ and $V = 0.3$, the Holt-Winters method with $U = 0.3$ and $V = 0.7$, and the autoregressive model perform well for the historical data and has a fairly random pattern of residuals. The Holt-Winters method with $U = 0.3$ and $V = 0.3$ has the smallest values in MAD while the Holt-Winters method with $U = 0.3$ and $V = 0.7$ has the smallest S_{YX}. So either the Holt-Winters method with $U = 0.3$ and $V = 0.3$ or $U = 0.3$ and $V = 0.7$ would be a good model for forecasting.

16.48 (a) $\log b_0 = 2$. $b_0 = 10^2 = 100$. This is the fitted value for January 1998 prior to adjustment by the January multiplier.

(b) $\log b_1 = 0.01$. $b_1 = 10^{0.01} = 1.0233$. The estimated monthly compound growth rate is $(b_1 - 1)100\% = 2.33\%$.

(c) $\log b_2 = 0.1$. $b_2 = 10^{0.1} = 1.2589$. The January values in the time series are estimated to require a 25.89% increase above the value determined by the monthly compound growth rate.

16.50 (a) $\log b_0 = 3.0$. $b_0 = 10^{3.0} = 1,000$. This is the fitted value for January 2000 prior to adjustment by the quarterly multiplier.

(b) $\log b_1 = 0.1$. $b_1 = 10^{0.1} = 1.2589$. The estimated quarterly compound growth rate is $(b_1 - 1)100\% = 25.89\%$.

(c) $\log b_3 = 0.2$. $b_3 = 10^{0.2} = 1.5849$. The second quarter values in the time series are estimated to require a 58.49% increase above the value determined based on the quarterly compound growth rate.

16.52 (a)

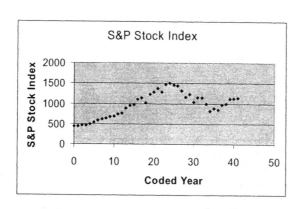

(b)

	Coefficients	Standard Error	t Stat	P-value
Intercept	2.7841	0.0485	57.4272	0.0000
Coded Quarter	0.0090	0.0015	6.0527	0.0000
Q1	-0.0128	0.0512	-0.2508	0.8034
Q2	-0.0062	0.0511	-0.1208	0.9045
Q3	-0.0200	0.0524	-0.3828	0.7041

$$\log_{10} \hat{Y} = 2.7841 + 0.0090X - 0.0128Q_1 - 0.0062Q_2 - 0.0200Q_3$$

16.52   (c) $\hat{Y}_{41} = 1356.0097$ (d) $\hat{Y}_{42} = 1405.8415$

cont.   (e)   2004: $\hat{Y}_{43} = 1390.2687$ $\hat{Y}_{44} = 1486.5076$

2005: $\hat{Y}_{45} = 1473.5496$ $\hat{Y}_{46} = 1527.7008$ $\hat{Y}_{47} = 1510.7782$ $\hat{Y}_{48} = 1615.3591$

(f) $\log_{10} b_1 = 0.0090$. $b_1 = 10^{0.0090} = 1.0210$. The estimated quarterly compound growth rate is $(b_1 - 1)\,100\% = 2.10\%$.

(g) $\log_{10} b_3 = -0.0062$. $b_3 = 10^{-0.0062} = 0.9859$. $(b_3 - 1)\,100\% = -1.4129$

The second quarter values in the time series are estimated to have a mean 1.41% below the fourth quarter values.

16.54   (a)

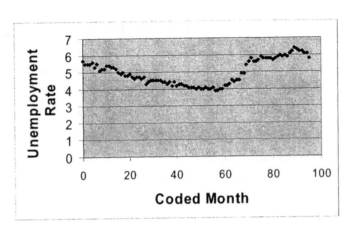

(b)

	Coefficients	Standard Error	t Stat	P-value
Intercept	0.656160	0.026242	25.004198	0.000000
Coded Month	0.000751	0.000241	3.120313	0.002485
M1	0.003547	0.032537	0.109023	0.913447
M2	0.003190	0.032518	0.098113	0.922079
M3	0.000033	0.032502	0.001004	0.999201
M4	0.000999	0.032486	0.030748	0.975545
M5	-0.001073	0.032473	-0.033045	0.973718
M6	0.000384	0.032461	0.011824	0.990594
M7	-0.001428	0.032452	-0.043991	0.965017
M8	-0.002460	0.032444	-0.075837	0.939731
M9	-0.004697	0.032437	-0.144809	0.885213
M10	-0.003683	0.032433	-0.113550	0.909868
M11	-0.000496	0.032430	-0.015293	0.987835

$$\log \hat{Y} = 0.656160 + 0.000751X + 0.003547M_1 + 0.003190M_2 + 0.000033M_3$$
$$+ 0.000999M_4 - 0.001073M_5 + 0.000384M_6 - 0.001428M_7$$
$$- 0.002460M_8 - 0.004697M_9 - 0.003683M_{10} - 0.000496M_{11}$$

(c) $\hat{Y}_{96} = 5.34\%$

16.54 (d) 2004: $\hat{Y}_{97} = 5.39\%$ $\hat{Y}_{98} = 5.40\%$ $\hat{Y}_{99} = 5.37\%$ $\hat{Y}_{100} = 5.39\%$

cont. $\hat{Y}_{101} = 5.37\%$ $\hat{Y}_{102} = 5.40\%$ $\hat{Y}_{103} = 5.39\%$ $\hat{Y}_{104} = 5.38\%$

$\hat{Y}_{105} = 5.36\%$ $\hat{Y}_{106} = 5.39\%$ $\hat{Y}_{107} = 5.44\%$ $\hat{Y}_{108} = 5.45\%$

(e) $\log b_1 = 0.000751$. $b_1 = 10^{0.000751} = 1.001731$. The estimated monthly compound growth rate is $(b_1 - 1)\,100\% = 0.1731\%$.

(f) $\log b_8 = -0.001428$. $b_8 = 10^{-0.001428} = 0.9967$. $(b_8 - 1)\,100\% = -0.33\%$.

The July values in the time series are estimated to have a mean 0.33% below the December values.

16.56 (a) The retail industry is heavily subject to seasonal variation due to the holiday seasons and so are the revenues for Toys R Us.

(b)

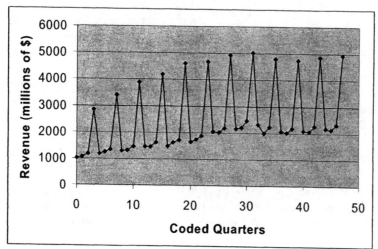

There is obvious seasonal effect in the time series.

(c) $\hat{Y}_i = 3007.9022(1.0149)^{X_i}(0.4051)^{Q_1}(0.4008)^{Q_2}(0.4322)^{Q_3}$

(d) $\log b_1 = 0.0064$. $b_1 = 10^{0.0064} = 1.0149$. The estimated quarterly compound growth rate is $(b_1 - 1)100\% = 1.49\%$

(e) $\log b_2 = -0.3924$. $b_2 = 10^{-0.3924} = 0.4051$. The 1st quarter values in the time series are estimated to have a mean 59.49% below the 4th quarter values.

$\log b_3 = -0.3971$. $b_3 = 10^{-0.3971} = 0.4008$. The 2nd quarter values in the time series are estimated to have a mean 59.92% below the 4th quarter values.

$\log b_4 = -0.3643$. $b_4 = 10^{-0.3643} = 0.4322$. The 3rd quarter values in the time series are estimated to have a mean 56.78% below the 4th quarter values.

(f) Forecasts for 2004: $\hat{Y}_{49} = 2480.3268$, $\hat{Y}_{50} = 2490.5146$, $\hat{Y}_{51} = 2725.5678$, $\hat{Y}_{52} = 6400.7917$

16.58 The price of the commodity in 2002 was 75% higher than in 1995.

16.60   (a) $I_U^{2004} = \dfrac{\sum_{i=1}^{3} P_i^{2004}}{\sum_{i=1}^{3} P_i^{1995}}(100) = \dfrac{43}{23}(100) = 186.96$

      (b) $I_L^{2004} = \dfrac{\sum_{i=1}^{3} P_i^{2004} Q_i^{1995}}{\sum_{i=1}^{3} P_i^{1995} Q_i^{1995}}(100) = \dfrac{240}{148}(100) = 162.16$

      (c) $I_P^{2004} = \dfrac{\sum_{i=1}^{3} P_i^{2004} Q_i^{2004}}{\sum_{i=1}^{3} P_i^{1995} Q_i^{2004}}(100) = \dfrac{227}{147}(100) = 154.42$

16.62   (a), (b)

Year	DJIA	Price Index (base = 1979)	Price Index (base = 1990)	Year	DJIA	Price Index (base = 1979)	Price Index (base = 1990)
1979	838.7	100.00	31.84	1991	3168.8	377.82	120.32
1980	964	114.94	36.60	1992	3301.1	393.60	125.34
1981	875	104.33	33.22	1993	3754.1	447.61	142.54
1982	1046.5	124.78	39.73	1994	3834.4	457.18	145.59
1983	1258.6	150.07	47.79	1995	5117.1	610.12	194.29
1984	1211.6	144.46	46.00	1996	6448.3	768.84	244.84
1985	1546.7	184.42	58.73	1997	7908.3	942.92	300.27
1986	1896	226.06	71.99	1998	9181.4	1094.72	348.61
1987	1938.8	231.17	73.62	1999	11497.1	1370.82	436.54
1988	2168.6	258.57	82.34	2000	10788	1286.28	409.61
1989	2753.2	328.27	104.54	2001	10021.5	1194.88	380.51
1990	2633.7	314.02	100.00				

      (c)   The price index using 1990 as the base year is more useful because it is closer to the present and the DJIA has grown more than 1000% over the 23-year period.

16.64   (a), (b)

Year	CPI	Price Index (base = 1990)	Price Index (base = 2003)	Year	CPI	Price Index (base = 1990)	Price Index (base = 2003)
1990	129.9	100.00	71.61	1997	160	123.17	88.20
1991	135.7	104.46	74.81	1998	164.4	126.56	90.63
1992	139.2	107.16	76.74	1999	167.3	128.79	92.23
1993	141.9	109.24	78.22	2000	172.2	132.56	94.93
1994	146	112.39	80.49	2001	173.4	133.49	95.59
1995	150.7	116.01	83.08	2002	176.3	135.72	97.19
1996	154.4	118.86	85.12	2003	181.4	139.65	100.00

      (c)   Both price indices are useful. The one using 1990 as the base year conveys a picture of how the CPI has grown since 1990 as a percentage of that year. The one using 2003 as the base year reveals what the CPI in prior years was as a percentage of the current level. Since the price index is usually used to compare the growth of price from some base year in the past, the price using 1990 as the base is more useful.

      (d)   The CPI in UK has grown 39.65% from 1990 to 2003 compared to the 1.45% growth in Japan over the same period.

16.66 (a), (c)

Year	Price	Price Index (base= 1980)	Price Index (base= 1990)	Year	Price	Price Index (base= 1980)	Price Index (base= 1990)
1980	0.703	100.00	40.52	1993	1.141	162.30	65.76
1981	0.792	112.66	45.65	1994	1.604	228.17	92.45
1982	0.763	108.53	43.98	1995	1.323	188.19	76.25
1983	0.726	103.27	41.84	1996	1.103	156.90	63.57
1984	0.854	121.48	49.22	1997	1.213	172.55	69.91
1985	0.697	99.15	40.17	1998	1.452	206.54	83.69
1986	1.104	157.04	63.63	1999	1.904	270.84	109.74
1987	0.943	134.14	54.35	2000	1.443	205.26	83.17
1988	0.871	123.90	50.20	2001	1.414	201.14	81.50
1989	0.797	113.37	45.94	2002	1.451	206.40	83.63
1990	1.735	246.80	100.00	2003	1.711	243.39	98.62
1991	0.912	129.73	52.56	2004	1.472	209.39	84.84
1992	0.936	133.14	53.95				

(b)   The average price per pound of fresh tomatoes in 2004 in the U.S. is 109.39% higher than it was in 1980.

(d)   The average price per pound of fresh tomatoes in 2004 in the U.S. is 15.16% lower than it was in 1990.

(e)

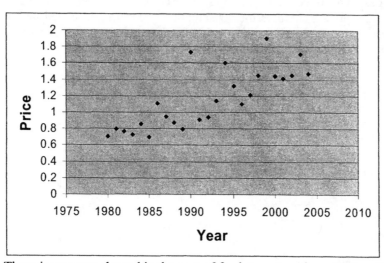

There is an upward trend in the cost of fresh tomatoes from 1980 to 2004.

16.68 Forecasting methodology is important as a tool for planning for the future.

16.70 Trend is the overall long-term tendency or impression of upward or downward movements. The cyclical component depicts the up-and-down swings or movements through the series. Any observed data that do not follow the trend curve modified by the cyclical component are indicative of the irregular or random component. When data are recorded monthly or quarterly, an additional component called the seasonal factor is considered.

16.72 The exponential trend model is appropriate when the percentage difference from observation to observation is constant.

16.74 Autoregressive models have independent variables that are the dependent variable lagged by a given number of time periods.

16.76 The standard error of the estimate relies on the squared sum of the deviations, which gives increased weight to large differences. The mean absolute deviation is the mean of the absolute value of the deviations.

16.78 An index number provides a measure of the value of an item (or group of items) at a particular point in time as a percentage of the item's (or group of items') value at another point in time.

16.80 Both the Laspeyres price index and Paasche price index are weight aggregate price indexes. The Laspeyres price index uses the consumption quantities associated with the base year as the weights while the Paasche price index uses the consumption quantities in the year of interest as the weights.

16.82 (a)

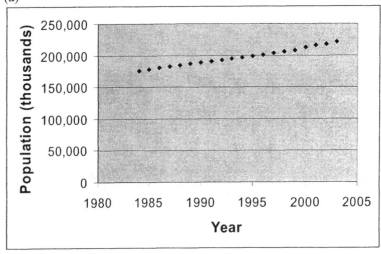

(b) Linear trend: $\hat{Y} = 175{,}224.1714 + 2{,}266.7662X$, where X is relative to 1984.

(c) 2004: $\hat{Y}_{2004} = 175{,}224.1714 + 2{,}266.7662(20) = 220{,}559.4947$ thousands

2005: $\hat{Y}_{2005} = 175{,}224.1714 + 2{,}266.7662(21) = 222{,}826.2609$ thousands

16.82   (d)   (a)
cont.

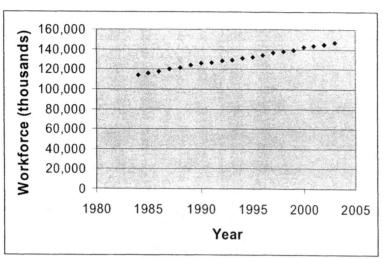

(b)   Linear trend: $\hat{Y} = 114,399.0286 + 1,695.1759X$, where X is relative to 1984.

(c)   2004: $\hat{Y}_{2004} = 114,399.0286 + 1,695.1759(20) = 148,302.5474$ thousands

2005: $\hat{Y}_{2005} = 114,399.0286 + 1,695.1759(21) = 149,997.7233$ thousands

16.84   (a)

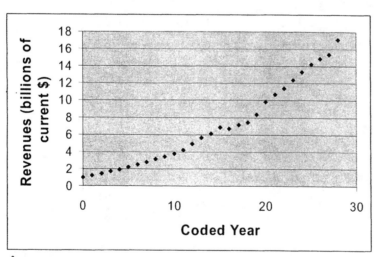

(b) $\hat{Y} = -0.8821 + 0.5588X$ where X = years relative to 1975

(c) $\hat{Y} = 1.2129 + 0.0933X + 0.0166X^2$, where X = years relative to 1975

16.84 (d) $\hat{Y} = 1.3251(1.1022)^X$, where X = years relative to 1975

cont. (e) AR(3): $\hat{Y}_i = 0.1984 + 1.2280Y_{i-1} - 0.3930Y_{i-2} + 0.2273Y_{i-3}$

Test of A_3: p-value = 0.4197 > 0.05. Do not reject H_0 that $A_3 = 0$. Third-order term can be deleted.

$\hat{Y}_i = 0.1699 + 1.1673Y_{i-1} - 0.1146Y_{i-2}$

AR(2): Test of A_2: p-value = 0.6322. Do not reject H_0 that $A_2 = 0$. Second-order term can be deleted.

AR(1): $\hat{Y}_i = 0.1880 + 1.0588Y_{i-1}$

Test of A_1: p-value is virtually 0. Reject H_0 that $A_1 = 0$. A first-order autoregressive model is appropriate.

(f)

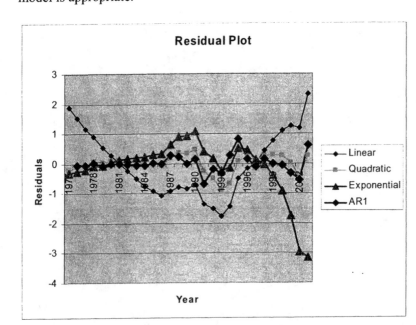

(g)

	Linear	Quadratic	Exponential	AR1
SSE	33.9875	2.6723	27.2235	2.3708
Syx	1.1220	0.3206	1.0041	0.3020
MAD	0.9264	0.2237	0.5904	0.1905
k	1	2	1	1

(h) The residuals in the first three models show strings of consecutive positive and negative values. The autoregressive model performs well for the historical data and has a fairly random pattern of residuals. It also has the smallest values in the standard error of the estimate, MAD and SSE. Based on the principle of parsimony, the autoregressive model would probably be the best model for forecasting.

(i) $\hat{Y}_{2004} = 0.1880 + 1.0588Y_{2003} = 0.1880 + 1.0588(17.1) = \$18.2940$ billions

16.86   (a)

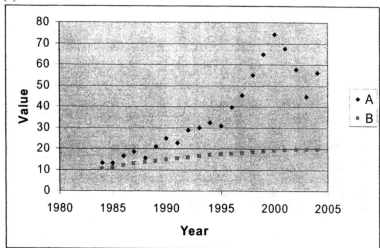

(b)   Variable A: $\hat{Y} = 8.5765 + 2.8170X$, where X = years relative to 1984

Variable B: $\hat{Y} = 11.4482 + 0.4732X$, where X = years relative to 1984

(c)   Variable A: $\hat{Y} = 8.2424 + 2.9225X - 0.0053X^2$, where X = years relative to 1984

Variable B: $\hat{Y} = 10.3022 + 0.8351X - 0.0181X^2$, where X = years relative to 1984

(d)   Variable A: $\hat{Y} = 13.6166(1.0889)^X$, where X = years relative to 1984

Variable B: $\hat{Y} = 11.6639(1.0314)^X$, where X = years relative to 1984

(e)   Variable A:

AR(3): $\hat{Y}_i = 5.1180 + 1.2487Y_{i-1} - 0.4886Y_{i-2} + 0.1586Y_{i-3}$

Test of A_3: p-value = 0.69 > 0.05. Do not reject H_0 that $A_3 = 0$. Third-order term can be deleted.

AR(2): $\hat{Y}_i = 5.2495 + 1.1723Y_{i-1} - 0.2653Y_{i-2}$

Test of A_2: p-value = 0.30 > 0.05. Do not reject H_0 that $A_2 = 0$. Second-order term can be deleted.

AR(1): $\hat{Y}_i = 4.7661 + 0.9267Y_{i-1}$

Test of A_1: p-value is virtually 0. Reject H_0 that $A_1 = 0$. A first-order autoregressive model is appropriate.

Variable B:

AR(3): $\hat{Y}_i = 1.1414 + 1.9239Y_{i-1} - 1.6231Y_{i-2} + 0.6482Y_{i-3}$

Test of A_3: p-value = 0.04 < 0.05. Reject H_0 that $A_3 = 0$. A third-order autoregressive model is appropriate.

16.86   (f)   Variable A:
cont.

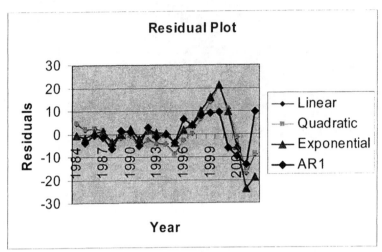

Variable B:

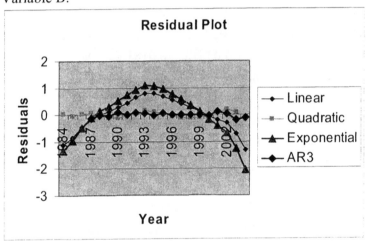

(g)   Variable A:

	Linear	Quadratic	Exponential	AR1
SSE	1380.9889	1380.3645	1902.5397	805.0368
Syx	8.5255	8.7571	10.0067	6.6876
MAD	5.9916	6.0414	6.1069	5.1562
k	1	2	1	1

Variable B:

	Linear	Quadratic	Exponential	AR3
SSE	7.5331	0.1887	15.4917	0.0998
Syx	0.6297	0.1024	0.9030	0.0844
MAD	0.4888	0.0814	0.7164	0.0495
k	1	2	1	3

16.86 (h)   Variable A: The residuals in the linear and quadratic trend models show strings of
cont.   consecutive positive and negative values. There is no apparent pattern in the
        residuals of the exponential trend and autoregressive AR(1) model . The
        autoregressive model has the smallest values in the standard error of the estimate and
        MAD. Based on the principle of parsimony, the autoregressive model would
        probably be the best model for forecasting.

        Variable B: The residuals in the quadratic and exponential trend models show strings
        of consecutive positive and negative values. There is no apparent pattern in the
        residuals of the linear trend and autoregressive AR(3) model. The autoregressive
        model AR(3) has the smallest values in the standard error of the estimate and MAD.
        Based on the principle of parsimony, the autoregressive model would probably be the
        best model for forecasting.

(i)   Variable A: $\hat{Y}_{2005} = 4.7661 + 0.9267 Y_{2004} = 56.6564$

        Variable B: $\hat{Y}_{2005} = 1.1414 + 1.9239 Y_{2004} - 1.6231 Y_{2003} + 0.6482 Y_{2002} = 19.5860$

CHAPTER 17

OBJECTIVES

- To be able to use the payoff table and decision trees to evaluate alternative courses of action
- To be able to use several criteria to select an alternative course of action
- To be able to use Bayes' theorem to revise probabilities in the light of sample information
- To understand the concept of utility

OVERVIEW AND KEY CONCEPTS

Some Basic Features of Decision Making

- **Alternative courses of action:** The decision maker must have two or more possible choices to evaluate prior to selecting one course of action.
- **Events or states of the world:** The decision maker must list the events that can occur and consider each event's possibility of action.
- **Payoffs:** The decision maker must associate a monetary value or payoff with the result of each event.
- **Decision criteria:** The decision maker must determine how the best course of action is to be selected.

Payoff Table

- A payoff table contains each possible event that can occur for each alternative course of action.

Consider a food vendor determining
whether to sell soft drinks or hot dogs.

Event (E_i)	Course of Action (A_j)	
	Sell Soft Drinks (A_1)	Sell Hot Dogs (A_2)
Cool Weather (E_1)	$x_{11} = \$50$	$x_{12} = \$100$
Warm Weather (E_2)	$x_{21} = \$200$	$x_{22} = \$125$

x_{ij} = payoff (profit) for event i and action j

Decision Tree

- A decision tree pictorially represents the events and courses of action through a set of branches and nodes.

Food Vendor Profit Tree Diagram

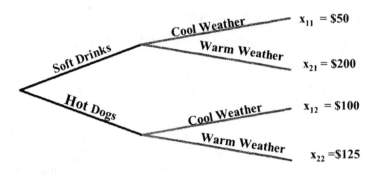

Soft Drinks

Cool Weather — $x_{11} = \$50$

Warm Weather — $x_{21} = \$200$

Hot Dogs

Cool Weather — $x_{12} = \$100$

Warm Weather — $x_{22} = \$125$

Opportunity Loss

- The opportunity loss is the difference between the highest possible profit (payoff or monetary value) for an event and the actual profit obtained for an action taken.
- The opportunity loss table:

Event	Optimal Action	Profit of Optimal Action	Alternative Course of Action	
			Sell Soft Drinks	Sell Hot Dogs
Cool Weather	Hot Dogs	100	100 - 50 = 50	100 - 100 = 0
Warm Weather	Soft Drinks	200	200 - 200 = 0	200 - 125 = 75

Some Decision Criteria

- **Expected monetary value (EMV):**
  - The expected profit (payoff or monetary value) for taking an action.
  - $$EMV(j) = \sum_{i=1}^{N} x_{ij} P_i$$

  where

  $EMV(j)$ = expected monetary value of action j

  x_{ij} = payoff that occurs when action j is taken and event i occurs

  P_i = probability of occurence of event i

- **Expected opportunity loss (*EOL*):**
  - $$EOL(j) = \sum_{i=1}^{N} l_{ij} P_i$$

    where

    $EOL(j) = $ expected opportunity loss of action j

    $l_{ij} = $ opportunity loss that occurs when action j is taken and event i occurs

    $P_i = $ probability of occurence of event i
- **Expected profit under certainty (*EPUC*):** The expected profit one could make if one has perfect information about which event will occur.
- **Expected value of perfect information:**
  - The expected value of perfect information is the expected opportunity loss from the best decision, i.e. the minimum *EOL* among all the courses of action.
  - It also represents the maximum amount one would pay to obtain perfect information.
  - The difference between expected profit under certainty and the expected monetary value from he best action.
  - $$EVPI = EPUC - \max_{j} EMV(j) = \min_{j} EOL(j)$$
- **Return to risk ratio:**
  - Expressed the relationship between the return (expected payoff) and the risk (standard deviation).
  - $$RRR(j) = \frac{EMV(j)}{\sigma_j}$$
- **Coefficient of variation:**
  - Coefficient of variation is the inverse of return to risk ratio.
  - $$CV(j) = \frac{\sigma_j}{EMV(j)} = \frac{1}{RRR(j)}$$

Decision Making with Sample Information

- Decision maker chooses the best course of action A_j using some prior probabilities of events $P(E_i)$. When new information becomes available in the form of conditional probabilities of an action given a specific event, $P(A_j \mid E_i)$, one can update the probabilities of the events using the Bayes's theorem to obtain the posterior probabilities of events, $P(E_i \mid A_j)$, and re-evaluate all the decision criteria.

Utility

- Each incremental amount of profit or loss does not have the same value to every individual.
  - A **risk adverse** person, once reaching a goal, assigns less value to each incremental amount of profit.
  - A **risk seeker** assigns more value to each incremental amount of profit.
  - A **risk neutral** person assigns the same value to each incremental amount of profit.

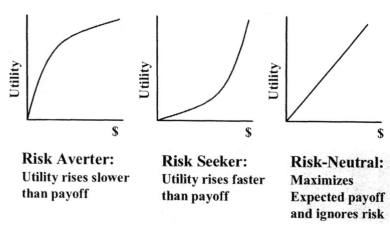

Risk Averter:
Utility rises slower
than payoff

Risk Seeker:
Utility rises faster
than payoff

Risk-Neutral:
Maximizes
Expected payoff
and ignores risk

SOLUTIONS TO END OF SECTION
AND CHAPTER REVIEW EVEN PROBLEMS

17.2   (a)   Opportunity loss table:

Event	Optimum Action	Profit of Optimum Action	Alternative Courses of Action	
			A	B
1	A	50	50 − 50 = 0	50 − 10 = 40
2	A	300	300 − 300 = 0	300 − 100 = 200
3	A	500	500 − 500 = 0	500 − 200 = 300

   (b)

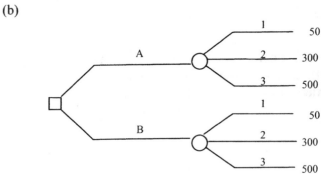

17.4   (a)-(b) Payoff table:

Action

Event	Company A		Company B	
1	$10,000 + $2•1,000 =	$12,000	$2,000 + $4•1,000 =	$6,000
2	$10,000 + $2•2,000 =	$14,000	$2,000 + $4•2,000 =	$10,000
3	$10,000 + $2•5,000 =	$20,000	$2,000 + $4•5,000 =	$22,000
4	$10,000 + $2•10,000 =	$30,000	$2,000 + $4•10,000 =	$42,000
5	$10,000 + $2•50,000 =	$110,000	$2,000 + $4•50,000 =	$202,000

   (c)

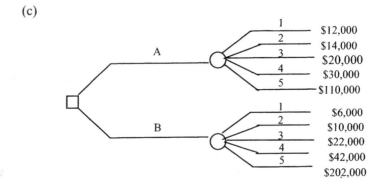

17.4 (d)   Opportunity loss table:
cont.

		Profit of	Alternative Courses of Action	
	Optimum	Optimum		
Event	Action	Action	A	B
1	A	12,000	0	6,000
2	A	14,000	0	4,000
3	B	22,000	2,000	0
4	B	42,000	12,000	0
5	B	202,000	92,000	0

17.6 (a) $EMV_A = 50(0.5) + 200(0.5) = 125$ $\qquad$ $EMV_B = 100(0.5) + 125(0.5) = 112.50$

(b) $EOL_A = 50(0.5) + 0(0.5) = 25$ $\qquad$ $EOL_B = 0(0.5) + 75(0.5) = 37.50$

(c) Perfect information would correctly forecast which event, 1 or 2, will occur. The value of perfect information is the increase in the expected value if you knew which of the events 1 or 2 would occur prior to making a decision between actions. It allows us to select the optimum action given a correct forecast.

EMV with perfect information $= 100\,(0.5) + 200\,(0.5) = 150$

$EVPI = EMV$ with perfect information $- EMV_A = 150 - 125 = 25$

(d) Based on (a) and (b) above, select action A because it has a higher expected monetary value (a) and a lower opportunity loss (b) than action B.

(e) $\sigma_A^2 = (50 - 125)^2\,(0.5) + (200 - 125)^2\,(0.5) = 5625$ $\qquad$ $\sigma_A = 75$

$CV_A = \dfrac{75}{125} \cdot 100\% = 60\%$

$\sigma_B^2 = (100 - 112.5)^2\,(0.5) + (125 - 112.5)^2\,(0.5) = 156.25$ $\qquad$ $\sigma_B = 12.5$

$CV_B = \dfrac{12.5}{112.5} \cdot 100\% = 11.11\%$

(f) Return-to-risk ratio for $A = \dfrac{125}{75} = 1.667$

Return-to-risk ratio for $B = \dfrac{112.5}{12.5} = 9.0$

(g) Based on (e) and (f), select action B because it has a lower coefficient of variation and a higher return-to-risk ratio.

(h) The best decision depends on the decision criteria. In this case, expected monetary value leads to a different decision than the return-to-risk ratio.

17.8 (a) Rate of return $= \dfrac{\$100}{\$1,000} \cdot 100\% = 10\%$

(b) $CV = \dfrac{\$25}{\$100} \cdot 100\% = 25\%$

(c) Return-to-risk ratio $= \dfrac{\$100}{\$25} = 4.0$

17.10 Select stock A because it has a higher expected monetary value while it has the same standard deviation as stock B.

17.12 (a) EMV(Soft drinks) $= 50(0.4) + 60(0.6) = 56$

EMV(Ice cream) $= 30(0.4) + 90(0.6) = 66$

(b) EOL(Soft drinks) $= 0(0.4) + 30(0.6) = 18$

EOL(Ice cream) $= 20(0.4) + 0(0.6) = 8$

(c) $EVPI$ is the maximum amount of money the vendor is willing to pay for the information about which event will occur.

17.12 (d)   Based on (a) and (b), choose to sell ice cream because you will earn a higher
cont.   expected monetary value and incur a lower opportunity loss than choosing to sell soft
               drinks.

(e) $CV(\text{Soft drinks}) = \dfrac{4.899}{56} \cdot 100\% = 8.748\%$

$CV(\text{Ice cream}) = \dfrac{29.394}{66} \cdot 100\% = 44.536\%$

(f)   Return-to-risk ratio for soft drinks $= \dfrac{56}{4.899} = 11.431$

Return-to-risk ratio for ice cream $= \dfrac{66}{29.394} = 2.245$

(g)   To maximize return and minimize risk, you will choose to sell soft drinks because it
has the smallest coefficient of variation and the largest return-to-risk ratio.

(h)   There are no differences.

17.14 (a) $EMV_A = 500(0.3) + 1{,}000(0.5) + 2{,}000(0.2) = 1{,}050$
$EMV_B = -2{,}000(0.3) + 2{,}000(0.5) + 5{,}000(0.2) = 1{,}400$
$EMV_C = -7{,}000(0.3) - 1{,}000(0.5) + 20{,}000(0.2) = 1{,}400$

(b) $\sigma_A^2 = (500 - 1{,}050)^2 (0.3) + (1{,}000 - 1{,}050)^2 (0.5) + (2{,}000 - 1{,}050)^2 (0.2)$
$= 272{,}500$
$\sigma_A = 522.02$
$\sigma_B^2 = (-2{,}000 - 1{,}400)^2 (0.3) + (2{,}000 - 1{,}400)^2 (0.5) + (5{,}000 - 1{,}400)^2 (0.2)$
$= 6{,}240{,}000$
$\sigma_B = 2{,}498.00$
$\sigma_C^2 = (-7{,}000 - 1{,}400)^2 (0.3) + (-1{,}000 - 1{,}400)^2 (0.5) + (20{,}000 - 1{,}400)^2 (0.2)$
$= 93{,}240{,}000$
$\sigma_C = 9656.09$

(c)   Opportunity loss table:

| | | Profit of | Alternative Courses of Action | | |
Event	Optimum Action	Optimum Action	A	B	C
1	A	500	0	2,500	7,500
2	B	2,000	1,000	0	3,000
3	C	20,000	18,000	15,000	0

$EOL_A = 0(0.3) + 1{,}000(0.5) + 18{,}000(0.2) = 4{,}100$
$EOL_B = 2{,}500(0.3) + 0(0.5) + 15{,}000(0.2) = 3{,}750$
$EOL_C = 7{,}500(0.3) + 3{,}000(0.5) + 0(0.2) = 3{,}750$

(d) EMV with perfect information $= 500(0.3) + 2{,}000(0.5) + 20{,}000(0.2)$
$= 5{,}150$

$EVPI = EMV$ with perfect information $- EMV_{B \text{ or } C} = 5{,}150 - 1{,}400 = 3{,}750$
The investor should not be willing to pay more than $3,750 for a perfect forecast.

(e) $CV_A = \dfrac{522.02}{1050} \cdot 100\% = 49.72\%$ $CV_B = \dfrac{2498.00}{1400} \cdot 100\% = 178.43\%$

$CV_C = \dfrac{9656.09}{1400} \cdot 100\% = 689.72\%$

(f)   Return-to-risk ratio for $A = \dfrac{1050}{522.02} = 2.01$

Return-to-risk ratio for $B = \dfrac{1400}{2498} = 0.56$

Return-to-risk ratio for $C = \dfrac{1400}{9656.09} = 0.14$

17.14 (g)-(h) Actions B and C optimize the expected monetary value, but action A minimizes the
cont.   coefficient of variation and maximizes the investor's return-to-risk.

(i)

	(1) 0.1, 0.6, 0.3	(2) 0.1, 0.3, 0.6	(3) 0.4, 0.4, 0.2	(4) 0.6, 0.3, 0.1
(a) Max EMV	C: 4,700	C: 11,000	A or B: 800	A: 800
(b) σ Max EMV	σ_C: 10,169	σ_C: 11,145	σ_A: 548 σ_B: 2,683	σ_A: 458
(c) Min EOL & (d) $EVPI$	C: 2,550	C: 1,650	A: 4,000 or B: 4,000	A: 2,100
(e) Min CV	A: 40.99%	A: 36.64%	A: 54.77%	A: 57.28%
(f) Max Return- to-risk	A: 2.4398	A: 2.7294	A: 1.8257	A: 1.7457
(g) Choice on (e), (f)	Choose A	Choose A	Choose A	Choose A
(h) Compare (a) and (g)	Different: (a) C (g) A	Different: (a) C (g) A	Different: (a) A or B (g) A	Same: A

17.16 (a) $EMV_A = 12{,}000(0.45) + 14{,}000(0.2) + 20{,}000(0.15) + 30{,}000(0.1)$
$\qquad\qquad + 110{,}000(0.1) = 25{,}200$
$\qquad EMV_B = 6{,}000(0.45) + 10{,}000(0.2) + 22{,}000(0.15) + 42{,}000(0.1)$
$\qquad\qquad + 202{,}000(0.1) = 32{,}400$

(b) $EOL_A = 0(0.45) + 0(0.2) + 2{,}000(0.15) + 12{,}000(0.1) + 92{,}000(0.1)$
$\qquad\qquad = 10{,}700$
$\qquad EOL_B = 6{,}000(0.45) + 4{,}000(0.2) + 0(0.15) + 0(0.1) + 0(0.1)$
$\qquad\qquad = 3{,}500$

(c) EMV with perfect information $= 12{,}000(0.45) + 14{,}000(0.2) + 22{,}000(0.15)$
$\qquad\qquad + 42{,}000(0.1) + 202{,}000(0.1) = 35{,}900$
$\qquad EVPI = EMV$, perfect information $- EMV_B = 35{,}900 - 32{,}400 = 3{,}500$
The author should not be willing to pay more than \$3,500 for a perfect forecast.

(d) Sign with company B to maximize the expected monetary value (\$32,400) and
minimize the expected opportunity loss (\$3,500).

(e) $CV_A = \dfrac{28{,}792}{25{,}200} \cdot 100\% = 114.25\%$ $\qquad\qquad CV_B = \dfrac{57{,}583}{32{,}400} \cdot 100\% = 177.73\%$

(f) Return-to-risk ratio for $A = \dfrac{25{,}200}{28{,}792} = 0.8752$

Return-to-risk ratio for $B = \dfrac{32{,}400}{57{,}583} = 0.5627$

(g) Signing with company A will minimize the author's risk and yield the higher return-
to-risk.

(h) Company B has a higher EMV than A, but choosing company B also entails more risk
and has a lower return-to-risk ratio than A.

17.16 (i)
cont.

Payoff table:

	Pr	A	B
Event 1	0.3	12,000	6,000
Event 2	0.2	14,000	10,000
Event 3	0.2	20,000	22,000
Event 4	0.1	30,000	42,000
Event 5	0.2	110,000	202,000
	EMV	35,400	52,800
	σ	37,673	75,346
	CV	106.42%	142.70%
Return-to-risk		0.9397	0.7008

Opportunity loss table:

	Pr	A	B
Event 1	0.3	0	6,000
Event 2	0.2	0	4,000
Event 3	0.2	2,000	0
Event 4	0.1	12,000	0
Event 5	0.2	92,000	0
	EOL	20,000	2,600

The author's decision is not affected by the changed probabilities.

17.18 (a) $P(E_1 \mid F) = \dfrac{P(F \mid E_1) \cdot P(E_1)}{P(F \mid E_1) \cdot P(E_1) + P(F \mid E_2) \cdot P(E_2)} = \dfrac{0.6(0.5)}{0.6(0.5) + 0.4(0.5)} = 0.6$

$P(E_2 \mid F) = 1 - P(E_1 \mid F) = 1 - 0.6 = 0.4$

(b) $EMV_A = (0.6)(50) + (0.4)(200) = 110$
$EMV_B = (0.6)(100) + (0.4)(125) = 110$

(c) $EOL_A = (0.6)(50) + (0.4)(0) = 30$
$EOL_B = (0.6)(0) + (0.4)(75) = 30$

(d) $EVPI = (0.6)(100) + (0.4)(200) = 30$
You should not be willing to pay more than \$30 for a perfect forecast.

(e) Both have the same EMV and the same EOL.

(f) $\sigma_A^2 = (0.6)(60)^2 + (0.4)(90)^2 = 5400$ $\qquad \sigma_A = 73.4847$
$\sigma_B^2 = (0.6)(10)^2 + (0.4)(15)^2 = 150$ $\qquad \sigma_B = 12.2474$
$CV_A = \dfrac{73.4847}{110} \cdot 100\% = 66.8\%$ $\qquad CV_B = \dfrac{12.2474}{110} \cdot 100\% = 11.1\%$

(g) Return-to-risk ratio for $A = \dfrac{110}{73.4847} = 1.497$

Return-to-risk ratio for $B = \dfrac{110}{12.2474} = 8.981$

(h) Action B has a better return-to-risk ratio.

(i) Both have the same EMV, but action B has a better return-to-risk ratio.

17.20 (a) P(forecast cool | cool weather) = 0.80
P(forecast warm | warm weather) = 0.70

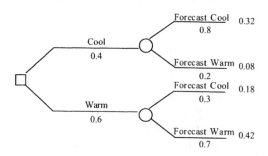

	Forecast Cool	Forecast Warm	Totals
Cool	0.32	0.08	0.4
Warm	0.18	0.42	0.6
Totals	0.5	0.5	

Revised probabilities: P(cool | forecast cool) = $\dfrac{0.32}{0.5}$ = 0.64

P(warm | forecast cool) = $\dfrac{0.18}{0.5}$ = 0.36

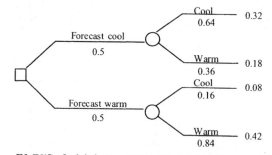

(b) EMV(Soft drinks) = 50(0.64) + 60(0.36) = 53.6
EMV(Ice cream) = 30(0.64) + 90(0.36) = 51.6
EOL(Soft drinks) = 0(0.64) + 30(0.36) = 10.8
EOL(Ice cream) = 20(0.64) + 0(0.36) = 12.8
EMV with perfect information = 50(0.64) + 90(0.36) = 64.4
$EVPI = EMV$, perfect information $- EMV_A$ = 64.4 − 53.6 = 10.8
The vendor should not be willing to pay more than $10.80 for a perfect forecast of
the weather.
The vendor should sell soft drinks to maximize value and minimize loss.
CV(Soft drinks) = $\dfrac{4.8}{53.6} \cdot 100\%$ = 8.96%
CV(Ice cream) = $\dfrac{28.8}{51.6} \cdot 100\%$ = 55.81%

Return-to-risk ratio for soft drinks = $\dfrac{53.6}{4.8}$ = 11.1667

Return-to-risk ratio for ice cream = $\dfrac{51.6}{28.8}$ = 1.7917

17.20   (b)   Based on these revised probabilities, the vendor's decision changes because of the
cont.   increased likelihood of cool weather given a forecast for cool. Under these
               conditions, she should sell soft drinks to maximize the expected monetary value and
               minimize her expected opportunity loss.

17.22   (a) $P(\text{favorable} \mid 1{,}000) = 0.01$ $P(\text{favorable} \mid 2{,}000) = 0.01$
              $P(\text{favorable} \mid 5{,}000) = 0.25$ $P(\text{favorable} \mid 10{,}000) = 0.60$
              $P(\text{favorable} \mid 50{,}000) = 0.99$
              $P(\text{favorable } and \text{ } 1{,}000)$ $= 0.01(0.45) = 0.0045$
              $P(\text{favorable } and \text{ } 2{,}000)$ $= 0.01(0.20) = 0.0020$
              $P(\text{favorable } and \text{ } 5{,}000)$ $= 0.25(0.15) = 0.0375$
              $P(\text{favorable } and \text{ } 10{,}000)$ $= 0.60(0.10) = 0.0600$
              $P(\text{favorable } and \text{ } 50{,}000)$ $= 0.99(0.10) = 0.0990$
              Joint probability table:

	Favorable	Unfavorable	Totals
1,000	0.0045	0.4455	0.45
2,000	0.0020	0.1980	0.20
5,000	0.0375	0.1125	0.15
10,000	0.0600	0.0400	0.10
50,000	0.0990	0.0010	0.10
Totals	0.2030	0.7970	

Given an unfavorable review, the revised conditional probabilities are:

$P(1{,}000 \mid \text{unfavorable})$ $= 0.4455/0.7970 = 0.5590$
$P(2{,}000 \mid \text{unfavorable})$ $= 0.1980/0.7970 = 0.2484$
$P(5{,}000 \mid \text{unfavorable})$ $= 0.1125/0.7970 = 0.1412$
$P(10{,}000 \mid \text{unfavorable})$ $= 0.0400/0.7970 = 0.0502$
$P(50{,}000 \mid \text{unfavorable})$ $= 0.0010/0.7970 = 0.0013$

(b)   Payoff table, given unfavorable review:

	Pr	A	B
1,000	0.5590	12,000	6,000
2,000	0.2484	14,000	10,000
5,000	0.1412	20,000	22,000
10,000	0.0502	30,000	42,000
50,000	0.0013	110,000	202,000
EMV		14,658.60	11,315.4
σ^2		31,719,333.50	126877326.67
σ		5,631.99	11263.98
CV		38.42%	99.55%
Return-to-risk		2.6027	1.0046

Opportunity loss table:

	Pr	A	B
Event 1	0.5590	0	6,000
Event 2	0.2484	0	4,000
Event 3	0.1412	2,000	0
Event 4	0.0502	12,000	0
Event 5	0.0013	92,000	0
EOL		1,004.40	4,347.60

17.22 (c)   The author's decision is affected by the changed probabilities. Under the new
cont.   circumstances, signing with company *A* maximizes the expected monetary value
($14,658.60), minimizes the expected opportunity loss ($1,004.40), minimizes risk
with a smaller coefficient of variation and yields a higher return-to-risk than choosing
company *B*.

17.26 A payoff table presents the alternatives in a tabular format, while the decision tree organizes
the alternatives and events visually.

17.28 Since it is the difference between the *highest* possible profit for an event and the actual profit
obtained for an action taken. It can never be negative.

17.30 The expected value of perfect information represents the maximum amount you would pay to
obtain perfect information. It represents the alternative course of action with the smallest
expected opportunity loss. It is also equal to the expected profit under certainty minus the
expected monetary value of the best alternative course of action.

17.32 Expected monetary value measures the mean return or profit of an alternative course of action
over the long run without regard for the variability in the payoffs under different events. The
return-to-risk ratio considers the variability in the payoffs in evaluating which alternative
course of action should be chosen.

17.34 A risk averter attempts to reduce risk, while a risk seeker looks for increased return usually
associated with greater risk.

17.36 (a), (c), (g), (h)   Payoff table:

Event		*Pr*	*A*: Buy 6,000	*B*: Buy 8,000	*C*: Buy 10,000	*D*: Buy 12,000
1	Sell 6,000	0.1	2,100	1,400	700	0
2	Sell 8,000	0.5	2,100	2,800	2,100	1,400
3	Sell 10,000	0.3	2,100	2,800	3,500	2,800
4	Sell 12,000	0.1	2,100	2,800	3,500	4,200
		EMV	2,100	2,660	2,520	1,960
		σ	0	420	896	1,120
		CV	0	15.79%	35.57%	57.14%
		Return-to-risk	undefined	6.3333	2.8111	1.7500

(d)   Opportunity loss table:

Event		*Pr*	*A*: Buy 6,000	*B*: Buy 8,000	*C*: Buy 10,000	*D*: Buy 12,000
1	Sell 6,000	0.1	0	700	1,400	2,100
2	Sell 8,000	0.5	700	0	700	1,400
3	Sell 10,000	0.3	1,400	700	0	700
4	Sell 12,000	0.1	2,100	1,400	700	0
		EOL	980	420	560	1,120

17.36 (b)
cont.

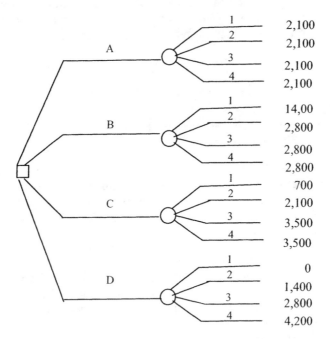

(e) *EVPI* = $420. The management of Shop-Quick Supermarkets should not be willing to pay more than $420 for a perfect forecast.

(f) To maximize the expected monetary value and minimize expected opportunity loss, the management should buy 8,000 loaves.

(i) Action *B* (buying 8,000 loaves) maximizes the return-to-risk and, while buying 6,000 loaves reduces the coefficient of variation to zero, action *B* has a smaller coefficient of variation than *C* or *D*.

(j) There are no differences.

(k) (a), (c), (g), (h)
Payoff table:

	Pr	*A*: Buy 6,000	*B*: Buy 8,000	*C*: Buy 10,000	*D*: Buy 12,000
Sell 6,000	0.3	2,100	1,400	700	0
Sell 8,000	0.4	2,100	2,800	2,100	1,400
Sell 10,000	0.2	2,100	2,800	3,500	2,800
Sell 12,000	0.1	2,100	2,800	3,500	4,200
	EMV	2,100	2,380	2,100	1,540
	σ	0	642	1,084	1,321
	CV	0	26.96%	51.64%	85.76%
	Return-to-risk	undefined	3.7097	1.9365	1.1660

17.36   (k)   (d)
cont.

Opportunity loss table:

	Pr	A: Buy 6,000	B: Buy 8,000	C: Buy 10,000	D: Buy 12,000
Sell 6,000	0.3	0	700	1,400	2,100
Sell 8,000	0.4	700	0	700	1,400
Sell 10,000	0.2	1,400	700	0	700
Sell 12,000	0.1	2,100	1,400	700	0
	EOL	700	490	770	1,330

(e) $EVPI = \$490$. The management of Shop-Quick Supermarkets should not be willing to pay more than $490 for a perfect forecast.

(f)   To maximize the expected monetary value and minimize expected opportunity loss, the management should buy 8,000 loaves.

(i)   Action B (buying 8,000 loaves) maximizes the return-to-risk and, while buying 6,000 loaves reduces the coefficient of variation to zero, action B has a smaller coefficient of variation than C or D.

(j)   There are no differences.

The management's decision is not affected by the changed probabilities.

17.38   (a)

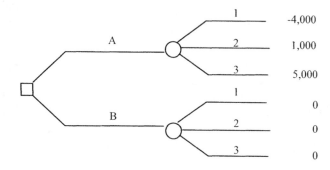

(c), (f) Payoff table:

	Pr	New	Old
Weak	0.3	− 4,000,000	0
Moderate	0.6	1,000,000	0
Strong	0.1	5,000,000	0
	EMV	− 100,000	0
	σ	2,808,914	0
	CV	− 2,808.94%	undefined
	Return-to-risk	− 0.0356	undefined

17.38   (b), (d), (e)   Opportunity loss table:
cont.

	Pr	New	Old
Weak	0.3	4,000,000	0
Moderate	0.6	0	1,000,000
Strong	0.1	0	5,000,000
	EOL	1,200,000	1,100,000

$EVPI = \$1,100,000$. The product manager should not be willing to pay more than $1,100,000 for a perfect forecast.

(g)   The product manager should continue to use the old packaging to maximize expected monetary value and to minimize expected opportunity loss and risk.

(h)   (c), (f)   Payoff table:

	Pr	New	Old
Weak	0.6	– 4,000,000	0
Moderate	0.3	1,000,000	0
Strong	0.1	5,000,000	0
	EMV	– 1,600,000	0
	σ	3,136,877	0
	CV	– 196.05%	undefined
	Return-to-risk	– 0.5101	undefined

(b), (d), (e) Opportunity loss table:

	Pr	New	Old
Weak	0.6	4,000,000	0
Moderate	0.3	0	1,000,000
Strong	0.1	0	5,000,000
	EOL	2,400,000	800,000

$EVPI = \$800,000$. The product manager should not be willing to pay more than $800,000 for a perfect forecast.

(g)   The product manager should continue to use the old packaging to maximize expected monetary value and to minimize expected opportunity loss and risk.

(i)   (c), (f)   Payoff table:

	Pr	New	Old
Weak	0.1	– 4,000,000	0
Moderate	0.3	1,000,000	0
Strong	0.6	5,000,000	0
	EMV	2,900,000	0
	σ	2,913,760.457	0
	CV	100.47%	undefined
	Return-to-risk	0.9953	undefined

17.38   (j)   (b), (d), (e) Opportunity loss table:
cont.

	Pr	New	Old
Weak	0.1	4,000,000	0
Moderate	0.3	0	1,000,000
Strong	0.6	0	5,000,000
	EOL	400,000	3,300,000

$EVPI = \$400,000$. The product manager should not be willing to pay more than $400,000 for a perfect forecast.

(g)   The product manager should use the new packaging to maximize expected monetary value and to minimize expected opportunity loss and risk.

(j) $P(\text{Sales decreased} \mid \text{weak response}) = 0.6$
$P(\text{Sales stayed same} \mid \text{weak response}) = 0.3$
$P(\text{Sales increased} \mid \text{weak response}) = 0.1$
$P(\text{Sales decreased} \mid \text{moderate response}) = 0.2$
$P(\text{Sales stayed same} \mid \text{moderate response}) = 0.4$
$P(\text{Sales increased} \mid \text{moderate response}) = 0.4$
$P(\text{Sales decreased} \mid \text{strong response}) = 0.05$
$P(\text{Sales stayed same} \mid \text{strong response}) = 0.35$
$P(\text{Sales increased} \mid \text{strong response}) = 0.6$

$P(\text{Sales decreased } and \text{ weak response}) = 0.6(0.3) = 0.18$
$P(\text{Sales stayed same } and \text{ weak response}) = 0.3(0.3) = 0.09$
$P(\text{Sales increased } and \text{ weak response}) = 0.1(0.3) = 0.03$
$P(\text{Sales decreased } and \text{ moderate response}) = 0.2(0.6) = 0.12$
$P(\text{Sales stayed same } and \text{ moderate response}) = 0.4(0.6) = 0.24$
$P(\text{Sales increased } and \text{ moderate response}) = 0.4(0.6) = 0.24$
$P(\text{Sales decreased } and \text{ strong response}) = 0.05(0.1) = 0.005$
$P(\text{Sales stayed same } and \text{ strong response}) = 0.35(0.1) = 0.035$
$P(\text{Sales increased } and \text{ strong response}) = 0.6(0.1) = 0.06$

Joint probability table:

	Pr	Sales Decrease	Sales Stay Same	Sales Increase
Weak	0.3	0.180	0.090	0.030
Moderate	0.6	0.120	0.240	0.240
Strong	0.1	0.005	0.035	0.060
Total		0.305	0.365	0.330

(j)   Given the sales stayed the same, the revised conditional probabilities are:
$$P(\text{weak response} \mid \text{sales stayed same}) = \frac{.09}{.365} = 0.2466$$
$$P(\text{moderate response} \mid \text{sales stayed same}) = \frac{.24}{.365} = 0.6575$$
$$P(\text{strong response} \mid \text{sales stayed same}) = \frac{.035}{.365} = 0.0959$$

17.38 (k)
cont.

(c), (f)   Payoff table:

	Pr	New	Old
Weak	0.2466	– 4,000,000	0
Moderate	0.6575	1,000,000	0
Strong	0.0959	5,000,000	0
EMV		150,600	0
σ		2,641,575.219	0
CV		1,754.03%	undefined
Return-to-risk		0.0570	undefined

(b), (d), (e)   Opportunity loss table:

	Pr	New	Old
Weak	0.2466	4,000,000	0
Moderate	0.6575	0	1,000,000
Strong	0.0959	0	5,000,000
EOL		986,400	1,137,000

$EVPI$ = $986,400. The product manager should not be willing to pay more than $986,400 for a perfect forecast.

(g)   The product manager should use the new packaging to maximize expected monetary value and to minimize expected opportunity loss and risk.

(l)   Given the sales decreased, the revised conditional probabilities are:

P(weak response | sales decreased) = $\frac{.18}{.305}$ = 0.5902

P(moderate response | sales decreased) = $\frac{.12}{.305}$ = 0.3934

P(strong response | sales decreased) = $\frac{.005}{.305}$ = 0.0164

(m)

(c), (f)   Payoff table:

	Pr	New	Old
Weak	0.5902	– 4,000,000	0
Moderate	0.3934	1,000,000	0
Strong	0.0164	5,000,000	0
EMV		– 1,885,400	0
σ		2,586,864.287	0
CV		– 137.21%	undefined
Return-to-risk		– 0.7288	undefined

(b), (d), (e)   Opportunity loss table:

	Pr	New	Old
Weak	0.5902	4,000,000	0
Moderate	0.3934	0	1,000,000
Strong	0.0164	0	5,000,000
EOL		2,360,800	475,400

$EVPI$ = $475,400. The product manager should not be willing to pay more than $475,400 for a perfect forecast.

(g)   The product manager should continue to use the old packaging to maximize expected monetary value.

17.40   (a)

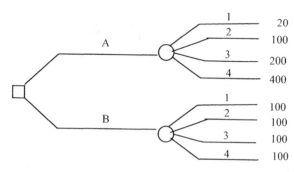

(c), (e), (f) Payoff table:*

Event		Pr	A: Do Not Call Mechanic	B: Call Mechanic
1	Very low	0.25	20	100
2	Low	0.25	100	100
3	Moderate	0.25	200	100
4	High	0.25	400	100
	EMV		180	100
	σ		142	0
	CV		78.96%	0
	Return-to-risk		1.2665	undefined

*Note: The payoff here is cost and not profit. The opportunity cost is therefore calculated as the difference between the payoff and the minimum in the same row.

(b), (d) Opportunity loss table:

	Pr	A: Do Not Call Mechanic	B: Call Mechanic
Very low	0.25	80	0
Low	0.25	0	0
Moderate	0.25	0	100
High	0.25	0	300
EOL		20	100

(g)   We want to minimize the expected monetary value because it is a cost. To minimize the expected monetary value, call the mechanic.

(h)   Given 2 successes out of 15, the binomial probabilities and their related revised conditional probabilities are:

	Pr	Binomial Probabilities	Revised Conditional Probabilities
Very low	0.01	0.0092	0.0092/0.6418 = 0.0143
Low	0.05	0.1348	0.1348/0.6418 = 0.2100
Moderate	0.10	0.2669	0.2669/0.6418 = 0.4159
High	0.20	0.2309	0.2309/0.6418 = 0.3598
		0.6418	

17.40   (i)   (c), (e), (f) Payoff table:
cont.

	Pr	A: Do Not Call Mechanic	B: Call Mechanic
Very low	0.0144	20	100
Low	0.2100	100	100
Moderate	0.4159	200	100
High	0.3598	400	100
	EMV	248	100
	σ	121	0
	CV	48.68%	0
	Return-to-risk	2.0544	undefined

(b), (d) Opportunity loss table:

	Pr	A: Do Not Call Mechanic	B: Call Mechanic
Very low	0.0144	80	0
Low	0.2100	0	0
Moderate	0.4159	0	100
High	0.3598	0	300
	EOL	1.15	149.53

(g)   We want to minimize the expected monetary value because it is a cost. To minimize the expected monetary value, call the mechanic.

CHAPTER 18

OBJECTIVES
- To understand the basic themes of quality management and Deming's 14 points
- To understand the basic aspects of the Six Sigma Management approach
- To be able to construct various control charts
- To know which control chart to use for a particular type of data
- To be able to measure the capability of a process

OVERVIEW AND KEY CONCEPTS
Themes of Quality Management
1. The primary focus is on process improvement.
2. Most of the variation in a process is due to the system and not the individual.
3. Teamwork is an integral part of a quality management organization.
4. Customer satisfaction is a primary organizational goal.
5. Organizational transformation must occur in order to implement quality management.
6. Fear must be removed from organizations.
7. Higher quality costs less not more but it requires an investment in training.

Deming's 14 Points for Management
1. Create constancy of purpose for improvement of product and service.

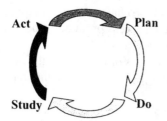

**The Shewhart-Deming Cycle
Focuses on Constant Improvement**

2. Adopt the new philosophy.
3. Cease dependence on inspection to achieve quality.
4. End the practice of awarding business on the basis of price tag alone. Instead, minimize total cost by working with a single supplier.
5. Improve constantly and forever every process for planning, production and service.
6. Institute training on the job.
7. Adopt and institute leadership.
8. Drive out fear.
9. Break down barriers between staff areas.
10. Eliminate slogans, exhortations, and targets for the workforce.
11. Eliminate numerical quotas for the workforce and numerical goals for management.
12. Remove barriers that rob people of pride of workmanship. Eliminate the annual rating or merit system.
13. Institute a vigorous program of education and self-improvement for everyone.
14. Put everyone in the company to work to accomplish the transformation.

Six Sigma Management
- A method for breaking processes into a series of steps in order to eliminate defects and produce near perfect results.
- Has a clear focus on obtaining bottom-line results in a relatively short three to six-month period of time.
- **The Six Sigma DMAIC model:**
  - **Define:** The problem to be solved needs to be defined along with the costs, benefits of the project, and the impact on the customer.
  - **Measure:** Operational definitions for each Critical-To-Quality (CTQ) characteristic must be developed. In addition, the measurement procedure must be verified so that it is consistent over repeated measurements.
  - **Analyze:** The root causes of why defects can occur need to be determined along with the variables in the process that cause these defects to occur. Data are collected to determine the underlying value for each process variable often using control charts.
  - **Improve:** The importance of each process variable on the CTQ characteristic is studied using designed experiments. The objective is to determine the best level for each variable that can be maintained in the long term.
  - **Control:** The objective is to maintain the gains that have been made with a revised process in the long term by avoiding potential problems that can occur when a process is changed.
- Its implementation requires a data-oriented approach using statistical tools such as control charts and designed experiments.
- Involves training everyone in the company in the DMAIC model.

Control Charts
- The **control chart** is a means of monitoring variation in the characteristic of a product or services by focusing on the time dimension in which the process produces products or services and studying the nature of the variability in the process.
- **Special (assignable) causes of variation:** Large fluctuations or patterns in the data that are not inherent to a process. They are often caused by changes in the process that represents either problems to be fixed or opportunities to exploit.
- **Chance (common) causes of variation:** The inherent variability that exists in a process. These consist of the numerous small causes of variability that operate randomly or by chance.
- An **out-of-control process** contains both common causes of variation and assignable causes of variation. Because assignable causes of variation are not part of the process design, an out-of-control process is unpredictable.
- An **in-control process** contains only common causes of variation. Because theses causes of variation are inherent to the process, an in-control process is predictable. An in-control-process is sometimes said to be in a **state of statistical control**.
- **Control limits:**
  - Statistical measure of interest $\pm$ 3 standard deviations

- **Identifying pattern in control charts:**

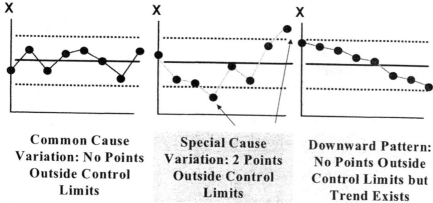

| Common Cause Variation: No Points Outside Control Limits | Special Cause Variation: 2 Points Outside Control Limits | Downward Pattern: No Points Outside Control Limits but Trend Exists |

  - A trend exists if there are 8 consecutive points above (or below) the centerline or 8 consecutive points that are increasing (or decreasing).
- **The first type of control error:** The belief that observed value represents special cause when in fact it is due to common cause.
- **The second type of control error:** Treating special cause variation as if it is common cause variation.
- When a process is out-of-control, the assignable causes of variation must be identified. If the assignable causes of variation are detrimental to the quality of the product or service, a plan to eliminate this source of variation must be implemented. If an assignable cause of variation increases quality, the process should be change so that it is incorporated into the process design and becomes a common cause source of variation and the process is improved.
- When a process is in control, it must be determined whether the amount of common cause variation in the process is small enough to satisfy the customers of the products or services. If it is small enough to consistently satisfy the customers, the control charts can be used to monitor the process on a continuous basis to make sure that it does not go out-of-control. If it is too large, the process should be altered.

Control Chart for the Proportion of Nonconforming Item (the p Chart)

- It is an attribute chart, which is used when sampled items are classified according to whether they conform or do not conform to operationally defined requirement.
- When used with unequal sample sizes over time, the unequal sample sizes should not differ by more than 25% from average sample size.

- $LCL_p = \max\left(0, \bar{p} - 3\sqrt{\dfrac{\bar{p}(1-\bar{p})}{\bar{n}}} \right)$, $UCL_p = \bar{p} + 3\sqrt{\dfrac{\bar{p}(1-\bar{p})}{\bar{n}}}$

  where

  X_i = number of nonforming items in sample i

  n_i = sample size for sample i

  $p_i = X_i / n_i$ = proportion of nonconforming items in sample i

  $$\bar{n} = \dfrac{\sum\limits_{i=1}^{k} n_i}{k}$$

  $$\bar{p} = \dfrac{\sum\limits_{i=1}^{k} X_i}{\sum\limits_{i=1}^{k} n_i}$$

  k = number of samples

Morals of the Red Bead Example
- Variation is an inherent part of any process.
- The system is primarily responsible for worker performance.
- Only management can change the system.
- Some workers will always be above average and some will be below.

The *c* Chart
- It is an attribute chart and a control chart for the number of nonconformities (or occurrences) in a unit (called an area of opportunity).
- $LCL_c = \bar{c} - 3\sqrt{\bar{c}}$, $UCL_c = \bar{c} + 3\sqrt{\bar{c}}$

  where

  $$\bar{c} = \dfrac{\sum\limits_{i=1}^{k} c_i}{k}$$

  $\bar{c}$ = average number of occurrences

  k = number of units sampled

  c_i = number of occurrences in unit i

Control Chart for the Range (R) and Mean $(\bar{X})$
- They are variable control charts.
- They are more sensitive in detecting special-cause variation than the *p* chart.
- They are typically used in pairs
- The R chart monitors the variation in the process while the $\bar{X}$ chart monitors the process average.
- The R chart should be examined first because if it indicates the process is out-of-control, the interpretation of the $\bar{X}$ chart will be misleading.

- **Control chart for the range (R chart):**
  - $LCL_R = D_3\overline{R}$, $UCL_R = D_4\overline{R}$
    where

$$\overline{R} = \frac{\sum_{i=1}^{k} R_i}{k}$$

    D_3 and D_4 are to obtained from a table.
- **Control chart for the mean ($\overline{X}$ chart):**
  - $LCL_{\overline{X}} = \overline{\overline{X}} - A_2\overline{R}$, $UCL_{\overline{X}} = \overline{\overline{X}} + A_2\overline{R}$
    where

$$\overline{\overline{X}} = \frac{\sum_{i=1}^{k} \overline{X}_i}{k}$$

$$\overline{R} = \frac{\sum_{i=1}^{k} R_i}{k}$$

    $\overline{X} = $ the sample mean of n observations at time i

    $R_i = $ the range of n observations at time i

    $k = $ number of subgroups

    and A_2 is to be obtained from a table.

Process Capability

- **Process capability** is the ability of a process to consistently meet specified customer-driven requirement.
- **Specification limits** are technical requirements set by management in response to customer's expectations.
- The **upper specification limit** (*USL*) is the largest value a characteristic of interest can have and still conform to customer's expectation.
- The **lower specification limit** (*LSL*) is the smallest value that is still conforming.

Estimating Process Capability:

- Must have an in-control process first before being able to estimate process capability.
- Estimate process capability by estimating the percentage of product or service within specification.
- **For a characteristic with an *LSL* and a *USL*:**
  P(an outcome will be within specification)

  $= \mathrm{P}(LSL < X < USL)$

  $= \mathrm{P}\left(\dfrac{LSL - \overline{\overline{X}}}{\overline{R}/d_2} < Z < \dfrac{USL - \overline{\overline{X}}}{\overline{R}/d_2} \right)$

  where Z is the standardized normal random variable.

- **For a characteristic with only an *LSL*:**

  P(an outcome will be within specification)

  $= \mathrm{P}(LSL < X)$

  $$= \mathrm{P}\left(\frac{LSL - \overline{\overline{X}}}{\overline{R}/d_2} < Z\right)$$

- **For a characteristic with only a *USL*:**

  P(an outcome will be within specification)

  $= \mathrm{P}(X < USL)$

  $$= \mathrm{P}\left(Z < \frac{USL - \overline{\overline{X}}}{\overline{R}/d_2}\right)$$

- A **Capability Index** is an aggregate measure of a process' ability to meet specification limits. The larger the value of a capability index, the more capable a process is of meeting customer requirement.

- **To measure a process' potential:**

  - **The C_p index:** $C_p = \dfrac{USL - LSL}{6(\overline{R}/d_2)} = \dfrac{\text{specification spread}}{\text{process spread}}$

    - C_p is a measure of process potential, not of actual performance, because it does not consider the current process average.
    - $C_p > 1$ indicates that if the process average can be centered, then more than 99.73% of the observations will be inside the specification limits.
    - $C_p < 1$ indicates that the process is not very capable of meeting requirement for even if the process average can be centered, less than 99.73% of the observations will be inside the specification limits.

- **To measure a process' actual performance:**

  - For one-sided specification limits:

    $$CPL = \frac{\overline{\overline{X}} - LSL}{3\left(\overline{R}/d_2\right)}$$

    $$CPU = \frac{USL - \overline{\overline{X}}}{3\left(\overline{R}/d_2\right)}$$

    CPL (*CPU*) >1 implies that the process mean is more than 3 standard deviation away from the lower (upper) specification limit.

  - For two-sided specification limits:

    $$C_{pk} = \min(CPL, CPU)$$

    $C_{pk} = 1$ indicates that the process average is 3 standard deviations away from the closest specification limit.

    Larger C_{pk} indicates larger capability of meeting the requirements.

SOLUTIONS TO END OF SECTION
AND CHAPTER REVIEW EVEN PROBLEMS

18.2   (a)   Proportion of nonconformances largest on Day 4, smallest on Day 3.

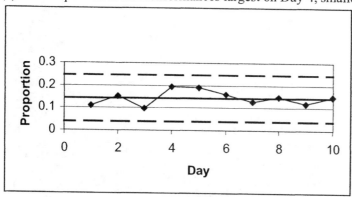

  (b) $\bar{n}$ = 1036/10 = 103.6, $\bar{p}$ = 148/1036 = 0.142857,

$$LCL = \bar{p} - 3\sqrt{\frac{\bar{p}(1-\bar{p})}{\bar{n}}} = 0.142857 - 3\sqrt{\frac{0.142857(1-0.142857)}{103.6}} = 0.039719$$

$$UCL = \bar{p} + 3\sqrt{\frac{\bar{p}(1-\bar{p})}{\bar{n}}} = 0.142857 + 3\sqrt{\frac{0.142857(1-0.142857)}{103.6}} = 0.245995$$

  (c)   Proportions are within control limits, so there do not appear to be any special causes of variation.

18.4   (a) $n = 500$, $\bar{p} = 761/16000 = 0.0476$

$$LCL = \bar{p} - 3\sqrt{\frac{\bar{p}(1-\bar{p})}{n}} = 0.0476 - 3\sqrt{\frac{0.0476(1-0.0476)}{500}} = 0.0190 > 0$$

$$UCL = \bar{p} + 3\sqrt{\frac{\bar{p}(1-\bar{p})}{n}} = 0.0476 + 3\sqrt{\frac{0.0476(1-0.0476)}{500}} = 0.0761$$

18.4 (a)
cont.

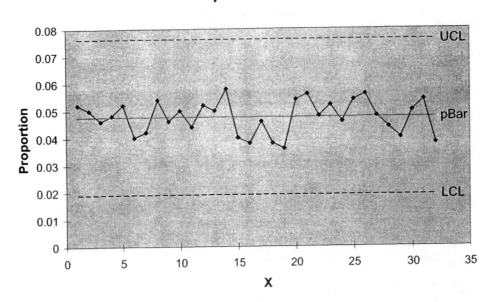

p Chart

(b) Since the individual points are distributed around $\bar{p}$ without any pattern and all the points are within the control limits, the process is in a state of statistical control.

18.6   (a) $\bar{n} = 113345/22 = 5152.0455,\ \bar{p} = 1460/113345 = 0.01288,$

$$LCL = \bar{p} - 3\sqrt{\frac{\bar{p}(1-\bar{p})}{\bar{n}}} = 0.01288 - 3\sqrt{\frac{0.01288(1-0.01288)}{5152.0455}} = 0.00817$$

$$UCL = \bar{p} + 3\sqrt{\frac{\bar{p}(1-\bar{p})}{\bar{n}}} = 0.01288 - 3\sqrt{\frac{0.01288(1-0.01288)}{5152.0455}} = 0.01759$$

PHStat output:

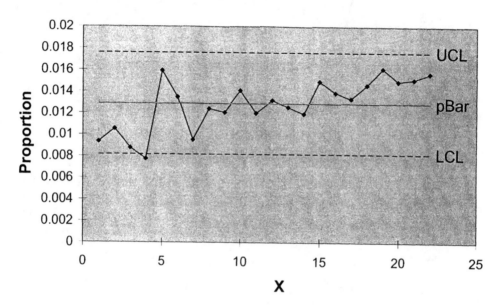

The proportion of unacceptable cans is below the LCL on Day 4. There is evidence of a pattern over time, since the last eight points are all above the mean and most of the earlier points are below the mean. Thus, the special causes that might be contributing to this pattern should be investigated before any change in the system of operation is contemplated.

   (b)   Once special causes have been eliminated and the process is stable, Deming's fourteen points should be implemented to improve the system. They might also look at day 4 to see if they could identify and exploit the special cause that led to such a low proportion of defects on that day.

18.8   (a)

p Chart

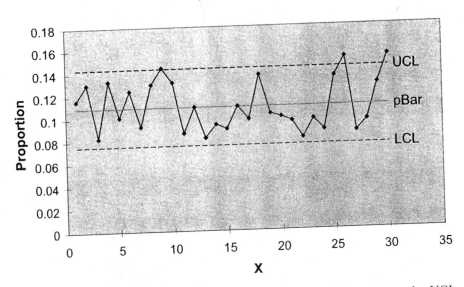

$\bar{p} = 0.1091$, $LCL = 0.0751$, $UCL = 0.1431$. Points 9, 26, and 30 are above the UCL.

(b)   First, the reasons for the special cause variation would need to be determined and local corrective action taken. Once special causes have been eliminated and the process is stable, Deming's fourteen points should be implemented to improve the system.

18.12   (a) $\bar{c} = 115/10 = 11.5$, $LCL = \bar{c} - 3\sqrt{\bar{c}} = 11.5 - 3\sqrt{11.5} = 1.32651$
$UCL = \bar{c} + 3\sqrt{\bar{c}} = 11.5 + 3\sqrt{11.5} = 21.67349$

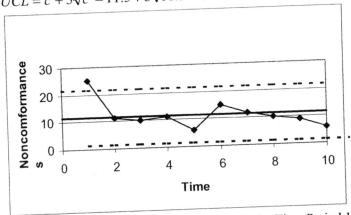

(b)   Yes, the number of nonconformances per unit for Time Period 1 is above the upper control limit.

18.14   (a)   The twelve errors committed by Gina appear to be much higher than all others, and Gina would need to explain her performance.

(b)

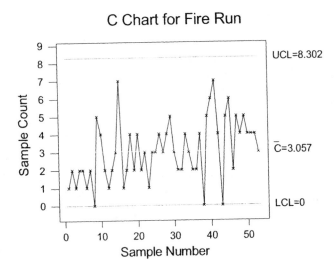

c-Chart

$\bar{c} = 5.5$, $UCL = 12.56$, LCL does not exist. The number of errors is in a state of statistical control since none of the tellers are outside the UCL.

(c)   Since Gina is within the control limits, she is operating within the system, and should not be singled out for further scrutiny.

(d)   The process needs to be studied and potentially changed using principles of Six Sigma® management and/or Deming management.

18.16   (a) $\bar{c} = 3.057$

(b)   Minitab output:

C Chart for Fire Run

UCL=8.302

$\bar{C}$=3.057

LCL=0

18.16   (c)   There is evidence of a pattern over time, since the first eight points are all below the
cont.   mean. Thus, the special causes that might be contributing to this pattern should be
                     investigated before any change in the system of operation is contemplated.

        (d)   Even though weeks 15 and 41 experienced seven fire runs each, they are both below
                     the upper control limit. They can, therefore, be explained by chance causes.

        (e)   After having identified the special causes that might have contributed to the first
                     eight points that are below the average, the fire department can use the c-chart to
                     monitor the process in future weeks in real-time and identify any potential special
                     causes of variation that might have arisen and could be attributed to increased arson,
                     severe drought or holiday-related activities.

18.18   (a) $d_2 = 2.059$ (d) $D_4 = 2.282$
        (b) $d_3 = 0.88$ (e) $A_2 = 0.729$
        (c) $D_3 = 0$

18.20   (a) $\bar{R} = \dfrac{\sum\limits_{i=1}^{k} R_i}{k} = \dfrac{66.8}{20} = 3.34,\ \bar{\bar{X}} = \dfrac{\sum\limits_{i=1}^{k} \bar{X}_i}{k} = \dfrac{118.325}{20} = 5.916.$

        R chart:
                $UCL = D_4 \bar{R} = 2.282(3.34) = 7.6219$

        LCL does not exist.

        $\bar{X}$ chart:
                $UCL = \bar{\bar{X}} + A_2 \bar{R} = 5.9163 + 0.729(3.34) = 8.3511$

                $LCL = \bar{\bar{X}} - A_2 \bar{R} = 5.9163 - 0.729(3.34) = 3.4814$

        PHStat R Chart output:

R Chart

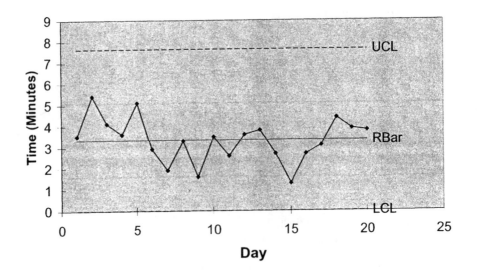

18.20   (a)
cont.

PHStat $\overline{X}$ Chart output:

XBar Chart

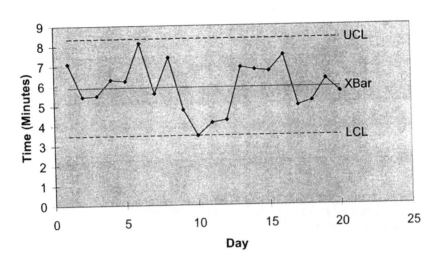

(b)   The $\overline{X}$ of sample 10 is slightly below the *LCL*. The process is out-of-control.

18.22   (a) $\overline{R} = 0.8794$, *R* chart: *UCL* $= 2.0068$; *LCL* does not exist

R Chart

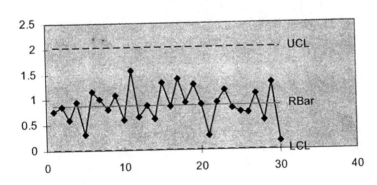

18.22   (b) $\overline{\overline{X}} = 20.1065$, $\overline{X}$ chart: $UCL = 20.7476$; $LCL = 19.4654$
cont.

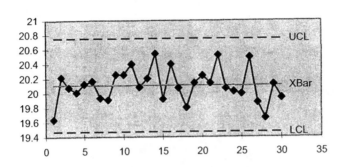

XBar Chart

(c)   The process appears to be in control since there are no points outside the lower and upper control limits of both the R-chart and Xbar-chart, and there is no pattern in the results over time.

18.24   (a)

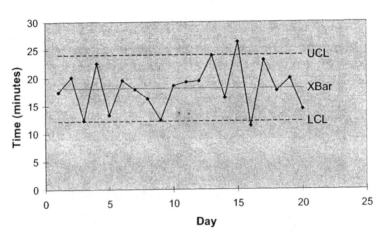

X Bar Chart

18.24 (a)
cont.

R Chart

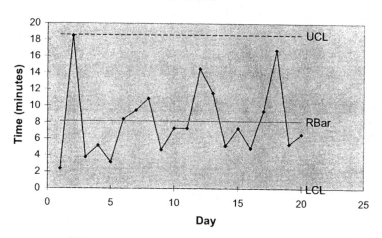

$\overline{R} = 8.145$, $\overline{\overline{X}} = 18.12$.

For R chart: $LCL = D_3 \overline{R} = 0\ (8.145) = 0$. LCL does not exist.

$UCL = D_4 \overline{R} = (2.282)\ (8.145) = 18.58689$.

For $\overline{X}$ chart: $LCL = \overline{\overline{X}} - A_2 \overline{R} = 18.12 - (0.729)\ (8.145) = 12.1823$

$UCL = \overline{\overline{X}} + A_2 \overline{R} = 18.12 + (0.729)\ (8.145) = 24.0577$

(b) There are no sample ranges outside the control limits and there does not appear to be a pattern in the range chart. The sample mean on Day 15 is above the UCL and the sample mean on Day 16 is below the LCL, which is an indication there is evidence of special cause variation in the sample means.

18.26 (a) $\overline{R} = 0.3022$, R chart: $UCL = 0.6389$; LCL does not exist

$\overline{\overline{X}} = 90.1317$, $\overline{X}$ chart: $UCL = 90.3060$; $LCL = 89.9573$

18.26 (a)
cont.

R Chart

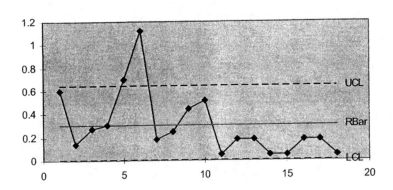

XBar Chart

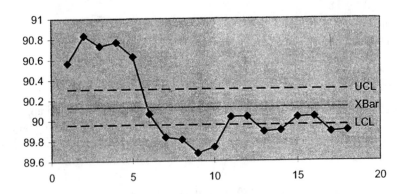

(b) The R-chart is out-of-control because the 5th and 6th data points fall above the upper
control limit. There is also a downward trend in the right tail of the R-chart, which
signifies that special causes of variation must be identified and corrected. Even
though the X-bar chart also appears to be out-of-control because a majority of the
data point fall above or below the control limit, any interpretation will be misleading
because the R-chart has indicated the presence of out-of-control conditions. There is
also a downward trend in the control chart. Special causes of variation should be
investigated and eliminated.

18.28   (a)   Estimate of the population mean = $\overline{\overline{X}} = 100$

Estimate of population standard deviation = $\overline{R} / d_2 = \dfrac{3.386}{1.693} = 2$

$$P(98 < X < 102) = P\left(\dfrac{98-100}{2} < Z < \dfrac{102-100}{2}\right) = 0.6827$$

(b) $P(93 < X < 107.5) = P\left(\dfrac{93-100}{2} < Z < \dfrac{107.5-100}{2}\right) = .9997$

(c) $P(X > 93.8) = P\left(Z > \dfrac{93.8-100}{2}\right) = .9990$

(d) $P(X < 110) = P\left(Z < \dfrac{110-100}{2}\right) \cong 1$

18.30   (a) $P(18 < X < 22) = P\left(\dfrac{18-20.1065}{0.8794/2.059} < Z < \dfrac{22-20.1065}{0.8794/2.059}\right)$

$= P(-4.932 < Z < 4.4335) = 0.9999$

(b) $C_p = \dfrac{(USL - LSL)}{6(\overline{R}/d_2)} = \dfrac{(22-18)}{6(0.8794/2.059)} = 1.56$

$CPL = \dfrac{(\overline{\overline{X}} - LSL)}{3(\overline{R}/d_2)} = \dfrac{(20.1065-18)}{3(0.8704/2.059)} = 1.644$

$CPU = \dfrac{(USL - \overline{\overline{X}})}{3(\overline{R}/d_2)} = \dfrac{(22-20.1065)}{3(0.8704/2.059)} = 1.4778$

$C_{pk} = \min(CPL, CPU) = 1.4778$

18.32   (a)

$$P(5.2 < X < 5.8) = P\left(\dfrac{5.2-5.509}{0.2248/2.059} < Z < \dfrac{5.8-5.509}{0.2248/2.059}\right)$$

$$= P(-2.830 < Z < 2.665) = 0.9938$$

(b)   According to the estimate in (a), only 99.38% of the tea bags will have weight fall between 5.2 grams and 5.8 grams. The process is, therefore, incapable of meeting the 99.7% goal.

18.34   Chance or common causes of variation represent the inherent variability that exists in a system. These consist of the numerous small causes of variability that operate randomly or by chance. Special or assignable causes of variation represent large fluctuations or patterns in the data that are not inherent to a process. These fluctuations are often caused by changes in a system that represent either problems to be fixed or opportunities to exploit.

18.36   When only common causes of variation are present, it is up to management to change the system.

18.38   Attribute control charts are used for categorical data such as the proportion of
nonconformances. Variables control charts are used for numerical variables and are based on
statistics such as the mean and standard deviation.

18.40   From the red bead experiment you learned that variation is an inherent part of any process,
that workers work within a system over which they have little control, that it is the system
that primarily determines their performance, and that only management can change the
system.

18.42   Process potential measures the potential of a process in satisfying production specification
limits or customer satisfaction but does not take into account the actual performance of the
process; process performance refers to the actual performance of the process in satisfying
production specification limits.

18.44   Capability analysis is not performed on out-of-control processes because out-of-control
processes do not allow one to predict their capability. They are considered incapable of
meeting specifications and, therefore, incapable of satisfying the production requirement.

18.46   (a)

p Chart

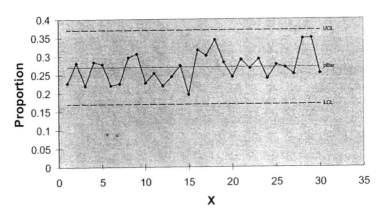

(b)   Yes, RudyBird's market share is in control before the start of the in-store promotion
since all sample proportions fall within the control limits.

18.46   (c)
cont.

p Chart

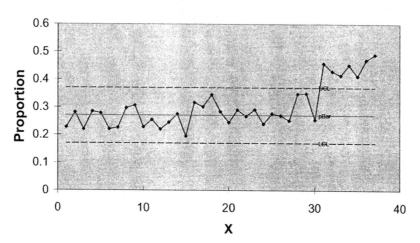

After including the data for days 31-37, there is an apparent upward trend in the p chart during the promotion period and all the market share proportions in that period are above the upper control limit. The process became out-of-control. This assignable-cause variation can be attributed to the in-store promotion. The promotion was successful in increasing the market share of RudyBird.

18.48   (a)

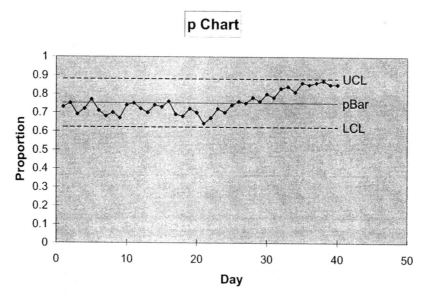

$\overline{p} = 0.75175$, $LCL = 0.62215$, $UCL = 0.88135$. Although none of the points are outside either the LCL or UCL, there is a clear pattern over time with lower values occurring in the first half of the sequence and higher values occurring toward the end of the sequence.

18.48   (b)   This would explain the pattern in the results over time.
cont.   (c)   The control chart would have been developed using the first 20 days and then, using those limits, the additional proportion could have been plotted.

18.50   (a) $\bar{p} = 0.1198$, $LCL = 0.0205$, $UCL = 0.2191$.

      (b)   The process is out of statistical control. The proportion of trades that are undesirable is below the LCL on Day 24 and are above the UCL on Day 4.

      (c)   Special causes of variation should be investigated and eliminated. Next, process knowledge should be improved to decrease the proportion of trades that are undesirable.